JUSTICE AND JUDGMENT

PHILOSOPHY & SOCIAL CRITICISM

Series Editor: David M. Rasmussen, Boston College

This series presents an interdisciplinary range of theory and critique emphasizing the interrelation of continental and Anglo-American scholarship as it affects contemporary discourses. Books in the series are aimed at an international audience, focusing on contemporary debates in philosophy and ethics, politics and social theory, feminism, law, critical theory, postmodernism and hermeneutics.

JUSTICE AND JUDGMENT

The Rise and the Prospect of the Judgment Model in Contemporary Political Philosophy

Alessandro Ferrara

SAGE Publications
London • Thousand Oaks • New Delhi

SAGE Publications Ltd
6 Bonhill Street
London EC2A 4PU

SAGE Publications Inc
2455 Teller Road
Thousand Oaks, California 91320

SAGE Publications India Pvt Ltd
32, M-Block Market
Greater Kailash – I
New Delhi 110 048

British Library Cataloguing in Publication data

A catalogue record for this book is
available from the British Library

ISBN 0 8039 7820 0
ISBN 0 8039 7821 9 (pbk)

Library of Congress catalog card number 99–71273

Typeset by M Rules
Printed in Great Britain by Redwood Books, Trowbridge, Wiltshire

For my daughter Giuditta

Contents

Preface

This book tells a story and contains a suggestion on how to carry it forward, not to a conclusion – for this particular story can have no conclusion – but to a new and different stage. The story is about political philosophy, its encounter with the change of philosophical horizon that goes under the name of the linguistic turn, the response of some of its leading theorists to that transformation, and what may come next. Started as a questioning of the representational capacity of language and as a discussion of the shaping function of linguistic forms over our representations of the world, the linguistic turn immediately shook our deep-seated and long-standing Western faith in the possibility of grounding the transcontextual cogency of general principles of theoretical and practical validity. This change in philosophical sensibility soon produced its effects in epistemology, in the philosophy of science and in the self-understanding of anthropological and social inquiry. Political philosophy came to be invested by the fall of Archimedean points and of the approaches that built on their existence relatively later – in the late 1970s and early 1980s. Nonetheless, it soon made up for that delay by producing, in the works of some prominent theorists, the seeds of quite a novel way of understanding the universalistic dimension of justice and, more generally, the universalistic nature of normative validity.

Looking at the last two decades of literature in the political philosophy of liberal, republican-liberal and democratic orientation one can see signs of the decline of an understanding of normative validity based on principles and the slow rise of an alternative view, based on judgment, not just in the debate over general theories of justice but in a number of distinct, and yet somehow interconnected, areas: for example, in the debates on constitutionalism, on deliberative democracy, on the revival of the republican tradition, on rights, on citizenship, on the public sphere, on the right to privacy, on cultural rights and on multiculturalism.

My effort, over the last few years, has been to elaborate a framework that could help to clarify the exact nature of this change and to make sense of its potential significance. I went back to Kant and found in his contrasting of two models of validity, based respectively on determinant and on reflective judgment, the basis for that framework. Kant's model of a normativity that is universalistic but not dependent on general principles – the model of reflective judgment that forms the object of the *Critique of Judgment* – was then further elaborated in order to bring it in line with the postmetaphysical premises of our own philosophical horizon. This enlarged reformulation, conducted in light of Rudolf Makkreel's reconstruction of what it means for reflective judgment to be *oriented* and on the basis of my own notion of *reflective authenticity*, enabled me then to characterize the current developments under way within political philosophy as a transition from an early modern model of generalizing universalism based on the power of principles, laws, norms and rules to transcend the particularity of contexts to a new model of exemplary universalism based on an oriented reflective judgment about the self-congruity or authenticity of an identity, be it individual or collective.

Considered from this vantage point, the internal development of the thought of theorists like John Rawls, Jürgen Habermas, Ronald Dworkin, Bruce Ackerman and Frank Michelman seems to point to a new configuration, not yet completed, but potentially capable of avoiding both the pitfalls of modern foundationalism and the postmodernist sirens that intimate the renunciation, along with the *subsumptive* model of 'context transcending', of all other notions of transcontextual validity as well. The judgment framework allowed me also to locate the junctures, within each of these theorists' work, where the older model of universalism survives within the new one and in tension with it. The reconstruction of these tensions between two incompatible models of normative validity often at work within the same framework gave impulse to the subsequent stage of my research, namely the attempt to plot a tentative course for the *completion* of the turn toward a reflective judgment view of justice and normative validity.

First, I tried to reconceptualize the 'context of justice' or the paradigmatic circumstances in which problems of justice are typically thought to arise by liberal thinkers. I tried to put to a better use the much invoked Davidsonian argument about the incoherence of total incommensurability, by linking it with an understanding of justice as an oriented reflective judgment concerning the optimal unfolding or flourishing of the identity, however minimal, originating in the area of overlap between the contending parties – an area of overlap that can be treated as a symbolic identity in its own right.

Furthermore, drawing on Charles Larmore's recent work on 'equal respect', but bending his argument to conclusions with which he need not necessarily agree, I developed the idea that reflective judgments on matters of justice differ from reflective judgments about the fulfilment or authenticity of identities in general, in that judgments on questions of justice are oriented not only by those intuitions concerning the flourishing or authenticity of individual and collective identities which I have tried to reconstruct in *Reflective Authenticity: Rethinking the Project of Modernity* (1998a), but also by an *additional* guideline – the ideal of 'equal respect' – which functions as an area of overlap between theories of justice. Another important moment in completing the turn toward a fully fledged judgment view of justice consists in uncoupling the distinction between the right and the good, which in a reformulated version remains at the centre also of the judgment view, from the assumption, generally taken for granted by all contemporary authors, that one of the two terms has necessarily to be given priority over the other. At the centre of the judgment view of justice, instead, is an understanding of the distinction between the right and the good as compatible with the *complementarity* of the two standpoints.

Finally, when it comes to presenting its own credentials for validity, the judgment view of justice undergoes a reflexive turn. One of the aspects of novelty that the judgment view, as a view *of justice*, receives from its being built on oriented reflective judgment is that it incorporates the same kind of radical self-referentiality that aesthetic objects, and primarily works of art, possess. At no point could the justification of a judgment view of justice appeal to anything beyond the intrinsic dynamic of judgment without forfeiting its own consistency. Consequently, the 'aesthetic analogy' is then pursued further and the judgment view is justified in a way not dissimilar from the one in which the more general *authenticity view of validity*, of which the judgment view of justice represents but one among several possible specifications, was defended in *Reflective Authenticity*, namely in terms of a situated appraisal of our identity as modern Westerners. In the course of this appraisal we come to the tentative and provisional conclusion that if we want to remain true to the project enshrined in that identity, 'we can do no other' – in Luther's sense – than embrace a judgment view of justice.

This whole line of reasoning may sound bizarre to ears used to the melody of contemporary liberalism, but to my mind it is just one among several possible ways of taking seriously Rawls's saying that the validity of a view of justice cannot but rest with 'its congruence with our deeper understanding of ourselves and our aspirations, and our realization that, given our history and the traditions embedded in our public life, it is the most reasonable doctrine for us' (1980: 519). Also, this way of approaching justice attests a return to the deepest spirit of Kant's lesson – a lesson that in the twenty-first century will most likely project a different meaning from the one attributed to it in the course of the twentieth. While Kant himself would have been horrified by the linkage of justice and aesthetics, it is not unreasonable to claim that, under conditions quite different from those under which he lived his intellectual life, in the spirit with which we turn to aesthetics some seeds survive of the spirit of modesty and willingness to learn with which Kant looked at the accomplishments of modern physics. He sought in Newtonian physics that nexus of certainty and experience that premodern metaphysics was unable to generate and placed that nexus, reconstructed as a theory of the knowing subject, at the centre of his transcendental philosophy. After the linguistic turn, with the same modesty and willingness to learn, we seek in aesthetics that nexus of *universality and radical pluralism* that modern thought in all of its variants seems unable to generate.

Several relations, institutional and personal, have made this book possible. Among the institutions, I am grateful to the Italian CNR and the Commissione per gli Scambi Culturali fra l'Italia e gli Stati Uniti for having financed, in the autumn of 1989, a semester spent as a Research Associate at the University of California at Berkeley, during which I worked on a preliminary draft called 'The Rationality of Judgment'; to the Department of

Philosophy of Boston College, to the Center for European Studies of the School of Government at Harvard University, to the Department of Political Science of Columbia University in New York, to the Department of Philosophy of the Universidad Autónoma Metropolitana of Mexico and to the Department of Government of the University of Manchester for having invited me to lecture on papers which later evolved to become Chapters 1, 2, 3, 4 and 6 of this book. I wish to thank also the Ministry for the University and for Scientific Research of the Italian government for having financed, in 1994, a research project on 'Models of Universalism Underlying Liberal Theories of Justice' that allowed me to draft other materials later included in the same chapters of this book.

Concerning individuals, I am very grateful to the participants of the Prague annual Conference on Philosophy and Social Science where a number of times I have presented work in progress from this book. The intellectual climate of these encounters, characterized by unrestrained dialogue and genuine pluralism, renders them uniquely stimulating opportunities for developing one's thoughts. Within that context, as well as on the occasion of other presentations, invited talks, and private conversations, I have benefited from comments by Ronald Beiner, Seyla Benhabib, Michelangelo Bovero, Hubertus Buchstein, Marina Calloni, Jean L. Cohen, Maeve Cooke, Peter Dews, Enrique Dussel, Pieter Duvenage, Paolo Flores D'Arcais, Gunther Frankenberg, Klaus Günther, Jürgen Habermas, Michael Halberstam, Axel Honneth, Maria Pia Lara, Sebastiano Maffettone, Giacomo Marramao, Virginio Marzocchi, Maurizio Passerin d'Entrèves, Stefano Petrucciani, Elena Pulcini, Richard Rorty, Nadia Urbinati, Salvatore Veca and Joel Whitebook.

Several people have had the patience to read through extensive parts of the manuscript and have offered me precious feedback which in some cases has led to a rethinking of parts of the argument. While responsibility for the results is obviously my own, their thoughts, questions and critical objections have very much contributed to the making of this book. I am very much indebted to David Rasmussen for having first encouraged me to embark on this intellectual journey, for his advice on the structuring of the materials and, last but not least, for having had the patience, as a series editor, to wait for the long detours and waystations that have separated the signing from the fulfilling of the contract. Giampaolo Ferranti and Rainer Forst have offered me extended and very insightful comments on Chapters 1 and 2. Massimo Rosati has been a constant and very stimulating partner in great discussions throughout the production of this manuscript – most likely, I owe him more thoughts than I can acknowledge. Furthermore, I am very grateful to Bruce Ackerman for having made the manuscript of his *Transformations* available to me, for a long conversation on the subject of justice that took place in Mexico City and for his comments on various parts of my manuscript. Frank Michelman has read every single line in this book and has led me to rethink many of them: his own work on the judgment view of higher lawmaking, again generously made available to me before publication, has been a great source of inspiration for my own. That is true also of Charles Larmore, to whom I owe with gratefulness many of my thoughts on 'equal respect' and on the right and the good: his copious and always perspicuous comments on the entire manuscript have accompanied me in the process of editing the final version and in more than one instance have occasioned substantial revisions – even, in one case, of structural import. Finally, I wish to thank Donatella Caponetti for her presence in my life: thoughts cannot flourish if emotions do not.

Alessandro Ferrara
Rome, February 1998

Introduction

In its course the twentieth century has demolished many of the certainties which it inherited from earlier stages of modernity. Progress, the universality of reason, the benign nature of science, the limitlessness of economic growth, the irreversibility of modernization and of secularization are among the ideas that have fallen victim to its critical axe. On the other hand, the somewhat facile image of a largely sceptical and iconoclastic century has to be balanced with the fact that the twentieth century has injected new substance into the notion of democracy – one notion that not only has survived its critical scrutiny but has emerged from it endowed with a renewed vigour and enriched with a new appreciation of social rights, of the role of the public sphere, of the right to privacy and of cultural difference.

In the realm of philosophical culture, the twentieth century has originated one event for which the often abused characterization as a new Copernican revolution is for once not entirely inappropriate – namely, the linguistic turn. Foreshadowed by Frege and Peirce and completed by the later Wittgenstein, the linguistic turn has dissolved the notion of a direct access, not mediated by the formative influence of one among a plurality of languages and cultures, to an uninterpreted reality. The Kantian 'transcendental' has undergone a process of pluralization, foreshadowed by Durkheim's *social genealogy* of the categories of time and space,[1] up to the point that 'facts' – facts as the *foci* of undisputable agreement to which evaluations are subsequently applied – have become, in the eyes of a contemporary philosopher, like the Kantian thing-in-itself: a chimera never to be attained.[2]

At the centre of this book is a concern for the correct assessment of the implications of the linguistic turn on our way of conceiving *justice* and, more generally, *normative validity*. Is there a way of understanding what we mean by justice that is consistent with the pluralistic intuitions embedded in the linguistic turn and yet continues to reflect that universalistic thrust that we usually associate with justice? Of course, the answer to this question – an affirmative answer, to anticipate the argument – depends on our understanding of the expression 'universalistic thrust'. The *judgment view of justice*, outlined in the second part of this book, is meant to reconcile our pluralistic intuitions with a new kind of *exemplary*, judgment-based universalism, different from and alternative to the *generalizing*, principle-based universalism that has largely prevailed in modern moral, political and legal theory.[3] The judgment view, furthermore, is understood as a conception of justice that builds on, and brings to completion, certain transformations – reconstructed

in the first part of the book – that have been under way in the political philosophy of the last third of the twentieth century.

The transformations at issue, though specific of political philosophy, draw
their impulse and meaning from a background context much broader than
political philosophy. The death of God, the normative disempowerment of
tradition, the disarray of history are distinct aspects of a predicament in
which to provide an account for the universalism of justice and normative
validity has become a difficult task. Traditional Archimedean points have lost
their cogency. Kant could still ground his categorical imperative on a substantive – 'metaphysical', in Rawls's terminology – view of the human subject
and of the nature of its rationality. Hegel could still rest the normative force
of the modern state on a normative vision of the historical process. Instead,
anyone who reflects on questions of justice and of normative validity after
Nietzsche, Heidegger and Wittgenstein is in a much more discomforting position. In this new predicament, however, we can observe the development,
over the last few years, of a way of going about the old task of providing
answers to practical questions whose novelty has often gone unnoticed.

If we try to weave the internal developments of the work of leading political philosophers such as Rawls, Habermas, Dworkin, Ackerman and
Michelman into a unitary and coherent narrative we do get a sense of a
common direction underlying the diversity of their positions, intellectual traditions and objects of inquiry. Such direction can be reconstructed as leading
to the decline of the once prevailing paradigm of *generalizing* universalism,
centred on principles, and to the beginning of a reorganization of the main
theories of justice and normative validity around a competing paradigm of
exemplary universalism, centred around the categories of reflective judgment, identity and authenticity. In other words, justice and normative validity
are less and less frequently understood as a matter of applying a set of universal principles to locally specific matters and instead are ever more
commonly understood as a judgment on the justness of local matters in the
light of a normative framework no less local and unique than the matters that
it should help us to assess.

The centrality of the notion of *judgment* to this new way of understanding
justice and normative validity makes the name of Kant loom large once
again. The twentieth century has already witnessed two resurgences of Kant's
philosophy, associated respectively with the debate on the role of values in science and with the attempt to reinterpret Kant's conception of moral rightness
as generalizability along postmetaphysical lines. What we can see emerging
from contemporary political philosophy is perhaps the beginning of a third
resurrection of Kant's philosophy, linked this time with a critical reappropri-
ation of themes and figures of thought drawn from the third *Critique*. In
Kant's *Critique of Judgment*, in fact, we can find answers – some of which still
await a reconstruction under new premises internal to the horizon of the linguistic turn – to many of the difficulties that have haunted early twentieth
century neo-Kantian philosophy and late twentieth century theories of justice
of Kantian descent.

Political theory and moral philosophy of liberal orientation generally conceive of justice as *impartiality*, *neutrality* or *fairness*. These concepts are not exactly equivalent, but we can say that for liberals the point of a theory of justice is to provide a neutral standpoint from which it becomes possible, under the condition of pluralism, (a) to set limits on the ends that can legitimately be pursued by actors who embrace competing conceptions of the good, (b) to outline ways of adjudicating conflicts of interest and of value, and (c) to provide some criterion acceptable to all for the evaluation of the legitimacy of norms. In order to understand the current debate on justice we should first distinguish two versions of this basic, elementary notion of justice understood as impartiality or neutrality: *absolute* impartiality or neutrality and *situated* impartiality or neutrality.

Absolute neutrality or impartiality is neutrality or impartiality *sub specie aeternitatis*, the 'view from nowhere', the impartial stance understood as the application of a purely formal principle. The view of justice thus obtained is supposed to be '*a priori* neutral', that is, neutral with respect to all conceivable conceptions of the good – present, past and future. This was the model of universalism underlying Kant's, Bentham's and Mill's liberal views of justice. It is hard to find contemporary defenders of this notion of neutrality, even though occasionally Rawls's and Habermas's early formulations convey a similar ring. Paraphrasing Constant, we could call this view 'the justice of the early moderns'.

Situated neutrality or impartiality, instead, is neutrality or impartiality with respect to a finite set of actual conceptions of the good. This category, still too broad for our purposes, applies to accounts of justice as diverse as those put forward in their most recent works by Rawls and Habermas, and also by Larmore, Walzer, Dworkin, Ackerman and others. In a sense, situated neutrality or impartiality captures what we might call – extending the relevance of Constant's saying beyond its temporal context – 'the justice of the contemporary moderns'. In order to grasp the polarity inherent in contemporary political philosophy and at the same time to make sense of its recent developments, we should further distinguish two rival versions of this notion. In one case neutrality or impartiality is understood as the *bracketing of controversial issues*, in the other it is understood as the search for an *expressive convergence*. This opposition is designed to reflect the polarization that opposes the more established modern model of *generalizing* or *determinant judgment* universalism on the one hand and the newly developing model of *exemplary* or *reflective judgment* universalism on the other. Strictly speaking, the exemplary as opposed to generalizing quality of reflective judgment universalism is nothing new. Kant worked it out in the *Critique of Judgment*. Furthermore, Aristotle's model of *phronesis* as a moral virtue can be said to parallel many of the points raised here. Yet there is something new in that for the first time the exemplary or singular type of universalism breaks free from the isolation and ineffectuality to which it had remained confined by the prevalence of the classical ontological and the modern generalizing and principle-based modes of justification, and candidates itself for becoming the paradigmatic model for understanding the normativity of norms in the context that follows the linguistic turn.

Going back to the liberal theories of justice, the difference between neutrality as uncontroversiality and neutrality as expressive convergence lies in the way the overlapping area, shared in common by the contending views of the good, is conceived and treated. Conceptions which equate the neutrality of justice with *uncontroversiality* usually understand the overlapping area as the product of careful abstention from any subject, assumption or implication which is controversial. Controversial issues are like dangerous underwater rocks which a skilful skipper must avoid.[4] Conceptions which view the neutrality or impartiality of justice as expressive convergence, by contrast, understand the overlapping area as a kind of hermeneutic horizon which possesses an expansive dynamic of its own. Interesting for our purposes is to note that the terms *neutrality* and *impartiality* assume different meanings in this debate and that these meanings are associated with two kinds of universalism ultimately linked with philosophical positions closer to the two polar opposites represented by the competing models of determinant and reflective judgment.

A word of clarification may be important at this point, concerning the Kantian distinction between determinant and reflective judgment. While judgment in general is for Kant 'the faculty of thinking the particular as contained under the universal',[5] in the case of *determinant* judgment such inclusion of the particular under the universal is understood as a relation of *subsumption*. By that term a specific relation is meant by Kant, which we can characterize on the basis of three aspects. First, a moment of *necessity* is associated with the universal: in other words, the universality of the universal is something which imposes itself on us, and enjoins our recognition, with inescapable cogency. Second, the conditions under which any relevant particular can be subsumed under the universal as an instance of it follow *deductively*, analytically or *a priori* from our understanding of the universal, thus allowing us to build a *method* for assessing every possible case with full certainty of reaching a valid judgment. And, third, the universal can be conceptually grasped *apart* from, and *prior* to, the occurrence of any particular instance of it. In this sense, it can be said to be conceptually separable from the particular.

Reflective judgment, instead, is a kind of judgment in which 'only the particular is given and the universal has to be found for it' (Kant 1986: 18). In this process of 'ascending from the particular in nature to the universal' we are in need of a guiding principle, argues Kant, but this principle cannot be borrowed from experience or from 'any other quarter', including conceptual analysis. For in that case our judgment 'would then be a determinant judgment' (1986: 19). Instead, in the case of reflective judgment, judgment must be a principle to itself.[6] Reflective judgment, in other words, obeys no law other than its own or, to use Georg Simmel's expression, is governed by an 'individual law'.[7] The meaning of this expression, and the sense in which it can be understood as a model of universalism, is well rendered in what Luigi

Pareyson, Umberto Eco's and Gianni Vattimo's mentor, says about the well-formed work of art:

> The work of art is as it should be and should be as it is and has no other law than its own ... The work of art is singular because the law that governs it is but its own individual rule, and is universal because its individual rule is really the law that governs it. The work of art ... is universal in its very singularity: its rule holds for one case only, but exactly in that it is universal, in the sense that it is the only law that should have been followed in its making. (1988: 140–1)

We can understand what is meant by conceptual separability of the universal and the particular by looking at two examples of the model of universalism based on determinant judgment and of the model of universalism based on reflective judgment: the case of assessing a work of art and the case of solving an equation. We can certainly discuss what the idea of the well-formedness of a work of art *generally* means – in fact, this has been the standard topic of aesthetics for quite a while. We can certainly sum up this meaning in the form of principles of aesthetic well-formedness. However, no one will then believe that the actual well-formedness of concrete works of art depends on their fulfilling any general idea of well-formedness reconstructed in terms of principles or concepts. An aesthetic conception of the well-formedness of the work of art is like a *poetics* – namely, a reconstruction, a summary of what we believe to inhere in any well-formed work of art. Poetics and aesthetic manifestos compete with one another in a contest over the title of 'best reconstruction of our intuitions concerning the necessary and distinctive constituents of a well-formed work of art' – a contest in which actual works of art are confined to the background, as illustrations of theses and counter-theses. It is nonsense to assess the concrete case of a work of art against the standard of its satisfying the requirements of a poetic, even of the best poetic that we have. It makes no sense to think that for the artist to follow the best available poetic manifesto means that the well-formed quality of the product is somehow guaranteed, or that following the wrong poetics condemns the artist to aesthetic failure, though not perhaps to commercial failure. Were this so, we could assess paintings without seeing them, musical works without hearing them performed, literary works without reading them.

In the case of solving an equation the opposite is true. The formal principles of algebra enable us to subsume the concrete single case without loss. The two planes, which remained incommensurable in the case of the work of art, here come together. When we master the relevant principles and the ensuing procedure for solving an equation it becomes possible for us to determine, for any given solution examined, whether it is correct. We do not need to know anything about the context within which the need to solve the given equation arose, about the history of the problem and its formulations, least of all about the concrete materiality of the symbols that represent the equation for us. All these aspects recede into the background. Knowledge of algebraic principles and procedures allows us to solve the equation from a distance, on the telephone, whereas pictorial expertise will never allow us to assess a painting without seeing it or even by seeing only a photograph of it.

It would be misleading, however, to think of determinant judgment as a form of judgment limited to mathematical procedures that take the form of algorithms.[8] Syllogistic reasoning, analytic relations between concepts, juridical and administrative rules, as well as rules that are constitutive with respect to games provide other examples of areas in which validity is conceived in terms of determinant judgment. If I say 'All men are mortal, Socrates is a man, therefore Socrates is mortal', the validity of the conclusions rests on the subsumption of the quality 'being a man' under the broader quality 'being mortal', and that conceptual relation allows me, via the principle of transitivity, to subsume a particular – 'Socrates' – under a universal, in this case 'being mortal'. Second, dictionary definitions, when carefully worded, offer us criteria for telling whether a certain word – for example, 'drive shaft' – can be appropriately used in order to refer to a member of a certain class of objects, in this case a member of the class constituted by metal bars designed to transmit motion from the engine to the wheels of a vehicle. A third example is offered by legal provisions and administrative regulations, ordinances and decrees that have the status of *rules* as opposed to *principles*.[9] Rules such as those which establish that one must be at least 18 years old in order to obtain a driver's licence, that an academic course has to include a certain number of hours of teaching, or that a specific authority will assume the functions of chief executive in the case of an impediment of the head of the government, are rules which, again, allow us to subsume a particular individual under the more general category of being a bearer of specific rights or the incumbent of specific duties. Finally, another area where validity is understood in terms of determinant judgment is given by the rule governed performances of the players of games. In chess as in soccer, in basketball as in tennis, the acts of players that have a relevance for the game are construed as allowed or forbidden ones according to rules that in principle enable us to assign in a clearcut way all the particular cases to the class of the allowed or forbidden moves. All of these cases of determinant judgment fall somehow within the scope of 'rule following' in Wittgenstein's sense,[10] and for Wittgenstein rule following is never just a mindless algorithmic application: it is linked with sensitivity to a context, to a practice, ultimately to a form of life.

Much as determinant judgment is not exclusively characteristic of mathematical algorithms, so reflective judgment is not just an aesthetic phenomenon. Let us consider another set of questions: has a soldier distinguished himself in battle for his martial valour, has a manager fulfilled her mandate, has a politician acted responsibly, has a parent brought up her daughter well, has a teacher educated his pupil well, has a friend acted with real care, has a therapist truly helped his patient, has a lawyer assisted her client well in a complicated transaction, has an interpreter expressed the meaning of a text appropriately, has an architect designed a house that really meets the needs of his client? All of these questions are such that no appeal can be made to any general notion – any 'universal', in Kant's terminology – that functions in the same way as do the rules of a game, rule-like statutes and regulations, the definitions in a dictionary or the premises in a syllogism. Not that general notions – such as courageously facing danger in battle, furthering the prosperity of the company, acting in the service of the public good, raising a competent and autonomous person, attending the interests of a client, grasping the core meaning of a text, designing a functional and beautiful home – do not play a role in our assessment; but the guidance that they provide never seems to come down to the kind of fine-grained indications of basically uncontested perceptual stimuli, spatial distributions or time lapses that are contained in the rules of tennis, basketball or checkers. The relevance of general notions seems at best that of *guiding* or *orienting* a kind of judgment that is much more open than the judgment that can fall back on established rules, but not as open as the judgment about the well-formedness of a work of art.[11]

Where does judgment about the justness or normative validity of an institutional order, of a norm, of a maxim of conduct fit within this picture? For a long time the ambition of modern moral and political philosophy has been to offer an account of rightness, fairness, or normative validity which, for all the enormous distance that separates complex, meaningful and subjectivity-forming 'objects' like institutions from equations, would nonetheless treat their case as somehow closer to the case of solving an equation, unfolding a syllogism, checking whether a certain thing can be referred to by way of using a given term, determining whether I am legally eligible for a certain benefit or deciding whether my move on the chessboard is legitimate than to the cases of assessing a work of art, evaluating the interpretation of a text, determining whether a politician has acted responsibly or whether an educator or a manager, let alone a parent, has fulfilled her mandate. Certainly this was the ambition of Kant's moral and political philosophy. On Kant's view, the categorical imperative, if understood and applied correctly, must, like the rules of algebra, give us one and only one correct solution for any practical problem to which it is applied. The principle of publicity, discussed in *Perpetual Peace*, is designed to offer us one clearcut criterion for assessing the fairness of policies. Removed as it can be from a deontological inspiration, utilitarianism shares the same ambition. This ambition can be found, for example, in Bentham's moral theory, which pivots on the principle of the 'greater happiness for the largest number of people'.[12] But about contemporary philosophy? Contemporary political philosophy – so I would begin a historical narrative concerning the overall direction toward which political philosophy seems to be headed during the last three decades of the twentieth century – finds itself in a sort of uncharted territory between these two models of justice and normative validity. Evidence for this statement comes from the increasing uneasiness that prominent authors such as Rawls, Habermas, Dworkin, Ackerman and Michelman have recently been feeling *vis-à-vis* the Kantian notion of determinant judgment and its generalizing kind of universalism as a model for moral and political philosophy.

One proviso is necessary at this point. Strictly speaking, none of these authors subscribes to a model of normative universalism based on the notion of determinant judgment as articulated by Kant. In fact, who among those who philosophize from within the horizon of the linguistic turn could conceive of the general principle, the 'universal' (in this case, a principle of justice), as a principle whose universality is given, before and beyond interpretation, by virtue of its reflecting some deep structure of subjectivity? Who could understand the relation between a general principle and the candidate norms submitted to its test as a strictly deductive relation, a relation which is deductive *more geometrico*? Nevertheless, underlying this book is the assumption that the distinction between determinant and reflective judgment continues to be relevant for the purpose of understanding the diversity underlying the various approaches to justice that exist today. Such distinction continues, in my opinion, to capture a real polarity between two types of current conceptions of justice.

On the one hand we have universalist approaches inspired by the model of determinant judgment – the 'weakest' of which is the *deontological* approach in the two versions offered respectively by Rawls and by Habermas. The proponents of deontological theories of justice share the conviction that it is possible to identify certain principles of justice (for example, the two principles of justice which constitute the core of 'justice as fairness') or a kind of 'procedural principle' governing our selection of substantive principles of justice (the principle of dialogical generalization 'U') and that one can claim the validity of such principles across contexts and cultures without invoking strong transcendental arguments incompatible with the perspective opened by the linguistic turn. At least at the moment when their paradigm was first formulated (Rawls 1971; Habermas 1990) they appear to have shared the conviction that a sharp distinction can be drawn between the *universality, abstractness, dialogical, rationally demonstrable* quality of justice versus the *particularity, context boundedness, monological and prudentially intuitive* quality of the good. They differ, however, on their substantive characterization of the principles of justice and the strategy adopted for justifying them. But to this we will come back below.

More important for our present purposes is to note that, concerning their stance *vis-à-vis* the model of determinant judgment, the proponents of contemporary theories of justice generally renounce claiming (a) that they provide unobjectionable foundations for the general principles and (b) that the relation between the principle and its application is one of deduction. However, one essential feature of the model of determinant judgment which they retain is the conceptual distinction between principle and application, general principles of justice and what is just on a concrete occasion or, in Kantian parlance, the conceptual separability of the universal and the particular. Even when the perspective suggested is explicitly 'constructivist' (Rawls) or 'reconstructive' (Habermas), we can still observe a substantial difference between the kind of argument developed for grounding the principle of justice and the kind of arguments developed in order to justify any of its applications. The cogency of the principle has a separate origin from the cogency of its applications. Furthermore, both the adequacy of the principle and the inclusion of some intended line of conduct within the scope of the principle are assumed to be possible objects of *demonstration* – where by demonstration I mean an argument which, if valid, would thereby make it *unreasonable* for anyone to reject its conclusions.[13]

On the other hand we have liberal theories of justice and normative validity which follow a different strategy for their own justification. Their proponents do not rely, as the authors mentioned above, on a sharp *discontinuity* between principles of justice and intuitions concerning the good. Their approaches continue to presuppose a distinction between the right and the good, but their mode of justifying their understanding of the right seems to fall more on the side of reflective judgment and exemplary universalism than on that of determinant judgment and generalizing universalism. The justness of justice is understood not simply as uncontroversiality and compatibility with independently established principles, as in the deontological theories, but as a sort of *expressive convergence* which is then conceived along different lines by Dworkin, Ackerman and Michelman. Although it is never mentioned, the idea of authenticity or exemplary self-congruence occupies a central place in these conceptions. In Dworkin's, Ackerman's and Michelman's views neutrality comes close to the principle of the least disruption of the realization of the collective identity which encompasses all parties to a distributive conflict. This principle, in turn, cannot be reduced to a mere consistency requirement, but must be conceived as entailing an affirmative, albeit implicit, standard of *optimal unfolding* of a relevant identity. To anticipate what will be discussed in greater detail below, for Dworkin the main principles that concur to constitute the view of justice embedded in the constitution – freedom of conscience and of speech, due process, equality before the law – are like the critical, as opposed to volitional, interests of a *collective* life-project.[14] We constantly have to reinterpret these principles in light of our new predicaments, but integrity demands that in our interpretation we remain faithful to them, not because they possess a validity independent of us, but rather because 'we', the members of the political community, and them are bound up in an inextricable nexus. Without them we would not be 'we'. Justices who assess the compatibility of a statute with those principles act then as an institutionalized analogue of that part of each of us which assesses whether and how the taking up of a new interest or project will fit with the core sector of our life-project. And while Hercules is free to *interpret* the constitution as he sees fit, at the same time he is not free to *change* the meaning of the document.

Like Rawls and Habermas, so too does Ackerman, as we will see, start with a stronger model of normative validity, indeed of distributive justice, and subsequently turns to a view of normative validity, now considered under the aspect of legitimacy in higher lawmaking, which is more receptive to a notion of universalism based on the model of reflective judgment. In *Transformations*, the second volume in the trilogy of *We the People*, Ackerman eventually comes to an understanding of legitimacy in higher lawmaking that is entirely couched in terms of reflective judgment – a view justified in turn on the basis of a radically self-reflexive argument which appeals to a reflective judgment on the history of, and the prospect for, an optimal fulfilment of the political identity of the American people.

Finally, Frank Michelman's republican-liberal conception of deliberative democracy is the view of normative validity in which we find validity, considered also in his case predominantly under the aspect of legitimacy in higher lawmaking, most closely connected with reflective judgment. Distinctive of Dworkin's, Ackerman's and Michelman's approaches seems to be the fact that problems of justice and of normative validity are assumed to be solvable by appealing to a normative framework which is understood as being no less connected with the flourishing of a collective identity than the specific claims which, by coming to a clash, have determined the problem in the first place.

In the part of the book dedicated to the rise of the judgment model in political philosophy – which includes Chapters 1–5 – I will reconstruct the deontological and the more expressivist approaches. Over and beyond the polarity mentioned above, in this part I will try also to highlight the internal transformations undergone by the approach developed by each of the authors considered. In fact, in the case of the two authors who at the beginning of their intellectual trajectory were more sympathetic toward the traditional model of generalizing universalism – namely, Rawls and Habermas – these transformations provide perhaps the most convincing evidence for the thesis that a shift is under way in our contemporary understanding of justice and normative validity.

The second part of the book – dedicated to the prospects of the judgment model – is designed to serve two ends: first, to point out the limits and obstacles against which the rise of the judgment model has thus far run; and, second, to outline a possible way of completing the turn toward a fully fledged judgment view of justice and normative validity.

In Chapter 6 those junctures are traced out, within the work of each of the authors considered, at which the resistances against the judgment model and the relapses into the older model of generalizing universalism become more visible. In fact, momentous and impressive as they might look, the modifications undergone by the frameworks initially developed by all our authors, but especially by Rawls and Habermas, should not be mistaken for what they are not. These transformations cannot be interpreted as suggesting that political philosophy has undergone a sudden and thorough change in perspective. There has been no revolution thus far. Rather, the theoretical transformations discussed in Chapters 1–5 are to be understood as symptoms of an awareness of the difficulties raised by the model of generalizing universalism and as indicators of a growing, but still somewhat reluctant, readiness to adopt a few aspects of a universalism based on the model of reflective judgment. In Chapter 6 this reluctance provides the thematic focus of a reappraisal of our authors' work and is shown to surface in different ways: for example, in the form of a tension between a stronger and a weaker model of reason, in the form of an ambiguous concept of generalization, in the form of residues of a moral realist understanding of justice and of an ambiguous concept of the People's will, or as the perception of a problem of infinite regress.

In Chapters 7 and 8 I try to sketch a view of justice entirely based on the model of reflective judgment and hopefully capable of reconciling our universalistic intuitions about justice with the pluralistic intuitions generated by the linguistic turn. More specifically, in Chapter 7 I present the basic intuition on which the judgment view of justice rests, namely the idea that what we call justice can be understood as a reflective judgment concerning what is required, for its own optimal fulfilment, by the overarching identity which contains the contending identities that have come to a conflict of interest or of value – provided that such reflective judgment is oriented not only, as every reflective judgment on the fulfilment of identities, by our grasp of certain dimensions of the authenticity of identities, but also by the ideal of *equal respect*. Several aspects of this basic notion of justice are illustrated. For example, the different conceptualization of the context of justice and of the ordering function of justice in the conceptions reconstructed in Part I and in the judgment view of justice are contrasted; then a number of forerunners of the judgment view of justice are briefly discussed; and, subsequently, the problem of identifying a new source of cogency, alternative to the cogency of general principles, for the judgment view of justice is addressed. In this context the notion of 'oriented reflective judgment' will be introduced in order to illustrate the characteristics of the kind of judgment underlying the judgment view of justice. This overview of the judgment approach to justice will be completed by a twofold distinction between moral and political conceptions of justice on the one hand, and elementary and fully fledged conceptions of justice on the other, and by a discussion of some aspects of the analogy of aesthetic judgments and judgments about justice.

In Chapter 8 some of the main presuppositions and implications of the judgment view of justice will be explored. The nature of the ideal of equal respect that orients our judgments concerning matters of justice and normative validity will be probed in greater detail and the ideal will be shown to provide a neutral ground between competing accounts of *justice*, much in the same way as political liberalism understands 'justice as fairness' to constitute an area of overlap between rival comprehensive *conceptions of the good*. Among the implications of the judgment view of justice, its consequences for the distinction between the right and the good will be investigated and the conclusion will be advanced that all appearances notwithstanding, the judgment view by no means presupposes a priority of the good. To anticipate the point, the judgment approach will be argued to uncouple the formulation of the distinction from the postulation of a hierarchization of the two terms along the lines either of a priority of the right or of a priority of the good, and to imply rather a complementarity thesis about the right and the good.

Finally, in the last section of Chapter 8, I address the problem of what justifies the judgment conception of justice. More particularly, what justifies the cogency of the idea of equal respect as an orienting guideline for our assessment of competing solutions to questions of justice? Without pretending to offer a fully fledged argument, and taking the observation that it would be a performative contradiction for a judgment conception of justice to seek justification in terms of *principles* as my point of departure, I will outline a defence of the general validity of the judgment view of justice in terms of a *radically reflexive form of self-grounding*, namely in terms of a situated judgment on our identity that leads us to the conclusion that *we* 'can do no other' than sum up our intuitions about justice and normative validity in a kind of 'judgment view' for reasons that are entirely *internal to*, or *immanent in*, a certain reading of the project-like component of our identity as Westerners on the eve of the twenty-first century.

PART I

THE RISE OF THE JUDGMENT MODEL IN CONTEMPORARY POLITICAL PHILOSOPHY

1

A Reasonable View of the Reasonable

Rawls's conception of 'justice as fairness' is today the most influential version of a liberal view of justice based on deontological premises and the main opponent of all consequentialist, utilitarian and non-utilitarian, conceptions of morality. It has rightly been called the most important contribution to political philosophy since John Stuart Mill. Justice as fairness is also a work in progress. Over more than two decades Rawls has revised various aspects of his project, which today has reached a level of complexity unequalled among the competing accounts of justice. Yet this complexity never amounts to a cumbersome quality of Rawls's style of theorizing. On the contrary, the recent recasting of his position in terms of 'political liberalism' gives Rawls's view of justice an elegant quality of self-containedness. At the same time one can find, throughout the intellectual trajectory that has led Rawls to his present position, a remarkable quality of openness and receptivity to the problems posed by other approaches and to the general philosophical climate. In none of the existing accounts of justice is the sense of the *contingency* of justice and of the futility of the dream of a purely formal or procedural view of justice so clear as in Rawls's recent writings. Even the difficulties which such a view incurs are extremely instructive. In this Chapter I will reconstruct the internal developments that his view of justice as fairness has undergone over the past two decades and will highlight some of the questions that it leaves unanswered.

Rawls's Conception of Justice as Fairness in its Development

Since the time he published his first paper (Rawls 1951), Rawls has kept emphasizing one basic idea. We happen to live in complex societies in which whatever conflicts may arise between competing interests, as well as between competing conceptions of the good, are not likely to be solved through an appeal to a shared horizon of values. We are therefore in need of a procedure, a method, or simply a way of adjudicating such conflicts that may prove acceptable to all the parties involved, despite the fact of their adopting diverse standpoints. Furthermore, Rawls wishes that that procedure, method or way of adjudicating conflicts, unlike a *Hobbesian* contract, be acceptable to all the parties involved as a matter of *principle* rather than *prudence*. The view of justice called *justice as fairness* is, in Rawls's opinion, the moral-theoretical construct more susceptible of performing such a function. With a variety of nuances, throughout the past 40 years Rawls has always emphasized this basic line of thought. Along with it Rawls has remained faithful to a certain *normative minimalism* or *restraint*. Underlying his project has always been the intuition that the less the conflict adjudicating procedure presupposes in terms of moral and metaphysical ideas, the greater chances it has of being acceptable to contending parties who subscribe to different and sometimes rival worldviews and moral outlooks.

The internal development of his thought concerns the different ways in which he has come to formulate and defend this basic idea. It can be reconstructed as a sequence of three stages. In the first stage, epitomized by *A Theory of Justice* (1971), Rawls constructs his case for justice as fairness by combining a contractarian standpoint with the notion of a thought experiment. Then a long transitional stage follows, within which I find appropriate to include, for the purposes of my present reconstruction, what some commentators have discussed as two separate phases (Kukathas and Pettit 1990). At this stage the previous contractarian, Kantian emphases gradually give way to a new strategy for grounding justice as fairness which hinges on the notion of an *overlapping consensus*. A new stage is finally entered with the publication of *Political Liberalism* (1993). This stage is marked by a pronounced distancing from Kantianism and by a thorough shift of emphasis on the question of *stability*, which now becomes the paramount question – a shift of emphasis which accompanies Rawls's perception of a change of the terrain of his own inquiry from *moral* to *political* philosophy. The object of Rawls's argument becomes now a *political* conception of justice capable of solving our conflicts, of constituting the normative core of the institutional order of a democratic society, and to do this not by way of defeating its rivals in philosophical battle but rather by virtue of its ability to dodge any battle over 'metaphysical' questions and proving acceptable from the standpoint of any among the reasonable comprehensive conceptions that are present in the culture of a modern democratic society.

The Model of the Thought Experiment

In *A Theory of Justice* Rawls conceives of his theory of justice as a *recapitulation of the results of a thought experiment concerning the arrangements which self-interested and rational actors deliberating behind a veil of ignorance would select as just.* Some clarifications are necessary concerning the meaning of the terms used in this formula.

First, in the context of deliberation, called the *original position*, the object of discussion is the fairness of what we have called 'arrangements'. The social, normative, political arrangements that are up for dispute are not concrete institutions, but what Rawls calls the *basic structure of society*, understood as 'the way in which the major social institutions distribute fundamental rights and duties and determine the division of advantages from social cooperation' (1971: 7).[1]

Second, the method by which we are to evaluate the competing reconstructions of the outcome of discussion in the original position involves, according to Rawls, checking the suggested moral-theoretical constructs against our considered judgments as stabilized in *reflective equilibrium* (1971: 48–51). This means that we are to avoid the misguided ideal of having all of our moral ideas *immediately* dictated by, or fitted with, our moral theory (as in extreme intuitionist and comprehensive conceptions of the good), for this would in the end lead to a relativistic outcome. The guiding methodological ideal is rather that of going back and forth from our intuitions to our theory of justice, of thinking of our moral ideas in light of the theory, and of the theory in light of our intuitions, until a *reflective equilibrium* is reached in which all the principles assumed to capture our sense of justice match with all the considered judgments we may form about their consequences and applications.

Third, the actors stand in a certain relation to one another – a relation described in the section on 'The Circumstances of Justice' (1971: 126–30). As Rawls puts it, these circumstances or presuppositions of justice as fairness include the assumption of a moderate scarcity and of certain relations between the deliberating actors. Now, as far as the relation between the deliberating actors is concerned, the central point is that these actors, who are assumed to have roughly similar needs and wants but different rational, long-term life-plans or conceptions of the good, *take no interest in one another's interests* (1971: 127). This does not mean that each actor's aims are selfish or egoistic – they may or may not be so – but that the actors have no preordained propensity to advance or hinder each other's interests. They simply ignore or tolerate the other person's interests and are not willing to have their own interests sacrificed to others. Now, among the circumstances of justice is another factor which Rawls mentions in passing but which is of crucial importance within his whole argument. Justice as fairness takes for granted 'the fact of pluralism', namely the existence of a plurality of irreconcilable and perhaps incommensurable conceptions of the good:

> In an association of saints agreeing on a common ideal, if such a community could exist, disputes about justice would not occur. Each would work selflessly for one end as determined by their common religion, and reference to this end (assuming it to be clearly defined) would settle every question of right. (1971: 129–30)

A modern society, however, is characterized by the lack of any such overarching common ideal, and thus within it questions of justice are questions to which we have to find answers acceptable to individuals who subscribe to different conceptions of the good.

Fourth, deliberation takes place *behind a veil of ignorance*, that is without knowing certain information about one's own place in society, or one's life-plans, or the economic and political circumstances of one's society, or to which generation one belongs (1971: 136–42). On the other hand, the parties are assumed to know 'the general facts about human society', 'political affairs and the principles of economic theory', 'the basis of social organization and the laws of human psychology' (1971: 137). The veil of ignorance, combined with the assumption that 'the deliberation of the parties must be similar' (1971: 139), is designed to yield a *'unanimous* choice of a particular conception of justice' (1971: 141). At this stage in the development of Rawls's thought this deliberation is thought of as taking place within the frame of *rational choice*. The model of universalism underlying the normative cogency of justice as fairness is thus the model of determinant judgment.

Fifth, in the original position different candidate views of justice are compared pairwise (1971: 123). Rawls's own substantive proposal – the two principles of justice – is weighed against two competing forms of utilitarianism (the classical and the average principle) and against perfectionism as well as other so-called mixed theories.

I cannot go here into the problems raised by these five aspects of Rawls's theory, and in fact each of them has aroused much debate and lots of criticisms.[2] Instead, I will recall the substantive outcome of deliberation in the original position. According to Rawls, the parties would agree that the best way of conceiving 'the basic structure' of a society is in terms of two principles of justice. The first principle states that

> Each person is to have an equal right to the most extensive total system of equal basic liberties compatible with a similar system of liberty for all. (1971: 302)

The second principle states that

> Social and economic inequalities are to be arranged so that they are both:
> (a) to the greatest benefit of the least advantaged, consistent with the just savings principle, and
> (b) attached to offices and positions open to all under conditions of fair equality and opportunity. (1971: 302)

One of the questions raised by Rawls's argument is: How does this outcome of the discussion taking place in the original position bind *us* who are *not* under a veil of ignorance? Much has been written about this and some of the most interesting remarks are offered by Dworkin, but for our purpose suffice it to say that the way Rawls thinks of this relation is in terms of *modelling*: the choice of a certain conception of justice made by actors deliberating under a veil of ignorance is supposed to *model* or emulate the choice that knowledgeable actors would make *if* they were oriented toward justice.[3]

The Transitional Stage

The conception of justice as fairness presented in *A Theory of Justice* underwent significant changes over the successive two decades. Some of the reasons for the modification are to be found in the internal structure of the theory. As Kukathas and Pettit (1990) have pointed out, a certain tension traverses Rawls's uneasy combination of a contractarian model with 'feasibility arguments'.[4] Feasibility arguments attribute superiority to 'justice as fairness' over utilitarianism and other competitors on the basis of its greater likelihood to be *stabilized* in consistent conduct under changing circumstances and configurations of interest once the veil of ignorance is lifted. If we imagine the selection of principles of justice as involving (a) the identification of conceptions of justice that are 'feasible' or subsceptible to institutionalization and (b) the contractarian choice of the one conception most in line with our considered judgments in reflective equilibrium, then the tension becomes apparent. On the one hand the contractarian elements of Rawls's theory cannot help us with the first task. Feasibility is a property of conceptions of justice which is independent of our preference for one conception over another. On the other hand, if we can establish the superiority of 'justice as fairness' on feasibility grounds, why would we need to select it via a contract?[5] The diagnosis of this tension seems accurate and is certainly corroborated by the undeniable fact that one of the main directions of change in Rawls's work over the two subsequent decades is a diminishing of importance of the metaphor of the contract with respect to the central role it played in *A Theory of Justice*.

Following Kukathas and Pettit, we can identify two distinct phases in the lapse of time that separates *A Theory of Justice* from *Political Liberalism*. In the first phase – including 'The Basic Structure as Subject' (1978), 'Kantian Constructivism in Moral Theory' (1980) and 'The Basic Liberties and their Priorities' (1982) – Rawls fine-tunes the Kantian aspects of 'justice as fairness' and tries to strengthen it against the standard Hegelian critique of Kant's moral philosophy.[6] The appropriateness of the principles of justice identified by the theory is now evaluated against a more *situated* context. As Rawls puts it,

> What justifies a conception of justice is not its being true to an order antecedent to and given to us, but its congruence with our deeper understanding of ourselves and our aspirations, and our realization that, given our history and the traditions embedded in our public life, it is the most reasonable doctrine for us. (1980: 519)

In this passage – to which Rorty has appealed in order to claim a thorough reversal of point of view on Rawls's part [7] – the author of *A Theory of Justice* now claims that the validity of a theory of justice should be understood as *congruence* with who we are, as its being the best theory *for us*. The goal of attaining a sort of *absolute impartiality* for the theory, inherent in the Kantian deontological approach and still somewhat ambiguously present in Rawls's earlier work, is now thoroughly replaced by a kind of *situated impartiality*. Furthermore, the procedure of construction now proceeds not only from the expository device of the original position but also from 'a model conception of the person'. Kantian constructivism follows in the footsteps of Kant in that it constructs a view of justice from a certain normative view of the moral actor as endowed with a sense of justice, but departs from Kant in seeking to articulate a view of justice which is valid not *sub specie aeternitatis* but only against the basic assumptions built into the political culture of our democratic societies. Also, Rawls's view of justice continues to be characterized by a Kantian colouring in the assumption that the two principles demand our allegiance not in view of instrumental considerations – not even in view of their conduciveness to collective well-being – but in so far as they bring to expression certain fundamental traits of our moral constitution. Another important aspect of the passage quoted above is the occurrence of the term 'reasonable'. The quality of being 'reasonable for us', typical of the view of justice at which we seek to arrive, stands in a complex relation to the *rational*. What is reasonable for us to hold is certainly broader in scope than what is merely rational for us; it is public in nature while the rational has a private nature; and, finally, it cannot be derived from the rational, though it is not entirely separate from it. Later, in *Political Liberalism*, Rawls specifies the relation: the reasonable becomes synonymous with a certain moral sensibility 'that underlies the desire to engage in fair cooperation as such, and to do so in terms that others as equals might reasonably be expected to endorse' (1993: 51).

In the second phase of the transition toward *Political Liberalism* Rawls emphasizes even more the situated quality of the construction of our principles of justice and at the same time veers away from an understanding of 'justice as fairness' along Kantian lines (Rawls 1987a; 1987b). In a footnote to 'Justice as Fairness: Political Not Metaphysical', Rawls retracts his suggestion that justice as fairness is part of the broader theory of rational choice: he calls an assertion to that effect, contained in *A Theory of Justice*, an 'incorrect' statement. Rather, the reconstruction of the arguments developed by the parties in the original position must be understood as part of a *political* conception of justice. The principles underlying that political conception of justice, continues Rawls, cannot be derived from 'an idea of the rational as the sole normative concept' (1985a: 237). The notion of the *reasonable* is needed.

The sense of the transition from the first to the second and the third stage in Rawls's thought is further reflected in the meaning of the term *political*, now introduced by Rawls in order to characterize the kind of liberalism and theory of justice that he endorses. 'Political' means, among other things, that a certain conception of justice, or a certain view of the person, is not bound up with controversial evaluative and factual assumptions – a requirement which can be satisfied only if we take a *situated* perspective. Uncontroversial can only mean uncontroversial 'among us', the citizens of a modern democratic society. A more detailed elucidation of the term 'political' will be offered below in the discussion of *Political Liberalism*.

Parallel to this realignment of emphasis we can notice a relocation of justice as fairness from the realm of moral philosophy into that of *political* philosophy.[8] The question of institutional stability for the basic structure founded on the two principles becomes now the paramount question. The task of political philosophy in a constitutional democracy becomes the formulation of

> a political conception of justice that can not only provide a shared public basis for the justification of political and social institutions but also helps ensure stability from one generation to the next. (Rawls 1987a: 1)

At this stage Rawls also draws for the first time the distinction between *political* and *comprehensive* conceptions of justice[9] and distances himself from the Kantian interpretation of his own project, but wishes to maintain the distinction between a political conception of justice and a mere *modus vivendi*. The public of a democratic society is still supposed to adhere to justice as fairness out of considerations of *principle*, not of expediency in achieving and stabilizing peace among the warring factions of society. These 'warring factions' are now identified with two main strands of modern political theory: the Lockean tradition which stresses negative freedom and the liberty of the moderns and the Rousseauian tradition which stresses equality and the liberty of the ancients. Reconciling these two traditions is presented as the chief challenge of contemporary political philosophy. The case for justice as fairness is now based no longer on its ability to win a contest over utilitarianism and intuitionism, but on its superior potential for becoming the focus of an *overlapping consensus* among the competing views of justice present in the political culture of modern democratic society. All these threads are finally woven together into a new systematic position in *Political Liberalism*.

The Model of the 'Overlapping Consensus'

Political Liberalism represents the end point of the trajectory initiated after the publication of *A Theory of Justice*. In this section I will discuss the elements of continuity and discontinuity between *A Theory of Justice* and *Political Liberalism* and then will examine in greater detail three central concepts in Rawls's latest work: namely, the concepts designated by the terms 'political', 'political constructivism' and 'public reason'.

The starting point of *Political Liberalism* is still the 'fact of pluralism' – or of 'reasonable pluralism', in the more recent formulation.[10] The 'fact of reasonable pluralism' is constituted (a) by the existence of an irreducible plurality of reasonable opinions concerning the good, the human being and the desirable ends of social life, and (b) by the permanence of this plurality which, far from representing a 'catastrophe' or a contingent state to be overcome in the future, constitutes instead a constant in the public culture of any democratic society.[11] Acknowledging the fact of pluralism makes it impossible for us to understand the fair solution to conflicts of interest and of value in terms of the realization of some kind of commonly shared evaluative horizon. Modern justice is a kind of justice that must be given to subjects who inhabit diverse ethical universes.

The *difference* between the two texts is best brought out by the question:

how is it possible to identify principles of justice that can be shared by individuals who dissent over the good for a human being and for the society in which they live? While in *A Theory of Justice* the idea of a mental experiment was prominent, in *Political Liberalism* this argumentative strategy moves to a less central role: it becomes *one* among various components of a normative picture which now contains an important historical dimension. This *historical* dimension does not merely amount to the demand that our political conception of justice be the most reasonable 'for us' rather than the most reasonable of all times and places, but pervades the *structure of the argument* in support of justice as fairness. The 'original position' argument for justice as fairness is now recast as representative of, and appropriate for, the first of two stages in the emergence of a *political* conception of justice from the early modern context of the religious wars.

In this first stage the contending parties start by accepting the intuitions embedded in justice as fairness in the same spirit as one accepts a compromise or *modus vivendi* (Rawls 1993: 159, 163) which appears capable of ending an otherwise hopeless conflict between opposing conceptions of the good and eventually end up forming a *constitutional consensus*, i.e. a consensus of a *procedural* kind. This kind of consensus allows polities to articulate *democratic constitutions* which express a common vision concerning (a) the way in which conflict of interest should be handled and (b) a common desire to expel religious issues from the political agenda. There remain, at this stage, large areas of disagreement concerning other areas of constitutional relevance, for example the scope and the ranking of rights.[12] This is the stage that best describes the current state of Western democratic societies, in which basic liberties are secured and thus the 'rules of political contest' are established clearly and firmly. Even so, however, there remains a large area of disagreement concerning 'the more exact content and boundaries of these rights and liberties, as well as on what further rights and liberties are to be counted as basic and so merit legal if not constitutional protection' (1993: 159).

Only at a further stage, not yet reached even by the most advanced among the advanced industrial societies, an *overlapping consensus* can emerge, which, without dedifferentiating the political culture – the plurality of comprehensive conceptions of the good remains in fact untouched – reflects a conception *no longer merely procedural*, but also *substantive*, and yet only *political*, of justice as fairness, a conception which now includes a shared interpretation of rights and social policies which respects the difference between the existent conceptions of the good. The motor of this development is the fact that once a constitutional consensus is reached, the need to form majorities around specific issues of political concern motivates groups clustered around a given comprehensive conception to 'move out of the narrower circle of their own views' (1993: 165) and to enter a dialogue with other groups. Since this motive is at work for all groups it generates a powerful drive toward the formation of a common understanding in matters previously divisive.[13] The object of the overlapping consensus is a political conception of justice, affirmed on moral grounds, and applied to the basic structure of society (1993: 147). It includes (a) the idea of society as a fair system of cooperation, (b) the idea of citizens as reasonable and rational, free and equal, and (c) the idea of taking certain matters off the political agenda, i.e. of no longer regarding them as appropriate subjects for political decisions by majority or other plurality vote (1993: 151).

The insertion of a temporal dimension in the argumentative framework introduces a Hegelian twist in a previously Humean and Kantian framework.[14] The Hegelian moment in *Political Liberalism* is twofold. First, we can see a marked emphasis on the necessity to start our quest for a political conception of justice from the existing traditions of our own society. Second, the internal dynamic which leads to the eventual formation of an overlapping consensus retroactively strengthens the original position argument about the two principles. This argument now gets cast in a more appealing light also because we are given a more articulate view of where the initial acceptance of the two principles leads.

Finally, aside from the already mentioned emphasis on the question of 'stability', which remained peripheral in *A Theory of Justice*, *Political Liberalism* is characterized by another powerful shift of accentuation. Its author is interested less in showing the superiority of 'justice as fairness' over the other competing conceptions of justice, using arguments that 'compel' the opposer either to agree or to accept being labelled 'unreasonable', than in showing that 'justice as fairness' is *not incompatible* with a number of other conceptions of justice embedded in a multiplicity of comprehensive ethical conceptions. The theory of justice as fairness no longer demands our allegiance *qua* winner of an ideal contest between rival conceptions, but rather by virtue of its being more capable than any other theory of staying away and keeping *us* away from the contest, by virtue of its leaving the question of superiority open – in other words by virtue of its remaining *neutral* with respect to all the other conceptions.[15]

It is now time to take a closer look at the meaning of the terms 'political', 'political constructivism' and 'public reason'. As was already the case during the transitional stage, the adjective 'political' stands first and foremost in opposition to 'metaphysical' (1993: 10), an opposition elucidated by Rawls through another conceptual pair: 'partial' and 'comprehensive'. A conception of justice which purports to constitute the core of a 'comprehensive' view of human subjectivity, of reason, of history and of the good is *metaphysical*. This is not to say that then it must necessarily be misleading or plainly wrong. It means, however, that that conception does not possess one quality which is essential for any view of justice fit for societies like ours. Its being enmeshed with comprehensive substantive assumptions makes it acceptable only by those who already agree with these substantive assumptions concerning subjectivity, reason, history and the good. *Political* is a conception of justice which does not depend on any assumption which turns out to be unacceptable to any of the reasonable conceptions of the good that coexist in a modern and democratic society.[16] More specifically, a *political* conception of *justice* is characterized by three distinctive features.

First, like the view presented in *A Theory of Justice*, it takes the 'basic structure of society' as its object – i.e. the set of the main political, social and economical institutions of a society and the sense in which these institutions form a unified system of cooperation that lasts over subsequent generations (1993: 11).

Second, a political conception of justice is susceptible of being *publicly* defended without any reference to values, to ideals of personality, of family, of friendship and of the social bond that are controversial, but this is not to say that conception does not presuppose any idea of the good (1993: 12–13).

Third, the argument in favour of a *political* conception of justice involves reference to 'certain fundamental ideas seen as implicit in the public culture of a democratic society' (1993: 13–15). Among these ideas, central is the notion of society as 'a fair system of cooperation over time, from one generation to the next' (1993: 14). Interesting, in this respect, is Rawls's warning that it would be a mistake to 'look to the comprehensive doctrines that in fact exist and then draw up a political conception that strikes some kind of balance of forces between them' (1993: 39). The procedure to be followed in outlining a *political* conception of justice cannot be conceived as a meeting halfway of the doctrines actually existing in a given society at a given time: 'This is not how justice as fairness proceeds,' warns Rawls (1993: 39). Understood along these lines, the notion of *overlapping consensus* would entrap us in a hopeless and uninspiring relativism. Rawls's idea of the overlapping consensus hinges, instead, on the hypothesis or 'hope' that if we work out *deductively* (a) the implications of the central idea of society as a fair system of cooperation, together with (b) the other interconnected ideas[17] and (c) the list of primary goods (basic rights and liberties, freedom of movement and occupation, powers and prerogatives of offices, wealth, income, and the social bases of self-respect), the resulting complex of assumptions can constitute the core of a generalized consensus which cuts across all the *reasonable* comprehensive conceptions present in our societies.

From a certain point of view, the term 'political' seems to acquire a peculiar *anti-political* ring. For a value, a conception of justice, a view of the person and of society, to be 'political' means to be acceptable by everybody by virtue of its being neutral with respect to the divisions that traverse the broader society and culture. The term 'political' takes on the meaning of 'unanimously acceptable', *au-dessus de la mêlée*. This meaning, intuitively opposite to the one commonly associated with the term 'political', in fact corresponds to a particular use of the term, which Rawls extends to cover the whole spectrum of the meaning of the term. He uses the term 'political' in a sense comparable to the one which we associate with the adjectives 'constitutional' and 'non-partisan', usually employed to designate a specific kind of political action – more exquisitely political than partisan politics – ideally associated with the function of the Supreme Court or any similar institution.

In the third chapter of *Political Liberalism* Rawls defends the methodological credentials of his constructivist theory of justice. By the term 'constructivism' is generally meant an approach to moral questions that, in a way that resembles what Habermas calls 'rational reconstruction', posits that the principles of justice are not something that we 'discover' or of which we 'become aware', but something which we cannot but postulate whenever we want to account for our intuitions concerning right and wrong. The main opponent of constructivism is the *moral realist* or *intuitionist* view according to which moral values exist in an ontological sense and are hierarchically ordered along lines which we can discover but not modify at our own will. From a moral realist or intuitionist standpoint, the fairness of the just social order is something to be discovered but not invented.

Constructivism can be understood in light of the distinction between three points of view: the standpoint of the parties in the original position; the standpoint of the citizens of a well-ordered society; and finally the standpoint of we who examine the various theories of justice, including justice as fairness, as candidates for the title of 'best political conception of justice'.[18] While the first two standpoints are *postulated* rather than constructed in the context of the theory of justice,[19] a constructivist perspective proper can be found only in the case of the point of view of we who evaluate the diverse conceptions of justice. In this context the constructivist alternative to moral realism, to relativism and to moral naturalism (the derivation of moral principles from non-moral notions) centres on the notion of 'reflective equilibrium'.[20] Reflective equilibrium is reached when the hermeneutic to and fro between our concrete moral judgments (the (in)justice of this practice, this policy, this statute) and our tentative formulation of general criteria or principles of justice (the Golden Rule, the maximization of utility, etc.) ceases to highlight discrepancies that call for new adjustments of our general conception of justice. This is still a *narrow* reflective equilibrium, however. A *wide* reflective equilibrium, instead, occurs when our concrete judgments on the one hand and the general principles on the other are reconciled with our most considered convictions concerning human nature, the nature of society, the meaning of rationality, and so forth. The wide reflective equilibrium which can ground *for us* the rightness of a certain conception of justice consists then, according to Rawls, in bringing three things together into a coherent whole: our own specific judgments, our tentative formulations concerning the possible general principles of justice, and a relevant set of background views. Understood along these lines, the notion of wide reflective equilibrium represents one of the main junctures at which the openness of the Rawlsian framework to a hermeneutic and more specifically judgment-based understanding of normative validity becomes evident.[21]

All these considerations apply to constructivism *in general*. *Political* constructivism is best characterized through contrast with other kinds of constructivist approaches, for example Kant's *moral* constructivism.[22] The main difference concerns the *scope* of the relevance of moral principles. For Kant the categorical imperative extends its cogency over the entire practical domain and thus is relevant for all the possible moral decisions that a moral actor may be confronted with. For Rawls, instead, justice as fairness has a much narrower relevance: it only accounts for our intuitions concerning the legitimate basic structure of a democratic society.

Another important notion introduced by Rawls in *Political Liberalism* is that of 'public reason'. Although this is not a term used by Rawls, public reason can be understood as a *universe of discourse* – namely, the universe constituted by all that is public knowledge, by the shared bases on which common decisions are made, and which marks the territory within which public deliberation must move. 'Politics in a democratic society,' maintains Rawls, 'can never be guided by what we see as the whole truth.' Only if we accept this fact can we fulfil a feasible ideal of legitimacy that Rawls describes as 'to live politically with others in the light of reasons all might reasonably be expected to endorse' (1993: 243). Public reason is not the same as overlapping consensus. It has a dynamic quality: it generates new consensus, it is not just a mere recording of existing convergences. Public reason is necessarily more limited than the other forms of reason which play a role in the process of the self-production of society. In its necessary limitedness, from which however its binding force originates, public reason stands opposite to the completeness and wholeness of partial reason.

Let us imagine a criminal trial. Public reason is here represented by the judicial procedure. It proceeds from the facts of the matter not 'as they are', but rather as they are represented in the legitimate trial records. The fairness of the criminal trial rests on the fact that for all the firmness of our private conviction concerning certain facts, the guilt of the respondent, or the cogency of a certain piece of evidence, this conviction carries no weight as far as our reasoning must proceed. Public reason is reasoning based on convictions formed only on the basis of legitimate evidence, of a representation of reality constructed according to certain rules. The facts of the matter count for nothing in a criminal trial if ascertained through the use of methods different from the procedure established as legitimate. Evidence illegally obtained through deception, for instance by wiring the respondent's telephone or violating the privacy of his mail, cannot count towards determining the judicial outcome of the proceeding but can only contribute to the formation of our own *private* convictions. In a similar way, in any official meeting of a deliberative body the only past which can publicly and legitimately count for the purpose of the deliberation at hand is the past represented in the regularly approved minutes. The point of both examples is that, in the area of public deliberation, to act on a basis more limited than the 'whole truth', yet a shared basis, may be preferable to acting on the basis of a representation of broader scope but of contested validity. This is the point of public reason.

The idea of public reason is also an original way of reformulating the theme of the 'common good'. For the self-limitation entailed by submitting one's claims to public reason is undergone, neither out of strategic considerations nor *despite* our broader political ideals, but, on the contrary, just out of respect for our ideals. Both the examples mentioned are cases in which we feel not merely that it is to our advantage, but that it is *fair* to act not on the basis of our private beliefs concerning the 'matter of fact' but on the basis of what turns out to be a 'shared construal of the matter of fact'. The main example of a deliberative body functioning according to public reason is once again the Supreme Court or any similar body to which in a constitutional regime the function of assessing the constitutional legitimacy of statutes approved by the legislative bodies is assigned.

The chapter on public reason is one of the sections of *Political Liberalism* in which the presence of a newly developing judgment-oriented understanding of the operation of reason, alongside and in tension with the generalizing and principle-based understanding, is most visible. 'What public reason asks,' argues Rawls, 'is that citizens be able to explain their vote to one another in terms of a reasonable balance of public political values' (1993: 243). This requirement screens out those comprehensive doctrines which fail to generate such a 'reasonable balance of political values'. Furthermore, Rawls concedes that 'not all reasonable balances [among the political values at issue in a controversy] are the same'. One problem arises in this connection. First, the grounds on which the reasonableness of the 'reasonable balance of political values' can be established remain unclear. It should be noted that Rawls does not offer a direct definition of the reasonableness of abstract ideas and political arrangements or solutions to practical problems, but highlights its features by way of defining what it means for *persons* to be reasonable. Since persons are deemed reasonable when (a) they are willing 'to propose fair terms of cooperation and to abide by them provided that others do' (1993: 54) and (b) when they are willing to accept 'the burdens of judgment and to accept their consequences for the use of public reason' (1993: 54), we can draw the conclusion that for a solution to a practical problem to rest on a 'reasonable balance of political values' means that the solution in question does not violate the terms of what reasonable people would regard as 'fair cooperation' and does purport to originate in a standpoint above the burdens of judgment.[23] Rawls does not clarify, however, how we are to understand the notion of the 'better balance', in situations in which several ways of balancing the political values involved in a controversy are supported by different sectors of the public, and all meet the requirement of reasonableness. His discussion of abortion shows the difficulty. According to Rawls, (a) 'the due respect for human life', (b) 'the ordered reproduction of political society over time, including the family', and (c) 'the equality of women as equal citizens' are the political values which require 'balancing' in the context of the abortion issue. Rawls maintains that 'any reasonable balance of these three values will give a woman a duly qualified right to decide whether or not to end her pregnancy during the first trimester' (1993: 243). This is because at 'the early stage of pregnancy the political value of the equality of women is overriding'. The description of the three political values involved is believed by Rawls to generate, in and of itself, the conclusion that 'any comprehensive doctrine that leads to a balance of political values excluding that duly qualified right [i.e. a woman's right to terminate her pregnancy] in the first trimester is to that extent unreasonable' (1993: 243). The argument is that the right to terminate pregnancy is 'required' in order to give 'force and substance' to the political value of the *equality* of women. Assuming that the political equality of women hinges on their right to terminate pregnancy, the idea that that right and with it the political equality of women would be undermined if its exercise were restricted to the first 10 weeks, as some demand, in lieu of the first three months, is not supported by any specific argument.

The Exchange with Habermas

In the March 1995 issue of *The Journal of Philosophy* Rawls engaged in a debate of historical importance with Jürgen Habermas. Interesting in this context is the fact that in his reply Rawls further develops some of the ideas presented in *Political Liberalism* and introduces some new distinctions. Furthermore, the tone of his reply corroborates the anti-foundationalist reading of *Political Liberalism*.

First, in response to Habermas's questioning the sharpness of his distinction between the *normative* acceptability of a political conception of justice and its *factual* acceptance within a given context, Rawls distinguishes three senses in which the term 'justification' can be used in connection with a political conception of justice. In the first sense, the political conception of justice can be made the object of a *'pro tanto* justification' – namely, a kind of justification offered within the bounds of public reason through recourse to political values only (1995: 142–3), and as such always susceptible of being 'overridden by citizens' comprehensive doctrines once all the values are tallied up' (1995: 143). In the second sense, the justification is offered by an individual citizen by means of binding the political conception of justice 'in some way to the citizen's comprehensive doctrine, as either true or reasonable, depending on what the doctrine allows' (1995: 143). This form of justification is beyond the reach of a *political* conception of justice, in that it involves the weighing of political values against non-political ones. In the third sense, a political conception of justice can be publicly justified by a political society – and this version of justification is at the centre of political liberalism. 'Public justification happens when all the reasonable members of political society carry out a justification of the shared political conception by embedding it in their several reasonable comprehensive views' (1995: 143). More specifically, the political conception is justified in this third sense when all the reasonable citizens 'taken collectively (but not acting as a corporate body) are in general and wide reflective equilibrium in affirming the political conception on the basis of their several reasonable comprehensive doctrines' (1995: 144). The occurrence of such a justification presupposes the existence of an overlapping consensus among the citizens. This leads Rawls to specify a second idea that was only implicitly present in *Political Liberalism*.

Rawls distinguishes now two kinds of consensus in a clearer way than was done in *Political Liberalism*.[24] One is consensus as found in everyday politics, whenever a politician 'looking to various existing interests and claims' brings together 'a coalition or policy that all or a sufficient number can support to gain a majority' (1995: 145). The other is a *reasonable overlapping consensus* and is the kind of consensus whose occurrence renders a political conception of justice publicly justified.

A reasonable overlapping consensus is also a necessary condition for a democratic society to acquire 'stability for the right reasons'. *Stability for the right reasons* is the new version of the concept of the 'stability of a well-ordered society' (1993: 38, 65). The new element introduced via this concept is a specification of the conditions under which a political conception of justice can be considered endorsed by an overlapping consensus. To the overlapping consensus must concur 'all the reasonable comprehensive doctrines in society' and these must be 'in an enduring majority with respect to those rejecting that conception' (1995: 147). Should instead a given conception of justice fail to gain endorsement on the part of any of the reasonable comprehensive conceptions, or should the unreasonable comprehensive conceptions that reject the political view of justice outnumber the reasonable ones, then society would not benefit from 'stability for the right reasons', but would be integrated merely via a *modus vivendi*, subject to the contingent fluctuation of a balance of forces and powers.

I will not deal with Rawls's important reflection on the concept of legitimacy in its relation to that of justice (1995: 148, 175–7) or with his reconstruction in six steps of the relation of basic liberties to a fully adequate system of the two kinds of liberties (of the ancients and of the moderns) (1995: 167–8). Rather, I would like to recall briefly one point made by Rawls in response to Habermas's accusation of weakening excessively the normative claim of justice as fairness. 'Political liberalism does not use the concept of moral truth applied to its own political (always moral) judgments' (1995: 149). Such use of a strong concept of validity 'is not rejected or questioned, but left to comprehensive doctrines to use or deny, or use some other idea instead' (1995: 150). The point of the political conception of justice embedded in political liberalism is simply to articulate a reasonable view of the reasonable and entrust it to a 'politics of hope' – the hope that it might win the consensus of all the citizens who evaluate it from within their reasonable comprehensive conceptions.

At the same time Rawls urges us not to confuse this minimalist attitude of 'normative restraint' with the Habermasian claim, rejected by him, that a theory of justice could and ought to be formulated in purely *procedural* terms. The opposition between procedural and substantive justice, i.e. the justice of a procedure and the justice of the ensuing outcome, is misleading in that there is, according to Rawls, no way of determining whether the requirements of procedural justice have been satisfied unless we also evaluate the (substantive) justice of the outcomes.[25] The point is illustrated with reference to the debate which opposes defenders of majoritarian democracy to constitutionalists. In their seemingly 'procedural' assessment of the fairness of generalized and fairly unchecked majority rule, both parties in fact, suggests Rawls, bring substantive evaluations concerning the outcomes of majority rule into play. The majoritarian argument, for example, has to rely on the assumption that 'constitutional devices are unnecessary and would, if anything, make those outcomes worse' (1995: 172–3). Thus the attainable ideal of the impartiality of a conception of justice should not be equated with the unrealistic demand that such a conception be free of substantive elements.[26]

Finally, Rawls replies to Habermas's criticism concerning the failure, on the part of the political conception of justice articulated in *Political Liberalism*, to give equal consideration to the private and the political notions of autonomy. Habermas claimed, in his article, that on Rawls's view the full exercise of the political autonomy of the people, the exercise of its sovereignty, takes place only at the stage when the principles inspiring the constitution are selected and at the subsequent stage of framing the constitution. All subsequent generations of citizens will enjoy only a dimidiated chance of exercising their communal autonomous political will, in that they will have to act within the boundaries set for them by the existent constitution, which is to say that in the context of democratic societies the sovereignty of the citizens is constrained from the outside by a basic set of negative liberties, or liberties of the moderns, established by a previous generation of citizens. Hence within the Rawlsian framework the constitution cannot be understood as 'an unfinished project' and citizens 'cannot reignite the radical democratic embers of the original position in the civic life of their society' (Habermas 1995a: 128). To this criticism Rawls responds that even though the outcome of the exercise of the citizens' political autonomy at the first two stages of the founding of a well-ordered society – the stage of the selection of principles and that of the framing of a constitution with a bill of rights – does indeed place constraints on the popular sovereignty of subsequent generations as expressed in the legislature, these constraints cannot be understood as pre-political ones imposed from outside, such as in natural law views. Rather, they are also the outcome of 'the will of the people expressed in democratic procedures such as ratifications of a constitution and enacting amendments' (Rawls 1995: 158). While it is true that the public and autonomous political will that has framed the constitution is that of *another* generation of citizens, different from those who will inherit the constitution and the constraints therefrom ensuing, it would be a misunderstanding – Rawls continues – to think that the 'citizens' conception of justice can be fixed once and for all'. Justice and a just constitution can never be 'fully realized', and the existing ones will always be 'subject to being checked by our reflective considered judgments' (1995: 153). Nothing prevents citizens from 'reigniting the radical democratic embers of the original position in civic life', and in fact citizens continually discuss publicly whether the existing arrangements of their time fit or fail to fit their view of justice and the constitutional embodiment of it. Even in the case of an 'already just society', where no fundamental injustices are present, it cannot be maintained that citizens do have a lesser chance to exercise political autonomy if they find a just constitution already framed by earlier generations. For the tasks of 'fully comprehending' and 'intelligently and wisely executing' a constitution are no less expressive of political autonomy than the act of framing it. And the less mechanistically we understand the task of executing a constitution, the more it appears to require public autonomy. If applying a constitution is seen as a task which involves a hermeneutic assessment of a network of meanings much broader than the meanings of the sentences that compose it, if we understand the constitution as a 'constitution of principle', as Ronald Dworkin has put it, then applying it does not involve any lesser degree of political autonomy than framing it.

The Overlapping Consensus and the Tension between Two Models of Normative Validity

I will now move on to discuss some of the questions raised by Rawls's political conception of justice from the vantage point of the emergence of a reflective judgment understanding of validity in political philosophy. These questions – some smaller, others of larger import, some already albeit partially taken up, others still neglected by Rawls – can be grouped under three main headings. Some of them relate to various aspects of the notion of *overlapping consensus*. Others concern the conceptual boundaries of a number of relevant categories in the theory. Finally, a third set of questions arises as a manifestation of an unsolved tension, underlying Rawls's intellectual trajectory, between a *constructivist* inspiration and a *contextualist* sensibility that underlie two different understandings of normative validity.

There are several questions raised by the complex of issues dealt with by Rawls under the title of *overlapping consensus*. The first concerns the *range* of comprehensive conceptions of the good and comprehensive views of justice which are admitted to concur to the formation of the overlapping consensus. We will recall that for Rawls the formation of an overlapping consensus cannot be understood as a meeting halfway of existing conceptions of justice: such a procedure would mire the resulting view of justice in a hopeless relativism and at best would produce the kind of 'ordinary consensus' that politicians try to secure by articulating a still latent convergence of interests. The correct way of proceeding, instead, involves a deductive derivation of the implications generated by the idea of society as a fair system of cooperation, by some of its related notions, and by the list of primary goods, in the *hope* that the resulting complex of assumptions will be shared by all the *reasonable* comprehensive conceptions that exist in a democratic society and that these will outnumber the comprehensive conceptions that reject it. Incidentally, this latter clause points to a contextual feature – the relative proportion of reasonable comprehensive conceptions to 'unreasonable comprehensive conceptions that reject justice as fairness' – which is totally *contingent* and beyond the ability of a liberal political philosopher to affect or theoretically neutralize. It makes for the ultimate contingency of the soundness of a political conception of justice.

Initially, at the stage of *A Theory of Justice*, the range of comprehensive conceptions to be bridged via justice as fairness seemed to include only conceptions that, in relation to the basic structure of a just society, emphasize either the value of *liberty* (Locke) or the value of *equality* (Rousseau). To call this range reductive, in light of the positions left out, is an understatement. However, with the distinction, drawn in *Political Liberalism*, between 'the fact of pluralism' and the 'fact of *reasonable* pluralism', the set of comprehensive conceptions with which justice as fairness should prove compatible, if it is to function as the normative core of the political culture of a democratic society, is extended to include *all* the comprehensive conceptions – past, present and future – which are or will be *reasonable*, namely do or will include a recognition of their own partiality and of the legitimacy of the other, equally reasonable, perspectives. Indeed, more than just the two traditions emphasizing 'the liberties of the moderns' and the 'liberties of the ancients' meet the standard of reasonableness. One needs only recall, for example, Mosca's and Pareto's elitist view of the democratic process, Weber's conception of democratic legitimacy, Schumpeter's conception of democracy as an electoral contest of elites or Luhmann's view of the democratic process. Furthermore, in the Western democracies of our time, characterized not just by the presence of a multiplicity of ethnic communities (which was the case also in the past) but by the pervasive diffusion of a *multicultural* ideal, the political cultures that compete and meet the standard of reasonableness are much more distant from one another. Finally, in many contemporary Western societies we find political conceptions (some reasonable, others unreasonable) that cannot be easily assigned to one or the other polarity of the dichotomy of freedom and equality. Take the cases, just to mention the examples that most readily come to mind, of the Scandinavian social democracies, of the European Christian democratic parties with their Catholic ethic of solidarity, of the privatism typical of the regular 'non-voters', of the postmodernist aesthetic subcultures, of fundamentalist ecology and environmentalism, of 'identity politics'. If the political conception of justice were not compatible with many of these conceptions, the *overlapping consensus* which, according to Rawls, makes the theory of justice as fairness convincing *for us* would narrow down that 'us' not only to the inhabitants of advanced industrial societies, or even to supporters of modern and reasonable comprehensive conceptions, but to an exceedingly restricted subset of them. The question concerns here the burden of proof. It seems plausible to claim that it is incumbent on the defender of political liberalism to show that the political conception of justice is compatible with the above mentioned and possibly other reasonable comprehensive conceptions present in democratic societies. An implicit confirmation of the plausibility of this way of assigning the burden of proof comes from Rawls's own arguments to the effect that the political conception of justice embedded in political liberalism is compatible with the comprehensive liberal conceptions that stress respectively rights and popular sovereignty, private and political autonomy, the liberties of the moderns and those of the ancients. Such arguments implicitly suggest the acceptance, on his part, of a burden of proof with respect to the actual compatibility of justice of fairness with at least those two families of reasonable comprehensive conceptions. However, in order to vindicate Rawls's claim that his 'political liberalism' is to count as the outline of a political conception of justice for Western democratic societies as such, it seems necessary either to produce a compatibility argument also with respect to *other* families of comprehensive conceptions, some of which were mentioned above, or to produce an argument that convincingly denies them the status of *reasonable* comprehensive doctrines.

The *overlapping consensus* approach, however, raises also a *second* series of questions. These questions concern the line which should in principle separate the views and opinions relevant within political discussion from those which are irrelevant and unacceptable. The issue is addressed in the section of *Political Liberalism* devoted to 'The Limits of Public Reason'. Rawls distinguishes two versions of the notion of public reason. He rejects the 'exclusive view', according to which 'on fundamental political matters, reasons given explicitly in terms of comprehensive doctrines are never to be introduced into public reason' (1993: 247). That view appears excessively restrictive to him and fit only for the ideal case of a well-ordered society. The 'inclusive view', instead, is presented by Rawls as more flexible, in that it allows 'citizens, in certain situations, to present what they regard as the basis of political values rooted in their comprehensive doctrine, provided they do this *in ways that strengthen the ideal of public reason itself*' (1993: 247). The extended view of public reason is appropriate for those situations in which a society is either partially well ordered but plagued by controversies about the application of the principles of justice, or not well ordered at all. The rationale for waiving the unacceptability of bringing comprehensive conceptions into the public realm is a *pragmatic* one: under such circumstances, arguments that draw on comprehensive conceptions, if and to the extent that they result in an affirmation of the public values, may contribute to the strengthening of mutual trust between the contending parties. 'To explain in the public forum how one's comprehensive doctrine affirms the political values' (1993: 249) may result in a strengthening of the conditions for the emergence of an overlapping consensus. The role that comprehensive conceptions may *legitimately* play in the public arena is thus primarily a *social-psychological* one: the citizens' exposure to experiencing how adherence to the political values can be generated *from their tenets*, as opposed to *bracketing them away*, strengthens mutual trust.

Two points seem here in need of further elaboration. First, on the social-psychological level, it is not clear why the result of such experience has to be necessarily the one described by Rawls. Depending on how removed from the political values a given comprehensive conception is generally perceived to be, the experience of seeing its leading representatives present in a public forum 'how their comprehensive doctrine does indeed affirm those values' may be cause for *alarm*, more than anything else – as for example when the leaders of an Italian 'post-fascist' party join the celebrations in memory of the victims of fascism.

Second, the price paid for confining the relevance of comprehensive views in the public arena to a trust-enhancing role could be the risk of overlooking their possible role in bringing about political change. How can the political values of a well-ordered society ever change? If all the actors follow 'public reason', it seems difficult to conceive how the various 'partial reasons' which, in the civil society of partially well-ordered societies like ours, move the conflict of interests and depend on rival comprehensive conception, could ever affect the substance of the overlapping consensus on which rest the basic structure of the society and its public political culture, including its political conception of justice. Significant political change would then be bound to always occur in an 'illegitimate' or 'unreasonable' way. If one subscribes to Rawls's view of public reason, can political *change* ever be 'political'?

The difficulty of distinguishing with sufficient sharpness between political and non-political views surfaces most clearly in the section of *Political Liberalism* in which Rawls argues that 'the abolitionists and the leaders of the civil rights movement did not go against the ideal of public reason' (1993: 250–1). Now, the abolitionists could not draw as unambiguously on the Constitution as the civil rights leaders of the 1960s, but had to rely on *religious* conceptions of the person. The legitimacy of their drawing on comprehensive conceptions in order to defend values that became 'political' only much later – which is just another way of saying that they were *not* political at all at the relevant time – is justified by Rawls on the basis of (a) the abolitionists' own understanding of 'their actions as the best way to bring about a well-ordered and just society in which the ideal of public reason could eventually be honored' and (b) the assumption that 'the political forces they led were among the *necessary historical conditions* to establish political justice'.[27] Neither of these reasons, which supposedly justify the abolitionists' recourse to comprehensive conceptions in order to justify collective action aimed at not-yet-political values, seems entirely convincing. First, subjective conviction of the conduciveness of one's political action to a well-ordered and just society seems an exceedingly inclusive criterion, to say the least. Second, on what basis, other than from within one among many comprehensive conceptions, can the political philosopher, or we the citizens, for that matter, ever ascertain whether the action and results of certain political movements are *necessary historical conditions* for establishing political justice?

A third set of questions raised by Rawls's conception of political liberalism concerns the boundaries of a number of concepts and their interrelations. Such questions concern primarily the concepts of 'comprehensive conceptions', of the 'publicity condition', and of society as 'a system of fair cooperation'. Let us take the case of comprehensive conceptions. A *political* conception of justice must be independent of ideas about human nature, about rationality and of values like the Kantian value of autonomy which are part of *comprehensive doctrines* not shared by all the citizens. On the other hand, however, a political conception of justice is not an abstract construction. Its principles must rest on ideas that are part and parcel of the public culture of a democratic society. Some of these ideas are: the model conception of the person as endowed with a capacity for a sense of justice and a capacity for a conception of the good, what Rawls calls 'the facts of com-

monsense political sociology' (1993: 193), the belief in the persistence of pluralism, the bindingness of a 'duty of civility' (1993: 217), not to mention the
shared 'general beliefs about human nature and the way political and social
institutions work' (1993: 66) required by the 'publicity condition'. Yet, how is
one to draw the line between the so-called comprehensive conceptions and
ideas as general as these? In the absence of a substantive criterion, the distinction between even quite general ideas that nonetheless are part of a
democratic culture on one hand, and comprehensive conceptions on the
other, seems to depend entirely on the *contingent* extension of the *actual, de
facto* consensus on a given belief or value – with relativistic consequences
which reflect on the rest of the theory.

Related to this point is Rawls's assumption that the boundaries of the
political – given his definition of the term 'political' – are themselves above
controversy. While no *ad hoc* argument is offered in support of such an
assumption, its counter-intuitive nature must be noted. The boundaries of the
political do not seem to lie at the frontier of politics, as it were: on the contrary, they are metaphorically at the *centre* of politics, in the sense that they
constitute one of the main themes of political debate and more often than not
are *contested* boundaries. Social, scientific-technological and *moral* changes
constantly raise new challenges: for example, the need for a measure of environmental protection, the need to set proper limits to genetical
experimentation, the need to establish a threshold beyond which human life
can no longer be considered fully human, and thus worth preserving, or the
minimal threshold before which the life of the foetus is not yet considered
human, and so forth. Now, these problems – for which Ronald Dworkin has
aptly coined the phrase 'the life's dominion' – arise at the interface between a
political culture and more comprehensive philosophical conceptions of the
person and of human dignity. Often the conflict is between those who maintain that their position is *within* the bounds of the political and those who
challenge that claim. The philosopher who wishes to argue in favour of a
political conception of justice may then not be in a position – as Rawls seems
to presuppose – to fall back on an agreed understanding of what constitutes
shared ground and what counts as controversial.[28]

Furthermore, in *Political Liberalism* Rawls resorts, more often and at
more decisive points than in his previous work, to certain essential ideas of
sociological theory. For instance, *Political Liberalism* is presented as a solution to the same problem (1993: xviii) on which social theory has been
interrogating itself for well over a century: how is it possible to ensure the stability or the integration of a complex society in which no unified and shared
horizon of meanings and value orientations exists any longer? That such
stability or integration can rest on the general consensus over a political
conception of justice is certainly a very interesting thesis, but if we are to take
it seriously, this thesis must also prove superior to other theses that have
been advanced and which suggest, instead, that the stability or integration of
complex societies is best guaranteed by market (Smith), functional (Spencer)
or systemic (Luhmann) interdependence, by the general consensus on a set of

substantive value orientations (Durkheim, Parsons), by the operation of the legal subsystem (Weber), and so forth.

Finally, also the idea of society as a 'system of fair cooperation that lasts over time' has constituted – under the heading of the 'problem of the division of labour' – one of the foci of sociological theory. Rawls seems to assume that from this idea – which he, quite optimistically, takes to be simple and self-evident – a coherent and unique set of implications can be drawn for the purpose of understanding the conditions for the stability and integration of a democratic society. The names of Adam Smith and Auguste Comte, of Herbert Spencer and Emile Durkheim, of Karl Marx and Georg Simmel, however, stand for as many reminders of the multiplicity of the implications, not necessarily compatible with one another, that one can draw from the seemingly elementary notion of 'fair cooperation'. The suspicion arises that the function played by the idea of 'fair cooperation' within the whole argument presented in *Political Liberalism* can be served successfully only if the meaning of the adjective 'fair', as applied to the noun 'cooperation', already is understood, circularly, in terms of that view of justice (as fairness) which supposedly it should help legitimate.

In the light of these difficulties, and considering the interpretation of his own intellectual trajectory provided by Rawls, one wonders whether he does not in fact gloss over a certain tension that exists between the two models of normative validity underlying *A Theory of Justice* and *Political Liberalism*. *Political Liberalism* is itself traversed by a tension between a *constructivist* and a *contextualist* perspective – what used to be misleadingly called a *stronger* and a *weaker* model of reason, as though the stronger model was a viable option and the weaker was not in fact the only one compatible with the fact of pluralism – ultimately linked with the two models of determinant judgment or generalizing and reflective judgment or exemplary universalism. The constructivist emphasis survives in Rawls's characterization of the original position and in his deontological understanding of the *overlapping consensus*. The contextualist accent resounds in his conception of public reason, in the notion of wide reflective equilibrium and in the section on the 'burdens of judgment'. I will mention two instances of this tension.

First, while it is true that the substantive core of the overlapping consensus continues, in line with the constructivist inspiration of the *Theory*, to be *analytically* derived from the notion of society as a fair system of cooperation, in *Political Liberalism* the actual obtaining of consensus, and thus the legitimacy of the basic structure of society, depends to a much greater extent on contingencies related to the political cultures prevailing in a given context, their distribution and inherent inclinations. A decisive indicator of this shift toward a contextualist weakening of the framework is the fact that the argument in favour of justice as fairness has lost – in *Political Liberalism* – the normative power to pronounce unfair or unjust the political arrangements of a society wherein the overlapping consensus failed to materialize: in such case, we could only say that our 'hope' to the effect that the view of justice analytically drawn from the notion of fair cooperation and related ideas will be compatible with all the reasonable comprehensive conceptions has proven ungrounded.[29] This alone suffices to highlight the distance that separates *A Theory of Justice* from Rawls's later work.

Another example of the tension between a contextualist and a constructivist perspective is offered by the 'publicity condition' associated with the conception of justice typical of a well-ordered society. In a well-ordered society, the principles of justice are accepted by all the citizens and this acceptance in turn is known to everybody (1993: 66). At a second level, however, the publicity condition requires that the citizens of a well-ordered society also agree on those general beliefs 'about human nature and the way political and social institutions generally work' as well as on 'all such beliefs relevant to political justice' (1993: 66). Such consensus, according to Rawls, rests on the fact that the citizens of a well-ordered society share also the 'methods of inquiry' and the 'forms of reasoning' on the basis of which the beliefs that serve as standards for assessing the soundness of principles are assessed (1993: 67). Now, if this second level of the 'publicity condition' were actually satisfied, it would cease to be clear how in a well-ordered society the 'fact of reasonable pluralism' could ever persist, over and beyond temporary contingencies due to contextual limitations. Equally unclear is how this second level of the 'publicity condition' can be reconciled with Rawls's understanding of the so-called 'burdens of judgment'. The burdens of judgment, which he describes as part and parcel of the modern condition, are the factors primarily responsible for the rise of reasonable pluralism. They play a role somewhat analogous to Wittgenstein's notion of the self-containedness of language games. We can understand them as six features inherent in every modern context of theoretical or practical choice. First, 'the evidence . . . bearing on the case is conflicting and complex, and thus hard to assess and evaluate'. Second, even if we agree on the nature of the considerations that are relevant, 'we may disagree about their weight, and so arrive at different judgments'. Third, all our concepts are somehow 'vague and subject to hard cases'. Fourth, our way of assessing evidence and assigning priority to values is somehow 'shaped by our total experience . . . and our total experiences must always differ'. Fifth, in every dispute the contending parties often proceed from 'different kinds of normative considerations of different force'. And, sixth, there is no way to avoid, on the part of any system of social institutions, a certain measure of 'closure', i.e. the selective promotion of certain values to the detriment of others.[30] Assuming that the burdens of judgment define the context of every theoretical or practical deliberation in modern times, it becomes hard to see how the requirements of the 'publicity conditions' could ever be met.

Another of the points worth further consideration is the fact that Rawls's understanding of the political quality of his conception of justice as *uncontroversiality* puts him in no position to exclude the possibility of a *plurality* of political conceptions of justice which all satisfy the condition of being compatible with the existing reasonable comprehensive conceptions of the good: one need only remind here of the discursive model of justice developed by

Habermas in *Between Facts and Norms*, or Larmore's model of 'rational dialogue', or Ackerman's 'conversational constraint'.[31] It is hard to see how the
argument developed in *Political Liberalism*, even if successful in establishing
the neutrality of justice as fairness *vis-à-vis* the main comprehensive conceptions vying for recognition in our democratic societies, could succeed in
singling out justice as fairness as the reconstruction of our view of justice to
be preferred over these other equally political conceptions of justice for the
role of normative core of the public culture of a democratic society. One of
the most influential among those competing conceptions of justice will be
examined in the following chapter.

2

Democracy, Justice and Discourse

Along with Rawls's theory of justice as fairness, Habermas's 'discursive' approach to democracy and law is one of the most important attempts to salvage a universalistic perspective in a historical context marked by the declining credibility of all foundational discourses. Habermas's book *Between Facts and Norms: Contributions to a Discourse Theory of Law and Democracy* (1996a) seems to constitute the main point of destination after a number of waystations that the reader of Habermas had been asked to touch. Even major works such as *The Theory of Communicative Action* (1984) and *The Philosophical Discourse of Modernity* (1987) appear as waystations on the path to a 'critical' and 'discursive' reformulation of a theory of democracy for the advanced industrial societies. The book contains a comprehensive reconsideration of the practical sphere, which includes both a new distinction between *pragmatic, ethical* and *moral* discourses and an original distinction between law, morality and politics. More specifically, in the context of his discussion of law, Habermas introduces a new *normative* theory of the legitimacy of law, in which he addresses questions concerning the constitutional process, adjudication, and the foundations and catalogue of rights, and complements this normative account with a social-theoretical discussion of the functional significance of positive law for the integration of modern society. Furthermore, Habermas develops a new conception of politics, which addresses the relation of politics to morality and law, the separation of powers, as well as the communicative basis of power.

The aspects of novelty of *Between Facts and Norms* are not confined to its contents. The theory of democracy, law and politics developed in it introduces a number of significant changes in the philosophical and social-theoretical fresco that Habermas has been painting over the past few decades – changes which are directly relevant for a discussion of the paradigm shift under way in political philosophy. For example, in *Between Facts and Norms* we can observe a general softening of the strong elements of proceduralism, formalism and generalizing universalism which characterized Habermas's framework until quite recently. At the same time we can observe a parallel appropriation of basic mainstream liberal tenets, among which are a full acceptance and legitimation of strategic action and a correspondingly important role attributed to bargaining.

These changes, though quite significant and worth discussing, do not amount to a complete revolution within Habermas's communicative paradigm but rather represent a careful *completion* of the paradigm, which includes the revision of several doubtful positions and a general shift toward a tone of political realism. While other waystations, such as the *Tanner Lectures* or the *Erläuterungen zur Diskursethik*, might have suggested the view that through his distinction between *das Ethische* und *das Moralische* Habermas was merely *immunizing* the discursive conception of ethics from the consequences of his formalistic approach, such an interpretation would certainly be reductive with respect to *Between Facts and Norms*. In this case we have a genuine expansion and development of the discursive approach to validity and of a certain reading of modernity which remain true, however, to a set of assumptions mostly located in that fortified citadel of universalism which is the discourse view of validity.

With respect to Rawls's itinerary, however, Habermas's shift away from the generalizing universalism typical of the determinant judgment model and toward a conception of universalism closer to the model of reflective judgment is less explicit and more gradual. I will begin by reconstructing Habermas's argument about *moral* validity in the search for evidence of this kind of shift; then I will discuss Habermas's theory of law in the same vein; and finally I will survey his understanding of politics in the context of his radical democratic project for contemporary Western societies.

Morality and Discourse

Despite all the modifications, adjustments, expansions, specifications and further differentiations of its central categories, Habermas's project for a discursive reformulation of moral theory has always remained faithful to one central intuition. This central intuition can be captured as the proposition that moral universalism is best understood as resting on a postmetaphysical and dialogical revisitation of Kant's view of moral validity as generalizability.[1] But let me first recall some of the most significant developments that this project has gone through, before taking the shape that it has acquired in *Between Facts and Norms*.

Habermas's project in moral theory began originally as the project of drafting a 'discourse ethics'. In a 1985 paper – 'Morality and Ethical Life: Does Hegel's Critique of Kant Apply to the Discourse Ethics?' (1993: 195–215) – Habermas characterizes the fundamental aspects of his project on the basis of four properties. In addition to being *universalistic*, his 'discourse ethics' purports to be *deontological, cognitivistic* and *formal*.

First, it is *deontological*, albeit in a peculiar sense. Habermas uses the term 'deontological' not in opposition to 'consequentialist' – as in the received usage – but in opposition to 'comprehensive'. The 'discourse ethics' is deontological in that it embeds an attitude of 'normative restraint', as it were. The practitioner of it permanently renounces all ambition to prescribe a philosophically correct solution to any practical problem, especially in matters concerning the good life. Rather, she understands her philosophical task as limited to the rational reconstruction of our intuitions relative to a fundamental moral phenomenon – that is, the normative force that inheres in moral norms, moral principles and especially in the so-called *moral point of view*.

Second, the 'discourse ethics' is *cognitivist* not in the sense that it aspires to possess the qualities of a moral objectivism, or that it blurs the line between factual and evaluative propositions, but in the much weaker sense that it assigns to the special validity of moral utterances a status somehow 'equivalent' to that usually associated with the validity of assertions. Habermas does not clarify – at least in that context – what this 'equivalence' really amounts to, but on the whole it seems sensible to assume that he intends to refer to the susceptibility, on the part of a factual assertion or statement, (a) to be either valid (true) or non-valid (false), and (b) to be *demonstrably* so.

Third, the 'discourse ethics' is *formal* or *procedural* in the sense that it takes the justification only of a moral principle, and not also of specific substantive tenets, as its object. Communicative ethics is meant to provide us not with concrete precepts, but rather with a 'method' for choosing in a correct, universalistically valid, way between the rival orientations that strive for our allegiance in any problematic context.

Finally, the 'discourse ethics' purports to be *universalistic* in the sense that the principle of dialogical generalization underlying it is understood not as a reflection of the moral intuitions of a concrete historical epoch or culture, but as a principle 'valid in general'.[2]

The seminal essays collected in the volume *Moral Consciousness and Communicative Action* first appeared in 1983, but the development of Habermas's ethical thought spans a period of over two decades. We can trace some constitutive aspects of it back to the essay 'Wahrheitstheorien' (1972) and, at the other extreme, it is not unsound to say that the most original of Habermas's contributions to moral philosophy are to be found in his 1992 volume *Faktizität und Geltung*, quoted hereinafter by the title of the 1996 English edition as *Between Facts and Norms*. For clarity's sake, we can divide the development of Habermas's ethical thought into four major phases: an initial stage, spanning from the early 1970s to 1981; the 1982–3 stage; the years between 1984 and 1991; and the new stage inaugurated by the publication of *Between Facts and Norms*.

I will not discuss at length the first stage, because at that time Habermas was not interested in moral philosophy except occasionally: his investigations focused mainly on the theory of knowledge, on social theory and on the theory of moral development. Habermas has concerned himself with moral-theoretical issues during this first stage mainly in connection with the fact that some of the central concepts of his position – for instance, the notions of 'ideal speech situation', of 'interaction', of 'communicative action' and of 'presuppositions of argumentation' – do possess an ethical dimension and, at the same time, are of crucial importance for the task of grounding a universalistic standpoint in philosophy in general, and in the theory of knowledge in particular. It is possible to find embryonic references to a so-called 'universal ethic of speech' and to 'communicative ethics' in the 1972 essay

'Wahrheitstheorien' and in the 1975 volume *Legitimation Crisis*, as well as in several of the essays collected in the volume *Communication and the Evolution of Society* (1979). In Habermas's *Theory of Communicative Action* (1984) we find the most articulate formulation of the notion of communicative action and of its presuppositions, genesis, and function within the process of social reproduction, but we do not find any specific attempt to develop a *moral-theoretical* perspective based on that notion – with the exception of a few remarks offered by Habermas in the context of his discussion of Mead and Durkheim.

At this stage we find no systematic formulation of the main moral-theoretical concepts of the 'discourse ethics' and no mention is yet made of any *principle of universalization*. 'Communicative ethics' still revolves around the idea that 'just' is any maxim on whose 'normative rightness' (*Richtigkeit* – Habermas does not yet make use of the term *Gerechtigkeit*) a 'rational consensus' arises among all the potentially affected actors, where the rational quality of 'rational consensus' is understood as its emerging from a debate conducted under conditions that approximate the 'ideal speech situation'. As in Apel's dialogical ethics, also in Habermas's 'communicative ethics' of the first stage we find no distinction between the right and the good and no restriction imposed on the object of moral-practical discourse. It seems as though all practical conflicts can in principle be submitted to the test of the ideal speech situation with equal probability – actually, with equal *certainty* – of being solved. Finally, we find no formulation of a specific *moral* principle that might guide our assessment of the validity of moral norms.

The years 1982–3 – when essays such as 'A Reply to my Critics', 'Discourse Ethics', 'Moral Consciousness and Communicative Action', and 'Was macht eine Lebensform rational?' were published – correspond to a stage in Habermas's intellectual development at which the project of grounding the 'discourse ethics' is given a high, if not exclusive, priority. These are also the years in which the *Philosophical Discourse of Modernity* is conceived. Of this stage of the Habermasian project I will highlight only one point – one, however, which will remain substantially unchanged to the present time. Habermas suggests that moral discourse can indeed lead to rational consensus only if we evaluate the contending alternatives in light of an *impartial moral principle*. This principle – called 'U' – operates like a kind of categorical imperative reformulated along dialogical lines. It purports to be a sensible reconstruction of the meaning of the term 'fair' or 'just', as it occurs in an expression like 'This norm is fair (or just).' In *Moral Consciousness and Communicative Action* Habermas defines 'U' as the principle according to which a moral norm is valid, 'fair' or 'impartial', when:

> *All* affected can accept the consequences and side effects its *general* observance can be anticipated to have for the satisfaction of *everyone's* interests. (1990: 65)

I will leave aside the 'quasi-transcendental' argument developed by Habermas in order to justify 'U'. More important for the purpose of reconstructing the backdrop against which the innovative quality of *Between Facts and Norms* can be understood is to recall that in *Moral Consciousness and Communicative Action* Habermas tries, for the first time, to demarcate more clearly the sub-domain of the moral-practical realm over which 'U' extends its jurisdiction. The differentiation, brought about by cultural modernization, of the expert knowledge typical of the various domains of high culture from the relatively unreflexive and commonsensical mode of knowledge characteristic of the life-world is reflected, within the moral-practical realm, as a differentiation of 'decontextualized' *questions of justice* – which in principle can always receive a rational answer if addressed from the standpoint of the universalization test[3] – from the larger set of *questions concerning the good life*, which remain amenable to a rational answer only *from within* the momentarily unproblem-atical horizon of a concrete historical life-form or individual life-project.[4] 'U' is relevant only as far as *questions of justice* are concerned. This means that only when *questions of justice* are concerned does there exist a kind of *a priori* guarantee to the effect that, *if the ideal conditions of communication hold*, then for each and any specific conflict a solution *can* be found that meets with the 'rational', not just factual, consensus of all the concerned ones.

This is the point, within the development of Habermas's ethical thought, where a certain way of understanding the distinction between the right and the good has its beginning – an understanding of these two moral-practical notions that contrasts them in terms of the four dichotomies of *universalism* and *particularism, context-transcending abstractness* and *context-bound con-creteness, dialogical* as opposed to *'monological'* types of rationality, and *demonstrability* and *undemonstrability*. It is also the point in time at which Habermas's moral theory comes closest to a determinant judgment model of validity. The object of the theory is to account for our intuitions concerning the meaning of a norm's being fair, just or impartial (these three terms are treated by Habermas as equivalent) and this meaning is equated with dialog-ical generalizability. To the predicate fair, just or impartial specified along these lines are attributed characteristics of universality and context indepen-dence, and these rest on the presuppositions of discourse which provide a sort of method, in a loose sense, capable of guaranteeing the rationality of the consensus on the norm and thus its universal validity. Habermas, at this stage, maintains that the validity claim linked with the discourse ethics can even be observed *empirically* if one looks at the institutionalization of rights. 'The history of human rights in modern constitutional states,' writes Habermas, 'offers a wealth of examples showing that once principles are rec-ognized, their application does not fluctuate from one situation to another, but tends to have a stable direction' (1990: 115).

In a sense, the use of the expression 'guarantee of consensus' requires a word of justification.[5] To be sure, Habermas goes only so far as saying that in the context of discourse the validity of norms *could* be ascertained in a uni-versalistically binding way. The full meaning of his assertion – and, more specifically, of the term 'could' – can be understood, however, only against the backdrop of his theory of types of discourses. In *The Theory of*

Communicative Action Habermas characterizes his use of the term 'discourse' as connected with the assumption that 'a rationally motivated agreement could in principle be achieved, whereby the phrase "in principle" expresses the idealizing proviso: if only the argumentation could be conducted openly enough and continued long enough' (1984: 41). This statement sheds light on the intended meaning of the word 'could'. Habermas obviously never meant to say that discourse guarantees that rational consensus be achieved *in the real world*. As long as the idealizing conditions are satisfied, however, there seem to exist no longer any obstacles that prevent us from being able to tell, via consensus, which among our claims possess a universalistic validity. The problem is that the obstacles to the formation of universalistically valid con-clusions are exclusively located, in a reductive way, in the *real world*. Instead, the *counterfactual* world in which the idealizing conditions of discourse are satisfied remains a Platonic world where there exist no intractable questions, no warring gods, no incommensurable frameworks and standpoints, no plu-rality of language games standing in the way of reconciling our viewpoints. Given 'unlimited time, unlimited participation, disinterested motivation, equal respect, etc. etc.' (that is, under ideal conditions) there seem to exist *no* theoretical or moral questions that *in principle* could *not* be solved. This reading of Habermas's assertion and of his use of the verb 'could' is what the expression 'guarantee of consensus' is designed to capture.

Evidence in favour of such an interpretation comes also from the fact that, were 'could' interpreted as meaning 'might or might not', it would then become difficult to understand how moral discourse differs from ethical dis-course, where even if all the idealizations are met, still we may or may not eventually come to an agreement. Let me push the point further. The Habermasian moral cognitivism of this stage resembles the cognitivism of pre-Kuhnian epistemology, when philosophers of science also believed that *under ideal conditions* – namely, barring incomplete information, time limita-tions, unscientific motivations of the scientists, lack of resources, etc. – a correct use of the scientific method ensured that no empirical question could not *in principle* be answered in a valid way. Now, the methodical *in*fallibility of the empiricist understanding of science is transferred to the presupposi-tions of communication, we have dialogue instead of monological observation, but the Habermasian moral universe remains a monistic one, where the only intractable contradictions, the only incompatible perspectives, are those originating in the limitations of the 'real world'. To interpret Habermas's discourse theory of morality of the early 1980s along these lines does not mean to attribute it the status of a determinant judgment model of validity *tout court*, however. That would certainly be an inaccurate reading of Habermas. Rather, the interpretation propounded above suggests that the discourse theory of validity fails to distance itself from *two* aspects of deter-minant judgment – namely, the methodizability of the search for validity and the dimension of necessity associated with the universal (in our case the quasi-transcendental 'inevitability' of the presuppositions of communica-tion) – while it certainly distances itself from other aspects, such as the deductive quality of the subsumption of the particular and the strong demonstrability of the conclusions.

The attempt to respond to a number of criticisms marks the beginning of a third stage in the development of Habermas's moral-theoretical thought – a stage which extends roughly between 1984 and 1991. Typical of this stage is the attempt to fine-tune the distinction between the right and the good, to introduce a new distinction between moral and legal discourse, and to engage in a fruitful dialogue with the proponents of other models of moral universalism, mainly Rawls and Dworkin.

These adjustments and corrections are mainly to be found in the essays collected under the title *Justification and Application* and in the *Tanner Lectures*. In a way not dissimilar from the path followed by Rawls during the 1980s, Habermas now presents the principle of universalization as the expression, within a controlled vocabulary, of our intuitions *qua* participants in the culture of modernity. Above all, characteristic of this phase is an increasing legitimation of the realm of the good as a domain of moral-philosophical relevance. In the texts of the 1982–3 period questions about the good life were understood as a residual area on which practical reason, if conceived post-metaphysically, has little to say. They constitute the object of a 'critique' of values or, better said, the subject matter of a reflexive articulation of the eudaemonistic intuitions inherent in a given culture. From this initial dichotomous understanding of the moral-practical realm Habermas moves soon to a tripartite model, first outlined in the section of the Howison Lecture *On the Concept of Practical Reason* (1988) which bears the subtitle 'Individual Will Formation in Terms of What Is Expedient, What Is Good and What Is Just'.[6] To these three moments or vantage points of practical will correspond now three distinct *kinds of discourse*: *pragmatic*, *ethical* and *moral* discourse. These three kinds of discourse address different understandings of the same paradigmatic practical question: 'What should I do?' *Pragmatic* discourses – the moral-practical reflection of *instrumental* and *strategic* action – address this question from the perspective of the best way of attaining what is *useful*. For example, what should I do in order to repair a broken car or to recover from a disease? *Ethical* discourses address the question 'What should I do?' from the perspective of a life-project oriented to one's own *good*. For example, given my abilities and weaknesses, what career should I choose? Given a certain dilemma, to which values should I accord priority in shaping my conduct? Differently than in the previous case, at the centre of my consideration are not hypothetical but unconditional imperatives, such as: 'You ought to undertake a career which makes you feel you are helping other people.' These are imperatives which are relatively independent of *individual* goals and preferences.[7] Finally, *moral* discourses begin when my actions happen to violate the interests of others and to lead to conflicts which stand in need of a consensual regulation. At the centre of these discourses is yet another sense of the question 'What should I do?' Now I have to determine for myself whether also others – indeed, *everybody else* – would agree on my choosing a certain course of action.

To contrast these three points of view, let us take the example of a tax-payer confronted with the task of filling out her income tax return form. Suppose the taxpayer has the possibility of hiding a certain revenue. From a *pragmatic* standpoint the question is whether the benefit of paying less out-weighs the risk of being caught and the sanctions attached to tax cheating. From an *ethical* standpoint, the question is whether the taxpayer would like to see herself as the kind of person whom we call a tax-cheater. From a *moral* point of view, finally, the question is whether everybody else would want that whoever finds herself in such a situation would try to hide a source of income. The watershed between ethical and moral discourse consists then in the difference between assessing the competing lines of conduct in 'ego-centric' terms and assessing them from the standpoint of their generalizability.[8]

The tripartition of the moral-practical sphere outlined by Habermas at this time is in fact a *twofold tripartition* – the two tiers being disposed along the opposition of *individual* and *collective* will. Thus far we have considered only the formation of an *individual* will. When we move on to the level of col-lective will things get more complicated. In fact, if we conjugate the practical question *par excellence* in the plural – 'What should we do?' – it appears that it can receive three different kinds of answers, in which three different processes of collective will formation are reflected: namely, the formation of a *political*, a *moral* and a *juridical* will.

Politics is understood by Habermas, at this point, as a pragmatic discourse on the means and strategies most conducive to the attainment of communally pursued goals. But this is not the only meaning of politics for him. Where an agreement on the ends of action or on the way of assigning priorities to pref-erences cannot be reached, we can either negotiate a compromise or accede to a second level of political will formation – the level at which we reassess our communal identity – and enter a kind of discourse centred around the ques-tion 'Who are we and who do we want to be?' Politics breaks down, then, in pragmatic discourses about means and strategies on the one hand, and prac-tices of negotiation and ethical-political discourse on the other. Hence Habermas defines the *rationality* of a policy as the quality of being both instrumentally expedient and 'good for us'. At this point, however, Habermas introduces the dimension of justice, understood as *political justice* in a sense quite different from Rawls. Beyond being expedient and appropriate to us, a programme or a policy is *just* if the outcome of its implementation is *equally good for all*.[9]

The question 'What should we do?' can be understood also in *moral* terms. Then it means something like 'According to which rules do we want to live together and regulate our conflicts?' This is the theoretical locus of univer-salistic moral discourse proper, of a public morality centred on the assessment of the fairness of norms. This is also the domain of politics understood as a process of *legislation*. The *application* of legal norms falls within the third domain of collective practical discourse, i.e. within the domain of *juridical* discourse – the kind of discourse entered by courts and judges, when they are required to establish whether and how a fact can be said to fall under the heading of a given norm. This third type of discourse of collective will formation rests, according to Habermas, on a so-called 'principle of impartial application'.

Finally, it must be noted that while in Habermas's early ethical writings the distinction between 'grounding' and 'application' seemed to overlap with the distinction between 'questions of justice' and 'questions concerning the good life', in the context of the Howison Lecture the relation between the two distinctions becomes much clearer. Both moral discourse and ethical discourse have a separate moment of grounding and one of application. The grounding dimension of *moral* discourse resides in the testing of the generalizability of a maxim. The 'application' of the norm or maxim thus grounded requires an 'additional' argumentation, which has to be conducted under the aegis of a 'principle of appropriateness' (or of 'impartial application') which constitutes the 'applicative' equivalent of the notion of impartiality in 'grounding' discourses. Also in the *ethical* realm a grounding and an applicative moment can be found. Habermas conceives of the process of existential deliberation as a discourse which embeds a moment of grounding. For example, he refers to the existence of 'better reasons', in abstract and general terms, for deciding in favour of one life-plan over another and, as we have seen, to ethical imperatives of a non-hypothetical kind. Ethical discourses, finally, also have an applicative moment, in which general maxims concerning the good life are brought into a relation with one's own case.

In *Between Facts and Norms* the process of upgrading and integrating the ethical realm within Habermasian moral theory finds its completion. It is possible to find a systematic niche for what is now termed ethical *discourse*, as well as a systematic role assigned to *pragmatic* discourses and *moral* discourses. Not only does ethical discourse concerning the good cease to be a mere residual category, but we find an attempt to go beyond a mere analytic distinction between moral and ethical discourse – namely the attempt to trace genealogically the realm of *das Ethische* back to a tradition of authenticity and self-realization which until now Habermas had hesitated to recognize as a distinct strand in the development of the modern practical sphere. *Das Ethische* has its source in the tradition that expresses itself mainly through the autobiographical literature of the 'confessions' and 'self-examinations' inaugurated by Rousseau and carried on by Kierkegaard and Sartre. At the centre of this tradition we find a fully modern question on the nature of the good life, in response to which these authors do not bring up models of the good life to be imitated but rather put forward the proposal – abstract and formal as any – that the moral actor reflexively appropriate the uniqueness, irreplaceability and contingency of his or her life history. The moral-practical discourse of modernity, at this fourth stage of Habermas's theory of moral validity, appears to be a kind of discourse 'always already' fractured in two competing traditions which pivot around the two concepts, non-reconcilable and thus in tension, of 'self-determination' or autonomy (*Selbstbestimmung*) and 'self-realization' or authenticity (*Selbstverwirklichung*) (Habermas 1996a: 99).

Furthermore, Habermas must be credited for having contributed to the
further differentiation of our perception of the *extramoral* moment of the
practical sphere. Not only have we a clear perception that the moral-practical
realm cannot be reduced to the narrow boundaries of moral discourse understood as a generalization test, but also we can better discern the other
components that compose it. Beyond *ethical discourse*, we now can identify
pragmatic discourses, discourses of *application*, discourses of *legitimation*,
and *political* discourses as distinct components of the practical.

Finally, in *Between Facts and Norms* Habermas conceives the *principle of
universalization* which guides our assessment of moral norms – the principle
'U' of 1983 – as a special case of a broader *principle of discourse* 'D', which
is supposed to be neutral between morality and law, i.e. topographically prior
to their bifurcation. The *principle of discourse* 'D' runs:

> Just those norms are valid to which all those possibly affected persons could agree
> as participants in rational discourses. (Habermas 1996a: 107)

This principle is understood by Habermas as a reconstruction of the intuitions of postconventional actors regarding what it means for both a moral
and a legal norm to be justified. The specification of 'D' for the *moral* realm –
which I will call hereinafter 'Dm' – is formulated by Habermas in the following form:

> A norm is just if all can will that it be obeyed by each in comparable situations.
> (1996a: 200)

This process, whereby the account of the moral point of view has over the
years been purified of all the spurious elements and functions which at the
beginning Habermas conflated with it, is not without problems. Above all, the
discourse-theoretic reconstruction of the moral point of view continues to be
affected by an ambiguity not yet removed or even addressed by Habermas,
which will be discussed in Chapter 6. Before addressing this ambiguity, however, we need to complete the reconstruction of the Habermasian discourse
approach to justice by looking at his conception of law and of democracy.

Habermas's Discourse Theory of Law

The overall point of Habermas's theory of law is to articulate the relation of
law, politics and morality in the context of a theory of communicative rationality, of modern society and of democracy. This is certainly quite a wealth
of terms of trade, yet it is true to the complexity of Habermas's attempt.[10]
Between Facts and Norms contains in fact an account of the actual function
of law in modern society as well as a normative argument about law and
democracy. In this normative vein Habermas discusses several layers of problems. He discusses the question of the legitimacy of law, of the nature of
political autonomy and political legitimacy, derives a 'system of rights' from
the presuppositions of communicative reason, and outlines a normative
theory of democracy in which again he combines a descriptive sociological

account of the functioning of democratic institutions and a normative project for a *deliberative democracy*.

The Integrative Function of Law in Modern Society

Habermas's sociological theory of law revolves around two theses, which touch on the genealogy of modern law and the function of law in contemporary society. Modern law draws its normative force no longer from natural law, from morals or from religious world views, but entirely 'from a legislative procedure based for its part on the principle of popular sovereignty' (Habermas 1996a: 83). Modern law is inherently positive law. Its function in contemporary society is twofold. On the one hand, it unburdens individuals from the strong constraints of communicative action, by creating realms of social action where strategic action is legitimate. On the other hand, by regulating the interplay between these spheres of social action it secures the integration of society in a context in which integration cannot be secured through shared values alone. Habermas equates the function of the 'legal medium' with that of a 'power transformer that reinforces the weakly integrating currents of a communicatively structured lifeworld' (1996a: 176). This function is performed by allowing for the transfer, without loss of binding force, of 'familiar structures of mutual recognition' rooted in face-to-face interaction onto the plane of the 'anonymous, systemically mediated interactions among strangers' (1994a: 136).

The normative argument developed in *Between Facts and Norms* presents an integrative or reconciliatory thrust in which the reader familiar with Habermas's previous work will recognize more than a family resemblance with other ambitious projects pursued by Habermas in the past. Habermas's aim is to reconcile *private* and *public* autonomy at a fundamental conceptual level – a challenge as exciting as the reconciliation of the paradigm of social action and the system-theoretical paradigm which he tried to bring about in *The Theory of Communicative Action*. One way of placing *Between Facts and Norms* in the context of Habermas's theory of modernity is to understand it as a further development in the reconstruction of the process of differentiation of the metaphysical worldviews into the cognitive-instrumental, moral-practical, and aesthetic-expressive spheres. Habermas now focuses on the second sphere and investigates the internal differentiation of law and morality and politics, as well as the interconnections between these elements of the practical realm. Be that as it may, modern positive law and modern morality both branch out from the 'substantial ethical life' of societies bound together primarily through shared traditions. But both modern morality and modern law carry from the beginning the marks of a vertical fracture. The practical discourse of modernity appears inherently split in the pursuit of two kinds of questions – questions of justice and questions of the good – and thus splits into an ethical discourse aimed at ascertaining the line of conduct most conducive to the good or the self-realization for an individual or for a group, and a moral discourse aimed at ascertaining whether a line of conduct is fair in the sense of being equally responsive to the interests of all the concerned ones. This fracture finds its equivalent in the public realm as well, in the form of a split between human rights and popular sovereignty.

In the first two chapters of *Between Facts and Norms* Habermas develops his account of the transformation undergone by law in modern society. In traditional societies,

> even the law still feeds on the self-authorizing force of the religiously sublimated sacred realm . . . According to this idea, the law made by the ruler remained *subordinate* to the Christian natural law administered by the Church. (1996a: 26)

In modern society, however, that force is exhausted and no longer available to provide legitimation for law: 'Even lifeworld certainties, which in any case are pluralized and ever more differentiated, do not provide sufficient compensation for this deficit' (1996a: 26). Hence Habermas's reformulation of the problem of the integration of a complex society – a reformulation which provides him with a starting point similar to the one adopted by Rawls in *Political Liberalism*:

> How can disenchanted, internally differentiated and pluralized lifeworlds be socially integrated if, at the same time, the risk of dissension is growing, particularly in the spheres of communicative action that have been cut loose from sacred authorities and released from the bounds of archaic institutions? (1996a: 26)

Furthermore, because modern societies from the times of Adam Smith onward depend more and more on the existence of large areas of social action regulated via interests rather than via common values, integration cannot be effected through the extension of processes of 'unrestrained communicative action'. 'The only way out of this predicament,' argues Habermas, 'is for the actors themselves *to come to some understanding* about the *normative regulation of strategic interaction*' (1996a: 26–7). Law in this sense carries out further, and on a broader societal plane, the evolutionary task achieved at the *cultural* level by Puritanism. Whereas Puritanism had provided a *cultural* acceptability and legitimation for strategic conduct in the context of economic and political relations, modern positive law sanctions, institutionalizes and protects areas of social action in which strategic conduct is allowed. Thus 'the core of modern law consists of private rights that mark out the legitimate scope of individual liberties and are thus tailored to the strategic pursuit of private interests' (1996a: 27).

If modern law draws its integrating force from its capacity for binding, orienting and coordinating action, the question arises: given the obsolescence of religiously anchored forms of legitimation, from what sources does modern law draw its legitimation? Before answering the question, however, a closer examination of the way in which modern law exerts its integrative function is needed. The equivalent of the combination of awe and terror inspired by the sacred, which in primitive and premodern societies formed the basis of law's capacity to influence conduct, can be found, argues Habermas, in the peculiar combination of freedom and coercion bound up with modern law. Law presents itself with the certainty of a fact linked with predictable consequences to the actor who acts strategically. At the same time, it presents itself with the deontologically binding character of a normative expectation – an expectation somehow linked with a 'rationally motivated consensus among the legal subjects' – to the actor who acts communicatively (see 1996a: 30–1). More specifically, the terror induced by a spell-binding authority finds an equivalent, under modern conditions, in the state's guarantee to enforce the law. There is an important difference, however. Unlike ancient and premodern kinds of law, which were backed up by religious worldviews, modern law regulates action not through conformity of motives but merely through sanctions and thus leaves the 'motives for rule compliance open while enforcing observance' (1996a: 31).

If considered along these lines, as an institution that relieves social actors from the burden of subjectively orienting themselves toward integration – namely, of selecting social-integrative goals and choosing means that also have a social-integrative valence – then law reveals its Janus-faced nature, its partaking both of the realm of 'facts' and of that of 'norms'. Law is anchored in the realm of facts through its *positive* character, in the realm of norms through its claim to *rational* acceptability. On the one hand, in all law there inheres an intrinsically voluntaristic moment: in fact 'the validity of positive law appears as the sheer expression of a will that, in the face of the ever-present possibility of repeal, grants specific norms continuance until further notice' (1996a: 38). On the other hand, if law is to indeed play an integrative function, its positive, fact-like quality, points out Habermas, 'cannot be grounded solely on the contingency of *arbitrary* decisions'. Rather, the integrative function of law in modern society requires both moments: it requires an 'alliance that the facticity of law forms with the claim to legitimacy' (1996a: 39).

These two sides of modern law often come apart in two kinds of one-sided approach to law. On the one hand, there exist sociological approaches to law that emphasize its positivity and overlook its normative dimension. They can account for the empirical effects of the working of the legal system as an autonomous system, but cannot explain its integrative function. On the other hand, there exist normative theories of justice and law which overlook the social and positive dimension of the legal system and thus remain at an abstract level. Luhmann and Rawls impersonate these two forms of one-sidedness which Habermas's approach aims at overcoming. Both aspects, instead, can be adequately accounted for, argues Habermas, within the discursive framework.

The Co-originality of Rights and Popular Sovereignty

The normative dimension of law – namely, law's claim to legitimacy – is itself traversed by a deep cleft. In modern times a new account of the legitimacy of law has developed which derived the legitimacy of positive law from its relation to a secularized natural law. On the one hand, this line of argument perpetuates the premodern subordination of law to a moral order, albeit a

rational and secularized one, external to it. On the other hand, the fact of pluralism, and in our century the linguistic turn, have spelled an end to the
possibility of a comprehensive moral framework capable of grounding the
legitimacy of positive law for all the members of a modern society. The only
solution left is to conceive the legitimacy of law as stemming from the idea of
self-determination, namely the idea that 'citizens should always be able to
understand themselves also as authors of the law to which they are subject as
addressees' (Habermas 1994a: 137). Yet at this level, too, the same alternative
surfaces again. We have theories that understand self-determination in the
guise of a contract subscribed to either on pragmatic grounds (Hobbes) or on
moral grounds (Rousseau, Kant). Even in this latter case, however, 'the break
with the tradition of rational natural law is incomplete, as long as *moral*
argumentation remains the exemplar for a constitution-founding discourse'.
In Kant, for example, 'positive law remains subordinate to, and is oriented by,
the moral law' (1994a: 137). This subordination is indefensible not so much
for *geschichtsphilosophisch* reasons – i.e. because it sets back the modern
trend towards differentiation – but because it overlooks a number of constitutive dissimilarities between law and morality. First, while in the moral realm
rights and duties are symmetrical, 'legal duties only result as consequences of
the protection of *entitlements*, which are conceptually prior' (1994a: 138).
Second, while moral autonomy amounts to the persons's 'capacity for rational self-binding', the individual's *legal* autonomy includes (a) a share of the
jointly exercised autonomy of the citizens, (b) the capacity for rational choice
and (c) the capacity for 'ethical self-realization'.[11]

Third, while the scope of moral norms encompasses humanity in its
entirety, legal norms only have effect within a given legal community. Fourth,
law is more complex than morality in that beyond constituting and setting
limits on individual liberty, it also 'incorporates goal-setting, so that its regulations are too concrete to be justifiable by moral considerations alone'
(1994a: 140).

Habermas's own discursive model of the legitimacy of law takes a different route. It views law not as subordinate but as *complementary* to morality:

> If the legitimacy of positive law is conceived as procedural rationality and ulti-
> mately traced back to an appropriate communicative arrangement for the
> lawgiver's rational political will-formation (and for the application of law), then the
> inviolable moment of legal validity need not disappear in a blind *decisionism* nor
> be preserved from the vortex of temporality by a moral *containment*. The leading
> question of modern natural law can then be reformulated under new, discourse-
> theoretic premises: what rights must citizens mutually grant one another if they
> decide to constitute themselves as a voluntary association of legal consociates and
> legitimately to regulate their living together by means of positive law? (1994a: 140)

In this question rights and popular sovereignty are joined together as two
interlinked categories. This is no accident, points out Habermas. Rights and
popular sovereignty represent, in fact, 'the precipitate left behind, so to speak,
once the normative substance of an ethos embedded in religious and metaphysical traditions has been forced through the filter of posttraditional

justification' (1996a: 99). These two ideas are also at the core of two competing traditions – the liberal and the republican – which interpret the legitimacy
of law and the working of democracy in light of opposing priorities.

> Whereas on the liberal view human rights all but impose themselves on our moral
> insights as something given, anchored in a fictive state of nature, according to
> republicans the ethical-political will of a self-actualizing collectivity is forbidden to
> recognize anything that does not correspond to its own authentic life project.
> (1996a: 100)

Habermas then proceeds to reconstruct Kant's and Rousseau's political
thought. They both tried to bring together the idea of human rights and the
principle of popular sovereignty, under the heading of autonomy, but both
failed to produce a fully complementary relation. For Kant the starting point
is the postulation of a fundamental 'right owed to each human being "by
virtue of his humanity"', which is construed as 'the right to equal subjective
liberties backed by authorized coercion' (1996a: 100). This fundamental right
to the respect of one's subjecthood enjoins respect for the inner nature of the
individual and, when applied to the external relations of the self, generates
the other rights included in the liberal catalogue. The point stressed by
Habermas is that these rights are understood as legitimate antecedently to
their being embedded in positive law, legitimate 'on the basis of moral principles, and hence independently of that political autonomy of citizens first
constituted only with the social contract' (1996a: 101). In this sense rights,
continues Habermas, for Kant precede sociation and the will of the sovereign.
They bind that will, but are not constituted by it.

For Rousseau, instead, there exists no such thing as an innate right. Yet
whatever Kant's human rights are meant to protect is also somehow protected
in Rousseau's theory through the various constraints that the formation of
the general will must satisfy in order to be correct. The problem is that
Rousseau conceives the general will along *ethical* more than moral lines:
'Rousseau imagines the constitution of popular sovereignty through the
social contract as a kind of existential act of sociation through which isolated
and success-oriented individuals *transform* themselves into citizens oriented
to the common good of an ethical polity' (1996a: 102). One of the difficulties
of this account is that it presupposes, according to Habermas, a homogene-
ity of value orientations that can be found only in small integrated
communities. Rousseau can explain neither 'how the postulated orientation of
the citizens toward the common good can be mediated with the differentiated
interest positions of private persons' nor 'how the normatively construed
common will can, without repression, be mediated with the free choice of
individuals' (1996a: 102). This reading of Rousseau is not without problems.
While it is true that 'the substantive legal equality that Rousseau took as
central to the legitimacy claim of modern law cannot be satisfactorily
explained by the *semantic* properties of general laws' (1996a: 102), Habermas
overlooks the fact that Rousseau's constraints on the correct process of the
formation of the general will are not merely 'semantic'. Among the additional
constraints Rousseau envisages also a certain equality of social station,

understood as equality of chances to influence one another, and a subjective orientation to the common good.[12] Furthermore, Habermas's claim that Rousseau's account of the self-constitution of a political community provides an inadequate basis for understanding the workings of a complex society over-looks the crucial distinction that Rousseau draws between the general will and the 'will of all' – an equivalent of aggregate preferences. There is nothing wrong with the will of all as such. Rousseau's negative appraisal of it refers only to the case in which the will of all falsely presents itself in the guise of the general will.

There is, however, a deeper-seated reason why both Kant and Rousseau could not articulate the internal connection between popular sovereignty and human rights in a fully adequate way. According to Habermas, the philoso-phy of the subject cannot grasp a connection that is inherently *communicative* and *intersubjective*.

> If the rational will can take shape only in the individual subject, then the individ-ual's moral autonomy must reach through the political autonomy of the united will of all in order to secure the private autonomy of each in advance via natural law. If the rational will can take shape only in the macrosubject of a people or nation, then political autonomy must be understood as the self-conscious actualization of the ethical substance of a concrete community; and private autonomy is protected from the overpowering force of political autonomy only by the nondiscriminatory form of general laws. Both conceptions miss the legitimating force of opinion- and will-formation. (1996a: 103)

Hence Habermas's own suggestion: the conditions of the legitimacy of law must be understood as *communicative* conditions concerning the quality of the context within which a legal community is first created.

> As participants in rational discourses, consociates under law must be able to exam-ine whether a contested norm meets with, or could meet with, the agreement of all those possibly affected. Consequently, the sought-for internal connection between popular sovereignty and human rights consists in the fact that the system of rights states precisely the conditions under which the forms of communication necessary for the genesis of legitimate law can be legally institutionalized. (1996a: 104)

In other words, the substance of human rights resides, for Habermas, 'in the formal conditions for the legal institutionalization of those discursive processes of opinion- and will-formation in which the sovereignty of the people assumes a binding character' (1996a: 104). Consequently, rights pos-itivized in the form of constitutional norms are not to be understood as the juridical translation of antecedently established moral rights or moral norms. Rather they are just another branch of the same differentiation process.[13] Furthermore, the *function* of rights is not merely to guarantee the liberties accorded to the individual, but also to make these liberties compatible with one another. We touch here on Habermas's distinction between *communica-tive* and *subjective* liberty. Communicative liberty is the liberty 'responding to the utterances of one's counterpart and to the concomitantly raised validity claims, which aim at intersubjective recognition' (1996a: 119). Subjective lib-erty is the right-based, communicatively secured, entitlement to 'step out of communicative action' and to retreat to a position of 'mutual observation and reciprocal influence' in which one does not have to give others reasons for one's actions. Thus the (negative) rights embedded in the constitution of modern democracies are communicatively legitimated norms that delimit the realm within which the individual is entitled to subjective freedom – i.e. is authorized to act strategically. In this sense communicative reason appears to be a self-limiting form of reason. It gives itself its own boundaries and calls its own 'other' into being. Habermas proceeds then to spell out a way of grounding a *system of rights* capable of conferring *equal weight* to both the *private* and the *public* autonomy of the citizen.[14]

The System of Rights

The grounding of negative subjective rights understood as the outcome of 'politically autonomous law making' on the part of the citizens requires a *principle of democracy*, which Habermas derives as another specification, alongside the moral principle, of the discourse principle 'D'. The idea is that 'the principle of democracy derives from the interpenetration of the discourse principle and the legal form' (1996a: 121). Habermas understands this interpenetration 'as a *logical genesis of rights*' that can be reconstructed 'stepwise'.

The first step includes the testing of the 'right to subjective liberties in general' in light of the discourse principle. Once this 'right to have rights' is recognized as satisfying the principle 'D', the legal form as such can be considered established. The third step is then the legal institutionalization of conditions for a discursive exercise of *political* autonomy. To this follows a fourth step in which private autonomy can 'take on a legally organized shape'. With a final step the principle of democracy can appear as 'the heart of a *system* of rights' and should contain 'precisely the rights citizens must confer on each other if they want to legitimately regulate their living together by means of positive law' (1996a: 122).

Habermas then introduces the categories of rights that correspond to these steps. At the first stage of the derivation we find *rights to equal subjective liberties*. These are norms couched in legal terms that entitle actors to subjective liberties. The discourse principle here enjoins *equality* of the subjective liberties accorded to each citizen. These rights are insufficient, however, to institutionalize a complete legal code. Needed are specifications that allow members of a *specific* legal community to see their basic rights protected in courts.

At the second stage we find *membership rights*, which 'result from the politically autonomous development of the *status of a member* in a voluntary association of consociates under law' (1996a: 122). Legal rules are not binding on human beings in general, but on members of a 'geographically delimited legal area' and on members 'of a socially delimitable collective of legal consociates'. Hence boundaries of membership must be established, and the rights of membership allow one to differentiate 'between members and nonmembers, citizens and aliens' (1996a: 124). The application of the discourse principle in this case results, argues Habermas, 'in the circumstance that each person must be protected from unilateral deprivation of membership rights but must in turn have the right to renounce the status of a member' (1996a: 124).[15] Corresponding to the third step in the derivation are the *rights to guaranteed legal recourse*, designed to guarantee legal recourse against any infringement of rights. The discourse principle can ground here the basic right of *due process*, which includes (a) equal legal protection, (b) equal claim to a legal hearing, (c) equal treatment before the law, and so on.

Taken together, these three categories of rights ground the legitimacy of the legal code. Simply, 'there is no legitimate law without these rights' (1996a: 125). They are not equivalent to the classical liberal rights, however, because there is still no state authority against which they could be directed. According to Habermas, however, the classical liberal rights (life, liberty, bodily integrity, freedom of movement, property, etc.) 'are interpretations of, and ways of working out, what we might call a "general right to individual liberties"' (1996a: 125–6). In a similar way the universal right to membership is interpreted within the classical liberal tradition as a complex of norms such as the prohibition against extradition and the right to political asylum. Finally, the guarantee rights concerning legal recourse are actualized in the liberal tradition through basic legal tenets such as the prohibitions against retroactive punishment, against double jeopardy, special courts, etc. The status of the first three categories of rights within Habermas's discursive account of law is that of formal rights types that can be specified into rights tokens by the constitutional lawgiver according to the particular aspects of the context and of the background tradition. On the one hand, these three categories of rights are in a way like 'legal principles that guide the framers of constitutions' (1996a: 126). On the other hand they do not constrain the will of the constitutional lawgiver, rather they are presupposed by the idea of that will's legitimate functioning: 'enabling conditions do not impose any limitations on what they constitute' (1996a: 128).

There follows a fourth type of formal rights, corresponding to the fourth step in the derivation of rights from the discourse principle. These are rights to 'equal opportunities to participate in processes of opinion- and will-formation in which citizens exercise their *political autonomy* and through which they generate legitimate law' (1996a: 123). This type of rights is the last abstract type that can be specified from a discourse-theoretical point of view. From this point on, instead, 'the citizens themselves become those who deliberate and, acting as a constitutional assembly, decide how they must fashion the rights that give the discourse principle legal shape as a principle of democracy' (1996a: 127).

At this point we are in a position, concludes Habermas, to fully understand what is meant by the *co-originality of political and private autonomy*:

> The scope of citizens' political autonomy is not restricted by natural or moral rights just waiting to be put into effect, nor is the individual's private autonomy merely instrumentalized for the purposes of popular sovereignty. Nothing is given

prior to the citizen's practice of self-determination other than the discourse principle, which is built into the conditions of communicative association in general, and the legal medium as such. (1996a: 127–8)

The fact that basic rights mentioned in specific constitutions are understood as 'context-dependent readings of the same system of rights' does not mean that the system is 'given to the constitutional lawgiver in advance as natural law' or that the system exists somewhere in 'transcendental purity'. Rather, the system of abstract right types should be conceived as a 'generalizing reconstruction', based on 200 years of European constitutional law, 'of the intuitions that guide the intersubjective practice of self-legislation in the medium of positive law' (1996a: 129). In Habermas's view, normative validity in the context of law understandably acquires a contextual ring that it lacked when considered from the standpoint of moral theory.

Politics, Discourse and Deliberative Democracy

The Discourse Theory of Politics and the Role of the Executive

At the centre of Habermas's communicative approach to politics and democracy is the concept of 'communicative power'. He starts from an Arendtian-like model of communicative power and traces through discourse-theoretic concepts its transformation into legitimate legislation on the one hand, and into legitimate administrative power on the other. The principle of popular sovereignty, according to Habermas, if interpreted as the proposition that 'all political power derives from the communicative power of the citizens', yields three further principles. First, it yields the principle of *comprehensive legal protection* for individuals – a protection which must be guaranteed by an independent judiciary. Second, it yields the principles of the *legality of the administration* and of the *judicial monitoring of the administration*. Finally, it generates the principle of the separation of state and society – a principle designed to prevent *social* power from translating into communicative power. Each of these principles can be further specified.

Important is the fact that from the *principle of popular sovereignty* interpreted in discourse-theoretic terms it is possible to further derive: (a) the *parliamentary principle* (justified by the circumstance that face-to-face deliberations involving the totality of members are impossible in a modern society), which then opens up further questions, such as those concerning mode of election, immunity, mandate, parties, majority rule, repeated readings of bills, etc.; (b) the *principle of political pluralism*, which includes the subprinciple of the *guaranteed autonomy of the public sphere* (i.e. the preparing and monitoring of parliamentary and governmental activities on the part of public opinion) and the 'basic tenet' of a competition between rival parties.

At this juncture Habermas provides also a discourse-theoretic formulation of the rationale for the separation of legislative and judicial power. These two forms of power represent public equivalents of the distinction between 'questions of justification' and 'questions of application'. The need for a separate institutionalization of legislative and judicial power derives then from the different logic underlying the two kinds of argumentation involved. While discourses of application demand that all facets of a case be represented before 'a judge who acts as the impartial representative of the legal community' (1996a: 172), in discourses of justification 'there are in principle only participants' (1996a: 172). Also, because in order to enforce its decisions the judiciary needs to use the means of repression, and thus to use somehow also *administrative* power, it must be prevented from programming itself through forms of self-legislation.

The meaning traditionally attributed to the separation of powers is captured, however, by the principle of the *legality of the administration*. The function of the separation, for Habermas, is to bind 'the use of administrative power to democratically enacted law in such a way that administrative power regenerates itself solely from the communicative power that citizens engender in common' (1996a: 173). Habermas now focuses on the relation of the legislative to the *executive* power. The priority of laws (the nullity of the government's ordinances, decrees, and measures that contradict a valid law or the constitution) is meant to prevent the administration from having 'access to the premises underlying its decisions'. Also, the act of creating an executive authority causes the civil rights stemming from the right to equal subjective liberties to 'acquire the additional meaning of liberal rights *against* the State' (1996a: 174) – those rights which historically 'make up the core of human rights declarations'.

Finally, the principle of the *separation between state and society* is meant to prevent 'social power', which is unequally distributed, from influencing processes of political will formation and thereby restricting the formation of communicative power. Among the further specifications of this principle we find (a) the *principle of democratic responsibility* before voters and parliaments (duty to stand for re-election) and (b) the *government's responsibility* for the acts of subordinate officials. Taken together these principles spell out the meaning of the *constitutional state*, whose function is to serve the politically autonomous self-organization of society (cf. 1996a: 174–5) by way of institutionalizing the 'public use of communicative freedom' on one hand, and of regulating 'the conversion of communicative power into an administrative one' (1996a: 176) on the other hand.[16]

The conversion of communicative into administrative power is one of the points in Habermas's discussion of politics that raises some questions. Habermas appears to have a very reductive and undifferentiated view of the executive power – one branch that often, even in contexts where it does not reach the dramatic prominence typical of the American Presidency, plays a fundamental role in the political life of the country, not to mention the fact that in several democratic countries the heads of government are the only office holders to receive a direct mandate from the entire electoral body. There is no notion of *governance* in Habermas's view of the executive power, not even in the minimal form of contributing, along with the public sphere, to setting the agenda for public legislative discussion. While legislative assemblies and the judiciary are expected to address and assess, among others, moral and ethical questions in their activity of justifying and applying norms, administrative activity in Habermas's account is reduced almost exclusively to pragmatic discourses about realizing goals that are already set in all their details by the legislator. 'An administration limited to pragmatic discourses,' argues Habermas, 'must not disturb anything in this universe [of differentiated kinds of discourses] by its contributions' (1996a: 192). The same reductionism appears in one of the passages of the 'Postscript' in which Habermas addresses the point. Habermas criticizes liberal conceptions that emphasize human rights, conferring them priority over popular sovereignty, for failing to distinguish popular sovereignty proper, which should be considered co-original with and not potentially antagonistic to human rights, and the state's monopoly on violence – something which belongs conceptually to a subsequent level in the design of a just institutional order. In so doing, continues Habermas, mainstream liberalism 'misses the *inherently technical*, and in any case non-repressive, meaning of an administrative power appearing in the form of law' (1994a: 143).

This understanding of the executive as a moment of mere administration, based on formal rationality alone, appears more adequate to capture the function of a *bureaucracy* than the function of *governance*. The difference between a government and a bureaucracy is overlooked by Habermas because he fails to realize that the programmatic points on which a head of government receives a mandate from the legislature or from the electorate are not to be understood as *exhaustive* of the governmental action. They should rather be understood as a tentative articulation of a broader mandate to do all that is necessary to preserve the common weal of the political community for a certain period. The difference between a government and a bureaucracy lies precisely in the interpretive leeway, much larger in the former case and significantly narrower in the latter, that each is allowed in interpreting its own mandate. The government mandate is always too comprehensive to be reducible to a set of formulas, though of course it is limited by the normative constraints set by law and by the constitution. Furthermore, an understanding of the function of the executive along merely technical lines clashes with the obvious fact that government is also entrusted, during its term of office, with dealing with all unforeseen and unforeseeable contingencies (international crises, natural calamities, economic crises, environmental emergencies, etc.) in the service of protecting the common good. No bureaucracy or other merely technical instance of executive power is ever entrusted with such legitimate power to decide in the name of the political body. It makes sense then to include the executive branch in the complex interplay of the democratic process, as the recipient of a *prudential* (in the sense of *phronesis*) and not merely technical mandate, and as one of the main contributors to the setting of the political agenda, not to mention the cohesive function that it often performs of symbolizing the unity of purpose and the moral cohesiveness of the polity (we need just recall the cases of Churchill and De Gaulle) – a unity and cohesion that inherently divided legislative assemblies can hardly symbolize.

In particular if we conceive, as Habermas urges us to do, the constitution as an *unfinished project* to be fulfilled by the generations to come, it seems somewhat implausible to understand such fulfilment as including only the moments of lawmaking and of judicial review. The executive action of government can also be a major force contributing to translate constitutional principles into living realities, as the American experiences of the New Deal, the New Frontier and the Great Society indicate. These were hardly slogans for selling packaged techniques aimed at tackling social problems: they were creative interpretations of constitutional possibilities that sometimes were far ahead of the understanding of the legislative assemblies and, in the case of the New Deal, even of the Supreme Court.[17] A head of the executive such as Franklin D. Roosevelt transformed the relation of the Presidency to Congress and the Supreme Court. As Bruce Ackerman points out, 'it became standard practice for the President to appeal over the heads of Congress for the support of the People in his struggle to enact his program into law' (1991: 106). As his Presidential Speech of 9 March 1937 shows, F.D. Roosevelt understood his mandate as including all measures that could effectively prevent 'the risk of another great depression'. So little was this task a technical one that it required, in Roosevelt's opinion, 'national laws' and a 'power to prevent and cure the abuses and the inequalities which had thrown that system out of joint'. In the way of enforcing those already enacted laws and basing on them policies devised to 'stabilize national agriculture, to improve the conditions of labor, to safeguard business against unfair competition, to protect national resources' stood a Supreme Court that would not enforce 'the Constitution as written' but would instead insist on 'reading into the Constitution words and implications which are not there, and which were never intended to be there' (Roosevelt 1937: 230–4). More on this episode of American constitutional history will be given in Chapter 4 in the discussion of Ackerman's view of normative validity. In the present context, it suffices to recall that in lieu of trying to institutionalize the changed perspective into a series of formal amendments, the President launched a campaign for gaining the support of the people for a measure, heavily opposed within Congress, that would allow him to nominate a substantial number of additional justices to the Supreme Court.[18] Shortly after, but – as historians claim – independently of such threat to 'pack' the Supreme Court, the justices changed their orientations and began to issue 'a series of transformative judicial opinions', which in the following years reassured 'the still-suspicious President, Congress, and electorate that the Justices had fully accepted the constitutional legitimacy of the New Deal and had committed the judicial system to the affirmative elaboration of its higher law implications' (Ackerman 1991: 119–20). Had Roosevelt subscribed to a view of constitutionalism and democracy like the one suggested by Habermas, we would have never had the New Deal.

Deliberative Democracy and the Public Sphere

Let me now turn to Habermas's outline of deliberative democracy. Deliberative democracy embeds an anti-utopian attitude. It is a project for a

radical democratic understanding of the political process of advanced industrial societies. As such it aims at reconciling the discourse principle on the one
hand, and the realities of complex societies, characterized by large scale
bureaucratic organization and the remoteness of politics from the everyday
life of the citizens, on the other. Habermas's perspective is rather different
from Rawls's view of a democratic society built around an overlapping consensus. For example, it does not make use of the 'method of avoidance' at all.
Rawls's view appears somewhat reductive and naive to Habermas, in that it
focuses merely on the link between a normative theory of justice and political *culture*. But there is more in the reality of contemporary society, according
to Habermas, that needs to be reconciled with the claims of theory than just
political culture. Habermas develops a *two-track model of democracy*, which
is basically a model of democratic lawmaking. The two tracks are not the
'ordinary lawmaking' and 'higher or constitutional lawmaking' which
Ackerman and Michelman, as we will see, distinguish, but rather the institutional bodies invested with formal decision-making prerogatives on the one
hand, and the larger public formed by individual and groups in civil society
who are concerned with public affairs on the other. The functioning of deliberative democracy, for Habermas, depends not only on the validity and
feasibility of norms and institutional designs, but also on conditions of a different nature, such as the presence of a 'vibrant civil society' and an
'unsubverted political public sphere' (1994a: 147). Deliberative democracy
depends also on the actual presence and vitality of processes of *opinion* formation that need not coincide with those formal processes of *decision* making
which, in a complex society, must necessarily remain the prerogative of office
holders, such as parliamentary representatives, members of the cabinet and
the like. The ongoing presence of processes of opinion formation, however, is
to be understood as a *necessary but not sufficient* condition for the establishing and stabilization of a deliberative democracy.[19] Another important
feature of the functioning of a deliberative democracy, according to
Habermas, is the 'anonymous' character of the communication processes
that lead to the formation of this public opinion and to decision making.[20]

Deliberative democracy is presented by Habermas as a third course
between mainstream liberalism and the republican view of the democratic
process. Both embed a different form of reductionism. While for mainstream
liberals the democratic process takes exclusively the form of a compromise
between particular interests, classical and contemporary republicans instead
equate the political process with a kind of ethical-political 'self-understanding'
writ large, i.e. carried out by the People understood as macro-subject.[21] The
liberal model underplays the moment of democratic will formation on the part
of the citizens: it understands democracy merely as a matter of *regulating* the
confrontation of particular interests. In this respect Habermas sides with
republicanism in defending the view that democratic theory ought to embed a
theoretical consideration of the process of collective will formation and self-
determination. He distances himself from his own understanding of
republicanism, however, in the way that process is conceived. The process of

self-clarification and self-determination must be conceptually severed, in his opinion, from the notion of a collective subject and the assumption of action in concert on the part of this subject. Rather, it is understood as a *subjectless* web of communication events which encompasses both the institutional decision makers and the public sphere:

> The 'self' of the self-organizing legal community disappears in the subjectless forms of communication that regulate the flow of discursive opinion- and will-formation in such a way that their fallible results enjoy the presumption of being reasonable. This is not to denounce the intuition connected with the idea of popular sovereignty but to interpret it intersubjectively. (1996a: 301)

The originality of the deliberative conception of politics lies in the relation between the institutional actors of politics and the general public. The function of the public, of the citizens, is neither the minimal one of legitimating the decisions of the institutional subjects through their electoral choices, nor the unrealistic one, assigned to it by what Habermas presents as 'republicanism', of binding the action of governmental institutions through a specific and self-expressive mandate. The public cannot *rule* by itself, Habermas points out, but can only *control* the operation of the administrative power of governmental institutions and *orient* it in certain directions.[22] The division of labour that Habermas envisages between institutional (or 'strong') and informal (or 'weak') publics or the public opinion as formed in the public sphere[23] resembles the distinction between the *context of justification* and the *context of discovery*. The organized, formal, 'strong' publics entrusted with decision-making prerogatives have to provide justified and legitimate *solutions* to problems. The unorganized, informal, 'weak' publics that concur in the formation of a public opinion have to *identify* the new problems that deserve formal consideration in a process that is relieved from the constraints of decision making. Characteristics of this public sphere are its *openness*, *inclusiveness*, *spontaneity* and intrinsic *pluralism*. The public sphere should be thought of as

> an open and inclusive network of overlapping, subcultural publics having fluid temporal, social, and substantive boundaries. Within a framework guaranteed by constitutional rights, the structures of such a pluralistic public sphere develop more or less spontaneously. The currents of public communication are channeled by mass media and flow through different publics that develop informally inside associations. (1996a: 307)

This means that the public sphere cannot be managed, organized, administered or artificially created by the powers that be, that it can be neither compartmentalized into separate non-communicating, ghetto-like communities nor fused into a unified and undifferentiated audience. Its pluralism comes from its composite character. The public sphere is always made of many subspheres, which function as public spheres in their own right, but communicate with each other in many other respects. Some of the subspheres that belong to the overarching network are delimited geographically (by national, regional, city and local boundaries), others are demarcated by way of a central theme of common concern (be it health care, art, religious experiences, science and technology, social policy, education, cinema, etc.), others by duration (from the transient public sphere of café discussions to the more organized public spheres supported by voluntary associations, periodicals, and social movements) and others by scope (ranging from public spheres that still do include face-to-face interaction all the way to the *abstract* public sphere generated by the mass media).[24] The public sphere is always a *public of publics*. It is unrestricted also in the sense that its communicative currents are not regulated by procedures, and thus it has a degree of flexibility that proves a great resource for the thematization of new needs and for the discussion of need interpretations (1996a: 314). As Habermas puts it,

> The public sphere cannot be conceived as an institution and certainly not as an organization. It is not even a framework of norms with differentiated competences and roles, membership regulations, and so on. Just as little does it represent a system; although it permits one to draw internal boundaries, outwardly it is characterized by open, permeable, and shifting horizons. The public sphere can best be described as a network for communicating information and points of view (i.e., opinions expressing affirmative or negative attitudes); the streams of communication are, in the process, filtered and synthesized in such a way that they coalesce into bundles of topically specified *public* opinions. Like the lifeworld as a whole, so, too, the public sphere is reproduced through communicative action, for which mastery of a natural language suffices; it is tailored to the *general comprehensibility* of everyday communicative practice. (1996a: 360)

Habermas then moves on to clarify the concept of the public sphere in relation to the notions of the *life-world* and of *civil society*. If we understand the life-world as a 'reservoir for simple interactions' (1996a: 360), then we can conceive of the various subsystems either as linked with one of the reproductive functions of the life-world (this is the case for religion, the educational system and the family) or as linked with one of the distinct validity claims embedded in the communicative use of language (this is the case of science, morality and art). The relation of the public sphere to that life-world from which it has originally branched out follows neither of these patterns. Rather, the public sphere remains linked to the life-world as the enlarged reflection of yet another feature of the everyday communicative use of language, namely the creation of a *social space* (see 1996a: 360). In this social space, which in the context of complex societies can no longer be conceived after the metaphors of *closed* public spaces such as the forum, the arena, or the stage, but should rather be thought of as a *virtual* space supported by the electronic media, the reciprocal offer and acceptance or motivated refusal of linguistic acts extends to each and any potential participant the possibility to intervene.

In its contemporary use the term 'civil society', as Cohen and Arato (1992) have pointed out, should not refer to the 'bourgeois society' which had formed the object of Hegel's and Marx's attention. The web of economic relations that traverse contemporary society are best thought of in terms of systems theory, leaving the term 'civil society' for designating the web of associations, organizations and movements that find their *raison d'être* in the elaboration of the themes most relevant in public debates. While the public sphere refers to the virtual space in which themes of public interest are elaborated and discussed and public opinion is formed, *civil society* designates the *associational infrastructure* which supports such space: the life of the public sphere takes place neither in formally institutionalized or system-like contexts nor in private interpersonal, familial and face-to-face settings.

Finally, Habermas distinguishes between three main kinds of actors who operate in the public sphere. Resorting once again to the image of the theatre, two kinds of actors can be metaphorically imagined to enter the stage from behind the wings or to accede to it directly from the audience. One kind of actor acts on the scene of the public sphere while coming from some formally structured and organized context in order to secure the one resource that circulates in the public sphere: influence. It is the case of organized lobbies, political parties, unions, members of parliament or of cabinet, and other institutional actors who *use* in an instrumental sense the public sphere for advancing their ends through the influence acquired in it. These actors usually enter the stage with an already formed and readily recognizable identity, for they represent interests that already enjoy public acknowledgment. As Habermas has put it more recently, these actors 'press, as invaders, from the outside onto the political public instead of acting from its midst' (1995b: 141). Another kind of actor reaches the stage from the ranks of the audience. Often these actors lend their voice to as yet unrecognized interests and have thus to generate their own marks of identification. Their primary task is to explain to the audience (and sometimes to themselves) who they are and what they stand for. The point is, however, that they are motivated not only by the intention to advance their goals and assert themselves, but also by an interest in 'revitalizing and enlarging civil society and the public sphere' (1996a: 370) – a revitalization and enlargement that include the preservation of existing associational and public structures, subcultural counter-publics, and the promotion of new collective identities, new rights and institutional reform. This dual attitude is typical of the new social movements and the associations that are formed around themes of public interest. There is, finally, a third kind of actors – the *Publizisten*, that is the journalists, publicity agents, and members of the press – who

> collect information, make decisions about the selection and presentation of 'programs', and to a certain extent control the entry of topics, contributions, and authors into the mass-media-dominated public sphere. (1996a: 376)

The Habermasian model of a democratic society includes an outline of the entire process of the circulation of power (*Machtkreislauf*), which is itself constitutionally regulated. The core of the political system is constituted by the 'familiar institutional complexes of administration (including the incumbent government), judicial system, and democratic opinion- and will-formation (which includes parliamentary bodies, political elections, and party competition)' (1996a: 354–5). It is a core that, following Dahl's terminology, Habermas characterizes as 'polyarchical'. The different parts of this political core of society also dispose themselves on a centre/periphery axis. The centre of the core is occupied by those institutions which rest on the classical powers. Of them, parliaments are the institutions most receptive to needs and stimuli arising from the public sphere, but the administration is by far the locus of effectiveness in problem-solving. At the periphery of the core, also called the *internal periphery*, we find various kinds of institutions entrusted with 'rights of self-governance or with other kinds of oversight and lawmaking functions delegated by the state (universities, public insurance systems, professional associations, chambers, charitable organizations, foundations, etc.)' (1996a: 355). Moving now to the *external* periphery, where the public sphere is located, we find a sector relatively closer to and more connected with the political sphere – constituted by a network including public institutions and private organizations, lobbies, interest groups and the like. Further removed from the political core, finally, we find those private associations, some of which function as lobbies who enter a dialogue with institutional actors in the service of special interests, and other circles, cultural organizations (academies, intellectual clubs, radical professionals), churches, philanthropic associations and 'public interest groups' (interested in environmental protection, animal rights, consumer protection, product safety), which instead address themselves primarily, though not exclusively (sometimes they resort to lobbying and to judicial action), to general problems and to the larger public.

Power and *influence* are the two resources that circulate throughout the political system, with a tendency for power to concentrate at the centre and influence to spread across the entire system. While *power* – understood as capacity to make decisions and render them binding – is found at the centre of this concentrical view of society, *influence* is the resource and medium through which the public sphere in general comes to affect the political core. Habermas appears here to accept the 'realistic' idea that a legitimate democratic political process may be compatible with the presence of vast 'weak' publics whose sole function is that of forming an opinion of their own and thereby influencing the circles of those who will actually make the decision about lawmaking and policy matters, but such division, if made into a rigid one, involves the risk of forfeiting the ideal of popular *sovereignty*. In one of the most interesting commentaries written on *Between Facts and Norms*, Bohman (1994) argues that somehow Habermas has already travelled too much in the direction of enervating the concept of 'popular sovereignty'[25] and that the framework developed by him needs to be recast in a more decidedly radical-democratic direction.[26] Bohman takes issue with the distinction between *opinion* and *will* formation, calling it 'a distinction without a difference'. In fact, to the extent that formal institutions are really democratic, the will formation process will reflect exactly the opinion formation process. Finally, points out Bohman, 'it is difficult to see why Habermas continues to call his democratic theory "deliberative", since the public is given only opinion-forming capacity' (1994: 925). Sovereignty, however, need not be idealistically imagined to be exerted all the time. Election times suffice, along with special occasions such as *referendums* and what Ackerman would call *constitutional politics* or higher lawmaking.

Deliberative Democracy and Pluralism

The crucial test of a conception of deliberative politics, however, is how it measures up to the predicament called by Rawls 'the fact of pluralism'. Habermas's 'solution' is to invoke at this point an all-encompassing 'communication model' capable of mediating between the various publics and the lawmakers. As Habermas puts it, this way of thinking takes

> a *structuralist approach* to the manner in which institutionalized opinion- and will-formation is linked with informal opinion building in culturally mobilized public spheres. This linkage is made possible neither by the homogeneity of the people and the identity of the popular will, nor by the identity of a reason that is supposedly able simply to *discover* an underlying homogeneous general interest. The discourse-theoretic conception is at cross-purposes with the classical views. If the communicatively fluid sovereignty of citizens instantiates itself in the power of public discourses that spring from autonomous public spheres but take shape in the decisions of *democratic, politically accountable* legislative bodies, then the pluralism of beliefs and interests is not suppressed but unleashed and recognized in revisable majority decisions as well as in compromises. The unity of a completely proceduralized reason retreats into the discursive structure of public communication. This reason refuses to concede that a consensus is free of coercion and hence has legitimating force, unless the consensus has come about under the fallibilistic proviso and on the basis of anarchic, unfettered communicative freedom. In the vertigo of this freedom, there is no longer any fixed point outside that of democratic procedure itself – a procedure whose meaning is already implicit in the system of rights. (1996a: 185–6)

One of the important points of this long quote is Habermas's explicit admission that majority decisions and compromises have full legitimating force, and that political legitimacy in a complex society cannot be measured by the strict standard of the discourse principle. This creates some tensions, on which more will be said below. For the time being, let me rather indicate some points of convergence and divergence with respect to Rawls's approach to the problem of pluralism. First, both take the fact of pluralism as the point of departure of their accounts of justice and democracy, both place their faith in some sort of 'public reason' of a more modest sort than the kind of Reason that metaphysical or comprehensive accounts claim to embed, but the main difference consists in the way in which they conceive the workings of such public reason.

For both, furthermore, public reason is essentially dialogic in nature, but while for Rawls the locus of public reason is constituted by the main institutions of political society, and especially the Supreme Court, Habermas's public reason primarily inhabits the public sphere – a domain which for Rawls would have to count as the locus of a non-public, though certainly not private, kind of reason. For Habermas, instead, public reason is really the public's reason.

Furthermore, Rawls's public reason works on the basis of a voluntary limitation in the themes to which it applies. Not only can public reason be invoked only when issues of a *recognizedly* public nature are involved, but it requires of the participants in deliberation that they defend their theses only through recourse to 'political values' and 'grounds' that everyone can reasonably be expected to endorse. Public reason enjoins us to draw on less than what we see as 'the whole truth' of the matter, in order to meet others on the common ground of a 'more limited truth'. One of the results of examining matters from the standpoint of public reason is that certain topics and issues are screened out as 'controversial' and are thus supposed 'to be bracketed away' in communal deliberation. Generalizing the paradigmatic case of the removal of religious issues and debates from the political agenda which made it possible to put an end to the religious wars at the beginning of the modern era, Rawls understands public reason as something that repeats over and over that marvellous feat which allowed for the coexistence side by side of competing religious views. Public reason screens out of the political agenda all that is potentially divisive.

Habermas's approach to the reality of pluralism in complex societies, instead, rests on a far more optimistic view of public or dialogic reason. There is no such thing as an intractable question. Every issue, including values, need interpretations and the requirements of identities, as Habermas points out in his 'Excursus on Procedural Neutrality', is amenable to public discussion and should be brought to the public forum if someone so desires. According to Habermas,

> not only informal, but also procedurally regulated opinion- and will-formation should be open to ethically relevant questions of the good life, of collective identity, and of need interpretation. (1996a: 313)

Any restriction on the topics acceptable as objects of public discussion and deliberation, instead, is likely to produce three kinds of negative results. First, if questions concerning the good were excluded from the public forum and left only for comprehensive conceptions to elaborate, political discourse would lose 'its power to rationally change prepolitical attitudes, need interpretations, and value orientations' (1996a: 309). Second, the boundary that separates questions of public relevance from questions of merely private interest would be taken for granted and a merely contingent distribution of areas of consensus and dissent would thereby be permanently frozen into a kind of ontological partition, impermeable to future change. Consequently, the public agenda would be implicitly biased toward a traditional understanding of what is public and what is private.[27] Third, a conception of public reason such as Rawls's, as well as similar views of public discourse as 'conversational restraint' (Ackerman) or 'gag rules' (Holmes),[28] runs against the fact that very often the boundary between public issues and private concerns is itself at the centre of controversy – as, for instance, the debate on pornography or many multiculturalist disputes (the *chador* issue in French schools, the Sikh turban issue in the Canadian armed forces, etc.) illustrate. Habermas's conception, instead, avoids these pitfalls and at the same time is quite responsive to the classical liberal suspicion of any public scrutiny over terrains that should remain the exclusive territory of the individual.[29] Habermas, in fact, draws a distinction between *thematizing* and *regulating* competences, needs and practices:

> to talk about something is not necessarily the same as meddling in another's affairs. Certainly the intimate sphere must be protected from intrusive forces and the critical eyes of strangers, but not everything reserved to the decisions of private persons is withdrawn from public thematization and protected from criticism. Rather, every affair in need of political regulation should be publicly discussed, though not every legitimate object of public discussion will in fact be politically regulated. (1996a: 313)

In the end, however, Habermas's approach to the question of pluralism appears more capable than Rawls's of accounting for the fact that the common ground on which an overlapping consensus may grow is not something that is given and that can only be defended through limiting public discussion to certain topics, but is something that as time passes and contexts change may also undergo reduction or even disappear. As McCarthy has noted, Habermas's understanding of the relation between deliberative democracy and pluralism presupposes a different set of democratic virtues than Rawls's:

> An ideal of mutual respect balancing commitment with openness is no less capable of accommodating reasonable pluralism and reasonable disagreement than Rawls's ideal of citizenship with its duty of civility. And it has the advantage over the latter of avoiding the sharp split between public and private reason that runs clear through Rawls's construction. Rather than obligating citizens to treat views publicly as reasonable that they regard privately, or in the background culture, as 'plainly unreasonable or untrue', it encourages them to propose and defend publicly whatever views they think reasonable and relevant to deciding public issues. (1994: 62–3)[30]

Concluding Remarks

The reader who has followed the trajectory of Habermas's thought from his early writings to *Between Facts and Norms* cannot but be impressed by the extraordinary variety of theoretical and disciplinary landscapes which it has spanned as well as by the distance that separates his current position from some of his earlier views. Habermas is a prolific and generous writer who allows the reader to see the threads of the woof, as it were. On the one hand, he has always been one of the most determined and sophisticated defenders of a universalistic standpoint in moral and political philosophy and has from time to time engaged in vigorous confrontations with all those who, from one perspective or another, questioned the very possibility of 'context-transcending' rules, assumptions, presuppositions and generalization tests that 'would burst the provinciality of their context asunder'. One need only recall the Habermas–Gadamer debate of the late 1960s and early 1970s, Habermas's polemics against French postmodernists and his ongoing controversy with

Rorty's brand of postfoundationalist thought. On the other hand a slow, halting and tension-ridden shift toward a model of universalism quite different from the one defended in philosophical combat – a kind of universalism of reflective judgment really not too remote from a hermeneutics with a critical colouring – can be observed. In his 1983 essay on the 'Discourse Ethics', included within *Moral Consciousness and Communicative Action*, Habermas still claimed for the presuppositions of argumentation on which the discourse ethics rests the status of 'unavoidable presuppositions',[31] defined the principle of dialogical universalization 'U' as 'a knife, that makes razor-sharp cuts between the good and the right' (1990: 104), and distinguished between the *necessity* or *inevitability* linked with the grounding of the moral principle and the *prudence* that must guide its *application*. Habermas distinguished between 'questions of justice' – which 'can in principle be decided [*entschieden*] rationally in terms of justice or the generalizability of interests' (1990: 108) – and 'evaluative questions' that can rationally be discussed (not *entschieden*) only *within* a particular ethical horizon and, as we have seen above, maintained that the 'transcending force' of the validity claim linked with the discourse ethics can even be observed *empirically* if one looks at the institutionalization of rights.

This discourse-theoretical understanding of the practical – split at this stage in moral discourses about questions of justice, where under ideal conditions that satisfy the presuppositions of argumentation an expectation of reaching final consensus is given, and discussions on the good life, where no such expectation exists – was still significantly enmeshed with the determinant judgment model of universalism. The 'universal' – in this case the principle of dialogical generalization 'U' – was conceptually linked with a dimension of necessity (the unavoidability of the presuppositions on which it rests), and certainly it was formulated antecedently and independently of the particular. As far as the deductive nature of the specification of the conditions of subsumption is concerned, Habermas's initial model of the discourse ethics had a more ambiguous status. On the one hand, the outcome of each concrete running of the test of dialogical universalization is left for the participants to determine. The theory cannot give any anticipation of it. On the other hand, however, as we have seen above, in a way a quasi-methodological 'guarantee of validity' is connected with the discourse approach to normative questions in the weaker sense that, *if certain idealized conditions are met*, there is no reason why a dialogical deliberation should not result in the formation of a 'rational consensus' on the best argument.[32]

The contrast with Habermas's present position is not difficult to notice. In lieu of the residual category of 'evaluative questions' Habermas has felt compelled to introduce a whole new subdomain of practical reasoning – *das Ethische* – where the object of discussion is the appropriateness of practical projects to concrete identities, individual or collective. Furthermore, over the years, the lower status of ethical questions – a lower status signalled, among other things, by the fact that the term 'discourse' would not apply to them – has been constantly upgraded, until the recent use, in *Between Facts and*

Norms, of the term 'ethical discourse'. More important, however, is the fact that the guarantee of reaching a rational consensus is no longer assumed to exist for moral questions, 'even under ideal conditions' (Habermas 1996a: 165), and that justice is said to consist of *what is equally good for everybody*. The knife that supposedly would sever the right from the good has lost its sharpness. One wonders how long that last vestige of the determinant judgment model of universality – the conceptual separability of the universal and the particular – will survive the demise of the rest of the paradigm. After all, it is not easy to see how we could establish 'what is equally good for everybody' independently of an ethical conception of the good.[33] On this specific difficulty more will be said in Chapter 6.

3

An (Almost) Aesthetic Model of Normative Validity

With Ronald Dworkin we move to a theorist who has been couching his view of normative validity very explicitly in terms of singular or exemplary universalism from the outset. There is a core of ideas to which Ronald Dworkin has remained tenaciously faithful throughout the span of the nearly two decades which separate his 1977 book *Taking Rights Seriously* from his 1996 volume *Freedom's Law*. The most significant is the idea that the activity of interpreting the US Constitution can be best made sense of if we understand the Constitution as a set of moral principles that need to be applied to concrete situations. This *moral* reading of the Constitution, which is actually an *aesthetic* reading in prudent disguise, stands over against a narrower approach to the constitution as a document containing specific provisions (the *Constitution of detail*) to be applied with reference to the state of affairs that the framers can be thought to have intended to bring about.

A second thematic thread that runs throughout Dworkin's work is a strong hermeneutic understanding of law as something which is always in need of interpretation: Dworkin is prepared to state that no descriptive statement of the form 'the law prescribes that *p*' can sharply be separated from evaluative statements of the type 'the law ought to prescribe that *p*'. In fact, the identification of what is to be included in the law is subject to interpretation in the first place. Judges confronted with a statute must still construe what the printed words mean and what their implications for the matter at hand are. At times, his radical anti-positivism colours Dworkin's account of rights and law with natural law overtones.[1] Yet his hermeneutic and, as we shall see, almost aesthetic approach to validity in matters of constitutional adjudication is counterbalanced by a powerful *moral realism* that runs throughout his work. Over and over again Dworkin emphasizes that for him right decisions exist and are *discovered*, and that in any legal case there is one right solution in need of being identified.[2] This peculiar combination of radical hermeneuticism and moral realism will be explored more closely in this chapter, for in it lies an equally peculiar combination of the determinant and the reflective judgment models of universalism.

Principles and Rules

As early as in *Taking Rights Seriously* Dworkin has stated that the problem with mainstream (mostly positivist) approaches to constitutional law is their failure to recognize that ultimately legal problems are bound up with the interpretation and application of moral principles. Legal problems are reducible neither to a technique of rule application nor to policy-making problems of rational choice.[3] They are rather problems of balancing conflicting *principles*. There is almost no word that recurs more often in Dworkin's writings than the word 'principle', and thus at first sight it might seem odd to assign Dworkin to the reflective judgment approach to normative questions. On closer inspection, however, the meaning of the word 'principle', as it occurs in all of Dworkin's writings, appears to be quite distant from the ordinary one. As will become clearer, Dworkin's definition of a legal problem is best understood if we invert the emphasis: legal problems are problems of *balancing* conflicting principles.

Dworkin's 'principles' – for example the principle according to which no one can profit from her own infringement of the law, or the principle 'no liability without fault' – stand in opposition to *rules*. They are not simply rules that happen to be more general than others. Rather, principles are *qualitatively different* from rules in three important respects. First, nothing can be *subsumed* under principles of the sort Dworkin has in mind. In fact, only valid *rules*, if relevant to the facts of the matter, unequivocally and unambiguously determine our judgment. Let's take the chess rule to the effect that the king moves only one step at a time. If the context is such that the rule is *relevant* – namely, if chess is the game we are playing – then no one, whether player, umpire or bystander, can claim at the same time that the rule holds and that someone who has moved the king diagonally across the whole board has made a valid move. To be sure, rules can have exceptions: when castling, the king can be moved two squares. Characteristic of rules is the fact that exceptions can be included in a more detailed, yet internally consistent, elucidation of the rule.[4] The legal positivists and all those who consider the Constitution a 'Constitution of detail' – the true representatives of a determinant judgment view of legal and constitutional validity – think that the Constitution operates as a system of rules. On this view, without much effort in interpretation, but merely adhering to the plain meaning of the words contained in the text of the Constitution, we can determine what the law, if it is valid law, prescribes and forbids. Two rules can come into conflict, but then, barring cases in which one of the conflicting rules is erroneously thought to be valid, the legal system solves the conflict by conferring priority on one rule over the other on the basis of several possible *criteria* that also function on the basis of determinant judgment – for example, the criteria according to which the rule issued by the higher authority, or the most recent rule, or the most specific rule ought to prevail.[5]

This property of allowing for subsumption, instead, does not apply to legal *principles*. Consider the principle according to which no one can profit from his or her unlawful act. If I know that I'm included in a will and kill the person, even after serving my time in prison I will be prevented from enjoying what would be the advantage of an unlawful act. Yet – continues Dworkin – consider the case of *adverse possession*. If I trespass on your property and pass through it for years and years and you do not protest, in the end I acquire the right to continue to do so. It appears as though I have benefited from an unlawful act. As Dworkin points out, we do not react to the example of *adverse possession* by denying that the principle is a valid one. Nor do we understand the case of *adverse possession* as an *exception*. Another example mentioned by Dworkin is when someone breaks a contract with her employer in order to sign another, more advantageous, contract with another employer. In court usually the person is forced to pay some compensation to the former employer, but not to renounce the benefits of the second contract. Once again, has the principle that no one can benefit from his or her unlawful act been violated, or do we have another 'exception'? Neither is the case, argues Dworkin. Our belief that the principle is a valid one in our legal culture is not undermined by these instances, nor do they constitute exceptions, because no further elucidation of the principle, no matter how detailed, can encompass all of them. These counter-examples simply show that principles are normative prescriptions that operate in a way different from rules. The difference lies in the fact that a principle 'does not even purport to set out conditions that make its application necessary' (Dworkin 1977: 26). The deductive aspect of its application to the relevant facts of the matter – a crucial component of determinant judgment – is lacking. A principle operates rather as 'a reason for', alongside other reasons 'for' or 'against' deciding a legal issue one way or another. In this sense, continues Dworkin, a principle 'states a reason that *argues* in one direction, but does not *necessitate* a particular decision' (1977: 26, my emphasis). In fact, there may be *other* reasons that push in the opposite direction – the protection of property rights, for example – and these other reasons might in certain circumstances, yet not in others, deserve priority over the principle that one should not benefit from one's unlawful acts.

Interesting is also the fact that, according to Dworkin, there are no principles that are subtracted, by virtue of their importance or generality, to this fate. The First Amendment provides that Congress shall not abridge freedom of speech. Only if we interpret the Constitution as a set of rules – as some positivists might do – are we entitled to conclude that *any* law introducing any restriction on freedom of speech would automatically have to be deemed unconstitutional. If we treat the Constitution as containing a set of principles then even the most fundamental rights, such as freedom of speech, may be balanced against other rights and principles, in contexts where this becomes important. The right of free speech was never meant to allow someone to divulge sensitive military information in war time, and is obviously limited by laws against libel, slander and defamation.

The second difference between rules and principles concerns the mode of their application. Rules apply or do not apply in an 'all or none' fashion. If they are overridden by higher-order rules, then they simply disappear from the normative picture with which we assess the case at hand. Furthermore, they can be neatly embedded into hierarchies of rules. Again, this does not apply to principles. Principles do not apply in an 'all or none' fashion. They possess a dimension that rules lack: the dimension of *weight* or *importance*.[6]

The more important principle takes precedence over the less important one, without annihilating the latter's normative significance for the matter at hand. Where rules are concerned, instead, from a descriptive standpoint we can certainly say that in a given practice one rule is more important than another, but what we mean by that is simply that *more* depends on that rule than on another, or that the rule coordinates more action than another. In fact, if two rules come into conflict, we do not say that the more important prevails 'by virtue of its greater weight' (1977: 27). If a rule prevails over another, it does so by virtue of being selected by some *criterion of precedence* which in turn operates as a distributional rule. The interesting point in this context is that Dworkin's 'principles', much like Nozick's 'reasons',[7] do not come with weight tags attached to them. We must *assign* weight to them, and there can't be a *method* for exactly measuring the weight that should be accorded to a principle. Decisions about the relative priority of principles, then, are bound, like *aesthetic* judgments, to be controversial and *undemonstrable*, which is not to say unarguable or arbitrary. In fact, evidence can be brought in support of our claim that a certain principle has relevance and even priority in the matter at hand. For example, we can mention precedents in which the principle has been used or we can mention statutes that exemplify or embed that principle.[8] As Dworkin suggests, in a legal argument a complete failure to produce any such evidence would most likely prevent us from succeeding in justifying our 'principle'. More generally, the *number* and *quality* of such occurrences of the principle in the relevant judicial or statutory provisions plays a role in our assigning it weight *vis-à-vis* other principles that are also relevant to the case at hand.

A third facet of the distinction between rules and principles is that while the rules that regulate a practice are always *finite* in number, principles seem to be artificially abstracted bits and pieces of a *legal culture* which is best understood in a *holistic* vein. Let us go back for a moment to the previous point. It is not the case, argues Dworkin against Hart, that we could identify valid principles through a *pedigree test* like the one which helps us to recognize valid statutes and rules.[9] Valid principles do not strictly depend on the kind of evidence mentioned above or on 'recognition rules'. Being embedded in precedents or in statutes, in fact, is a *necessary* but not as such *sufficient* condition for validity. The precedent decision might itself be wrong, or the statute unconstitutional. In lieu of identifying a Hartian 'rule of recognition' that might function as a *pedigree test* for legal principles, we could understand valid principles as *constituting* such a rule of recognition by means of which we identify valid lower-order rules. But, continues Dworkin, if following this tack we tried to enumerate all the valid principles operative in our legal system, we would be bound to fail in our task. The totality of valid principles is law, *droit, Recht* itself. We would only generate the tautology that law is law.[10] Valid principles in our legal system

> are controversial, their weight is all important, they are *numberless*, and they shift and change so fast that the start of our list would be obsolete before we reached the middle. (1977: 44, my emphasis)

To sum up, more than resembling overarching and very general rules, and without being beliefs, principles function *like* those common, taken for granted beliefs out of which what phenomenology-oriented social theorists call the *life-world*, what John Searle has called the *background* or what Gadamer has called a *tradition*, is made. These beliefs cannot be apprehended *in toto*, all at once, but only selectively, and they cannot be listed in a *finite* series, because each one mentioned by us brings in new ones. Our understanding of law, thus, is no less holistic than our understanding of a text, of a culture or of a tradition. Imagine, continues Dworkin,

> that you have read a long book about geology, and I ask you to tell me what information it contains. You will do so in a series of propositions of fact. But now suppose I ask you first how many propositions of fact the book contains, and what theory you used in counting them. You would think me mad, not simply because the question is preposterously difficult, as if I had asked you how many separate grains of sand there were in a particular beach, or because it requires a difficult conceptual discrimination, as if I had asked you how many human beings there were in a group that included a woman in early pregnancy. You would think me mad because I had asked entirely the wrong sort of question about the material at hand. The book contains a great deal of information; propositions are ways of presenting that information, but the number of propositions used will depend on considerations independent of the content of the information, such as, for example, whether one uses the general term 'rocks' or the names of particular sorts of rocks. In the same way, lawyers use rules and principles to report legal information, and it is wrong to suppose that any particular statement of these is canonical. (1977: 75–6)

One problem that Dworkin's account leaves open is the following. Normative utterances do not come with structural features that single them out as principles or rules: they come as 'ought' utterances such as 'No one can draw an advantage from his or her unlawful act' or 'No one can obtain a driver's licence before being 18 years old.' Only the first has to be balanced against other principles. The second is a rule, a statute that does not have to be balanced against anything else. There are no exceptions and no other considerations to be taken into account: no one under 18 can be given a licence, period. But how do we decide on the status of a normative utterance, on whether it should be treated as a principle or as a rule? Let us consider Dworkin's answer for the time being. More will be said on this question below. Many of the clauses of the Bill of Rights, points out Dworkin, are drafted in exceedingly abstract moral language. The First Amendment refers to the 'right of free speech', for example,

> the Fifth Amendment to the process that is 'due' to citizens, and the Fourteenth Amendment to protection that is 'equal'. According to the moral reading, these clauses must be understood in the way their language most naturally suggests: they refer to abstract moral principles and incorporate these by reference, as limits on government's power. (1996: 7)

The language of these clauses is not the sole kind of language to be found in the Constitution, however. For example,

> Article Two specifies that the President must be at least thirty-five years old, and the

Third Amendment insists that government may not quarter soldiers in citizens' houses in peacetime. (1996: 8)

The language of these clauses is not that of moral principle, and they should be taken as legal rules to be applied as their literal meaning dictates. No one could legitimately infer from the language of the Third Amendment that the real good being protected is the privacy of citizens, and thus conclude from the Third Amendment to a more general 'right to privacy'.

What is the basis and the justification for our claims concerning the status of legal norms? How can we be sure, about any given clause of the Constitution, whether it ought to be regarded as a principle or as a rule? Dworkin's answer is that this is itself 'a question of interpretation or, if you prefer, translation' (1996: 8). Here is one juncture where what used once to be the target of Dworkin's irony – namely, the framers' intention – somewhat unexpectedly reenters the picture: we find nothing in history, argues Dworkin,

> to cause us any doubt about what the framers of the Third Amendment meant to say. Given the words they used, we cannot sensibly interpret them as laying down any moral principle at all, even if we believe they were inspired by one. They said what the words they used would normally be used to say: not that privacy must be protected, but that soldiers must not be quartered in houses in peacetime. The same process of reasoning – about what the framers presumably intended to say when they used the words they did – yields an opposite conclusion about the framers of the equal protection clause, however. Most of them no doubt had fairly clear expectations about what legal consequences the Fourteenth Amendment would have. (1996: 8–9)

Dworkin construes the meaning of the Fourteenth Amendment as a principle 'of quite breathtaking scope and power', namely as the principle 'that government must treat everyone as of equal status and with equal concern' (1996: 10). Not much more is to be found in the whole of Dworkin's work on the questions, crucial for his approach, 'How do we tell a rule from a principle?' and 'How do we decide the issue in controversial cases?', and I will return to this point in Chapter 6.

Interpretation and Integrity: Making the Most of the Constitution

Having reconstructed Dworkin's case for the interpretive, and thus judgment-based, nature of all legal argumentation we need to examine now the nature of the process of interpretation as conceived by Dworkin. In fact, Dworkin propounds an original account of interpretation and interpretive validity which rests on the notion of *valorizing* or 'making the most' of the object of interpretation by way of enhancing its *integrity*. This account has a *pars destruens* and a *pars construens*.

Starting with the *pars destruens*, in *Law's Empire* (1986) we find a critical assessment of the inconsequentiality of the view according to which the normative content or meaning of a statute is equivalent with the legislator's intention in conceiving the statute. For one thing, it is difficult to demarcate precisely who is to count among the authors of a statute. Every member of the Parliament that enacted it, including those who voted against it? Only those who approved it? But isn't a statute an expression of the will of the Parliament as a whole, as determined by majority rule? Whose intentions are we to take into account? Those of the members of Parliament who publicly took the floor and declared their views, as reported in the official record? Couldn't the intentions of those who didn't speak, but were the target of lobbying, have played a larger role? Should a legislator's intentions as expressed in a speech before an empty Parliament count more toward defining the meaning of the statute than his responses in an interview broadcast on the evening news and watched by millions of people?[11]

Second, even if we reach an agreement on who the real authors of the statute are, their intentions in voting the statute may be very different and even conflicting. Should we then take the intention shared by the greater number as the one that defines the meaning of the statute, or should we construe a kind of 'average' intention that 'comes closest to those of most legislators, though identical to none of them?' (Dworkin 1986: 320).

Third, suppose an agreement can be found on this issue too. Then, should spoken words as recorded on the Congressional Record be taken as reliable indicators of the real intentions of the legislators? What about the congressman who wishes that a certain goal be reflected in the statute but has no power to have a clause or amendment to that effect inserted? He may have voted for the final version of the statute, though his intention was that the statute should be read as to imply certain things that he did not have the power to have it say explicitly. Should that intention count?[12]

The alternative suggested by Dworkin is close in certain respects to Gadamer's view. It relies on reflective judgment and it is a view of adjudication as ultimately guided by *integrity*. Judgment as to the meaning of single constitutional provisions must start, as a first step, from what the framers *said*. 'History is therefore plainly relevant. But only in a particular way. We turn to history to answer the question of what they intended to *say*, not the different question of what *other* intentions they had' (1996: 10). Distancing himself from the positivist approach to the Constitution, Dworkin adds then that 'we have no need to decide what [the framers] expected to happen, or hoped would happen, in consequence of their having said what they did, for example; their purpose, in that sense, is not part of our study' (1996: 10).

As a second step, and here we enter the core of the *pars construens* of Dworkin's position, a judge must check his or her interpretation of the Constitution against the requirement of *integrity*, about which more will be said below.[13] Integrity for the time being can be understood as the requirement of the self-congruency or authenticity of the political identity that the Constitution reflects and at the same time contributes to shape. Authenticity as exemplary self-congruency cannot be reduced to a mere mirror-like projection of a kind of 'essence' of a collective identity – it is not just like Montesquieu's *esprit general d'une nation* or Herder's *Volkgeist* – because inherent in every identity is also a future-oriented, project-like component.

Self-congruency presupposes congruence also with this component and thus
with a volitional moment of identity which cannot be reduced to an objec-
tivist description. The abstract principles to which the judge has recourse in
order to buttress her interpretation of the Constitution, however, still have to
fit with the whole of the Constitution as defined by its written text, by our
historical knowledge about the context and by authoritative precedents. For
example,

> a judge who believes that abstract justice requires economic equality cannot inter-
> pret the equal protection clause as making equality of wealth, or collective
> ownership of productive resources, a constitutional requirement, because that
> interpretation simply does not fit American *history* or *practice*, or the rest of the
> constitution. (1996: 11, my emphasis)

We are thus thrown back to a crucial definition of what the expression 'fit'
might mean, the best account of which is to be found in Dworkin's discussion
of *integrity* in *Law's Empire* (1986) as well as in his more general discussion
of validity in interpretation in *A Matter of Principle* (1985).

The analogy between justice and aesthetic judgment is explicitly addressed
by Dworkin when, in discussing the notion of the fairest sentence in controversial constitutional cases, he suggests that the judge 'deciding what the law
is' can be usefully compared 'with the literary critic teasing out the various
dimensions of value in a complex play or poem' (1986: 228). In other passages
judges are said to be like writers who inherit a half completed manuscript and
decide to add a chapter of their own: their aim is to create 'a single unified
novel that is the best it can be' (1986: 229). Among the many different chapters which can possibly be written, the best is the one which *makes the most*
of the entire narrative, stylistic, and literary texture of the existing manuscript.[14]

According to Dworkin, the impartiality or fairness of the just solution
cannot be justified solely in terms of avoiding controversial ideas, but must be
justified in an affirmative way, as the one solution which *maximizes the degree
of convergence of a contingent plurality of value orientations*.

Let us examine Dworkin's view more closely. First, what does the judge do
exactly? In his acting as a chain novelist writing the next chapter his aim must
be that of making of the novel 'the best novel it can be construed as the work
of a single author rather than, as is the fact, the product of many different
hands' (1986: 229). Furthermore, the judge

> must take up some view about the novel in progress, some working theory about its
> characters, plot, genre, theme, and point, in order to decide what counts as con-
> tinuing it and not as beginning anew . . . He will aim to find layers and currents of
> meaning rather than a single, exhaustive theme. (1986: 230)

The judge then forms a projected structure – his intended sentence, with all its
supporting legal argumentation – and tests it against two distinct interpretive
standards. First, the sentence must be tested in terms of 'fit':

> This does not mean his interpretation must fit every bit of the [previous] text . . .
> But the interpretation he takes up must nevertheless flow throughout the text; it

> must have general explanatory power, and it is flawed if it leaves unexplained some major structural aspects of the text, a subplot treated as having great dramatic importance or a dominant and repeated metaphor. (1986: 230)

If more than one interpretation 'fits the bulk of the text', then our judge must resort to the second standard and determine 'which of these eligible readings makes the work in progress best, all things considered'. In this second test he enjoys more degrees of freedom:

> His more substantive aesthetic judgments, about the importance or insight or realism or beauty of different ideas the novel might be taken to express, come into play. But the formal and structural considerations that dominate on the first dimension figure on the second as well, for even when neither of two interpretations is disqualified out of hand as explaining too little, one may show the text in a better light because it fits more of the text or provides a more interesting integration of style and content. (1986: 231)

Thus a legal judgment concerning the constitutionality of a statute is really *a blend of several types of judgment*. It is a 'judgment of judgments' in which 'judgments about textual coherence and integrity' are rendered alongside 'more substantive aesthetic judgments that themselves assume different literary aims' (1986: 231). In the overall judgment expressed in the judge's sentence these more partial kinds of judgments 'check one another' and, as Dworkin points out, it is the possibility of a tension and 'a contest, particularly between *textual* and *substantive* judgments, that distinguishes a chain novelist's assignment from more independent creative writing' (1986: 232, my emphasis).

This tension – which is not to be construed as the tension between aspects of interpretation that depend on subjective aesthetic convictions and aspects of interpretation that are less dependent on them, or as the tension between uncontroversial and controversial aspects of an interpretation – is perhaps the distinctive trait of legal judgment in constitutional cases. Is the judge free to give effect to her vision of what the Constitution ought to be like? Is she bound to ignore such vision because she is enslaved by a text that cannot be ignored? According to Dworkin 'neither of these two crude descriptions – of total creative freedom or mechanical textual constraint – captures' the judge's situation. A judge will sense creative freedom when she compares her task with 'some relatively more mechanical one, like direct translation of a text into a foreign language'. On the other hand, the same judge will sense constraint when she compares her task 'with some relatively less guided one, like beginning a new novel'.[15] To anticipate a point which will be addressed in Chapter 7, Dworkin's characterization of the judgment rendered by the Supreme Court justice seems to fit perfectly in that intermediate area between the closedness and inherent necessity of determinant judgment and the unconstrained openness of pure reflective judgment – a third type of judgment constituted by a reflective judgment guided or oriented by certain normative constraints.

Another interesting quality inherent in the kind of judgment presupposed by the 'law as integrity' approach is, according to Dworkin, that it is not a judgment on 'whether and how far' one should depart from the Constitution as a received body of law. For, as Dworkin notes, a judge 'has nothing he *can* depart from or cleave to until he has constructed a novel-in-progress from the text, and the various decisions we have canvassed are all decisions he must make just to do this' (1986: 238).

Similar considerations are developed in *A Matter of Principle* (1985). An explicit reference is made to literary criticism as a field of interpretive activity where more theories are present that avoid the kind of rigid separation of descriptive and evaluative stances from which, according to Dworkin, legal theory has suffered. Also in the case of literary criticism, *mutatis mutandis*:

> an interpretation of a piece of literature attempts to show which way of reading (or speaking or directing or acting) the text reveals it as the best work of art . . . Interpretation of a text attempts to show *it* as the best work of art *it* can be, and the pronoun insists on the difference between explaining a work of art and changing it into a different one . . . An interpretation cannot make a work of art more distinguished if it makes a large part of the text irrelevant, or much of the incidents accidental, or a great part of the trope or style unintegrated and answering only to independent standards of fine writing. (1985: 149–50)

In *A Matter of Principle* Dworkin also takes up two objections that are often raised against interpretive accounts of normativity such as his. It is interesting to follow his response, because his thesis enters a certain tension with the moral realism which later he will embrace in *Foundations of Liberal Equality*. The first objection runs as follows: since on the integrity approach a legal text speaks to us only through interpretations, the text cannot successfully set limits on our interpretations. Thus the activity of interpretation is not qualitatively different from *reinventing the text anew*. Dworkin responds to the objection by recalling that in post-Kuhnian philosophy of science it is widely accepted that scientific facts are not really independent from theories. This predicament is not thought to prevent lower-level scientific propositions, purported to portray 'facts' but not really independent from certain theoretical definitions of their subject matter, from corroborating or disproving higher-level theoretical generalizations. All that is required of the post-Kuhnian epistemologist is the awareness that at no point are theories assessed against 'facts' or uninterpreted reality, but the process of scientific testing consists rather of matching theoretical propositions against lower-level descriptive languages, all the way down to 'observational' languages that are images of reality about which we are more confident – but are languages and constructions nonetheless. Thus, as Dworkin points out, 'there is no paradox in the proposition that facts both depend on and constrain the theories that explain them' (1985: 169).

In the realm of constitutional adjudication things are not much different. Dworkin emphasizes, however, that the difference between interpretive convictions concerning the structure and form of the text and broader interpretive convictions concerning what is of value, and thus susceptible of improving the text, is enough to ensure that one set of convictions acts as a check and constraint over the other set. The difference between *interpreting* and *changing* a text lies in allowing the first set of considerations to limit the second.

The second objection touches on the question of *objectivity* in interpretation: if the soundness of interpretation depends on the extent to which it succeeds in making a text 'better', then there is no such thing as objectivity in interpretation because such betterness is a matter of an entirely subjective kind of judgment. Dworkin's answer takes on a Rortyan flavour. 'I see no point,' argues Dworkin,

> in trying to find some general argument that moral or political or legal or aesthetic or interpretive judgments *are* objective . . . In fact, I think that the whole issue of objectivity, which so dominates contemporary theory in these areas, is a kind of fake. (1985: 171–2)

The reason why this is so is that there is, according to Dworkin, no real difference between 'the claim that slavery is unjust, offered as a move in some collective enterprise in which such judgments are made and debated, and the claim that slavery is really or objectively unjust in the actual world' (1985: 174). In other words, if I am really convinced, on the basis of some moral argument, that slavery is unjust, I must also believe that this is not just 'my opinion', but something on which everybody ought to agree. It is unclear then, concludes Dworkin, what the adverb 'objectively' would add to the adjective 'unjust' so understood.

Integrity as Making the Most of One's Life

The notion of integrity at work in Dworkin's view of constitutional adjudication cannot be fully understood unless we place it in a broader context. It is not a strictly legal notion, but really a broader normative notion – defined by Dworkin in ways very close to what I have called *authenticity* – which encompasses the domain of individual ethical-existential decisions, of individual moral decisions, of public ethical-political decisions, of public moral decisions, and of course of legal adjudication. The interesting thing, from the standpoint of a judgment view of justice, is that Dworkin, differently than Habermas and Rawls, is prepared to use the same notion for all these domains and to thereby emphasize that underlying normative decisions we find a unitary logic of judgment. Although this function of integrity as a guiding ethical ideal is partially visible in *Foundations of Liberal Equality* (1990), in no work by Dworkin does it become clearer than in *Life's Dominion* (1993).

One of the theses defended in the book is that in the abortion controversy the contest is not really between two different ways of answering the question 'Is the fetus a human person with rights and interests that the state must protect?', but rather between two different ways of understanding how a common, shared reverence for the *sanctity of life* ought to be expressed.[16] Dworkin supports this statement by pointing at some of the inconsistencies into which opposers of abortion fall if the ground of their opposing abortion is voiced in terms of the fetus's rights or interests being violated.[17] First, there is a fallacy in the argument that having now an obvious interest in survival, 'it must have been in my interest not to be aborted when I was a just conceived fetus'. In fact, 'whether abortion is against the interests of a fetus must depend on whether the fetus itself has interests at the time the abortion is performed, not whether interests will develop if no abortion takes place' (1993: 19). For it is in my interest 'that my father didn't go on a long business trip the day before I was conceived. But it would not have been against anyone's interests, in that way, if he had done so because there would never have been anyone whose interests it could have harmed' (1993: 19). Second, the idea that abortion is permitted only 'in self-defence' as it were, in order to save the mother's life – which only the most extreme anti-abortionists would deny – is inconsistent with 'any belief that a fetus is a person with a right to live' (1993: 32). Self-defence is a legitimate option if it is *self*-defence. But unless a woman procures herself an abortion by herself, the notion of self-defence cannot vindicate what the doctor who performs an abortion does: no one is allowed, as a third party, to kill an innocent person in order to save another (see 1993: 32). Third, the same applies for those conservative positions which allow for the possibility of abortion in case of rape or incest. If the fetus has a right to life that counterbalances the mother's interest in not having her life ruined, it can hardly be understood how it would be legitimate to have the same fetus pay with its life for the crime committed by a third person.

Similarly, runs the second main thesis of the book, 'at the other end of life' the contest between supporters and opposers of euthanasia is really a contest between two different ways of understanding the sanctity of life – two competing conceptions from which the opposite conclusions follow that, under certain conditions, to allow someone to choose the time and manner of his death would be an insult to, or an affirmation of, the sanctity of life. Interesting for our purposes is the way in which the idea of the sanctity of human life is understood and connected with that of integrity by Dworkin.

Sanctity really means 'of ultimate value' or 'inviolable'. For something to possess 'sanctity' in this sense means to be not just *personally* important to its possessor, not even just *instrumentally* important, on account of the advantages that its possession brings to the possessor or to others, but *intrinsically* important, namely having value independently 'of what people happen to enjoy or want or need or what is good for them' (1993: 71). It means that 'its deliberate destruction would dishonor what ought to be honored' (1993: 74). Here we see a new light cast on the distinction – already drawn in *Foundations of Liberal Equality* – between 'the model of impact' and the 'model of challenge' as paradigmatic ways of thinking about the good life. The model of impact presupposes a view of human life as instrumentally valuable: we admire and consider good the lives of the world-historical figures because what they did was so useful to so many people. The model of challenge, instead, presupposes a view of human life as intrinsically valuable: we admire and consider good the lives of those who simply succeed in executing exemplarily well a self-chosen task, regardless of the practical contribution that such a task might bring to an external enterprise.[18]

Not just human life, but also works of art, cultures, languages, and natural species are *intrinsically* important in the latter sense, on account of their uniqueness and regardless of their practical contribution to any specific enterprise. We dread the idea of a work of art, a culture, a language or a species being permanently destroyed, not just on account of its usefulness to us, but in and of itself, even if no dimension of practical loss is involved.[19] According to Dworkin,

> the nerve of the sacred lies in the value we attach to a process or enterprise or project rather than to its results considered independently from how they were produced. We are horrified at the idea of the deliberate destruction of a work of art not just because we lose the art but because destroying it seems to demean a creative process we consider very important. Similarly, we honor and protect cultures, which are also, more abstractly, forms of art, because they are communal products of the kinds of enterprise we treat as important. (1993: 78)

Against this backcloth we can now discuss the sanctity of each *individual* human life. We treat every single human life as something that possesses *personal*, *instrumental* and *intrinsic* value. The third component is the most important. We treat a single life as the joint product of two kinds of creativities at work in shaping it: the creativity of *nature* in shaping the biological aspects of it and the *human* creativity displayed by its bearer in *conducting* that life within the human context of norms, codes and expectations. The conjunction of, and at the same time the different importance accorded to, these two components of the value of each human life can shed light both on our shared sense of a gradient of tragedy in the loss of specific lives and on our disagreements about what honouring the sanctity of a human life requires of us. On a merely naturalistic approach we would sense that the loss of a life is more of a tragedy in proportion to its being premature. But while we feel that the death of a 40-year-old man is more tragic than that of an 80-year-old, we don't feel that the death of a newly born infant is more tragic that than of a 40-year-old man. In fact we perceive it as less tragic. Dworkin's understanding of the value of a single life as being formed at the crossroads of the natural and the human creative processes helps us to make sense of this intuition. The dimension of tragedy involved in the loss of a human life is also a function of the aspects of human creativity enshrined in it and a function of what has already happened in that life. We feel that 'the death of an adolescent girl is worse than the death of an infant girl because the adolescent's death frustrates the investments she and others have already made in her life – the ambitions and expectations she constructed, the plans and projects she made, the love and interest and emotional involvement she formed for and with others, and they for and with her' (1993: 87). On the whole, Dworkin's 'investment view' of the value of human life suggests that we regard it as a 'waste of the natural and human creative investments that make up the story of a normal life' when the progression of that life across what we consider its normal biosocial stages of growth is frustrated by death.[20] And it can also account for the fact that the degree of tragedy associated with that frustration 'depends on the stage of life in which it occurs, because the frustration is greater if it takes place after rather than before the person has made a significant personal investment in his own life, and less if it occurs after any investment has been substantially fulfilled, or as substantially fulfilled as is anyway likely' (1993: 88). Thus the real criterion that corresponds to our intuitions in matters concerning the occurrence of death is not the mere 'absence' of life but the 'degree of frustration', both quantitative and qualitative, of life; or, in other terms yet, the degree of frustration of a human being's capacity for attaining authenticity or self-realization.

This approach can help us make sense also of the disagreements that divide those who think abortion and euthanasia are permissible and their opposers. The former and the latter disagree about the relative balance of the contribution brought to the value of an individual human life by the two components:

> If you believe that the natural investment in a human life is transcendently important, that the gift of life itself is infinitely more significant than anything the person whose life it is may do for himself, important though it may be, you will also believe that a deliberate, premature death is the greatest frustration of life possible, no matter how limited or cramped or unsuccessful the continued life would be. On the other hand, if you assign much greater relative importance to the human contribution to life's creative value, then you will consider the frustration of that contribution to be a more serious evil, and will accordingly see more point in deciding that life should end before further significant human investment is doomed to frustration. (1993: 91)

When we consider euthanasia, the model should be complemented by the special role played by our notion of dying 'with dignity'. By this expression Dworkin understands a life-ending which is *appropriate* to, or congruent with, 'the way we want to have lived'. Authentic death is part and parcel of authentic life: that is why we usually worry about the effect that what a person does on that last scene projects on the character of her life as a whole, much in the same way 'as we might worry about the effect of a play's last scene or a poem's last stanza on the entire creative work' (1993: 199). What people who prefer to be allowed to die rather than be artificially kept in life through intrusive medical machinery really care about is to be saved from a kind of life – either totally passive, or unconscious, or disfigured by pain – 'stunningly inadequate to the conception of self around which their own lives have so far been constructed' (1993: 211). Furthermore, the idea of a death with dignity or a good death includes considerations not just about the mode of death, but also about the timing of death. Sometimes, as we all know, people put the most strenuous effort into living to 'see' some particular event – the birth of a grandchild, the graduation of a child, the completion of a work of theirs or of a communal project. The event, *for* which the person truly continues to live, is chosen for its special symbolic significance in light of the value or values that the person has been trying to affirm during a lifetime. The event expresses a theme, the theme to which the integrity or authenticity of the person is tied. The same considerations can help us to understand why for someone it may become urgent to die, once the possibility of expressing those core values at the basis of his or her authenticity or integrity is barred by physical or mental conditions so adverse that any further stretch of life lived under them could only *subtract* something from the value of one's life. From this standpoint we can give a new sense to Nietzsche's saying, in a fragment by the title 'A Moral Code for Physicians', that 'In a certain state it is indecent to go on living' (1968: 88).

Now, as we have observed in the case of abortion, we can also understand what to respect the sanctity of life means in two quite different ways. If we prize nature's creative shaping of a human life over the human investment then 'any human intervention – injecting a lethal drug into someone dying of a painful cancer or withdrawing life support from a person in a persistent vegetative state – cheats nature' and thus 'insults' the sanctity of life (1993: 214). From this vantage point, 'preserving life supersedes living the "good life"' (1993: 215). On the contrary, if we assume that the human creativity contributes just as much or perhaps even more to the intrinsic value of human life, then we will be inclined to admit that

> someone who thinks his own life would go worse if he lingered near death on a dozen machines for weeks or stayed biologically alive for years as a vegetable . . . is showing more respect for the human contribution to the sanctity of life if he makes arrangements in advance to avoid that, and that others show more respect for his life if they avoid it for him. (1993: 216)

From this second standpoint, dying may be the best way to *affirm* the sanctity of life.

To sum up, we find a remarkable unity of inspiration at work in Dworkin's view of constitutional adjudication, in his ethical notion of the good life, in his view of the person, and in his account of the contested issues of abortion and euthanasia. In all these discussions, the principle of *authenticity* or *integrity* holds centre stage and, consequently, judgment also holds centre stage as the specific competence and practice capable of discriminating what fits and what doesn't, what is appropriate and what isn't, what is congruent with the integrity of an individual or collective identity and what isn't. The internal congruence of Dworkin's position shows also in the fact that much of what he suggests at one level, for example concerning the role of integrity in ethical choice, applies at other levels as well, for example at the level of constitutional adjudication. Two points are particularly interesting for our purposes.

First, the good for a human life is ultimately equated by Dworkin with self-realization, authenticity, integrity or self-congruency. All of these notions point to one fundamental aspect of the good: the recognizable presence of a chosen theme that runs underneath all facets of one's life and one's death. This understanding of the good as responding well to the challenges arising from the tension between one's chosen life-plan and the actual circumstances of one's life operates as a kind of overarching criterion that selects our *critical*, as opposed to *experiential* or *volitional*, interests. Namely, although they can certainly evolve in one chosen direction or another, the interests rooted in the particular challenge that my way of life presents me with – the interest in developing a certain talent, in cultivating a certain relation, and so on – are not disposable, like my interest in sailing or in travelling to the Far East, without a serious risk for the overall successfulness of my life. For they contribute to the uniqueness of my life, to its being *that* unique human life, and thus any change in their structure reflects on the overall quality of my life. Critical interests are such that failing to satisfy them or failing to recognize them detracts from the value of my life: missing out on them means missing out on something *objectively* or *intrinsically* important, not just important because I am interested in it.[21]

This statement should not be interpreted in terms of a crude moral realism. The expressions 'objectively' and 'intrinsically' really mean 'necessitated by the structure of meanings around which I have constructed my life', much in the same sense in which we could say that a certain turn in the plot, a certain final scene or a certain style of acting or photography are *necessitated* by the rest of a movie project that we try to realize. I can change my critical interests along with changing my life-project, but I cannot change them in the same way as I can change my other interests. They vary with my life-project – the central set of values through which I direct my life. To change that cluster of values is to change one's identity – a lesson that we have learnt first from Rousseau.[22] Different is the sense in which the value of integrity or authenticity as such is said by Dworkin to be of *objective* significance. Its objectivity is bound up with the notion that it is *intrinsically* important that we live well or at least don't waste our life, because human life itself is something that we, being the beings we are, cannot but regard as important, perhaps the most important thing we have.

The same regulative idea is at the basis of the assessment of constitutional decisions. Dworkin's discussion of the relation of *integrity* and the sanctity of life to the issues of abortion and euthanasia helps us understand better what he means by integrity in the context of constitutional adjudication. The main principles asserted in the Constitution – freedom of conscience and of speech, due process, equality before the law – are like the critical interests of a *collective* life-project. We constantly have to reinterpret them in light of the new predicaments we find ourselves in, but integrity demands that in our interpretation we remain faithful to them. We the People and them are bound up in an inextricable nexus. Without them we wouldn't be 'we'. Justices who assess the compatibility of a statute with those principles act as an institutionalized analogue of that part of us which assesses whether and how taking up a new interest will fit with the core sector of our life-project.

Now, a life-project, whether individual or collective, can only be understood if it is encoded in some *objectified* form. It is never the letter of that objectification that is binding, but rather the meaning underlying it. Justices are thus not bound by the letter of the Constitution: Dworkin is right in underscoring that that would be an impossible task. They are free to *interpret* the document as they see fit, but at the same time are not free to *change* the meaning of the document as they see fit on account of political or philosophical reasons. Only the People can change their own collective life-project.

Furthermore, Dworkin's integrity approach to normative validity presupposes a sharp distinction between the pleasure dimension and the integrity or authenticity dimension of the good life. Pleasure, in the sense of the gratification of our desires, may or may not be there in a life that we regard as exemplarily well lived. Certain exemplary lives that we admire – the life of Father Kolbe, for example – are fraught with very severe frustrations. And, going to the other extreme, Tolstoy's Ivan Illich ends his life in despair for having wasted it over attaining the kinds of things he aimed at having. Self-realization, authenticity or the attainment of integrity, instead, are inextricably bound up with the good life: they *are* the good life under the conditions of modernity. This way of thinking brings us back to the role of judgment in recognizing – 'discovering' is indeed the Sandelian expression Dworkin at some point uses (1993: 205) – our critical interests. *Judgment* is indeed the third alternative sought by Dworkin between the two wrong ideas of critical interests that he wants to avoid:

> The first of these two ideas – that critical interests are personal – seems to pull us toward the annihilating idea that critical interests are only subjective, only matters of how we feel. The second seems to pull us toward the equally unacceptable idea that everyone's critical interests are the same, over all history, that there is only one truly best way for anyone to live. The remedy is to embrace neither of these two extreme positions but instead to remind ourselves of how it feels to believe that a given life is the right one. We feel this not as a discovery of a timeless formula, good for all times and places, but as a direct response to our own specific circumstances of place, culture, and capacity. (1993: 206)

Underlying the 'direct response' mentioned by Dworkin is reflective judgment applied to the task of ensuring that one's life has 'a structure that expresses a coherent choice' among the different combinations of achievable ends, for example that it should 'display a steady, self-defining commitment to a vision of character or achievement that the life as a whole, seen as an integral coherent narrative, illustrates and expresses' (1993: 205). At work in Dworkin's view of ethics and of justice is really a notion, left implicit, but susceptible of being brought to fuller fruition, of reflective judgment in the service of 'making the most' of one's lives, reflective judgment in the service of tuning the whole of one's life to the 'individual law' – partly discovered but partly constructed – that underlies one's life. In a similar way what a constitutional judge does is rendering such a judgment about the fitness of a single normative moment – a statute, a decree, an ordinance, an act of government – within that larger picture of the meanings that we collectively want our collective life to reflect. The difference is, of course, that the judge cannot think of this communal life in the unbounded and open terms in which we can think of our individual lives but must think of the integrity of a *special* kind of life, which is part of the whole of the communal life of a community, namely the *political* life that we collectively and jointly lead.[23]

From the reconstruction conducted above it is not difficult to notice how Dworkin's (almost) aesthetic way of thinking about normative validity, when compared with Rawls's model of the overlapping consensus and with Habermas's discursive approach, represents a much clearer and unambiguous indicator of a shift, under way in the political philosophy of liberal inspiration, from a generalizing and principle-based model of universalism to a new exemplary and judgment-based model of universalism. It is not, however, a thoroughly aesthetic model, as the adverb 'almost' signals. In fact, it contains an important tension that betrays the presence of a significant residue of the older model – a tension and a residue which will be illustrated in Chapter 6, after examining the views of normative validity put forward by Bruce Ackerman and Frank Michelman.

4

From Fictive Dialogue to Situated Judgment

With the liberal theory of justice developed by Bruce Ackerman we go back to a two-step pattern of development of the kind already observed in the case of Rawls and to some extent also in Habermas. We can see a view of normative validity more heavily influenced by the model of determinant judgment in *Social Justice in the Liberal State* (1980), and a significantly changed framework underneath the more recent *We the People* (1998). Much of this shift is accounted for by transformation of the object of inquiry. While at the centre of Ackerman's early work was a general pattern of justification for normative claims concerning distributive patterns, citizenship, and intergenerational justice, the object of his latest work is historical and hermeneutic from the outset. In *We the People* Ackerman articulates a 'dualistic' understanding of the constitutional experience of the United States: the distinctive characteristic of that experience consists in the separation of the level of ordinary politics on the one hand and constitutional or higher lawmaking on the other. The question of normative validity, in this new context, is understood as a question concerning the validity of context-bound and singular political decisions at the level of higher lawmaking. In this chapter this difference of perspectives will be examined and the ground will be laid for highlighting, in the next chapter, some persisting continuities between Ackerman's notion of legitimate higher lawmaking and the modern model of generalizing universalism which make of his position a peculiar judgment approach without judgment proper.

The Model of Constrained Dialogue

The starting point of Ackerman's *anti-utilitarian, anti-atomistic* and *anti-contractarian* account of a liberal theory of justice is somewhat similar to Rawls's way of posing the problem of justice in his earlier work. The problem of grounding normative validity in a context marked by 'the fact of pluralism' is understood as the problem of establishing a principle of distributive justice capable of matching our intuitions concerning what justice requires and of consensually settling disputes about conflicting priorities in the allocation of scarce resources. Also Ackerman sets up a mental experiment designed to test, under controlled conditions, the fit between three principles and our intuitions concerning distributive justice. The mental experiment – and here is an element in common with Habermas's 'discourse theory' of normative validity – is understood along discursive lines. For both Habermas and Ackerman, rational consensus originating in discourse is supposed to ground normative validity. A second element of convergence seems to consist in the fact that for both authors there exist crucially significant sources of normativity that remain external to discourse. In the case of Habermas, however, the assertion to the effect that validity in the modern sense has a dialogical nature is not grounded in discourse – but rather in a derivation of the indispensability of the presuppositions of discourse based on the notion of 'performative contradiction'. In Ackerman's case, the model of the constrained conversation is supposed to be itself, in a fully reflexive way, the outcome (provisionally anticipated by the author) of a dialogue about modes of solving controversies. However, the three principles that constrain conversation – both the conversation about distributive justice and the metaconversation about possible ways of solving problems of just distribution – seem to be given antecedently to the occurrence of any conversation. They seem to govern conversation 'from the outside', as it were, not being themselves the outcome of any conversation, but being a reflection of a fictional spaceship commander's intuitions about the best way to discipline the oncoming contest among the passengers over a new planet's resources. As we will see below, however, this impression does not stand closer scrutiny.

In *Social Justice in the Liberal State* Ackerman understands the problem of justly distributing a scarce resource as a problem of *legitimation*: what kind of answers to questions concerning the legitimacy of a certain pattern of distribution can be called valid? The occurrence of the terms 'question' and 'answer' already indicate a dialogical perspective. The liberal dialogue about the legitimacy of arrangements, however, is no real one, but a decontextualized conversation which takes place in a controlled and fictive context that Ackerman characterizes in great detail.

In Ackerman's hypothetical construction we are on a spaceship that is circling around a newly discovered planet on which we, the fellow travellers on the spaceship, are seeking refuge. The spaceship's scanning devices inform us that the planet contains only one useful but quite peculiar resource, called 'manna', 'infinitely divisible and malleable, capable of transformation into any physical object a person may desire' (1980: 31). The bad news is that the supply of manna is not unlimited. Only a finite amount of goods can be drawn from a given quantity of grains of manna. Thus one fundamental characteristic of the fictive context devised by Ackerman is that 'there won't be enough manna to satisfy the total demands of all the members of our party' (1980: 31) – a characteristic analogous with the notion of 'moderate scarcity' counted by Rawls as one of the circumstances of justice.

Within such a context then the question arises: what initial distribution of manna is legitimate – a term here roughly equivalent to the sense in which Rawls uses the term 'fair' in *A Theory of Justice*? All the passengers of the spaceship are participants in the constrained conversation within which an answer is sought. Chaired by the commander of the spaceship, the conversation is structured or 'constrained' by three 'preliminary announcements' or assumptions. First, the commander announces the existence of what Ackerman calls a 'perfect technology of justice'. Namely, technical problems of feasibility and implementation of any just solution to the distributive problem need not worry the participants. The function of this assumption is to let the disagreements about *values* emerge without the confusing interference of divergences concerning problems of implementation – divergences which often are of a pragmatical and empirical nature. Second, the commander announces that she will self-limit her role to that of an enforcer of three regulative principles that jointly define the notion of a legitimate contribution to the discussion – namely, the principle of *rationality*, the principle of *consistency* and the principle of *neutrality*, to be illustrated below. Third, the commander announces the unrevisability of these three principles.

Artificial as it may seem, this deliberative context is not altogether removed from the 'real world' conditions under which the legitimacy of distributive schemes is assessed. While it certainly differs from a real liberal polity in that the metarules of the conversation are not grounded in a collectively agreed constitution, but are enacted through the will of a commander who plays the role of a Rousseauian legislator, on the other hand, just as happens in any 'real world' deliberation on distributive justice, also on Ackerman's spaceship one must assume the condition of moderate scarcity mentioned above. And once again, just as is the case in the real world, and unlike what happens in Rawls's original position, each participant takes part in the discussion which will shape the basic structure of society with the full endowment of her capabilities, competences, knowledge, values and beliefs. No 'veil of ignorance' is assumed to be necessary in order for a liberal theory of justice to operate.

Ackerman's model of conversational legitimacy is based on three principles, as we have seen. For the outcome of a constrained dialogue to be normatively valid and legitimately binding, the proposal put forward by the party which meets the largest consensus must in the first place satisfy the *principle of rationality*, according to which

> whenever anybody questions the legitimacy of another's power [to have access to and use certain resources], the power holder must respond not by suppressing the questioner but by giving a reason that explains why he is more entitled to the resource than the questioner is. (1980: 4)

The principle of rationality is indeed a principle of accountability: it is part of the idea of a just and legitimate distribution that each party be able, on demand, to account for her claims to an unequal share of resources that are not unlimited. Interesting here is the reference to the concept of *power*. Ackerman's rendition of the problem of justice echoes somehow what Parsons once viewed as the quintessential *political* problem, the problem that indeed defines the political aspect of social action – namely, the problem of attributing priority to the ends pursued by different social actors in a context in which the means available do not allow for the simultaneous pursuit of all ends.[1] By virtue of its enjoining *everyone* to offer good reasons for *any* of her powers to *anyone* who might feel put at a disadvantage by them, Ackerman's rationality principle provides a thoroughly discursive foundation for rights and thus marks the distance that separates his account from more traditional accounts of rights revolving around the ideas of a *state of nature* and of a *social contract*. The theory of constrained dialogue does not assume that people have 'rights' 'before they confront the harsh fact of the struggle for power' (1980: 5). In this sense, Ackerman's model of the constrained conversation shares another important characteristic with Habermas's view of deliberative democracy: all norms as well as the rights attributed to citizens originate in the democratic procedure of the conversation concerning legitimacy. No prepolitical rights are presupposed. However, this is only a partially accurate description. To be sure, the Ackermanian parties do not have political or even human rights before the constrained conversation has come to a conclusive end, but they apparently enjoy an overarching right to 'equal consideration', embedded – as we will see – in the principle of neutrality, as well as an even more fundamental right to demand an account of the legitimacy of any proposed arrangement – a right which follows implicitly from Ackerman's overall argument. Furthermore, differently from all contractualist approaches from Rousseau to Rawls, Ackerman's approach does not contain any reference to any 'privileged moment of promising – existing apart from ordinary social life – as the foundation of everyday claims of right' (1980: 6). The dialogue engendered by all questions of legitimacy is understood, instead, as a liberal 'way of talking about power' or a *'form of political culture'* within which we are constantly, and not just at some magic founding moment, immersed (1980: 6).

The second principle which a liberal dialogue about the legitimacy of distributive schemes must satisfy is the *principle of consistency*, which stipulates that

> the reason advanced by a power wielder on one occasion must not be inconsistent with the reasons he advances to justify his other claims to power. (1980: 7)

This principle serves the purpose of avoiding particularistic and *ad hoc* renditions of the proposed schemes.

The most important principle, however, is the *principle of neutrality*. According to it,

> No reason [for a given distributive scheme] is a good [i.e. legitimate] reason if it requires the power holder to assert:
> (a) that his conception of the good is better than that asserted by any of his fellow citizens, *or*
> (b) that, regardless of his conception of the good, he is intrinsically superior to one or more of his fellow citizens. (1980: 11)

This principle is designed to ensure what Rawls would call the 'political' quality of a conception of justice. It excludes claims to the intrinsic superiority of one participant *vis-à-vis* any other as well as any reference to substantive and controversial conceptions of the good. At the same time, the principle of neutrality presupposes that all participants possess a right to equal consideration – a right that obviously does not itself result from dialogue, but indeed constitutes one of the conditions that make dialogue possible.

This point offers a basis for comparing Ackerman's model with Larmore's own proposal for a 'neutral justification of political neutrality' (1987: 53). Also Larmore resorts to a dialogical model of legitimation or justification. His model is based on a 'universal norm of rational dialogue' and on an equally universal norm of 'equal respect'. The norm of rational dialogue prescribes, according to Larmore, that

> people should respond to points of disagreement by retreating to neutral ground, to the beliefs they still share, in order either to (a) resolve the disagreements and vindicate one of the disputed positions by means of arguments that proceed from this common ground, or (b) bypass the disagreement and seek a solution of the problem on the basis simply of this common ground. (1996: 135)

This norm of rational dialogue specifies one point that remained implicit in Ackerman's principle of rationality: the reasons which ought to be offered in response to an inquiry into the legitimacy of one of our power claims should be reasons that we believe to be *acceptable to the addressee*. In Larmore's account we also find an awareness, not equally reflected in Ackerman's model, that such a norm captures only *one* aspect of public dialogue – the aspect of the deliberative function, aimed at generating a solution to some practical controversy. There may be other aims, served at other times, by the liberal dialogue: for example, the aim of 'disclosure', where 'disclosure' designates the free articulation of conceptions of the good or relevant parts thereof in the public space, despite the expectation of reasonable disagreement, for the purpose of enabling the parties to accede to mutual recognition and enlightenment – the kind of function often emphasized by Habermas in his view of the public sphere and in his frequent emphasis on the 'fluidification of need interpretations' in the context of public discussion. By contrast, Ackerman's strategy for handling 'ethical pluralism', unlike Habermas's and in consonance with Rawls's 'method of avoiding', rests on a sharp opposition between *privately* held ethical convictions and *public* discourse. As Ackerman puts it in a later article, when normative disagreement occurs then

> We should not search for some common value that will trump the disagreement; nor should we try to translate it into some putatively neutral framework; nor should we seek to transcend it by talking about how some unearthly creature might resolve it. We should simply say nothing at all about this disagreement and put the moral ideals that divide us off the conversational agenda of the liberal state. (1989: 16)

Finally, the limits of dialogue are explicitly taken into account in Larmore's conception. The norm of rational dialogue 'does not suffice by itself . . . to yield the liberal principle of neutrality' (Larmore 1996: 136). In fact, it *presupposes* that we prefer to solve our disagreements dialogically but cannot enjoin us to give precedence to such a method over other possible ways of dealing with reasonable disagreement, including the use of force, deception, threats, and so on. A further norm is needed in order to ground the priority of dialogue. This norm, called by Larmore the norm of 'equal respect', pre-scribes in a Kantian vein 'that we should never treat other persons solely as means, as mere instruments of our will' but always 'also as ends, as persons in their own right' (1996: 136). Thus the norm of rational dialogue is parasitic on the norm of equal respect for all members of the polity.

Interesting is the different structural role assigned to this principle or norm by Ackerman and Larmore. For Larmore the norm of 'equal respect' is rooted in the premise – never fully specified in Ackerman's three principles – that the reasons or principles that justify our basic political arrangements 'ought to be rationally acceptable to all those whom they are to bind' (1996: 219). And if we ask the further question 'Why should they be acceptable to all?', the answer that seems to best match our intuitions is, according to Larmore, still the Kantian idea that it is unconditionally wrong to treat per-sons only as means and not also as ends, even if they were to be treated as means to the achievement of some very important social goal. Thus we want dialogue for the sake of 'equal respect' and not the other way around, because dialogue – this is a point that Larmore develops with reference to Habermas's discourse theory of normative validity – is the way of dealing with contested power claims that best ensures respect for everybody. And the standpoint of equal respect constitutes the 'core of our moral consciousness', the 'histori-cally situated point of departure for our moral reflection' as well as 'the framework within which we can conceive of moral argument' (1996: 221). I will come back to the crucial role that this principle of equal respect plays in our understanding of justice and will address the question of its normative credentials when, in Chapter 8, I will discuss some facets of a judgment view of justice.

In Ackerman we find the norm of equal respect embedded in the principle of neutrality – as the idea that no one can claim unconditional superiority with respect to another – but the 'duty to enter dialogue' is not defended on the basis of a norm antecedent and external to dialogue. To the question 'Why should our controversial claims and power struggles be regulated through dialogue, as opposed to force or anything else?', Ackerman answers that his dialogical account of justice has enough substance and *prima facie* plausibility to shift the burden of proof onto the questioner. It is for the questioner to say why she finds the model of constrained conversation 'unduly confining'. At this juncture, the impression, mentioned at the begin-ning of this chapter, that the three conversational principles govern the conversation from the outside can be seen in a different light. Engaging the reader, Ackerman expresses the hope that if she articulates her perplexities concerning the conversational model, then a chance may be offered to the defender of that model to show within a dialogue the inconsequentiality of such perplexities and to lead the interlocutor to recognize that the world *as construed by her*, and as not construed by the defender of the liberal conver-sation, 'makes Neutral dialogue [i.e. not *any* kind of dialogue, but dialogue as constrained by the principles of rationality, consistency and neutrality] the most sensible way of regulating our power struggle' (1980: 357). This point is completed by Ackerman's reconstruction of the paths that link four familiar philosophical stances – 'realism about the corrosiveness of power; recognition of doubt as a necessary step to moral knowledge; respect for the autonomy of persons; and skepticism concerning the reality of transcendent meaning' (1980: 369) – with the recognition of the sensibleness not just of a generic dialogical model, but of the model of *constrained* conversation. This reconstruction serves the function of defending the specific principles reconstructed by Ackerman over other competing principles that one could imagine to govern rival, but equally conversational, accounts of normative validity and of showing that the model is neutral with respect to a plurality of philosophical doctrines. But it is time to go back to the main thread of our reconstruction.

Within Ackerman's conversational model of normative validity a crucial role is played by the mechanism whereby a normative outcome can be established: in other words, by the way the constrained power talk legitimately *comes to an end*. The conversation ends when one of the parties has nothing more to say in support of her claim – when the victorious claim meets with the opponents' silence. Ackerman underscores that 'the dialogue does not end with an *unconditional* conversational victory by A [the power holder], but simply establishes that Q [the person who questions the legitimacy of A's command of a given resource] cannot expect to win his claim so long as he remains silent' (1980: 17, my emphasis). The legitimacy of arrangements that have been validated in a constrained conversation is always, as in Habermas's discourse theory of normative validity, a 'legitimacy for the time being'.

Social Justice in the Liberal State does not consist solely of a general discussion of the principles of legitimacy and justice. The model of the constrained conversation outlined in the first part of the book is then applied by Ackerman to a number of substantive controversies. People in the real world struggle not over abstract resources, but over concrete ones that are to be found and used within specific institutional contexts. In the end the reiterated, albeit counterfactual, application of the model of unconstrained dialogue outlines the contours of an ideal state of a liberal polity which Ackerman calls the state of *undominated equality*. If a society is characterized by undominated equality – a term somewhat reminiscent of what Michael Walzer calls 'complex equality'[2] – then no citizen *genetically dominates* another. Furthermore, each citizen receives a *liberal education* and begins his or her life under conditions of *material equality*. Finally, each citizen 'can *freely exchange* his initial entitlements within *a flexible transactional network*' and, at the moment of his death, 'can assert that he has fulfilled his obligations of *liberal trusteeship*, passing on to the next generation a power structure no less liberal than the one he himself enjoyed' (1980: 28).

I cannot reconstruct here the full range of Ackerman's arguments about these substantive issues. Particularly interesting from our point of view is his case for 'initial material equality'. It is constructed by Ackerman in the guise of an argument by elimination, directed obviously at egotistic worldviews, but also at utilitarian and contractarian positions. Somewhat problematic appears

Ackerman's rejection of utilitarianism, to which he assimilates a position that should be kept distinct from it and is best described as a *eudaemonistic* approach to justice based on a reflective judgment understanding of the authenticity of an identity. The reasons which, according to Ackerman, should incline us to reject utilitarianism are (a) the impossibility of finding a neutral yardstick for comparing utilities and (b) the underlying assumption 'that the good consists entirely in subjective satisfaction' (1980: 49). More generally, Ackerman takes issue with the *consequentialism* implicit in utilitarianism. As he points out, in a context characterized by the fact of pluralism, any conception of justice that links the just outcome with the goodness of its practical consequences cannot but find itself at a disadvantage. Ackerman, however, seems to underestimate the extent to which the same difficulty affects also the liberal conception of justice as neutrality, to which his model of constrained conversation belongs, unless these conceptions succeed in severing the notion of justice from that of the good in such a definitive way that not even John Rawls could accept.[3] In his exchange with Habermas, in fact, Rawls has pointed out that the neutrality of a conception of justice should not be equated with the unrealistic demand that such a conception be free of substantive elements. For even the simplest and strictest procedural approach to the task of dividing a cake by having one person cut it and the other choose ultimately could not be regarded as fair if it failed to generate a tacitly, and antecedently accepted, fair outcome, namely 'equal division' (Rawls 1995: 171).

The one possibility charitably considered by Ackerman in order to render utilitarianism, for the sake of the argument, as defensible as it can be is what he calls the 'equal fulfilment approach', of which there exist two variants. Common to both variants is the recourse to the notion of 'fulfilment' as the key index for interpersonal comparisons. Both variants of utilitarianism also share the idea that resources should be distributed in proportion to the extent to which they further the conception of the good that each citizen happens to endorse. The first version, however, specifies the 'in proportion' clause in the sense that the initial distribution of resources should leave each citizen at the same distance – e.g. halfway – from fulfilment as defined by her conception of the good. Thus people whose conception of the good requires more resources in order to attain fulfilment could legitimately get a larger share of the available resources. In Ackerman's example, someone who devotes his life to mountaineering (and needs expensive climbing gear) claims 10 times as much 'manna' as someone who aspires to be an armchair philosopher. The problem is, Ackerman points out, that not all conceptions of fulfilment are equally amenable to a quantitative, spatial assessment of the extent to which they are realized. Mountaineering and philosophizing can perhaps be looked at in terms of the number of significant mountain tops conquered and significant books written. Instead, the conceptions of the good endorsed by those who see the point of their life in struggling to achieve 'yet another goal' after the last one attained, or by those who endorse an irreducibly 'all or nothing' view of the value of life, cannot be accommodated within this framework. In the

case of the 'strugglers' that is because their notion of fulfilment takes the
form of an ever receding horizon, and no one can measure how close a certain distribution brings the present horizon to infinity. In the case of the
second group of people there might not be a conceivable point located
halfway to the achievement of their ultimate ends – as in the case of the
mystic who protests that she has achieved '*nothing* of value' until she has
achieved a *total* communion with God.[4]

The second version of 'equal fulfilment' utilitarianism partially avoids the
problem of selectivity by substituting the notion of 'equal chances for fulfilment' for the problematic one of 'equal distance from fulfilment'. The
conception of the good embraced by the mystic can thus be accommodated.
The egalitarian distributive scheme is now required to provide the mystic not
with the means for getting halfway to her ultimate goal, but with a 50 per cent
chance of attaining it. The conception of the good embraced by the 'struggler', however, remains problematical. The notion of 'equal chances' or 'equal
opportunity' cannot be easily applied to a conception of the good that denies
'that life is one long climb to a determinate peak' (Ackerman 1980: 53). In
sum, the ethical partiality of utilitarianism consists in its forcing everyone to
mould her conception of the good to fit 'a particular formal structure' – the
one most amenable to a quantitative assessment of the distance separating
the actor from fulfilment or of her chances to attain fulfilment. In so doing,
utilitarianism violates the principle of neutrality. In fact, as Ackerman points
out,

> in a liberal state I cannot define the terms of political conversation in a way that
> disparages my fellow's right to express his ideas *in the words that make most sense*
> *to him*. I cannot force him to argue his claims for manna in terms that require him
> to deny the validity of his own answer to the question of life's meaning. (1980: 54)

Ackerman, instead, rests his case for an egalitarian initial distribution on
the common realization, on the part of the participants in the constrained
conversation, of the fact that each affirms '*some* conception of the good' and
that, given the impossibility for anyone to claim possession of a yardstick for
assessing differential claims to resources, it seems sensible to assign an equal
amount of manna to everyone *just by virtue of his or her being a person who
has affirmed some conception of the good*: 'since I'm at least as good as you
are, I should get at least as much of the stuff we both desire – at least until
you give me some Neutral reason for getting more' (1980: 58). While this position cannot claim any kind of ultimate validity, it can certainly establish
itself as one position for which at least 'something rational can be said'. This
is enough, according to Ackerman, for shifting the burden of proof onto
those who wish to refute the initial 'equality of endowment' principle. It is for
them to come up with reasons why resources ought to be distributed
unequally. Short of any argument to that effect capable of meeting the three
conversational constraints, the assembly of fellow space travellers will be
legitimized in proceeding to distribute equal shares of manna. In the rest of
the book Ackerman discusses some of the cases that have actually been made

for an unequal initial distribution from the standpoint of genetic handicaps and of cultural disadvantage.

I will not discuss these cases, because I think that the general pattern thus far outlined already shows enough detail to highlight one central problem. The problem is that Ackerman fails to distinguish between a utilitarian kind of consequentialism and a *eudaemonistic* consequentialism. Utilitarian consequentialism remains vulnerable to the objection about the moulding of all conceptions of the good into the mountain climbing metaphor not on account of its taking fulfilment as a yardstick, but on account of its remaining tied to a determinant judgment model of the assessment of fulfilment. What Ackerman is really objecting to, but misleadingly assimilates to 'consequentialism', is the idea of a universal commensuration of all life-plans, including those of the 'strugglers', from the standpoint of 'subjective fulfilment' and in terms of a *calculable* and *demonstrable* level of their attainment. More specifically, there are two problematic points in Ackerman's anti-utilitarian objection. First, 'subjective fulfilment' could be spelled out in terms that avoid the utilitarian partiality in favour of certain structural qualities of life-plans. Elsewhere I have argued that, in our postmetaphysical context, the formal notion of the good life with which philosophy tries to reconstruct our ethical intuitions is best construed along psychological lines, and that evidence for this assertion lies in the difficulty of conceiving any answer to the question 'Why might we want fulfilment?'[5] Such difficulty indicates that the notion of fulfilment has come to acquire, in the context of late modernity, a role somehow analogous – albeit obviously not identical – to that of the good life or *eudaemonia* in the classical era. Namely, what Ackerman calls 'subjective' fulfilment has acquired the status of a substantively neutral good for the sake of which all other goods are sought. If radically detached from all sorts of hedonism and equated instead with a formal concept of *self-congruency* or *authenticity*, similar to the idea of artistic well-formedness presupposed by our critical assessment of the work of art, then fulfilment can indeed become a category equally relevant for asceticists and mystics, for hedonists and heroes of self-abnegation alike.[6]

Second, not all assessments of value need presuppose a notion of measurement based on the model of determinant judgment and thus allowing for calculability and demonstrability. Aesthetics is a whole area of human endeavour that has always functioned on a different basis. Each work of art has always been considered a world in itself, responding to laws of validity no less stringent for the fact of applying to one case only. This peculiar incommensurability – which prevents us from comparing the masterpieces of Michelangelo and Picasso on a scale that measures the different degree to which they approximate some kind of independently existing artistic perfection – nonetheless has never constituted an obstacle to the assessment of the quality of works of art. Art criticism is precisely the ability to tell a painting by Michelangelo from one by a second-rate painter working in Michelangelo's shop – which is in a way a measurement of sorts, though not of the kind amenable to calculation and demonstration. It is a measurement of excellence which the practitioners of art criticism and literary criticism – as well as the practitioners of clinical psychology, in so far as individual identities are concerned – do place at the centre of their concerns. The use of a notion of excellence as exemplary self-congruence within the practices of art and literary criticism, as well as clinical psychology, makes sense only against the assumption that the irreducible uniqueness of each work of art and of each individual identity does not ultimately prevent *all* kinds of comparisons, but only comparisons from the standpoint of external yardsticks. In the ethical realm, Dworkin's understanding of the good life in terms of the 'model of challenge', discussed above, as well as MacIntyre's 'model of the quest' – the good life as 'the life spent in a quest for the good life' (1981: 204) – bring to fruition the same intuition. Instead of referring to 'fulfilment' in the utilitarian sense, they refer to 'excellence' in doing well a self-chosen task and in turn understand excellence as a fully neutral dimension of assessment, neutral also with respect to the possible formal structures of a life-plan. In fact, while someone might object to the attribution of a conception of life as a work of art to her – indeed 'life as a work of art' is the name of a specific and far from neutral conception of the good – the idea that the worthiness of one's life is linked with one's ability to meet a challenge that one recognizes as one's own is something to which no modern actor could reasonably object. The radical mystic and the relentless struggler can conceive of their lives in terms of meeting the respective challenges of imbuing oneself deeper and deeper with the divine principle or of never giving up one's striving. Even the Dionysian postmodernist who seeks the limit experiences of annihilation of the self can conceive of her own life-project in terms of meeting the challenge of facing up to the threat of annihilation.[7] Finally, to the extent that they are modern and not premodern traditional actors, also those who take up a certain self-defining challenge only because they believe it is their *duty*, as opposed to their *choice*, to do so, in fact have exerted a preliminary choice – from which the obligation to face the unwelcome challenge then follows – by recognizing the duty in question as *theirs*.

It is time to draw the implications of these difficulties for the initially equal distribution of manna in Ackerman's fictional world. On the one hand, the problems linked with Ackerman's objection to utilitarianism leave us with an inconclusively argued case for initial distributional equality. If one of the participants in the assembly were to put forward the principle that manna ought to be distributed 'to everyone according to his needs', where 'according to his needs' means in a quantity that matches what is thought necessary – to the best shared knowledge available at the moment – in order to meet his chosen or recognized identity-defining challenge with the same chances of success as all his fellows have of meeting their own challenges, it is hard to see how Ackerman could argue that this principle – which potentially entails the assignment of different quantities of manna to different people – fails to pass the neutrality test.

On the other hand, there is something disturbing, for any democratic minded person, in the notion of an unequal distribution of resources being

legitimated on grounds other than the compensation of severe genetic handicaps or cultural disadvantages. The account of *why* that notion is disturbing,
however, cannot rest on its failing to meet the conversational constraints outlined by Ackerman. The reason, in my opinion, lies elsewhere – in a
consequence that Ackerman fails to draw from his specification of the conversational constraints. If one understands the second clause of the principle
of neutrality – forbidding participants to claim intrinsic superiority – as
implying a *strong* moral equality among all the participants, it is hard to
understand why it would not be possible to derive directly from that clause a
principle of equal distribution that outranks, from a normative point of view,
the life-plans individually chosen by the participants. Equal resource expen-
diture could then be treated as a fixed parameter – along with mortality, the
laws of physics, embodiment, and other uncontroversial features of the
human condition – that any conceivable and legitimate ethical life-plan must
accommodate. Any life-plan that requires a more than equal share of communal resources in order to have some chances of success could then be
legitimately embraced at the person's own risk. While the distribution of
communal resources would cover only the share that everybody else is obtaining, on a separate plane we would all admire the courage of those who have
the 'nerve of failure' of dedicating their life-plan to such ambitious pursuits.
Ackerman, instead, never explains why people's life-plans ought to be treated
as unquestionable independent variables. The issue is somewhat concealed by
the reasonableness of the differences in the amounts of manna claimed by the
participants in the dialogical exchanges envisaged by Ackerman. Someone
wants five grains of it and someone complains about getting just one. But at
no point in Ackerman's discussion do we get a sense that there might be a
legitimate limit on the amount of resources that an individual might claim on
the basis of his self-chosen conception of the good. The discussion is conducted as though no ground existed for questioning an individual's claim,
based on his conception of the good, to more than an equal share if the
individual managed to avoid claiming either the superiority of his conception
of the good or the intrinsic superiority of his own self.

On the contrary, to the extent that we speak of life-plans as *chosen* – even
though such choice occurs within the framework of conceptions of the good
that are chosen only in a more tenuous way – we need to introduce a dimension of *responsibility* which Ackerman's model fails to capture. Life-plans are
not things that happen to us in the same sense as conceptions of the good are
webs of meaning that we may find ourselves entangled in – though we can
always assume, at least in the context of modernity, the actor's capacity to
transform them. Consequently, the notion of moral equality presupposed
by the neutrality principle and by the idea of equal respect underlying the
model of dialogue are sufficient, in my opinion, to justify our treating – on
equality grounds – all life-plans that entail a more than equal share of
resources as plans that the actor chooses 'at her own risk'. Moral equality
taken seriously enjoins us to form our plans in light of the resources that we
can reasonably expect to be assigned to us *on an egalitarian basis*. It does not

authorize us to calibrate our claims for a share of the communal resources on the basis of needs stemming from a life-plan conceived in total independence from all concern for the claims of others.

Towards a Model of Normative Validity as Situated Judgment

With the transition to *Foundations*, the first volume of *We the People* (1991), we begin to see a shift at work in Ackerman's framework. In lieu of a general model of the liberal conversation on legitimacy we are offered a historical interpretation of the significance of American constitutionalism. Normative validity is explored not so much in terms of general distributive patterns as from the perspective of the political self-definition of a collective identity.[8] According to the *dualist* understanding of the workings of democracy put forward by Ackerman, when we talk of democratic legitimacy we ought to distinguish between two different kinds of political decisions: decisions by the people which concern matters of higher lawmaking and decisions by their government which are part of ordinary politics.[9] As in the older framework, the focus is on questions of legitimacy, but the questions of legitimacy have now become more contextualized. What constitutes a legitimate political decision at the level of constitutional politics?

The dualist account of political legitimacy enters in competition with two rival accounts – the monist and the foundationalist. The monist account – exemplified by constitutionalists of diverse political orientations such as Alexander Bickel, John Ely and Richard Parker – rejects the distinction as undemocratic. Democracy rightly understood, according to the majoritarian credo, places the whole power to make laws – regardless of the scope of their import – in the hands of the winner of the last general election, provided the election was 'conducted under free and fair ground rules', and keeps it there for the entire term until the next general election. Under this majoritarian view, every time that any non-elected institution places a constraint of any sort on the legislative will of the legitimate majority in Parliament a *prima facie* loss of democracy occurs. Special justifications are needed, then, for reconciling the practice of judicial review with the monistic picture.

The foundationalist account – a sort of postmetaphysical natural right approach, exemplified by Richard Epstein and Ronald Dworkin – shares the dualist understanding of democratic legitimacy, but conceives of the point of a constitution as the protection of certain rights singled out as fundamental: be they property rights or a right to equal respect, depending on the perspective adopted. From this perspective, rights can be then said to trump democratic ordinary legislation as well as any consequentialist consideration about the public interest.

Ackerman, instead, wishes to distance his dualist approach from all sorts of foundationalism and formulates the question of legitimacy in the following terms:

In elaborating the constitutional will of the People, the dualist begins neither with the will of the present legislature nor with the reason of some utopian assembly. Her aim is the kind of situated understanding one might reach after a good conversation. Only this time, the conversation is not between friends – or even enemies – who share the same moment of time and so can observe each other's tone of voice and gestures, continue tomorrow what is left unsaid today. The challenge, instead, is to locate ourselves in a conversation between generations. (1991: 23)

The shift in perspective involved in the transition to the dualist model underlying *We the People* is best highlighted if one separates the different components of the question of legitimacy. The legitimacy of statutes can be safely assumed to be a function of the procedural correctness of their enactment and of their substantive fit with the US Constitution – and thus falls within the bounds of a determinant judgment understanding of their normative validity. But how are we to conceive the legitimacy of a political decision of the People in matters of higher lawmaking?

What makes of a constitutional provision or of a constitutional amendment a legitimate one? In the context of *We the People*, the ruling out of both the monist and the foundationalist perspective leaves open just one basic route for conceiving the legitimacy of higher lawmaking. This intimation opens more problems than it solves, however. For example, it calls for a clarification of what is meant by higher law's responding to the People's will. Depending on whether this 'responding' is conceived as fitting with some basic constituents of a political identity that the People tries to enact in the form of higher law,[10] or is conceived along democratic-positivist lines as a reflection of what the will of the People contingently happens to be, we obtain different accounts that come closer to a reflective judgment model of normativity or continue to embed significant aspects of the older kind of determinant judgment view. In Ackerman's thought on constitutional legitimacy, as we shall see below, a residue of positivism – and, with it, of the determinant judgment model of normativity – survives in his way of conceiving the relation between legitimacy and its source, the will of the People. This limit emerges most clearly in his view of the legitimacy of constitutional amendments. Ackerman is among the constitutionalists most decidedly opposed to the possibility – suggested among others by Dworkin through his idea of a 'moral reading of the Constitution' – of conceiving structural, implicit limits to the modification of the Constitution. For Ackerman the Constitution in its present form – though future changes in the direction of the entrenchment of fundamental rights might be desirable – remains amendable in whatever direction the People want to amend it, provided that the amendment has been enacted in full respect of the required procedures and supermajorities. Even an amendment establishing Christianity as a state religion could not be rejected as illegitimate by the Supreme Court if enacted in accordance with the prescribed procedure.[11] In the light of the present constitutional culture, as reconstructed but not necessarily endorsed by Ackerman, the Constitution appears as an unquestionable reflection of the will of the People and no standpoint can be imagined from which to assess the legitimacy of higher lawmaking other than its reflecting that will understood as an empirical fact. The Supreme Court can make mistakes in interpreting the will of the People, and be corrected, but from Ackerman's perspective the People can never, strictly speaking, make mistakes. I will come back to this point in Chapter 6.

In Part II of *We the People*, Ackerman traces the origins of the dualistic view of politics back to the *Federalist Papers*, and especially to the original solution envisaged by the writers of the *Papers* to the familiar problem of stabilizing the political achievements of the revolution and securing them against deterioration through routine politics. Their political judgment led the Founders to devise a mixed model of 'mobilized deliberation' and institutional channelling of mobilization. At the time of their writing the political contest for the ratification of the draft of the Constitution was under way – a contest that the Framers successfully shifted from the terrain of state ordinary legislatures to that of the extraordinary and more informal 'constitutional conventions', which, as Ackerman points out, combined 'formal illegality, mass energy, public-spiritedness *and* extraordinary rationality' (1991: 177). From the midst of such a still uncertain battle, Hamilton, Madison and Jay looked ahead, to the times when the new political order, if successfully instated, would have to face the challenges of special interests, factionalism and corruption. They resisted the temptation to tread the two familiar paths of either envisaging the future of the republic as an eternal return of the revolution or treating the new order as a blueprint through which all political action could be 'normalized' and reduced to routine. Instead, they devised a third course, in which a great concern for institutional design was combined with a high value put on public-spirited participation and with the sober realization of the limits of any appeal to public virtue. At the crossroads of these motifs the bipartition of the political universe into constitutional and ordinary politics first took place.

Of all the evils of ordinary political life, the writers of the *Federalist Papers* appeared to fear factionalism above all – the factionalism of what Ackerman renames 'ideological groups' as well as of 'charismatic' ones, but even more the factionalism of *interest groups*. The recipe against the hold that factionalism might gain over republican politics was twofold. On the one hand, contrary to Montesquieu's doctrine, Madison maintained that the large size of the country represented a bulwark against the petty interests, feuds and schemes on which factionalism thrives. This protective function of size is due to the greater probability that in larger districts the voters will have to extend the horizon of their considerations and in the end to choose more public-interest-minded representatives, but also to another factor. The larger size of constituencies will make, according to Madison, for a greater variety of interests pressing their way to representation, and this in turn will make it easier for the public-minded representative to use *divide et impera* in the service of the public good. On the other hand, what social differentiation alone cannot ensure could be furthered by appropriate institutional design, and especially by a division of lawmaking, executive and judiciary power across the different branches of government. Such a distribution of prerogatives is aimed at 'economizing on civic virtue' and also responds, in Ackerman's reconstruction, to the intuition that no single branch of government, not even the legislative one, by itself can claim to represent the People's will and, on the other hand, each branch must be so designed as to give 'those who administer each department the necessary constitutional means and personal motives to resist encroachment of the others' (*Federalist Papers* no. 51, 321–2).

A special role in this connection was attributed to judicial review by the Supreme Court. The nine justices are the guardians of meaning of the Constitution against erosion through the wear and tear induced by normal politics. Hamilton, in particular, developed a case for the legitimacy of judicial review. Of all the 'departments of power', the judiciary is by far the weakest, so it can never 'attack with success either of the other two' or endanger the 'general liberty of the people'. And to those who objected that the ultimate say of the Court on the constitutionality of statutes would upset the balance of power between the three branches and establish what will later be called a 'judicial supremacy' over the legislative, Hamilton counter-argued that

> there is no position which depends on clearer principles than that every act of a delegated authority, contrary to the tenor of the commission under which it is exercised, is void. No legislative act, therefore, contrary to the Constitution, can be valid. To deny this would be to affirm that the deputy is greater than the principal; that the servant is above his master; that the representatives of the people are superior to the people themselves. (*Federalist Papers* no. 78: 467)

In this picture the Supreme Court is supposed to act as an 'intermediate body between the people and the legislature in order, among other things, to keep the latter within the limits assigned to their authority' (*Federalist Papers* no. 78: 467). The Supreme Court is thus not superior to the legislative bodies, but as subject to the will of the people as the legislature.

This last remark brings in the decisive point. Even the penultimate check of judicial review may sometimes, though conceivably rarely, fail to curb factionalism, organized interest or ideological sway. Even the justices are human beings after all, who can fall prey to ordinary politics. Or perhaps the representatives may be right in their claim that the People are with them in understanding the Constitution in a certain way. When such controversies arise, then the last word must go back to the source of all democratic power, to the People. The question is: how? Through which procedure?

In a passage quoted by Ackerman, Hamilton instructs the justices never to take at face value the claim of the 'representatives' that the People support their interpretation of the Constitution until the People themselves have 'by some solemn and authoritative act' provided evidence of their willingness to change the Constitution in that regard and along those lines. Ackerman points out that the characteristics of the people's acts of approval – being 'solemn and authoritative' – strikingly do not include the adjective 'legal'. In his interpretation, Ackerman suggests that

> Publius does not say that the judges should resist until the transformative move-
> ment satisfies all the *legal rules* for constitutional amendment that are contained in
> his new Constitution. He leaves open the relationship between these new rules and
> the kinds of 'solemn and authoritative' action that should convince the judges.
> (1991: 195)

In other words, there is no *a priori* set of criteria for determining when the
People have expressed their will: the procedures and supermajorities prescribed by Article Five are sufficient but not necessary conditions, according
to Ackerman. It takes an act of *political judgment* – of course, of a reflective
kind of judgment – to distinguish between cases when 'a momentary incli-
nation' in the orientation of constituencies constitutes no ground for
departing from constitutional usage, and cases when the People are exercising
their right 'to alter' the Constitution because 'they find it inconsistent with
their happiness' (*Federalist Papers* no. 78: 469). Two consequences of this perspective call for further scrutiny. First, a constitutional role for participation
and for social movements is carved out. Second, the need arises for what
Hamilton calls 'a constitutional road' to be 'marked out, and kept open', for
the people to express their will on 'certain great and extraordinary occasions'
(*Federalist Papers* no. 49: 314). But here we also reach a new formulation of
the problem of legitimacy in higher lawmaking in light of which we should
consider the above mentioned consequences:

> How to organize a process of public reasoning between the mass of Americans and
> their political representatives so as to identify those occasions when a movement
> has *earned* the authority to speak in the higher lawmaking voice of We the
> People? . . . What kind of institutional tests should Americans impose on a polit-
> ical movement before it is conceded higher lawmaking authority? (Ackerman 1991:
> 197)

The answer to this question involves three steps. First, Ackerman depicts the
democratic process in its normal state, that of ordinary politics. Then he proceeds to clarify how from the midst of normal politics a political process of
constitutional significance may arise. Finally, he discusses the standards that
ought to apply to constitutional politics and that define the legitimacy of
higher lawmaking.

As Frank Michelman has suggested, for Ackerman normal politics is to
constitutional politics as normal science is to scientific debate at times of paradigm revolution.[12] Namely, it is a sort of uninspiring puzzle-solving, from
the midst of which sometimes, unpredictably, anomalies arise that push the
whole process through creative paths. The functioning of a democratic polity
is described by Ackerman along lines similar in one further respect, aside
from the crucial role of dialogue, to those followed by Habermas. According
to both theorists, the functioning of a vital democracy cannot be grasped in
terms of institutions and principles alone. We need to presuppose the existence of a *public sphere* where interest groups, civic-spirited organizations,
ideological crusaders, disinterested and interested citizens all act and influence one another. According to Ackerman, the public space of a liberal
democracy is populated by three main types of characters. At one extreme of

participation we find *public citizens*, exemplified by Ralph Nader, who 'combines an emphatic asceticism in personal life with a more-than-fulltime commitment to the public good as he understands it'. At the opposite end of the spectrum are *perfect privatists*, who shun all involvement in enterprises that carry no direct advantage for them and assess all institutional allegiances in terms of costs and benefits. The bulk of the inhabitants of modern democracies, however, fall somewhere in between these two extremes: they are neither embodiments of Montesquieuian virtue nor total free-riders, they are just *private citizens.*[13]

By this expression, by no means self-contradictory, Ackerman designates citizens who do go so far as voting, but do so in a distracted manner, without spending too much time and effort in making sense of the alternatives before them, and thus are fully aware of their failing to form a considered judgment on the issues at hand. Aside from voting, for the rest private citizens do not participate much in any public debate or movement. They are like the characters that Tocqueville depicted as a threat to democracy, people who are content to be politically lethargic most of the time and then wake up periodically, every four years, just in time to choose their new rulers and retreat once again into their private concerns. For Ackerman, however, private citizens pose no threat to democracy and come in two versions: *private* citizens and private *citizens*. Sometimes

> Millions of private citizens may be provoked by their fellow Americans to scrutinize some of their received political opinions with care. Not, mind you, that they become public citizens, whose commitments may lead them to become full-time activists. Nonetheless, during periods of successful constitutional politics, there is an important difference in their political conversations, actions, attitudes. Their questions become more urgent, their conversations more energetic; their actions move beyond the ballot box to include money contributions, petitions, marches – all to express the fact that they now have a *considered* judgment that they want their would-be governors to recognize. If italics will do the trick, *private* citizens become private *citizens*. If jargon is any better, distinguishing between passive and active citizens will serve, so long as it is firmly recalled that even the passive citizen is not a perfect privatist, nor is the active one a public citizen – we are distinguishing between shades of grey. (Ackerman 1991: 243)

Yet public citizens, perfect privatists, and private citizens in their active or passive mode are not the only actors on the scene of modern democracy. Alongside them are a variety of collective actors. We find *private interest* groups which – much like the Habermasian actors 'coming from the wings' who try to use the public sphere to their own ends (Habermas 1996a: 367–8) – try to advance particular interests by putting their resources (money, where permitted, or just influence on the public) at the service of the politicians receptive to them. Ackerman reminds us that the Founders were well aware of this pathology but wisely 'did not seek its total eradication'. Their solution was to increase the proliferation of diverse special interests, so that the virtuous representative could be facilitated in playing one off against the other.

Furthermore, the public scene is inhabited by *public bureaucracies* which, 'acting on their interest in selfpreservation', 'will try to use the resources at their disposal to create powerful constituencies on their behalf', namely constituencies that 'will fight to maintain the private benefits they receive from the programs regardless of the broader public interest' (Ackerman 1991: 247). Also in this case eradication is a dangerous utopia. The committed liberal should rather devise means for controlling and containing such occurrences.

A third kind of aggregate actor that usually is present on the scene of normal politics is typically constituted by *single-issue* groups who coalesce around a cause, often coloured in ideological if not fundamentalist ways, and act in a very determined, value-rational way as though their cherished issue were and ought to be the centre of all political concerns. The potential influence and permanent mobilization of some of these groups makes it prudent for politicians to avoid antagonizing them and often to pay lip service to some of their moralisms.

Finally, other constant presences on the scene of normal politics are *parties*, which in the United States between elections are little more than 'a service organization helping local constituents with their personal dealings with the government' (1991: 250), and the *media*. The importance of the media comes, according to Ackerman's account, from their constituting, given the almost perpetual passivity of the private citizens, the 'essential mechanism by which would-be representatives can reach out, however superficially, to the bulk of their constituents' (1991: 249). Two effects, mostly negative, follow from this predicament: the constant reinforcement of a 'media personality' on the part of politicians and the rewarding of impressive but superficial 'sloganeering' over more complex forms of argument.

The picture of normal politics is completed by an analysis of the shifting roles of the major branches of government. Comparing the American and the British political systems on the three dimensions of 'responsibility', 'transparency' and 'decisiveness', Ackerman finds the current state of democratic politics in the United States wanting on all three scores. In contrast to the concentration of authority and imputability in the hands of the Cabinet and of the Prime Minister in particular, the American system, according to his analysis, 'invites buck-passing: President blames Congress, House blames Senate, the Court condemns them all, only to be excoriated in turn' (1991: 252). Second, while the centralized structure of the British system puts pressure on members of the party to run their electoral campaigns in close ranks with the themes of the candidate Prime Minister, 'opacity' is the norm in the American system: the fact that congressmen are elected in elections that are independent of presidential elections invites differentiation and a plurality of political themes, not all coherent with one another. Third, integration and close ranks make for incisiveness of legislative initiative and easier implementation. By contrast, observes Ackerman, the President's statutory initiatives seldom come out unscathed by congressional battles, and the result is that initiatives conceived as coherent and comprehensive plans become a patchwork of 'interstitial compromises' (1991: 254).

For all these apparent shortcomings, however, the American system has the advantage of avoiding recourse, according to Ackerman, to the 'utter fabrication' of a mobilized majority in the country that rallies behind the party of the Prime Minister and sustains its policies. Nothing of the sort is going on among a private citizenry that gives the parliamentary debates 'only passing attention'. Instead, the political process envisaged by the Founders embeds a full awareness that in normal politics '*the People themselves* have retired from public life' and consistently 'refuse to grant *any* single governor an effective monopoly over lawmaking in the manner of a victorious Prime Minister' (1991: 255). This lesser measure of imputability, transparency and decisiveness represents also a safeguard against the never entirely absent risk that the concentration of powers might result in concentrated, high-powered *factionalism*. Also, argues Ackerman, it constitutes a sensible solution for a country like the United States where political elites lack the qualities of being stable and continuous over time as well as of being intrinsically of a national character, but are rather alternating regional elites propelled onto the national stage by a victorious presidential election.

How is it then possible that once politics has fallen into the normal state – during which '*nobody* represents the People in an unproblematic way', not even the Supreme Court, let alone Congress or the President, for the simple reason that during that time 'the People simply do not exist' – a new stage of constitutional politics might arise during which a majority of the passive private citizens is activated and begins to participate in a constitutional discourse about contested and highly consequential issues of higher lawmaking? How can the embers of public autonomy, buried under the ashes of normal and factional politics, be rekindled and brought to generate a new flame of public-spirited discourse?

Ackerman conceives of this process as including four distinct stages which include a functional, albeit different in each case, role for social movements and pose specific problems of institutional design. The first is the stage of *signalling*, parallel somehow to Habermas's idea of a network of organizations and associations that in the public sphere bring to expression a dissatisfaction with certain present arrangements or the need to address new issues. For the whole process of higher lawmaking to be set in motion, someone has first to indicate the existence of a problem of potentially constitutional relevance. Ackerman points to a transformation that has deeply changed the received understanding of how this signalling function ought to be discharged. While in the *classical* system of the Founding era the role of signalling the need for a constitutional deliberation was played by a 'deliberative assembly meeting on the national level', in the *modern* system, inaugurated by Roosevelt and consolidated by the subsequent Presidents, 'the decisive constitutional signal is issued by a President claiming a mandate from the People' and getting under way a number of appropriate and transformative legislative initiatives which, as in the case of the New Deal, need not take the form of a proposal for constitutional amendment.[14]

At the next stage – the stage of *proposing* – the general current of opinion that signals the need for constitutional deliberation on some new issue or for a reconsideration of parts of the existent Constitution must bring the plurality of voices that compose it and the multiplicity of reasons and arguments offered in support for its claim down to the unity of *one specific proposal*. As Ackerman points out,

> it is not enough for the movement's proposal to gain the wholehearted support of its present adherents. It must be framed in a way that will prove acceptable to the millions of Americans who have yet to take the matter seriously, but whose support will be decisive at later stages in the higher lawmaking process. (1991: 281)

In the classical model this synthesizing function was discharged by Congress or by a constitutional convention of more informal standing than elected state legislatures. In the modern model from Roosevelt to Bush, a formal proposal has usually come from the President who, on the basis of a claim to be acting on popular mandate, 'convinces Congress to enact transformative statutes which give legal substance to the new movement's program for fundamental change' (1991: 283). There are other significant differences. Within the classical system the moment of truth of constitutional choice came soon after the formalization of the proposal and the proposal was couched from the beginning in the abstract language of constitutional law. Within the modern system the whole process spans over a significantly longer period and the task of capturing the constitutional gist of a 'mass of statutory material' shifts onto the Supreme Court. New constitutional principles emerge much later in the process, and only as part of Supreme Court opinions.

The third stage, after the transformative statutes have been approved by Congress and are now likely to be challenged by judicial review, is the stage of '*mobilized deliberation*'. According to Ackerman, this stage is perhaps the feature most distinctive of the American process of higher lawmaking. Other countries often utilize referenda for the purpose of verifying popular consent to a proposed constitutional amendment. Peculiar to the American experience, however, is the length of the period of deliberation, measured in years rather than in months, and the chance that this prolonged period of mobilized confrontation gives to the defenders of the status quo to effectively organize a counter-mobilization. Such counter-mobilization, argues Ackerman, produces an unequalled broadening and deepening of the political engagement of the People. It creates the conditions for a massive reclaiming of *active* private citizenship and for wakening the public from its lethargy:

> A year or two after the first higher lawmaking signal, much of the softness of normal public opinion will dissolve. The apathy, ignorance, selfishness that occlude the judgments of tens of millions of Americans will have been dissipated by hundreds of millions of arguments, counterarguments, insults, imprecations. Apathy will give way to concern, ignorance to information, selfishness to serious reflection of the country's future. (1991: 287)

Again, also this phase of higher lawmaking has undergone modifications. Within the classical system the stage of mobilized deliberation coincided with the struggle for ratification within the state legislatures. In the modern system, the debate around formal ratification is replaced by the debate – (a) focused from the beginning on the national level, and (b) institutional as well as (c) conducted informally by the public at large – about the proper response to be given to the first series of judicial invalidations coming from the Supreme Court and by the electoral debate stirred by the President's and Congressmen's electoral campaign, presumably centred on asking for the People's consent to their transformative effort. If this consensus materializes, the final stage of *codification* sets in.

At this stage the role of the Supreme Court is essential. In the classical system its function was top-down: the Court received a formally approved amendment couched in very abstract legal language and had to work out the 'middle-level' doctrines capable of rendering the new or modified principles operative and reliable as means for settling new lawsuits and controversies. In the modern system, 'the revisionary effort begins concretely', bottom-up so to speak:

> the judges confront particular statutes and explain how preexisting doctrine must be revolutionized to accommodate the new innovations that have won the support of the People. (1991: 290)

This process presupposes a political judgment, on the part of the justices, that in light of the consent coalescing around the President's and Congress's proposal 'it would be counterproductive to continue the constitutional crisis until the new movement ratifies formal constitutional amendments' (1991: 289). When this judgment is formed, then the Supreme Court, in the new script for constitutional change brought into being by the New Deal, decides to 'uphold the last wave of transformative statutes in a series of landmark opinions, which inaugurate the radical revision of preexisting doctrine' (1991: 289).

The reconstruction of development of Ackerman's understanding of normative validity has highlighted a by now familiar pattern. Like Rawls and Habermas, so too Ackerman starts with a stronger model of normative validity, indeed of distributive justice, and subsequently – perhaps in a more abrupt way than the other two authors – turns to a view of normative validity, now considered under the aspect of legitimacy in higher lawmaking, which is more receptive to a notion of universalism based on the model of reflective judgment. More specifically, a number of elements in Ackerman's thought point to, and provide evidence for, the rise of the judgment model of justice and normative validity in general. In *Social Justice in the Liberal State* the guiding ideal was still to ground the normative validity or justness of certain political arrangements – 'undominated equality' – in a decontextualized model of a conversation constrained by the overarching principle of neutrality. Despite the dialogical form in which many of Ackerman's philosophical points are presented, the basic move repeated over and over is a traditional one. A philosopher posits some guiding principles and assesses some of the leading views of the day in their light. These principles, that is, operate in the same way as *criteria* operate within the determinant judgment paradigm: that is, they are external to the matter under assessment and their operation allows for demonstration of the correctness of the results. It must be noted, however, that even in the initial version of Ackerman's approach to normative validity, reliance on the model of determinant judgment was mitigated in an important respect by three distinctive features. First, no dimension of necessity was associated with the three principles that structure the power conversation. In fact, Ackerman grounded the validity of his model in a reflexive way through the outcome of a metaconversation – whose outcome is not to be anticipated by the philosopher – about the viability of the conversational model. Second, no relation of derivation was assumed to hold between the general principles and the substantive contents and outcomes of the constrained conversation. As such, the principles are supposed to function as a substantively neutral generalization test. Third, although Ackerman relied on a sharp distinction between suitable objects for public discourse and private beliefs to be kept out of the public arena, his own version of the Rawlsian 'method of avoiding' lacks the unidirectional and cumulative thrust – as I will try to show in Chapter 6 – that distinguishes Rawls's view of public reason. Because the constrained dialogue never issues in an 'unconditional conversational victory' of one thesis over another, but rather with the contingent and provisional silence of the defeated party, a two-way crossing of the boundaries between public and private conceptions of the right is always possible and in fact to be expected.

In *We the People*, instead, the picture is quite different. The focus is no longer on a general model for the liberal polity, but on the legitimacy of the process whereby a legal community of free and equal citizens comes to the decision to modify its own political identity as reflected in the Constitution. Normative validity is now understood in terms of a *situated judgment* about whether the conservation or the transformation of a certain set of constitutional provisions is most appropriate for a given historical identity. At the level of higher lawmaking no external criteria can be provided for assessing the legitimacy of what might be called constitutional will formation. No external criteria can be used to gauge *when* it is appropriate for the People to initiate a transformative process. Drawing on the *Federalist Papers*, we could attribute to Ackerman the implicit answer: it is appropriate whenever they find the inherited Constitution 'inconsistent with their happiness'. No external criteria can be used to gauge when the complex institutional and informal process of higher lawmaking has come to a point that authorizes the supposition that the People have *conclusively spoken their mind* on the issues at hand. As Ackerman emphasizes, the identification of such a moment takes an act of '*political judgment*' on the part of the Supreme Court – especially in the context of what he calls the modern model of Constitution amending. No external criteria can prescribe how the Supreme Court ought to discharge its *codification* function at the end of a successful process of mobilized higher-law deliberation. Perhaps Dworkin's interpretive model based on the value of integrity could be helpful here, but certainly no determinant judgment understanding of the task could be adequate.

This tendency to move away from the model of a fictive dialogue about principles of distribution to a judgment model of normative validity becomes even more manifest, as we will see in the next section, in Ackerman's most recent work – *Transformations*, the sequel volume to *Foundations* in the *We the People* trilogy (to be completed by the forthcoming volume *Interpretations*).

The Space of Judgment

The Two Themes of Transformations

Transformations in a way implements a much more ambitious project than the declared purpose of supplying historical documentation for the theses of *Foundations*. It contains a reconstruction of the crucial moments of constitutional innovation in American history – the Founding, the Reconstruction and the New Deal – from the perspective of highlighting the unconventionality of the transformative path undertaken by the major actors that have shaped them, the Philadelphia Convention, Congress and the Presidency. *Transformations* identifies the distinguishing trait of the American experience of constitutionalism in a peculiar 'space of judgment' which combines adherence to the substance of democratic constitutionalism understood as 'government by the governed' with innovative ways of reasserting this basic principle against supervening institutional rigidities. The unique stability, over two centuries, of this 'revolutionary constitutionalism' can be explained neither from a legal-positivist perspective with the enduring adherence to one particularly felicitous set of 'rules of the game' – for in the transitions from the America of the Articles of Confederation to the America of the Constitution, from the America of slavery to the America of equal protection, from *laissez-faire* capitalism to the 'activist regulatory state', the rules of the game also underwent significant change – nor with the Schmittian understanding of the legitimacy of constitutional acts as a refraction of actual political success at stabilizing a new constellation of power. The main target of Ackerman's book remains the former view, however, which he renames 'hypertextualism' and characterizes as the 'naive, but orthodox, view that Article Five provides a framework within which modern lawyers can explain *all* valid amendments since the Founding' (1998: 115).

If we read Ackerman's reconstruction in the light of our interest in the transition from a principle-based to a judgment-based model of normative validity, two main themes acquire a striking significance. First, we can see a partial, though not complete, correction of the constitutionalist majoritarianism present in *Foundations*. Ackerman's scepticism about 'structural entrenchment', fuelled by his 'Article Five non-exclusivism', is mitigated by the need to account for the feeling of restraint that the historical material shows to have been experienced by all the forefront innovators of the Founding, the Reconstruction and the New Deal. As Ackerman formulates it, the question runs: 'if the participants weren't respectful of established legal norms, why did they feel any legal constraints at all?' (1998: 11). Nowhere in Ackerman's text is an explicit answer offered, but the answer that appears most plausible in light of the historical materials runs along judgment lines. The relevant actors felt constrained to stop short of exerting outright coercion on their opposers because they were primarily concerned neither (like the French or the Russian revolutionaries) with breaking away from a certain communal project – in this case, the political identity of the *demos*, as embedded in the old Constitution – nor with simply 'making the most of it' while leaving the project unchanged (like justices when deliberating on the constitutionality of statutes). Rather, they were concerned with enhancing the Constitution's potential to be conducive to the realization of the best part of the political identity of the People.

Second, in the course of Ackerman's reconstruction of the three fundamental junctures of constitutional change in the history of the United States we observe time and again the occurrence of a kind of paradoxically successful 'normative bootstrapping' – the establishing of the normative validity of a constitutional provision on the basis of a 'rule of recognition' created simultaneously with the provision to be enacted. This kind of radically reflexive self-grounding – whose background, structure and justification I have explored in more general terms in *Reflective Authenticity: Rethinking the Project of Modernity* (Ferrara 1998a) – really constitutes the normative backbone of Ackerman's book. In the last section of *Transformations*, Ackerman puts forward his own proposal for a reform of the rules for amending the Constitution and justifies his proposal along judgment lines as the best way to appropriate the lesson to be drawn from the Founding, the Reconstruction and the New Deal. Furthermore, his proposal is presented as the best way for the contemporary citizens of the United States to fulfil the political identity that they have developed due, among other things, also to those events. Consistently with his reconstruction, Ackerman reflexively expects the legal validity of the newly designed procedure to be ratified not through Article Five strictures, but by way of a new kind of 'unconventional adaptation', the ground for which is prepared by his judgment-based declaration of 'Article Five non-exclusivism'. As he puts it:

> None of [Article Five's] 143 words say anything like 'this Constitution may only be amended through the following procedures, and in no other way'. The Article makes its procedure sufficient, but not necessary, for the enactment of a valid amendment. It is up to us, not the text, to decide whether to convert a sufficient condition into a necessary one and give the Founding procedure a monopoly over future development. (1998: 15)

Again, the case for a non-exclusivist interpretation can only rest on judgment concerning the democratic prospect offered by a broader versus a strictly literal adherence to the constitutional text. In other words, the choice between exclusivism and non-exclusivism does not *follow* from any other part of the Constitution, nor is it maintained by Ackerman to be a matter of sheer arbitrary *preference* . In fact, his book of over 450 pages is an argument aimed at showing that it is *better* for the American polity to embrace non-exclusivism and to consider, in light of the experiences of the Reconstruction and the New Deal, the possibility of an enhanced role for the Presidency in the process of constitutional amendment. In a thoroughly reflexive way the whole book can then, at the last chapter, be discovered to provide the substance of a historical argument designed to serve as the background for a transformative Supreme Court opinion that should validate the new procedure. I will come back to this point below.

The Framing and Amending of the Constitution in Ackerman's Account

In order to clarify the two themes of *Transformations*, we need to take a closer look at the historical events that form the object of Ackerman's inquiry. More specifically, we need to briefly highlight the constitutional innovations brought about by the Federalists, the Republicans and the New Dealers and also the junctures at which total rupture of the existing legal framework was avoided even by the most radical innovators.

I cannot go into the wealth of historical materials taken into account in Ackerman's account of the Founding, the Reconstruction and the New Deal except for recalling just a few elements. In all three of these constitutional crises, normatively valid constitutional innovations were brought about in ways that were significantly at odds with the procedures envisaged by the extant Constitution and yet did not amount to a complete break. At work was a kind of 'unconventional adaptation' of old institutions to new substantive emphases and new contexts – an expression through which Ackerman felicitously captures both the moment of discontinuity and that of loyalty, and at the same time signals the inadequacy of the model of determinant judgment for the purpose of accounting for normatively valid constitutional change.

The distinctive rupture brought about by the Founding concerned the mechanism for political will formation at the constitutional level that was embedded in the Articles of Confederation – the higher-law arrangement that since 1781 governed the relations among the thirteen states of the Union. As to be expected in a document meant to regulate the life of confederate sovereign states, *unanimousness* was required for all modification of the constitutional status quo. All alterations of the Articles would have to be 'agreed to in a congress of the United States, and be afterwards confirmed by the legislatures of every state' (quoted in Ackerman 1998: 34). The new Constitution being hammered out in Philadelphia by the Federalists in 1787 contained a decisive break with this pattern in its Article Seven, which established that a majority of nine states out of thirteen would suffice in order to enact the new Constitution. Furthermore, the new constitutional text cut deep into the established procedure for amendment by eliminating 'the power over amendments granted by the Articles to the Continental Congress' (1998: 34–5) and by transferring the power of ratification from the state legislatures to special conventions to be held in each state. Finally, the framing of such a proposal went well beyond the limits, implicit but in many cases explicitly formulated, of the mandate with which the delegates were sent to the Philadelphia Convention by state legislatures which had a quite diverse understanding of the function and operating of conventions.[15]

How did it come about, under these conditions, that the new Constitution hammered out in Philadelphia by 1787 was accepted by the People of the United States? This is a fascinating question for any European scholar who pauses to reflect on the chances for the unification of Europe to ever pass the stage of a 'Confederation' which is a Union only by name in as much as no mechanism is yet accepted for important political decisions that prescind from the unanimous approval of the single states. Back in the 1780s, the chances for a Federalist Constitution to bypass the state legislatures in the process of ratification must have looked as slim as today's chances for a European Convention calling for a Constitution of Europe to become law without passing through the formal ratification of the member states and, worse, with some of the states openly disputing the legitimacy of the procedure and the substance of the Constitution. How was then success possible for the Framers, short of a revolution of the Leninist kind – of the kind of violent transformation that openly disclaims all linkages with the past and portrays itself as an altogether new beginning?

Ackerman's reconstruction points to two elements that the Founding experience shares in common with subsequent instances of unconventional constitutional transformations: (a) what he calls the *institutional bandwagon* effect, and (b) a protracted phase of constitutional alertness and participation in an otherwise not very involved citizenry – a phase that includes five distinct stages.

The 'institutional bandwagon' – which in another terminology might be called a 'chain reaction of institutional recognition' – consists in the sudden subsiding, in close succession, of the 'legalistic' or otherwise conservative resistance opposed by each or most of the leading institutions against constitutional change. In the case of the Founding,

> At each stage, the Federalists suffered great legal difficulties in advancing their enterprise. At each stage, some important institutions refused to cooperate on legalistic grounds. Nonetheless, the Federalists gained enough acceptance by enough standing institutions to sustain their momentum. Winning these *official confirmations* made it plausible for them to embark on another illegal initiative, which – confirmed once again by more standing institutions – made it plausible for them to proceed to another illegal initiative. And so forth, until they had earned a deep sense of constitutional authority even though they had not played by the rules. (1998: 39)

From this point of view, the trajectory followed by each of the major great cases of constitutional reform shows a similar pattern. The whole phase of constitutional alertness, from the origin of a constitutional crisis to its successful resolution, is now accounted for by Ackerman in terms of five stages. As in *Foundations*, the first is the stage of *signalling* – i.e. the formal placing of a constitutional problem on the public agenda. The second, once again, is the stage of *proposal* and of gaining legitimacy for a proposal to be taken seriously enough to become an object of public deliberation. What Ackerman in *Foundations* conceived as the stage of mobilization is now further differentiated into a stage of *triggering* and one of *ratification*. The *triggering* stage involves the unconventional securing of enough legitimation for a new, unconventional procedure of ratification, and the stage of *ratification* includes the actual struggle of the reformers to gain the kind of support necessary under the new rules. Finally, the process is crowned by a stage of *consolidation*, formerly called 'codification', during which residual opposition is won over and gradually the constitutional issue is removed from the public agenda as a settled matter.

Signalling the Need for Constitutional Deliberation

In the case of the Founding, the *signalling* was bound up with the bandwagon legitimation of the Philadelphia Convention. In 1785, four years after the Articles of Confederation had been enacted, delegates from the states of Virginia and Maryland met in Mount Vernon, at Washington's house, to negotiate a commercial agreement between the two states. The delegates far exceeded the bounds of their mandate in the agreement they worked out, but the legislatures of Maryland and Virginia both approved the proposal and for unclear reasons refused to give formal notice of the proceedings and of their result to the Continental Congress. Then in January of 1786 Madison and other Federalists managed to convince the legislature of Virginia to allow some Virginia delegates to call for a thirteen state meeting at Annapolis in order to explore further the possibility of a comprehensive plan for regulating interstate commerce. Reactions began to be mixed. Only nine states sent delegates; the others, including Maryland, declined and denounced the Annapolis Convention as a politically dangerous meeting bent on usurping prerogatives that belonged to the Continental Congress. The fiasco was evident when delegates from only five states appeared. Yet this dimidiated assembly agreed to Hamilton's suggestion to call for another convention, to be held this time in Philadelphia, in order to discuss not just matters of commercial regulation, but all possible problems raised by the Articles of Confederation. To the ever increasing doubts as to the legitimacy of such an assembly, the Annapolis delegates responded in a pre-emptive way by venturing a powerful signal of constitutional need. They declared that if in calling for such a convention the delegates 'seem to exceed the strict bounds of their appointment, they entertain a full confidence that a conduct, dictated by an anxiety for the welfare of the United States, will not fail to receive an indulgent construction' (Commissioner's Report, quoted in Ackerman 1998: 43). Immediately the Annapolis delegates sought some kind of institutional recognition for their signal to the nation that a moment of constitutional deliberation was impending. First and foremost, the Annapolis Commissioners asked Congress and the thirteen states to call themselves for such a convention in Philadelphia. Since there was obviously no legal quorum of states or Congress members to validate such a convocation, the Federalists' hopes were simply that a politically significant majority of states and the call of Congress would lend enough legitimacy to the convention.

Congressional support for the idea of a convention in Philadelphia was initially lukewarm. A special committee took no action and debated the merit of the initiative for months. Then the sudden conversion of some prominent congressmen led to an acceleration of the bandwagon effect. On 21 February 1787 two Massachusetts delegates formally moved that Congress call the states to send delegates to Philadelphia for the purpose of amending the Articles of Confederation 'wherever necessary'. The signal was sent and enough institutional recognition was secured for the Philadelphia Convention.

In the case of the Reconstruction, the activating of the signalling function dates back to the election of President Lincoln in 1860. As Ackerman points out, during the first half of the nineteenth century the initial understanding of the office of the Presidency as one to which men who distinguished themselves more for their past service to the republic, than for their promise of constitutional transformation, should ideally be appointed had undergone a gradual modification in a plebiscitarian direction.[16] The impact of powerful personalities such as those of Thomas Jefferson and Andrew Jackson, combined with the rise of the mass political party cemented around the quadrennial struggle for conquering the Presidency, began to modify the original picture in a populist direction, often 'allowing the winning Presidential candidate to claim a mandate from the People that would have horrified the Founders' (1998: 126). This new kind of 'plebiscitarian Presidency' formed the background against which the election of Lincoln functioned as a threat for the Southern states as well as like a *signal* in its own right for the approaching of a moment of constitutional choice. Ackerman draws an interesting analogy with the signalling function exerted by the Annapolis Convention in putting forth, and by the Continental Congress in endorsing, the call for the Philadelphia Convention:

> In calling for the Philadelphia Convention, these bodies did something that fell far short of a concrete constitutional proposal. Nonetheless, they did something terribly important – signaling that the new movement had gained sufficient political authority to demand that others take its constitutional intentions seriously. By midcentury, the capture of the Presidency had become a similar symbol of constitutional seriousness. (1998: 127)

More specifically, for the Southerners the election of Lincoln 'was a signal that the American people – at least in the North – were no longer willing to allow the old compromises with slavery to go unchallenged' (1998: 127). Their response took the direction of attempting to create a *counter-signal* through the use of the narrow window of feasibility allowed by the survival of the 'lame duck' Congress and Presidency in the period between election and inauguration day, and through the legislatures of the Southern states. The Southern opposers of Lincoln tried to tread the Founding path and called for a Philadelphia-like convention to be held in Washington. This

convention materialized immediately and in February 1861 sent a conservative proposal to Congress. After a bitter combat, the proposal did not win
the needed approval of Congress. Meanwhile in the South secessionist conventions met and urged that the issue of slavery be considered in a spirit of
compromise. In this connection the election of Lincoln proved to be a decisive variable. The President simply wouldn't allow enough time for the
conservative bandwagon effect to coalesce. While his predecessor had ruled
out the possibility of a military response to the secessionist challenge,
Lincoln went in the opposite direction. He built up the armed forces quar-
tered at Forts Sumter and Pickens, making a return to normal conditional on
the disbanding of the Virginia secessionist Convention. The military confrontation then became the only viable option.

Also in the case of the New Deal it was a presidential election that played
the key *signalling* role: the election of Roosevelt in 1932. As Ackerman points
out, however, neither in the case of Lincoln nor in that of Roosevelt

> did these initial triumphs represent a massive endorsement of the ultimate consti-
> tutional solutions consolidated a decade later. To the contrary, these signaling
> elections did not even focus on the proposals that would ultimately win the day.
> The Republican platform of 1860 disclaimed any intention to assault slavery in the
> states where it was established. The democrats did not put the voters on notice of
> Roosevelt's intentions for his first Hundred Days. In both 1860 and 1932, the
> Presidential victories served more to put new constitutional options on the agenda,
> rather than to legitimate new solutions. (1998: 266)

The fact remains that Roosevelt won the 1932 election with a mandate for
reconsidering the economic arrangements that had led to the disaster of 1929
and of the Depression, a mandate for 'bold persistent experimentation' in
order to 'correct, by drastic means if necessary, the faults in our economic
system' (quoted in Ackerman 1998: 284).

The Stage of Proposal

The *proposal* and the *triggering* function are almost indistinguishable in the
case of the Founding. The new constitutional proposal was so comprehensive – in fact the whole institutional architectonic of the American republic
and not just one amendment was its object – as to contain also the triggering
device of a new form of ratification, in the guise of Article Seven. I will thus
return to the Founding when discussing the triggering moment of constitutional change.

In the case of the abolition of slavery, instead, the two moments are distinct. Ironically, the Article Five path of proposing a formal amendment was
followed by the conservative legislatures of the Southern states which tried
to work out a compromise solution susceptible of salvaging the institution
of slavery. President Lincoln and the Republican Party tried instead an
alternative, entirely unconventional path. First, in 1862 Lincoln issued a
Proclamation which 'emancipated' blacks only 'where the Union writ did
not run, specifically exempting the four loyal slave states [Missouri,
Kentucky, Maryland and Delaware] and all Southern areas under Union

military control' (Ackerman 1998: 131). The legal status of this Proclamation appeared dubious from the beginning and from a substantive point of view it did not amount to an outright condemnation of slavery. Rather, in providing compensation for the loyal slaveowners who suffered a loss of slaves the Proclamation went in the opposite direction: indirectly, it did recognize the legitimacy of slaveowning. Yet, as Ackerman maintains, the Preliminary Proclamation of 22 September 1862 was 'neither a final decision, nor a meaningless symbol, but an unconventional proposal' (1998: 131). Such status turned it into one of the crucial issues in the 1862 congressional elections. After the elections confirmed the Republican majority in the House, though eroding it, on 1 January 1863 Lincoln reiterated his Proclamation in its final form. Turmoil followed. While the abolitionists hailed the decision as one of historical consequence, the Southerners saw the coming true of the worse scenarios in it. The Republicans tried unsuccessfully to convince Congress to back up the legally ineffective Proclamation by turning it into an ordinary statute. Eventually Lincoln decided to include an explicit call for a formal amendment to abolish slavery in the Republican platform for the 1864 presidential election. It was so that the 1864 election then acquired the meaning of a referendum for or against the abolition of slavery.

The Republicans won by an unprecedented landslide: Lincoln was re-elected, and the Republican majority in the Senate grew to 42 to 10 and in the House reached 145 to 40 counting only the Northern seats. The Republicans claimed that such results went beyond the vicissitudes of normal politics and represented a mandate on the part of the People to abolish slavery. Many Democrats then switched sides and the Thirteenth Amendment was formally proposed by Congress in January 1865. Yet Congress was not really Congress, because only 25 out of 36 states of the Union were represented in it. Thus

> the Congressional decision is best seen as part of the Republicans' effort to create an institutional bandwagon similar to the one generated at the Founding . . . Within the emerging pattern, the Presidency and the system of national elections had begun to interact together to generate a powerful legitimating dynamic. (1998: 134)

This was also the first time that a President had taken such an active part in Article Five processes of constitutional transformation, an exceptionality which was marked symbolically by the fact that for the first time a President had put his signature on a congressional proposal for an amendment to be sent out to the states.

In the case of the New Deal, we also see a landslide victory. The Democrats, led by Roosevelt, won 310 seats in the House (117 remained Republican seats) and a large majority in the Senate, where the number of Republicans went down from 56 to 35 – after which the newly elected President was faced with the choice of an appropriate policy capable of transforming his claimed mandate for activist-government experimentation into a clear proposal. At first Roosevelt tried out a radical experiment in government-led corporatism – the so-called National Industry Recovery Act

(NIRA). The government would preside over negotiations between labour organizations and the management of the prominent firms of every industry, and these negotiations were supposed to generate regulatory codes for economic activity in each sector. The scope of this act and the attack it entailed on the received constitutional view of economic relations soon became apparent, yet Congress passed NIRA in a few months and went along with equally ground-breaking statutory innovations in the areas of agriculture, energy and pensions, as well as with the attempt to regulate the Wall Street stock market through the Securities and Exchange Commission. The midterm election of 1934 cleared away most of the residual doubts about the mandate claimed by Roosevelt. The Democrats further strengthened their position both in the House and in the Senate. The impact of their influence was such that not only did the Republican minority shrink further, but it was forced to change qualitatively, from more to less conservative. The obstacles to the New Deal, however, came not from Congress but from the Supreme Court. Starting with NIRA, one after another of the many measures enacted by the Roosevelt administration came under fire and their constitutional credentials were called into question. In May 1935, in deciding *United States* v. *Schechter Poultry Corporation* the Court unanimously struck down NIRA. One of the objections was that NIRA dethroned Congress from its legislative role and altered the balance of legitimate authority too much on the side of the Presidency, and no alteration of this magnitude could be effected without going through the formal procedure for constitutional amendment.

In response to the Supreme Court, Roosevelt made his proposal much more sharply focused. During a historical press conference, held on 31 May 1935, Roosevelt conceded that the alteration of the balance between the branches of government in favour of the Presidency required some legislative provision in order to be fully legitimate, but reaffirmed the undiminished relevance of the state of economic emergency which prompted the New Deal measures, and above all challenged head-on the Court's indiscriminate condemnation of all forms of regulatory interference with interstate commerce. He defended 'the right to legislate and administer laws that have a bearing on and general control over national economic problems and national social problems' (quoted in Ackerman 1998: 298). At the same time, the rest of his first term was devoted by Roosevelt to the attempt to build an alternative to the much contested NIRA – an alternative which would then be put to test in the upcoming presidential election of 1936. The result of this strategy was a series of statutory provisions that Congress agreed to support: the Wagner Labor Act, the Social Security Act and the Public Utility Holding Company Act.

As Ackerman points out, the effect of the Court's opposition was to increase the public's awareness of the revolutionary character of the New Deal measures. And, indeed, the second wave of New Deal measures, though lacking the corporatist flavour of NIRA, did amount to a 'revolutionary redefinition of the citizen's relationship to the nation-state' (1998: 306). Given the enduring opposition of the Supreme Court, the 1936 elections acquired a heightened significance as a test for the popular approval of the President's policies: they acquired a new triggering function.

The Triggering Function and the Stage of Ratification

Let us go back to the Founding and consider the *triggering* moment of the process. At the Philadelphia Convention the Virginia Plan, calling for a strong national government independent of the states and departing from the Articles provision of equal representation for all the states in Congress, was soon to meet the opposition of the supporters of the New Jersey Plan, which extended the prerogatives of the federal government without infringing the principle of assigning equal voting power to the states in Congress. The confrontation soon assumed the tone of a dispute between defenders and challengers of legality. Then, in July 1787, the Great Compromise closed the controversy: the Virginia Plan was by and large accepted, but equal representation for the states was preserved in the Senate. The debate then turned to the procedure for ratifying the new proposal. Some delegates raised the point that the Articles of Confederation could be superseded, within the bound of legality, only through the unanimous procedure envisioned in the Articles of Confederation themselves. However, with the exception of Madison the Federalists did not make a serious attempt to construct a counter-argument. They simply used their majority in the Convention to vote for the bootstrapping solution of approving the new Constitution via the procedure specified in Article Seven of the Constitution yet to be ratified. Another dire passage was the actual handing over of the Convention approved text to Congress on the occasion of formally requesting Congress to call for the ratification process to start. The fear was that Congress might in turn amend the proposal before sending it out and leave the dissolved Convention with no recourse against such an assertion of Congressional authority. To avoid this outcome Madison argued that while Congress was indeed legally entitled to modify the proposed Constitution, if it did so it would automatically turn the end product into a congressional proposal, which would then require approval along the traditional and more impervious track – ratification by thirteen and not just nine states, and ratification in the state legislatures and not via state conventions. After much debate, on 28 September 1787 Congress resolved to transmit the unmodified Philadelphia proposal to the states, without any substantive endorsement of it, in order for the proposal 'to be submitted to a convention of delegates chosen in each state by the people thereof in conformity to the resolves of the Convention' (quoted in Ackerman 1998: 55). The struggle for ratification was uphill in many states. In Pennsylvania it took the Federalists to mob reluctant members of the legislature to attend the session and vote in favour of calling a ratifying convention. Pennsylvania was among the first group of states that ratified the Constitution, together with Delaware, Georgia, New Jersey and Connecticut. Instead, in New Hampshire, North Carolina and New York, not to mention Rhode Island, the prospect for ratification seemed quite bleak. Contested states like Massachussets and

South Carolina were won over by quite unconventional means such as luring undecided members of the Convention with the promise of high offices or sheer gerrymandering. A crucial turning point came with Congress's declaration, on 2 July 1788, upon ratification by the ninth state (New Hampshire), that under the newly ratified Constitution a presidential election would have to be called for. That declaration added institutional legitimacy to the nine states rule and accelerated the process of ratification. Under the changed circumstances and, as they pointedly said, because of the changed circumstances, the delegates of the New York convention approved the Constitution by a small margin. Something similar happened in Virginia. As Ackerman points out, the unconventional strategy of first drafting the nine states rule, then seeking congressional indirect recognition of it, and finally relying on a political bandwagon, eventually worked out not despite its dubious legal status, but because of the infringements of the law that were made by the Federalists. Had Congress trodden a more legalistic path, declaring itself bound by the Articles of Confederation, the Constitution as we know it would have never materialized.

In the case of the abolition of slavery, after Congress formally sent out the Thirteenth Amendment to the states, the prospects for ratification did not seem favourable to Lincoln and the Republican congressmen. Under Article Five, the eleven states of the South had a veto power over the abolition of slavery, unless – once again an unconventional solution – an argument could be made plausible to the effect that only the votes of the states that had remained loyal to the Union had to be counted. The assassination of Lincoln on 14 April 1865 further complicated the matter. Andrew Johnson, on taking up Lincoln's office, made it clear that he would take an active part in the process of ratification of the Thirteenth Amendment. The extralegal triggering moment in this case consisted in the use that President Johnson made of his North Carolina Proclamation. By that Proclamation the right to vote for delegates to the ratifying conventions belonged only to those 'loyal' citizens who could already vote before 20 May 1861, when the ordinance of secession was issued. 'Loyalty' was determined, according to a second Proclamation, by the willingness to sign a solemn oath in which the citizen would commit herself to 'abide by and faithfully support all laws and proclamations which have been made during the existing rebellion with reference to the emancipation of slaves' (quoted in Ackerman 1998: 139). The unconventional, to put it mildly, quality of this process of ratification is not difficult to discern. The right to vote for electing delegates was made conditional upon acceptance of a certain set of contested propositions. As Ackerman puts it,

> By insisting that North Carolina be organized by 'people . . . who are loyal to the United States, and no others', and defining loyalty as requiring support of emancipation, the President had shifted the constitutional baseline from the one established by Article Five. Under Five, state legislatures are free to accept or reject a proposed amendment without endangering their standing in the Union. But this was not the choice presented by the President and his agents: Southern legislators could exercise their Article Five veto and reject the Thirteenth Amendment *only at the risk of tainting themselves and their states as disloyal to the Union.* (1998: 140)

Furthermore, in each Southern state Johnson appointed a provisional governor, responsible to the President, to act as a representative of the 'national
interest'. The Southern states reacted to this 'unconventional delegitimation'
not by outright opposition – how could they after all? – but by electing mod-
erates and seeking compromise solutions. Eventually, South Carolina and in
its wake Alabama, Georgia and North Carolina did capitulate to presidential
pressure and ratified the Thirteenth Amendment. Here we have another case
of an unconventional process of constitutional ratification: part of that
process was neither totally legal nor completely bound up with coercion.[17] On
18 December 1865, finally, Secretary of State William Seward issued a
Proclamation to the effect that the Thirteenth Amendment, ratified by 27 out
of 36 states, was thereafter part of the Constitution. But the legal status of
the Proclamation was far from being universally accepted. A few days earlier,
on 4 December, upon meeting for the first time after election, Republican-led
Congress refused to admit representatives and senators from the Southern
states with the exception of Tennessee, on the ground that 'no legal state
government' existed in those states. If the Southern states were not states for
the purpose of sitting in Congress, how could they be counted as states in the
ratification process? Meanwhile, President Johnson had vetoed the act in
which Congress declared that no legal state government existed in the
Southern states. The struggle that took shape in the coming months, however,
soon took another course, centred around an even more controversial amendment. To this new cycle – from *signalling* to *consolidation* – we will now turn,
before looking at the triggering function exerted by the presidential elections
of 1936 in the context of the New Deal.

At stake in the struggle over the Fourteenth Amendment – a struggle
called by Ackerman 'the greatest constitutional moment in American history'
(1998: 160) – was the notion that emancipation was not enough, but needed
to be complemented by an anti-discriminatory provision for equal protection
and equal rights. The possibility for a new proposal in the form of a
Fourteenth Amendment to be approved required, however, that Congress
remain an anomalous 'assembly' of 25 states instead of 36. Once again the
entire cycle of unconventional higher lawmaking was set in motion. The
signal of the new approaching of a constitutional moment was provided by
the Republican majority's decision to keep the representatives and senators
from the Southern states from joining Congress. In so doing, Republicans
entered a collision course with President Johnson's moderate conservativism:
the President had twice vetoed this form of political exclusion. After the
sweeping majority won in the 1866 election, Republicans sought again to set
a bandwagon effect in motion by trying to convince President Johnson to
accept the exclusion of the formerly disloyal Southern states at least on a temporary basis. Republicans, however, had another enemy to fight – namely, the
conciliatory tendencies, within their own moderate wing, to strike a compromise with the conservatives, even at the cost of stopping emancipation before
the threshold of an actual right to vote for the freed blacks. Two statutory initiatives were sent to the President in this spirit – the Freedman's Bureau Bill

and the Civil Rights Act[18] – and with the understanding that their acceptance could lead to a removal of the ban of the Southern states. The strongly negative response of Johnson – who purported to offer a voice to the excluded eleven states – precipitated the confrontation that eventually led to the ratification of the Fourteenth Amendment. In Ackerman's reconstruction, in the months that followed the separation of powers 'had shifted into high gear as an engine of constitutional articulation. Rival branches were denouncing each other's authority to speak in the name of the People, launching a point–counterpoint that framed the next phase of popular debate, mobilization, and decision' (1998: 173). It soon came to a formal proposal for a constitutional amendment, whose radical character consisted in its giving blacks a right to vote at a time when 90 per cent of the freed blacks of the North lived in states that excluded them from voting, in its strengthening national citizenship up to the point of granting the freed blacks 'the right to break down borders by claiming citizenship in any state they wished', and in its making full representation of the states in Congress conditional upon their abstaining from discriminating anyone from the equal protection of the law. The formal proposal won the approval of Congress with the required supermajority only because of the exclusion of the Southern states. The question was then whether this was a formally valid proposal to be sent through the ratifying procedure. The unconventional claim to authority on the part of Congress was officially defended in the Report written by Senator Fessenden on behalf of the Joint Committee on Reconstruction – a Report which challenged the President's power to re-establish civil power in the South, denounced the treacherous and lip-service quality of the Southern states' allegiance to the Union, and in sum seemed to demand 'nothing less than a spiritual transformation of the South' (1998: 175). It is interesting to follow, at this point, Ackerman's defence of the reason why Federalists in 1787 and Republicans in 1866 constitute a case quite apart from the Robespierres and the Lenins:

> While Federalists and Republicans challenge normal procedure, they are unwilling to smash the legitimating structures within which they are embedded. Fessenden does not claim the authority to impose the Fourteenth Amendment on the South by brute force. Like the *Federalist Papers*, his *Report* seeks to adapt pre-existing institutions into a new and democratic ratifying pattern. (1998: 176)

In transmitting, through his Secretary of State, the text of the proposed amendment to the states for ratification, President Johnson issued an unprecedented formal protest against the legitimacy of the proposal – a kind of negative counterpoint to Lincoln's equally unprecedented endorsement of the Thirteenth Amendment. Moreover, the President was supportive of the Washington-based attempt to convene a 'National Union Convention' in Philadelphia, where delegates from the North and the South would walk in 'arm-in-arm' and discuss the platform of a new party aimed at competing electorally with the Republicans. The congressional election of 1866 was thus charged with constitutional meanings of the highest order. From an ordinary politics point of view, a Republican failing to achieve the required two-thirds majority regardless of the Southern votes would have spelled an end to their claim to represent the voice of the People. From the standpoint of higher law-making, the question at stake was one of identity definition: was the United States to be a country in which *racial* identity had an impact on political rights or one in which full citizenship solely depended on *political* identity, namely on having been loyal to the Union? The result of the election was a landslide victory for the Republicans, who carried every Northern legislature and every contested governorship.[19]

The electoral victory strengthened but did not decide the case for the Fourteenth Amendment. President Johnson appeared to have lost his battle. Had he conceded that, had he operated what Ackerman calls a 'switch in time', he could have recovered a measure of control over the situation. He decided, instead, to play down the electoral outcome as an irrelevant momentary 'aberration' and tried to gain time by a policy of postponing the steps necessary for the ratification process to move further on. His policy was clearly aimed at having the Republicans face the electorate again in 1868 with no ratification of the Amendment on their hands and chaos in the South widely perceived as their responsibility.

The Republican majority's response was the First Reconstruction Act of 1867, whereby full readmission to representation in Congress for the formerly secessionist states was made conditional upon the extension of the right to vote to black constituencies, upon the formation of new state legislatures on that basis, and upon giving evidence of loyalty to the Union by nothing less than ratifying the Fourteenth Amendment. Furthermore, readmission was conditional not on the single state's conduct but on the actual gathering of the required country-wide three-quarters majority for ratification, so that readmission was even conditional on something independent of the state's will. This again was a deeply problematic triggering move: 'the First Reconstruction Act told Southerners, in no uncertain terms, that they could not act as citizens of their individual states without affirming the priority of national citizenship by ratifying the Fourteenth Amendment' (1998: 199). Here again we see surfacing the theme of the priority of national citizenship over state citizenship which was at the fore in the ratification struggle for the Constitution in 1787. Yet, as Ackerman emphasizes, even this coercive aspect of the conduct of the Republican majority stopped short of outright coercion: the Southern states were still free to reject the Fourteenth Amendment, if they were willing to pay the political price of not being represented in Congress.

Republicans were well aware of the importance of time. Thus they passed a statute authorizing the newly elected Congress to meet right after the expiration date of the preceding one, without allowing for the usual lapse of several months. As a result, many states were not prepared to send representatives, and this lowered even further the number of states that were actually represented to a mere 20 out of 37. However, even under this condition, in little more than two weeks the new Republican majority enacted a Second Reconstruction Act, only to see it vetoed by the President. A second vote overran the veto. Under this Act, the Union Army was to supervise the registration of white and black voters, as well as the actual voting operations and the formation of a ratifying majority in the thus elected conventions of the Southern states. Again, the point was reiterated that these states could be represented in Congress again only after the Fourteenth Amendment was ratified with the help of their vote as well. The substance of this new triggering device, points out Ackerman, was that 'the People, speaking through national institutions, may rightfully intervene to safeguard the exercise of equal citizenship in the states' (1998: 204).

President Johnson and the Supreme Court, however, were as aware of the relevance of time as the Republicans. Much as the Republicans were trying to hasten the ratification process, the President (and to some extent the Court) were trying to slow it down through legalistic objections, in the hope that the upcoming elections of 1868, if taking place at a time when ratification was still an open issue, would give the conservatives another chance to fight an all-out and possibly final electoral battle on the Fourteenth Amendment. As Commander-in-Chief, the President had the privilege of instructing his generals on how the tasks enjoined on them by the Reconstruction Act had to be carried out, and the interpretation he suggested was designed precisely to undermine the efficacy of the statutes. In response to this presidential tactic there was a Third Reconstruction Act, purporting to offer the right interpretation of the previous one. Also this new effort to force the President to comply with the timetable of 'Congress' was off the mark. Johnson, who among other things resorted to purging the highest ranks of the Army in order to delay the Reconstruction process, showed an outstanding capacity to elude congressional guidelines, rules and instructions, while at the same time always presenting his opposition in legalistic and not defiant terms.

It was at this point that the Republicans escalated the confrontation and started the procedure for impeaching the President. When the President tried to replace Secretary of War Edwin Stanton, loyal to Congress, with Lorenzo Thomas, an Adjutant-General of conservative faith, Stanton barricaded himself in his office with a number of Republican senators and challenged the legitimacy of the President's order. The President tried to turn over the issue to the Supreme Court, but before he could do so a majority of 126 to 47 congressmen voted an impeachment act that, among other things, charged Johnson with disregarding 'the rightful authority of Congress' and publicly denying the legitimacy of a Congress without the Southern states.

Another battle was being fought in another theatre at the same time. The Supreme Court was scheduled to adjudicate the case of McCardle, a citizen of Mississippi arrested and tried by the military for publicly attacking in writing the Reconstruction Act. McCardle's lawyers had challenged the constitutionality of the whole Reconstruction Act. In an unprecedented attack on the separation of powers, the Republican Congress voted a statute that removed the case from the jurisdiction of the Supreme Court. The Court decided not to fight for its own independence, partly in fear of the consequences of further retaliation on the part of the Republican majority, and left the new jurisdiction-stripping statute unchallenged. When McCardle's lawyers then did challenge its constitutionality before the Court, the Court simply adjourned the matter to the next December, after the congressional election. As Ackerman observes, the Court's retreat made it more difficult for the President to resist. As the impeachment trial began on 30 March, Johnson faced the alternatives of almost surely being impeached if he continued his opposition to the Republicans, or preserving some chance of bringing his term to completion if he allowed the Fourteenth Amendment to be ratified. He too decided to give in, nominated a new Secretary of War loyal to Congress, committed himself to no longer interfering with the Reconstruction, and readily accepted the results coming from the first two Southern states – Arkansas and South Carolina – that had ratified the Fourteenth Amendment. Eventually Johnson was acquitted by a single vote and that event impressed its mark on American constitutional history by ushering in a long period of congressional supremacy which came to an end only with Roosevelt. The realignment of the Presidency and the Supreme Court enabled the Republicans to finally win the ratification struggle. Ironically, however, they had to use the votes of the quickly rehabilitated states of the South to compensate for the loss of votes from those Northern states that, like New Jersey and Ohio, had reversed their previous endorsement of the Fourteenth Amendment.

The last unconventional element in the ratification of the Amendment concerned its proclamation. When all the reports of the new Southern states were in, it was the institutional responsibility of Secretary of State William Seward to declare that the Amendment had officially become part of the Constitution. On 20 July 1868, Seward issued an ambiguous Proclamation which in fact challenged the validity of the ratification by delegitimating the votes of the Southern legislatures, by pointing to the case of Ohio and New Jersey and by making ratification conditional on these states going back to the original decision. In response, the Republican Congress issued a resolution, approved by both Houses, in which it declared the ratification of the Fourteenth Amendment. It was now up to the Secretary of State to challenge the legitimacy of this unconventional resolution and thus also of the Fourteenth Amendment. However, as the President and the Supreme Court had done earlier, so too the Secretary of State prudently backtracked before the Congress's determination and on 28 July signed a second Proclamation in which finally the higher-law status of the ratified amendment was put beyond doubt.

Let us now resume the course of our discussion of the triggering function in the context of constitutional reform. In the case of the New Deal the triggering function was played by the elections of 1936. The contest between Landon and Roosevelt focused on the constitutional import of the new measures of economic policy:

> Roosevelt's watchword was now the rebirth of freedom, not the imperative of central planning. But it was a new freedom, defined in the light of modern realities that would otherwise defeat the claims of equal opportunity. It was a freedom that

could not be achieved in opposition to the state, but only through democratic control of the marketplace . . . While Landon was willing to endorse a more activist version of Progressive republicanism, he was unwilling to revise the old constitutional definition of freedom – tightly linked to principles of limited national government, freedom of contract and private property. At most he could endorse a constitutional amendment that authorized state (not federal) regulation of hours and wages. But he was entirely unwilling to accept the New Deal claim that modern freedom could only be achieved through the state and not against it; or endorse Roosevelt's assertion that the old constitutional regime had degenerated into a legalistic smokescreen for a world in which 'life was no longer free; liberty no longer real; men could no longer follow the pursuit of happiness'. (Ackerman 1998: 310)

The victory of Roosevelt and the Democrats at the polls was the largest in American history. The Republicans were left with 89 seats in the House and 16 in the Senate.[20] The way in which Roosevelt chose to use his mandate to formally sanction the New Deal reforms was again unconventional. He shrunk from the prospect of a formal amendment and instead on 5 February 1937 proposed an ordinary act that would give him the authority to make six new appointments to the Supreme Court. Here the rupture with extant legality is less severe than in the former cases examined. The Constitution places no constraints on the size of the Supreme Court, which had varied before. Also, conservative Attorney-Generals had made similar proposals for accelerated turnover in the lower courts, and no one had ever contested the right of Congress to legislate a restructuring of the judiciary on grounds of efficiency. It was the timing and context that caused Roosevelt's proposal to meet with great suspicion and outright opposition in Congress. Leading Democrats like Wheeler joined the opposition and induced many others to prudently wait in order to see which side public opinion would finally settle on. Wheeler was a defender of the New Deal, however, and even came up with an alternative solution: to introduce via an amendment the possibility for a new Congress, elected after the Supreme Court had struck down a statute, to override the Court's judgment by re-enacting the statute with a two-thirds majority in each House. This would change the Court's veto power from a definitive to a mere suspensive one. Roosevelt was not in principle against this alternative path: in fact, he set two of his advisers to work on the text of a possible amendment. But eventually he took another course. In his address of 9 March he discussed the issue. He expressed doubts as to the viability of the amendment strategy, on account of the legal intricacies, of the difficulties of reconciling all the diverging views, and of the time it would take to go through all the steps prescribed by Article Five. And in the end, he added, the ultimate meaning of the amendment would depend once again on the Supreme Court's interpretation. Finally, he mentioned the uncertainty of the whole process and the veto power that Article Five assigned to too small a minority: 'thirteen states which contain only five percent of the population can block ratification even though the thirty-five states with ninety-five percent of the population are in favor of it' (quoted in Ackerman 1998: 732).

In the midst of the Senate hearings on the President's proposal, however, the great change – functionally equivalent to ratification – took place. The Court had backtracked. The two centrist justices, Hughes and Roberts, had switched sides and realigned themselves with the progressives, forming the necessary majority to approve first the Wagner Labor Act, then the Social Security Act. The public perception that the Court was permanently reorienting itself had the effect of making all proposals for a formal amendment fade out of the public attention. With this switch in time 'all three branches were now operating on the premise that the *New Deal spoke for the People in enacting revolutionary reforms like the Wagner Act and the Social Security Act*' (1998: 350).

The Stage of Consolidation

Finally, in all three instances of revolutionary constitutional reform the process comes to an end with a stage of *consolidation* of the new constitutional meanings. Even after the ratification of the 1787 Constitution there continued to be radical dissenters. Aside from Rhode Island's refusal to even call a ratifying convention, North Carolina did not ratify but, together with New York, called for a second convention that should consider a Bill of Rights. It took another three years of battles before these states eventually accepted the Constitution.

In the case of the Fourteenth Amendment, consolidation was achieved only with the elections in autumn 1868. In fact, Democratic vice-presidential candidate Blair publicly called for the Presidential candidate to declare the ratification of the Fourteenth Amendment 'null and void' if elected, to allow the white people of the South to reorganize their state governments to their liking, to readmit the representatives from the South into Congress, and only then to run the ratification process again. It was only the subsequent victory of the Republicans at the polls, by a large margin in Congress, by a small one in the election of President Ulysses Grant, that put an end to the dispute over the Fourteenth Amendment. A different result would have reopened the questions raised by Seward's Proclamation and perhaps led to a third counter-proclamation.

In the case of the New Deal, consolidation in a way was easier and yet more uncertain. Given the reality of the Supreme Court's 'switch in time', a public perception came into being that all the three branches of government were now at one in recognizing the fundamental legitimacy of the New Deal statutes. From this point of view, the controversy appeared to be solved. On the other hand, given the dynamics of this very unconventional acceptance of new constitutional contents, what could prevent a switch back to the older positions on the part of enough justices as to undermine the new stability? This new stability was finally consolidated with two new nominations to the Supreme Court that Roosevelt was able to make upon the announcement of the retirement of two justices and with the electoral victory of 1940.

Ackerman's Proposal

The intellectual trajectory that has brought Ackerman from a model of fictive dialogue about decontextualized distributive arrangements to a situated historical judgment based on a kind of radically reflexive self-grounding is perhaps the one most typical of the tendency of political philosophy that forms in part the object of this book. While Ronald Dworkin makes a more explicit use of the aesthetic analogy in order to illustrate his understanding of the practice of constitutional adjudication, Ackerman does not emphasize the analogy between the practice of constitutional innovation and that of artistic production. Yet the processes that he reconstructs are in a sense not very different, in structure, from the processes that lead to stylistic innovation within artistic traditions. In painting as in music, in literature as in filmmaking, we observe the phenomenon of stylistic innovation. A number of similarities immediately catch the eye. First, the legitimacy of innovation cannot be made the object of a conclusive demonstration that moves from the premises of the framework being transformed. Nothing in the aesthetic assumptions underlying the classical realist novel can as such be used to show that the innovations brought about by Joyce, Proust or Robbe-Grillet are what an artist of the twentieth century *ought to* have done. Similarly, there is nothing in the American Constitution of 1787 as such that enjoins subsequent generations of Americans to abolish slavery and to devise mechanisms of compensation for the inequalities created by the market. When I say 'there is nothing', I mean that no more could one claim that the Constitution had been violated if these innovations failed to be brought about than one could legitimately claim that all twentieth century novelists who did not try the path of Proust, Joyce or Robbe-Grillet were doomed to artistic failure.

Second, while innovators cannot be understood to be under a normative obligation to transform the inherited framework, political or artistic, no one can claim that their innovations are the mere products of arbitrary stylistic or political preference either. Innovations of consequence are regarded as enlarging and deepening our understanding of the world and of ourselves or, in a different terminology, to be *world disclosing*. But this capacity for world disclosure is not independent of who we, as recipients of art or evaluators of constitutional amendments, are and want to be.

Third, it being impossible to validate innovations by subsuming them in terms of determinant judgment, the validity of both artistic and constitutional innovations requires the setting in motion of a 'bandwagon effect' or a chain reaction of instances of authoritative *recognition*. This is the contingency element in the validation of innovation. It may just so happen that opportunities for innovation are lost for contingent reasons: the ship transporting Gauguin to Polynesia might have sunk in the ocean; those who smuggled the manuscript of Diderot's *Rameau's Nephew* from Russia to Germany might have sold the text to the wrong person instead of giving it to Schiller; a health problem might have prevented Madison from delivering his speech urging Congress to refrain from modifying the Philadelphia Convention's proposal. As a result, history might have been quite different. On the other hand, what is of philosophical interest is our sense that certain artistic or political innovations *deserve* recognition as valid, regardless of their unconventional character. Here we touch also on the most obvious difference between the two kinds of processes. While in art we seek innovation, and for some product to fail to be 'unconventional' is to fail at being artistically worthy, in constitutional politics we value the predictability that comes from convention and are willing to accommodate unconventional ways only for the sake of something else, of some greater value being realized only through unconventional means. What is it, then, that makes us think of certain constitutional innovations as *deserving* recognition?

An implicit answer can be gleaned from Ackerman's text, when he discusses at length Roosevelt's address at the celebration of the 150th anniversary of the Philadelphia Convention. Roosevelt had stressed, in a key passage, that 'the Constitution of the United States was a layman's document, not a lawyer's contract' (quoted in Ackerman 1998: 377), meaning that it is a 'charter of general principles' and not a collection of 'legalistic phrases'. Subsequently he mentions the many times when a broader than literal interpretation of the document has deservedly overruled the legalistic cries of unconstitutionality. 'Whenever legalistic interpretation has clashed with contemporary sense on great questions of broad national policy,' continues Roosevelt, 'ultimately the people and the Congress have had their way' (quoted in Ackerman 1998: 378). Yet that innocuous word – 'ultimately' – is the crux of the matter. Roosevelt mentions some examples: a Civil War was needed to abolish slavery, 20 years of 'taxation on those *least* able to pay to recognize the constitutional power of the Congress to levy taxes on those *most* able to pay', 'twenty years of exploitation of women's labor to recognize the constitutional power of the States to pass minimum wage laws for their protection' (quoted in Ackerman 1998: 378–9). Roosevelt's conclusion is that that temporal gap is intolerable, too much suffering is allowed to take place before appropriate and needed change is institutionalized or, in his language, before 'law catches up with life', and there is no justification for this delay in the reforms which American people need in 1937, the time when the New Deal is consolidating.

Ackerman agrees with the premises and the factual assumptions of Roosevelt, but comes to an entirely different conclusion – a correct conclusion, in my opinion, of which however he does not highlight all the facets. According to Ackerman that gap between the rise of a discontent with the Constitution and the acceptance of a remedy to such discontent is a necessary guarantee for the democratic life of a country. The reason for this is that, from Roosevelt, we are quite aware that the *life* with which time and again higher law has to catch up *for us only comes in the plural*. To catch up with one vision of life means to lose touch with another. To catch up with abolition is to lose touch with the life and culture of the plantation, to catch up with 'equal protection' means to lose touch with racism, to catch up with the idea of a life whose basic decency cannot be jeopardized by the market means to lose touch with a Darwinian view of life as a bottomless struggle for existence. That is why the process of constitutional transformation really constitutes a space of judgment. In a pluralized world where different visions of life coexist side by side, any deliberation and any argument concerning which life higher law has to catch up with, or distance itself from, presupposes a judgment concerning who we are and who we collectively want to be. I cannot discuss here the question of validity in this sort of judgment.[21] Rather, let me go back to the status of Ackerman's own proposal for constitutional reform.

At the end of the book, the whole reconstruction of the three most important junctures of constitutional reform in American history turns out to be a basis on which to build a new proposal for the present. This new proposal, which concerns the reform of the institutional mechanism for constitutional reform, builds on four lessons that can be drawn from the reconstructive sections. The first lesson is that the path leading to reform need not follow Article Five. The second lesson is that each of the subsequent turning points of American constitutional history has been about a more direct affirmation of the *national* dimension of the People's will over the idea of the People's will as the sum total of local political wills. The third lesson is that the Presidency, formally left out of the process of constitutional amendment as envisioned in Article Five, in fact has been playing an increasingly important role, on account of its being the one elective office whose constituency spans the entire nation: 'modern Americans put their national identity at the center and expect the Presidency to take a leading role in the process of articulating the nation's future' (Ackerman 1998: 413). That is the reason why Article Five, owing to the weight it attributes to state-based processes of political will formation, appears restrictive and biased in a conservative sense, as the case of ERA teaches. The fourth lesson is that to limit, as the presently predominant interpretation of the Constitution does, the formal avenues for the President's orienting function over processes of constitutional change to the nomination of prospective justices is both restrictive and dangerous.[22] Instead, Ackerman's proposal embeds a sober recognition of the 'rise of the Presidency to a plebiscitarian role' and at the same time tries to dilute this populist element by tying the exercise of presidential influence to a tight interaction with all the other branches.

Ackerman's proposal, already outlined in *Foundations*, is the following.[23] Assuming that the electoral confirmation of a President makes it plausible, though by no means necessary, that some sort of constitutional mandate is being given by the People, then Presidents at their second term ought to be allowed to put forward proposals for constitutional amendments. The potentially populist and plebiscitarian dynamics should then be held in check by the requirement that the presidential proposal be endorsed by a supermajority of two-thirds in Congress. Then comes 'the test of time', which supposedly extends a sort of 'veil of ignorance' over the original proponents of the amendment. Politics is an art of judgment in the short run. Ackerman's requirement that in order to be ratified the proposal has to be approved by three-fifths of the electorate in two national referenda run in conjunction with two consecutive presidential elections is designed precisely to inject a strong element of uncertainty in the partisan calculations that might possibly provide motivation for presidential and congressional action. It is simply too hard to predict the political climate of nearly 10 years in the future. Finally, the referendum format of ratification is designed to offset the residual weight attributed by Article Five to state-bound processes of will formation. As Ackerman puts it, 'each voter will be treated as an equal citizen of the nation' in that 'his judgment on the referendum-question will not count more if he happens to live in Wyoming than in California' (1998: 410).

Interesting for our argument is the fact that, consistently with his reading of American constitutional history, Ackerman would not see it necessary or advisable to effect such a reform of Article Five via an Article Five procedure. Learning from the patterns of 'unconventional adaptation' that have emerged over the Reconstruction and the New Deal, Ackerman envisages the enacting of a special statute called the Popular Sovereignty Initiative designed to supplement and not to suppress Article Five. Let us consider his proposal:

> Proposed by a (second-term) President, this Initiative should be submitted to Congress for two-thirds approval, and should then be submitted to the voters at the next two Presidential elections. If it passes these tests, it should be accorded constitutional status by the Supreme Court. (1998: 415)

On what ground could the Supreme Court uphold such a broad transformation of Article Five? Here in the last 10 pages the real status of the historical reconstruction provided by Ackerman is finally revealed. The Court should construct its transformative opinion precisely on the argument developed in the book: it should explain how Article Five has 'failed' to accommodate the nationalistic aspect of the American constitutional identity 'ever since the Civil War' and how the Popular Sovereignty Initiative can help future generations to gain 'a clearer sense of the steps they can take to speak for the People through a nation-centered process' (1998: 415–416).

To sum up, *Transformations* confirms and consolidates the shift of Ackerman's framework toward a reflective judgment model of normative validity.[24] It remains to be clarified, however, how certain processes of higher lawmaking that have occurred in the past, as well as the reflexively grounded proposal for the future put forward by Ackerman, can claim a normative validity that goes beyond the factual coalescence of a political consensus. It remains also to be clarified in what sense such consensus *ought to have materialized* or, in the case of Ackerman's own proposal, ought to emerge within the Supreme Court. The answer which implicitly can be gleaned from Ackerman's text is that all these transformative events are instances of a more and more complete realization of the political identity of the American People as a nation. Such a reorientation of the source of normativity from general principles to a situated judgment on the fulfilment of identity has a number of implications that need to be carefully unpacked. This task will be taken up, in a general form, after considering, in the next chapter, the work of the author who, in his conception of higher lawmaking, most explicitly and coherently connects normative validity and judgment, namely Frank Michelman. Also, despite the presence of such significant elements of a reflective judgment understanding of normative validity, Ackerman's thought – no less than Rawls's, Habermas's and Dworkin's mixed models – remains characterized also by important traces of the classical modern model for conceiving normativity. As we shall see in Chapter 6, they are located in Ackerman's way of conceiving the relation between the Constitution and the will of the People.

5

The Judgment View of Higher Lawmaking

Until now we have examined liberal conceptions of justice that by and large, with the exception of Dworkin, have their point of departure in a framework closer to the model of determinant judgment – though important differences, as we have seen, sever them from what Kant understood by that term – and then move some reluctant steps toward a different understanding of the normativity of justice. The picture is not complete, however, until we consider another contemporary author who, instead, from the very beginning closely weaves together normative validity and judgment: Frank Michelman. His 'judgment view of higher lawmaking', which is part of a broader 'republican-liberal' proposal, sometimes referred to as the 'complex (republican-liberal) ideal of constitutional democracy',[1] promises to deliver a fully postmetaphysical notion of normative validity based on reflective judgment. However, as we will see, his position still leaves us in need of a theoretical articulation of a notion of justice compatible with the new paradigm, a notion which I will try to sketch out in the last two chapters under the title of a 'judgment view of justice'.

If it were still possible to write a history of political philosophy within the nineteenth century paradigm of internal consequentiality, the work of Frank Michelman could be appositely said to take up precisely where many of the authors considered leave off. In fact, the work of Frank Michelman articulates a view of deliberative democracy and higher lawmaking that incorporates many of the insights that we have seen thus far emerge in the work of the authors considered – the contingency of justice, the interpretive approach to law, the dualist perspective – without falling prey to the old paradigm of modern universalism in any of the extensive ways that will be discussed in the next chapter, but, on the contrary, opening up a new vista on a fully fledged judgment view of normative validity.

Michelman's Conception of Deliberative Democracy

Frank Michelman's conception of deliberative democracy can be characterized on the basis of four basic features and one preliminary consideration of historical tenor. According to the latter, over and beyond Rawls's fundamental premise of the 'fact of pluralism', any sensible view of democracy as democratic constitutionalism – where democratic constitutionalism is sometimes equated with 'republicanly liberal constitutionalism' – must incorporate and respond to, according to Michelman, an additional and equally inescapable premise: namely, a realization of the 'inauspicious conditions' with which the classical liberal ideal of 'government by consent' is bound to be confronted in contemporary society. Partly converging with Ackerman's diagnosis, but substantially diverging from its implications, as we shall see, Michelman points out that any contemporary conception of democracy must come to terms with a fundamental tension that arises in modern societies but comes to full fruition in today's complex societies: the tension between the ideal, irrecusable for any conception of democracy which wishes to remain within the liberal family, of 'government by consent', and four 'inauspicious conditions' – namely, (a) the sheer extension of the body politic in complex societies, (b) the complexity of the institutional order, (c) the anonymous character of the processes of political will formation and (d) the irreducibility of cultural pluralism.[2] Just as the acceptance of the 'fact of pluralism' consisted in sharing the acknowledgement that it is extremely unlikely that basic disagreements about the good life will ever cease to exist, so the acceptance of the limits imposed by the 'inauspicious conditions' to the liberal ideal of government by consent consists in the realization that it is extremely unlikely that any form of accepted legitimation might ever cover every institutional aspect of a political order and every political act accomplished by any of the office holders operating within it. Under the 'inauspicious conditions' of contemporary society, then, any theory of democracy that wishes to remain faithful to the ideal of government by consent ought to renounce the unrealistic requirement that liberal institutions and policies be able to convincingly justify themselves to anyone anytime and ought, instead, to reconcile itself with the sober acknowledgement that there will always be aspects of governmental policies, of the legislative activity of parliaments, and of the adjudication process that some of the citizens will experience as unjust and unfair to their own person, to their political convictions or to the social group to which they belong. The liberal ideal of 'government by consent' can only survive if made into a *manageable* ideal, and the dualist understanding of constitutional democracy is designed precisely to that effect: it restricts the applicability of *direct justification* – via a political conception of justice, via discourse, via constrained dialogue, or any other procedural scheme – to the *higher* level of law and institutional design, namely the level that possesses *constitutional* relevance. For all the other levels of the legal and institutional order, including policies and administrative procedures, an *indirect* form of legitimation based on their compatibility with the provisions of higher law will be considered sufficient.

With this proviso in mind, let us proceed to examine the four features that distinguish Michelman's version of deliberative democracy, as presented in a number of recent papers, of which some have been published under the titles of 'Always under Law?' (1995a), 'Can Constitutional Democrats Be Legal Positivists?' (1996a), 'Thirteen Easy Pieces' (1995b) and 'The Subject of Liberalism' (1994a), while others are still unpublished.[3] Aside from embedding a dualist constitutionalist inspiration, Michelman qualifies his *republican-liberal* conception of deliberative democracy against the backdrop of a whole range of debates, including: (a) the contest between the classical liberal emphasis on *rights* and the republican emphasis on *popular sovereignty*; (b) the controversy between the *deontological* and the *teleological* understanding of political rightness, (c) the tension between the *liberal* and the *populistic, majoritarian* and *plebiscitarian* understandings of democracy, and (d) the confrontation between the *process-bound* and the *abstract* and *process-independent* quality of deliberative democracy.

Deliberative Democracy as Jurisgenerative

According to Michelman, a defensible notion of deliberative democracy must strike a balance between the classical liberal emphasis on 'government by consent' and the republican and democratic emphasis on 'government by the governed'. This balance, when successfully generated, yields the first of the distinctive features of deliberative democracy: its potential for attaining a *jurisgenerative quality.* As he quite appositely puts it,

> at the core of our constitutionalism lies a notion of rights entrenched in law, against politics, by a founding act of politics. (1995c: 18)

Michelman's starting point is not, as it is for Habermas, the classical opposition of Locke and Rousseau, but the intuitions embedded in American constitutional culture, which seems to contain 'a pair of seemingly disparate ideas about political freedom' (1995c: 19): namely, (a) the notion that 'a people are politically free insofar as they are their own governors' and (b) the idea that 'a people are politically free insofar as their government is one of laws and not of men' (1995c: 20). The tension between these two notions can easily be brought out if one thinks of the former as referring mainly to the unbounded exercise of a sovereign will and of the latter as pointing to limits to that exercise. Even if the limits, in the form of rights, can be understood as themselves flowing from the sovereign will, namely as *self-imposed* limits, still there is room for tension. The limitations that the people thought it right to self-impose on its own will at one time may become unbearable constraints a few generations later.

If we look at this tension through republican lenses, a possible way of allaying it emerges. Such a way

> could mean envisioning politics as a process in and through which private-regarding 'men' *become* public-regarding citizens and thus collectively a 'people'. It would be by virtue of this people-making quality that the process could confer upon its law-like issue the character of validity, of law binding upon all as self-given. (1995c: 22)

To this process that both transforms its own protagonists and yields normatively valid outcomes – thereby constituting a condition of the possibility that a 'government of the people by the people' might at the same time be a 'government of laws' – Michelman gives the name of *jurisgenerative* politics. The parallel with civic republicanism is highlighted by him in terms of a certain

'circularity' or reciprocal influence – very close to what Habermas calls 'complementarity' – that is supposed to hold between the 'idea of the people
acting politically as the sole source of law and guarantor of rights' and the
'idea of good laws and good legal rights as preconditional to good politics':

> those who desire freedom must concern themselves with the social and economic
> structures of a free state. The structures must be such as to sustain, across the
> whole citizenry, the political motivations and capacities required for the support of
> freedom. They must be such as to sustain collective resistance to domination of the
> whole, or of any part by any other, by or through government. But the requisite
> structures are themselves crucially conditioned by laws. That makes the structures
> themselves products of politics. Thus politics itself, through authorship of the
> legal order, shapes the social and economic conditions on which the political sup-
> port of freedom depends. (1995c: 24)

The kind of republican liberalism reflected in Michelman's notion of *jurisgenerative* politics which distinguishes Michelman's deliberative democracy is
thus not quite different from Habermas's thesis of the co-originality of private and public autonomy. Certainly, and contrary to the rendition of it to be
found in *Between Facts and Norms*, it is a conception of democracy which not
only is not oblivious of the role of rights, but also contains an explicit reference to what Michelman calls a 'distinctive republican attachment to
individual rights, including rights of speech, property, and privacy' (1995c:
25). Michelman very carefully distinguishes his notion of jurisgenerative politics from the communitarian overtones that sometimes Habermas attributes
to him. In fact, the whole point of a modern dualist constitutional democracy
is to detach the notion of jurisgenerative politics from the image of a 'sol-
idary community' or from the classical republican idea of disclosing a latent,
pre-existent, 'prepolitical' convergence of comprehensive views. The advocate
of jurisgenerative politics points not so much to a commonality of substantive normative orientations, but to a 'weaker' commonality of concrete
historical experiences that a citizenry has gone through together or possesses
in its collective memory – a shared political past 'that is present for all as
political memory' (1995c: 32). Such a 'fund' of common facts could suffice,
argues Michelman, both to 'supply participants with identity "as" a people or
political community' and to put a limit on the otherwise infinite variety of
possible interpretations of the common ends and meanings. Michelman
stresses here that while such a collective dimension of communally generated
meanings represents a prerequisite for the single participants' ability to exercise their political autonomy, agency remains 'ontologically individual': 'We
envision *individuals* persuasively *connected* through dialogic *exchanges* of rec-
ollective "imagination"' (1995c: 32).

In 'Traces of Self-Government' Michelman (1986) demarcates his position
from classical republicanism in a careful way. Classical republicanism as exemplified by James Harrington embedded an emphasis on self-government, on
practical deliberation as dialogue, on the equality of the rulers and the ruled,
on a realistic notion of the common good, on virtue, on proprietary independence as the social basis of virtue. The fundamental principle, however, is

the idea of positive freedom as consisting of self-government. The other notions are conditions of the possibility of positive freedom so understood.[4] Important modifications are needed if such a principle is to be adopted by a contemporary republican approach. Differently from Renaissance and Harringtonian republicanism, in fact, the republican-liberal view propounded by Michelman conceives of self-government not only in a 'negativized' way, as aimed at the preservation of rights – in this being the heir to the post-Harringtonian development of republicanism – but also as an institutionally channelled form of self-government, mediated by the role of the Supreme Court: 'the courts, and especially the Supreme Court, seem to take on as one of their ascribed functions the modeling of active self-government that citizens find practically beyond reach' (1986: 74).[5]

Deliberative Democracy as Embedding a Deontological Notion of Political Rightness

Michelman emphasizes the *deontological*, as opposed to *teleological*, nature of the view of normative validity implicit in his version of deliberative democracy. According to his account, deliberative democracy is deontological in spirit 'because it subordinates any and all pursuit of a social or collective or *good* to a prior distributive constraint of *right*, of doing justice to each taken severally of as many as there are to be considered of "the self-authenticating sources of claims" – the entities severally possessed of basic moral entitlements to consideration and respect – that it recognizes' (1997a: 152).

The supporting argument is that a teleological perspective, whose most typical form is the utilitarian claim that 'the right goal for government is the maximum feasible sum of experiential "happiness" or "satisfaction" across society in the aggregate' (1996b: 17), cannot 'unconditionally require' any notion of the indispensability of deliberative democracy, or in a weaker form, any sense in which involvement of the governed in lawmaking would be necessary. In fact, teleological views can consistently embed the view that 'there's no good reason to involve the mass of the governed in lawmaking, that indeed it's best if they're not only not involved but remain oblivious of lawmaking while it occurs' (1996b: 17). Historically, from a utilitarian perspective no case has ever been made for a stronger involvement of citizens in lawmaking than their passing judgment, at intervals of four or five years, on 'whether they are better off now than they were four years ago' (1996b: 18).

The deontological perspective thus becomes the one of choice by exclusion. It must be said, however, that what Michelman means by 'deontological' is quite different from what Habermas for example meant in his 1985 paper on the discourse ethics. First, it is a *minimalist deontologism*, in that it does not entail strict proceduralism as Habermas understands it. On the contrary, for Michelman the deontological quality of his view of political rightness allows for substantive normative contents – if these do not violate the priority of doing justice to the free and equal individuals 'taken severally'.

The sharp distinction between the justification of norms (which forms the domains of a deontological moral theory) and their application (where interpretation and judgment have jurisdiction) is explicitly rejected by Michelman.[6] Furthermore, the deontological quality of a view of political rightness does not presuppose, according to Michelman, the idea that that view rests on some kind of dialogical procedure capable 'under ideal conditions' of (a) transcending particularity and (b) carrying the guarantee that a rational consensus eventually will be reached. In this sense, from Michelman's perspective the right remains no less contingent and linked with the particularity of context than the good is from a Habermasian perspective. Finally, the deontological quality of a view of rightness is not set in opposition to the quality of being judgment-based, as in Habermas's distinction between the right, based on communicative, context-transcending reason, and the good, based on context-bound judgment concerning the appropriateness of projects to identities. Indeed, the originality of Michelman's approach to deliberative democracy consists, among other things, in its embedding a *deontological view of rightness based on judgment*.

Deliberative Democracy as Liberal Democracy

Third, the view of deliberative democracy put forward by Michelman is *liberal* and not populistic, majoritarian or plebiscitarian 'because only individuals, and not any supraindividual entity such as a people or a majority, figure as self-authenticating sources of claims in the view's derivations of rightness requirements for political regimes' (1997a: 152). This means that in our assessment of the rightness, legitimacy or justness of institutions, political arrangements, policies, legislative initiatives and so on, the proper object of consideration is their impact on the life of citizens *qua individuals*. Such a stance distinguishes deliberative democracy *with a liberal spirit* from *communitarian* and other versions of democracy,[7] but does not commit us to one substantive view of the individual – least of all to the *atomistic* view of subjectivity associated with classical liberalism. On the contrary, we can embrace the intersubjective view of the individual as always immersed in, and constituted by, a web of relation of reciprocal recognition – the view endorsed by Habermas no less than by Taylor – and still assume, for the purpose of evaluating the validity of normative orders, that our social and political world is populated by 'individuals severally possessed of minds and lives of their own and severally possessed, furthermore, of worthwhile . . . capacities for rational agency, for taking some substantial degree of conscious charge of their own minds and lives, making and pursuing their own judgments about what to do, what to strive for, what is good, and what is right' (1997a: 153). The priority of the individual is a priority of *concern*, not an *ontological* priority.

In 'The Subject of Liberalism' (1994a), Michelman spells out further the conception of the individual embedded in his republican-liberal view of democracy. He starts out with illustrating five basic aspects of every liberal conception of the individual. First, individuals are assumed to be *ethically several*, i.e. each capable of leading 'a life of its own that is conceptually distinct from the lives of other subjects' and that constitutes a 'distinct field of value' (1994a: 1812). Second, individuals are assumed to be *interest bearing*, i.e. to be 'differentially affected for better or worse by various events'. Third, individuals are assumed to be *self-activating*, a synonym of 'autonomous', namely to possess the ability to contemplate their interests, reflect on their implications and to initiate modifications of their own internal state or of the external world. Fourth, individuals are assumed to be *communicative*, in the sense of being 'capable of intentionally affecting other subjects' perceptions of reasons for action' and of being 'intentionally affected by others'. Fifth, individuals do possess a property of *self-consciousness* or *reflectiveness* understood as an awareness of oneself as an 'ethically several, interest bearing, self-activating and communicative' subject (1994a: 1812).

Taken together these features define a sort of minimal or 'default' liberal conception, which in its pure form can only be found in extremely individualistic versions of liberalism – perhaps only in Hobbes. As a component of a broader conception, however, these features recur in all conceptions of the individual that fall under the heading of liberalism broadly understood. As examples of these 'thicker' conceptions of subjectivity Michelman mentions the Kantian and the Romantic views. On the Kantian conception the individual 'cannot thrive without having before it principles of regard for the interests of particular fellow subjects, or for all subjects – principles of right or morality of justice – to which it can precommit itself and from which it can then draw preemptive reasons for action' (1994a: 1813). This is the view of the individual presupposed by Rawls and Habermas.[8] On the Romantic view, instead, for an individual to thrive means to attain 'self-creative accomplishments such as authoring one's life or setting apt challenges and meeting them well' (1994a: 1812–13). Relevant examples of liberal and democratic theorists espousing this conception are Dworkin, Raz and Kateb.[9] Although there is no explicit pronouncement on this point in his writings, it seems fair to attribute to Michelman a view of the individual that certainly goes beyond the minimal threshold constituted by the characteristics listed above and also tries somehow to combine what he calls the Kantian and the Romantic conceptions. In fact, in order to engage in jurisgenerative politics, in the assessment of alternatives at the level of higher lawmaking, Michelman's subject must be able to be concerned with the interests of other fellow participants in the democratic process and at the same time to take the Romantic standpoint of the political community's creative self-authorship.

Deliberative Democracy as Intrinsically Process-Bound

Within Michelman's conception of deliberative democracy the democratic process is not thought to follow as an outcome from correctly 'political-moral reasoning that we already accredit as right', but is understood as a 'validity condition for political-moral reasoning or authority in the first place' (1997a: 151–2). Just as for Habermas only 'actual' democratic processes of will formation do ultimately have normative significance, so for Michelman it is inconceivable that political philosophy could generate by its own internal development a blueprint for a legitimate system of higher law for any given political community. The difference, however, is that where Habermas sees a solution, Michelman detects the presence of a problem. In fact, a kind of *infinite regress* threatens to undermine the deliberative view of democracy by virtue of making the legitimate establishing of a democratic order a task that is practically impossible to achieve on account of its conceptual incoherence.

Deliberative constitutional democrats start from the assumption that

> No political philosopher or lawgiver, or select group of them, unaided by actual live dialogic encounter with the full range of affected others, can reliably presume to see and appraise a set of proposed fundamental laws as all those others will reasonably and justifiably see and appraise them. (1997a: 161)

Actual discourses and deliberations are needed, if the postulate of government by the governed has to be fulfilled. Even Habermas, notes Michelman, cannot go so far as to say that from the rationally accessible idea of a fair democratic procedure, understood as dialogue under idealized conditions, one could derive 'a set of fundamental laws for a given country in given times'. Now, the impasse originates precisely in the requirement that the justness or rightness of a legal order, i.e. its deserving to be 'approved by all citizens in a democratic discourse', be linked conceptually (a) with the law's passing *successfully* the test of an *actual* democratic discussion and (b) with the understanding of the democratic character of such discussion in *legal* terms.[10] How can then the enacting of the first law – that *legal big bang* represented by the framing of a constitution – ever amount to a jurisgenerative process, since the *democratic* quality of the discussion which supposedly should ground the rightness and justness of the constitution can only be defined, consistently with the premises of modern legal thought, in terms of an already existing law? The political task of establishing a deliberative democracy, from this perspective, appears as hopelessly unfeasible as the enterprise of writing a novel in which the opening sentence of each chapter should be identical with the closing one of the preceding chapter. There would simply be no way of legitimately writing the opening chapter of the novel.

The solution suggested by Michelman to the problem of infinite regress is to introduce a distinction between (absolute) *justice* and (situated) *validity*. The citizens of a constitutional democracy ought to 'settle for the pursuit of *validity*, instead of *justice*, as the condition of rightness in a political practice'. In order to escape infinite regress, we should strive for *relative or historicized* rightness, which I take to mean rightness *for us*, given who we are. The transition from the standpoint of justice to that of validity so understood, however, involves also a change in the actor's relation to its own political ends, a transition somehow from *choice* to *discovery*. We awaken one day or come of age in the context of a society where democracy is practised and we recognize in the political community around us the underlying intent to live under the premises of an 'intentional, if always necessarily imperfect, approximation of the deliberative-democratic ideal'. And although no 'original' instituting act existed, one can live one's political life *as if* such a founding act had existed and shape one's political conduct accordingly.

The next question is: if situated validity, or qualified social acceptance, is less than pure justice, under what conditions can we attribute value to it? The answer can't be 'never' and can't be 'always' either. Skipping a number of passages, Michelman's answer is: we can attribute value to validity when the acceptance of what Rawls would call the constitutional essentials would generate enough *stability* as well as a workable conception of political justice. The justification for valuing validity because of its stability generating properties lies in the fact that, under the conditions of a democratic polity characterized by 'stability for the right reasons', the individual's capacity for justice would be 'freely exercisable without insult to the same individual's capacity for steering by his or her own autonomously determined conception of the good' (1996b: 33). The good of situated validity, in so far as political arrangements are concerned, lies then in its allowing for the *harmonious* exercise of the individual's capacities for justice and autonomy.

Yet this very justification seems to presuppose a certain conception of the person and of what it means for a person to flourish or live well. Thus, and here comes Michelman's bleak closing remark, we are back to square one:

> either we are critically disposed toward any and all philosophical specifications of the relevant ('political') notion of the person, hence epistemically committed to democratic procedures all the way up and caught in the immobilizing regress, or we stop the regress with a philosophical-foundational conception of the political person. (1996b: 33)

In the last section of Chapter 6 I will return to Michelman's formulation of this problem and will suggest a different solution to it.

The Inner Logic of the Judgment View of Higher Lawmaking

The most interesting aspect of the conception of deliberative democracy developed by Frank Michelman is to be found, from my perspective, in the notion of normative validity that underlies it. In order to grasp the originality of that notion, we need to place it in the context of the transformation of political philosophy that I have tried to reconstruct thus far. Michelman is primarily interested not so much in an abstract scheme of distributive justice, but in the rightness, justness or normative validity of single occurrences and processes of higher lawmaking. The term 'higher lawmaking' designates the area of legislative activity having as its object what Rawls has called 'constitutional essentials' or, in other words, the setting of standards by which all other, lower-order acts of lawmaking are to be evaluated. As such, validity in higher lawmaking is not *per se* a new object of concern, and all the authors discussed above have something to say about it. In Dworkin, for example, and in Rawls as well, we have already encountered the notion that the normative acceptability of a constitutional amendment and the assessment of the constitutional compatibility of a statute are a matter of *judgment*: a judgment that concerns the fit between the amendment or the statute under review on the one hand, and the interpreted constitution on the other hand.

Michelman's question is located at a somewhat different level, in that it concerns the conditions of legitimacy of the act by which popular sovereignty enacts a constitution in the first place or by which later on it accepts, through some formal amendment procedure or other, substantive modifications of that initial constitution that are more than simple applications and adaptations of the original constitutional intent to new historical realities. If we pressed the question of what grounds validity *at this level* onto the frameworks developed by the authors thus far considered we would observe a polarization between two types of responses.

On the one hand, Habermas, Dworkin and to some extent Rawls would tend to capture the conditions that meet our intuitions concerning validity as a general set of transcontextual conditions. Habermas understands the normative validity of the historical expressions of the sovereign will(s) as their responding to a certain set of common transcultural intuitions concerning the relation of discourse to validity. Dworkin would replace discursive categories with a kind of overarching intuition concerning the primacy of equality: even majority rule is justified in terms of its *prima facie*, but not intrinsically necessary, connection with equal respect for everybody's opinion.[11] Rawls would perhaps take a more nuanced position: the legitimacy of the enactment of certain constitutional essentials, from his point of view, would be vindicated not directly by reference to their reflecting the principles of justice that pass the test of the original position, but *indirectly* through their being compatible with a political conception of justice which, in turn, is the object of an overlapping consensus among the most significant traditions of a democratic political culture. All these authors emphasize the role of a standard that, in one way or other, is not specific of and internal to the sovereign will to whose political expressions it should be applied. The criteria and background intuitions which come into play in this assessment are not linked in any significant way with the context within which that sovereign will is formed. Sometimes the criteria and the context are closely related, but that is most likely an effect of the fact that we are confronted with American philosophers reflecting on the American constitutional experience. Habermas's case is especially instructive in this sense: the philosophical background which nourishes his discursive intuitions is totally detached from the plane of any concrete context of evaluation. But, to repeat once more, common to the three approaches is the anti-positivist idea that the sovereign will of the people makes right and just choices when it is responsive to intuitions justifiable in a framework that *goes beyond the will itself*. In this sense, we can say that the sovereign will that acts and chooses rightly acts as if it were itself acting, to use Michelman's expression in a different sense, 'under law'.

The originality of Michelman's position lies in his charting a wholly different course. Just like Habermas, Dworkin and Rawls, he also conceives of higher lawmaking as being *always under law*, 'even when the higher lawmakers are the people themselves' (1995a: 231). Yet, differently than for Habermas, Dworkin and Rawls, for Michelman 'the law that even the highest politics is under is itself a *politically immanent* creation, not a deliverance of transcendent, transpolitical reason' (1995a: 231).

What remains to be clarified, then, and will form the starting point of my reflections on justice and normative validity in Part II of this book, is how it is possible at all for the will of the people to be sovereign while at the same time remaining responsive to a normative framework *more comprehensive than any of its single political acts*, including the framing of a constitution, and yet *not external to it*.

Notice the close analogy that exists here with the problem of accounting for aesthetic value – an analogy on which more will be said in the final section of Chapter 7. To account for the possibility of an exemplary aesthetic experience means precisely to show how the artistic intent or formative will of the artist can be 'sovereign' and, at the same time, responsive to a kind of framework of sorts, more comprehensive than any of the manifestations of the artist's will but at the same time immanent and not external to those manifestations. In both cases, the task is to account for the possibility of a practice that is responsive to an *individual law* in Simmel's sense.[12] In the rest of this section I will first review Michelman's case for a reflective judgment understanding, as opposed to a more traditional 'quasi-transcendental', 'right-foundationalist' or 'method of avoidance' understanding, of the 'always under law' thesis. Then I will try to unpack some of the assumptions inherent in his view and to highlight some of the problems that they raise.

Michelman's argument starts from the arguably uncontroversial claim that we understand a 'scheme of government' or a set of 'constitutional essentials' to depend, for its normative validity, on the actual availability of justifying reasons for it 'aptly attributable to all affected persons' (1995a: 234). This minimal threshold of validity can be called 'justification by reasons of the governed'. Constitutional democrats' intuitions, however, are usually more demanding than that. In order to acknowledge a 'scheme of government' as normatively valid, legitimate or just, constitutional democrats also require that it be a form of 'government under law'. In other words, the requirement is not simply that officials and institutions come up with single *ad hoc* and uncoordinated justifications severally acceptable to the governed, but also that these justifications be somehow coherent with one another, namely proceed from 'some *public and unified* set of *durable, antecedently binding* principles of justice and right' (1995a: 237) – some principles relevant for the justification of '*all* determinations, interpretations, and resolutions of a political society's operative scheme of constitutional essentials' (1995a: 237). The 'lawness' of 'government under law' lies then in this 'unity, publicity, durability and antecedence' of the principles used for justifying the constitutional essentials of a political society.

What distinguishes constitutional *democrats* from other kinds of liberal theorists, however, is a third requirement of the justness or normative validity of a 'scheme of government', namely that it proceeds from the sovereign will of the very people whose political life is to be regulated by it. But there are problems with the notion of self-government. Some concern the relation with the other two requirements, and I will leave these aside. More interesting is the problem of identity: for the sake of the argument, we assume that a people who by framing a constitution engage in an act of self-government will also establish legitimate procedures for subsequently modifying the product of their sovereign will – for example, the procedures outlined in Article Five of the Constitution of the United States. Now, just by virtue of the future-oriented and future-shaping moment of the framing of a constitution, the people as original charterers 'seem to stand on a different plane of authority from the chartered'. They seem to stand to the subsequent generations of people who will live under the constitution as 'creators to creatures' (see Michelman 1995a: 240). In what sense can we then speak of a practice and an ideal of 'self-government'?

We can speak consistently of self-government, contends Michelman, in so far as we 'confer an identity on "the People" that is continuous across an event of higher lawmaking, leaving them the same People after as they were before the event' (1995a: 239–40). This elucidation of the notion of self-government, in turn, indirectly provides a justification of the 'always under law' thesis. The argument goes in the following way:

> As a self-governing people, [the People] cannot accept laws from anyone save . . . themselves. But it seems they can know themselves as themselves – can know themselves as, so to speak, a collective political *self* – only by knowing themselves as a group of sharers, joint participants in some already present, contentful idea, or proto-idea, of political reason or right. This means that they can know their lawgivers as legitimate – as sharing political identity with them – only through the *lawgivers'* perceived or supposed participation in some political-regulative idea that is sufficiently distinct to be identifiable – identifiable, that is, as the same one as theirs. What we're saying, in effect, is that a population's conception of itself as self-governing, as legislating law *to itself*, depends on its sense of its members as, in their higher lawmaking acts, commonly and constantly inspired by, and aspiring to, some distinct regulative idea of political justice and right, but an idea that itself has sprung from the politics of the self-same self-governing People. (1995a: 241)

That's why it is necessary to consider both the present and the founding generations as responding, in their exercise of political sovereign will, to an already present but *immanent* framework capable of encompassing all their acts – namely, as responding to their own specific idea of 'political reason or right'.

This account of deliberative democracy and of higher lawmaking raises a number of questions and at the same time opens up new conceptual possibilities. The first among the questions is the following: how exactly are we to understand the pre-existent idea of political reason and right, of which the original constitution is supposedly an interpretation and an application? Two answers seem to be precluded to Michelman on consistency grounds. On the one hand, the judgment view must avoid a relapse into the invoking of an external framework or a philosophical idea of right that is not directly expressive of the people. On the other hand, the judgment view must also avoid the communitarian solution of attributing the quality of a shared ethos to the 'proto-law' to which the constitution stands in an interpretive relation. The one avenue that seems to remain open, in order to avoid these pitfalls and yet conceive of the 'prior idea of right' as a *legal* concept, is to understand the broader idea of political reason and right as equivalent to 'the constitution as the people *intended* it' as opposed to 'the constitution as it was *actually worded*' owing to the contingencies of the debate in the constitutional convention, to contextual limitations of the vocabulary available to the framers, and so on – much like the work of art as planned by the artist (to the extent that we can extrapolate it from various sources) can be compared with its actual realization.

The second question concerns the meaning of the identity of the people as *charterers* and as *chartered*. To what extent does the problem of the sameness of the charterers and chartered depend on the semantic ambiguity of a term such as 'people' – an ambiguity which characterizes also its cognates *peuple*, *pueblo* and *popolo*? These terms, in fact, bring together two aspects of a collectivity which for our purposes should be kept distinct – namely, the 'cultural' identity and the 'political' identity of one and the same social group. If we substitute the terms 'cultural identity' and 'political identity' for them, we observe a number of interesting shifts of meaning. We can still say that for a people *qua* collectivity endowed with a political identity to be self-governing means for them to legislate to themselves as the self-same collectivity endowed with a political identity as those who legislate. But the people *qua* collectivity endowed with a political identity did not exist prior to the enactment of a constitution. The people, back then, were just a collectivity endowed with a *cultural* identity. At some point in their history, however, the people *so conceived* constituted themselves as a people *qua* collectivity endowed with a *political* identity, and in that transformation, as in all transformations, something changes and something remains the same. The crucial change is the coming into being, by virtue of the enactment of the constitution, of the people *qua* collectivity endowed with a political identity. From now on all subsequent interpretations and adjustments of the constitution will have to issue from the people *so conceived* and be congruent with that original moment of founding.

But in what relation does the people *qua* collectivity endowed with a *political* identity stand to the people *qua* collectivity endowed with a *cultural* identity? They can't be identical and they can't be unrelated. Perhaps their relation can be described as follows, in a way that is consistent with Michelman's argument. The people *qua* collectivity endowed with a political identity is one aspect of the people *qua* collectivity endowed with a *cultural* identity or, better, one self-description (along with other self-descriptions couched in religious, cultural, ethical terms) that the people *qua* collectivity endowed with a cultural identity choose to adopt at some point. In so doing, however, the people *qua* collectivity endowed with a cultural identity inevitably changes itself: paraphrasing what Montaigne wrote about his own autobiographical work, we could say 'The constitution makes us, no less than we make the constitution.' But the formative impact of the constitution only affects the people *qua* collectivity endowed with a *cultural* identity – for the people *qua* collectivity endowed with a political identity do not have a life beyond that political practice which is regulated by the constitution. Consequently, we must come to the realization that 'We' are in a way always larger than 'the People' – in that respect the phrase 'we the People' contains a measure of ambiguity.

To sum up, there is a certain difficulty involved in conceiving an agent – in this case a collective agent – being left unchanged by the action that it performs. In the most banal sense, the agent has now acquired a new experience. The sameness that we are talking about must then be the sameness of an 'identity' in the cultural and historical sense, not in the logical sense. Among the possible ingredients of such an identity, Michelman mentions 'some substantially contentful normative like-mindedness' or a 'cultural or dispositional or experiential commonality'. How can one define that core of identity to which the framing of the constitution stands as an act of interpretation in such a way as not to make a collectivity endowed with a *political* identity stand to the same collectivity now considered under the aspect of its *cultural* identity as an attribute stands to an essence? Of course, the core of the people's identity can't be conceived as an ethical core, otherwise the judgment view of constitutional democracy would not be consistent with the fact of pluralism. A different but possible candidate is a commonality of historical experiences, including experiences of conflicts and divisions, from which a perceived commonality of destiny flows. Pointing to such a notion, however, constitutes only the beginning of an answer to the question 'How does a series of individuals come to think of themselves as a people?'

A second set of problems is raised by the conceptualization of the relation between the constitution *qua* expression of the public political autonomy of the people and that core of the people's identity. It is part of the notion of autonomy that the constitution cannot 'flow' or 'derive' from certain things that are *factually* true about the identity of the people. Since the relation of any subject, individual or collective, to itself is an inherently *practical* relation, in which the subject contributes to make itself by way of choosing certain self-descriptions over other possible self-descriptions, the constitution ought to be understood as the objectification of just *one* among several political identities that are congruent with the people's identity – namely, the one variant of the identity which is freely chosen as a project by the people itself. The appropriateness of an act of constitution framing would then be a matter of the *degree of congruency* of this one choice with who we are. The future-oriented project moment inherent in this choice frees the notion of fit from a naturalistic understanding in terms of 'reflecting' certain given identity components. Peoples, no less than individuals, can centre their identity upon projects of radical self-reform. The 'political identity' created by a constitution can be part of the project whereby a collectivity endowed with a cultural identity seeks a transformative deliverance from certain undesired, or no longer desired, aspects of its own identity. For this reason, a judgment view of higher lawmaking ought to operate with a notion of the identity of the people that goes beyond the Montesquieuian concept of the 'general spirit of a nation' or Herder's concept of *Volkgeist* and includes a stronger emphasis on the project-like and future-oriented component of identity – namely, on the component of identity which functions as the locus of the *practical* relation of the collective with itself.

A third order of considerations that Michelman's approach enjoins us to take into account concerns the dimension of time. Taking up again the aesthetic analogy, we can notice a significant difference between the case of artistic practices and that of higher lawmaking. Also in the case of the production of a work of art, no less than in the case of higher lawmaking, we have an initial project, then a conscious attempt to realize the project, and in the midst of that attempt several reconsiderations of the project may take place in light of new contingencies. The project is what gives aesthetic unity to our acts, but is also open to revision, up to a limit. The work of art, however, is expected to be completed within a certain time – which can span, in certain cases (for example, the construction of medieval cathedrals), more than one generation – and the project somehow gives the author a sense of what changes are still possible at any point without risking artistic failure altogether. In the case of an individual identity this time frame is provided by our expected life span. The accessibility of options that in principle, but only in principle, could be compatible with a revised project is thus determined also by biological factors (at my age, I can no longer change my life-project into that of becoming a professional pianist or soccer player, though I could still decide to write novels or to open a restaurant). In the case of the people, however, it is difficult to think of any similar time frame within which the political project underlying their identity has to be completed and judged a success or a failure. The disturbing effect of this lack of temporal closure is that any commitment, even the deepest one, could be written off as an incidental and marginal mistake in the context of a communal life potentially extended to the very end of time and based on quite different premises. A flagburning amendment devised to curb freedom of speech could then be justified in terms of a thorough reassessment of the background culture against which the First Amendment has traditionally been interpreted. The received reading could be placed in perspective by claiming that it suffers from an individualistic bias rooted in the liberal culture of the eighteenth and nineteenth century and that the new intersubjective conception of the individual assigns finally a proper relevance to the symbols of communal identity and to the vital role that such symbols play in shaping our chances to attain individuation via mutual recognition.

Finally, the metaphor of the work of art also helps us to elucidate better the distinction between two levels of higher lawmaking introduced by Michelman – a distinction which constitutes another element of originality with respect to the other authors considered. In 'Always under Law?'[13] Michelman refers to a 'lower layer' and an 'upper layer' of higher lawmaking and connects them with the jurisdiction of the Supreme Court and the juris- diction of what he calls the 'People's Court' – namely, the People's political capacity and legal prerogative to intervene directly at any time in the process of higher lawmaking via the established procedures for constitutional amend- ment. The criterion for the attribution of legal subject matters to one or the other jurisdiction cannot simply be that norm *origination* pertains to the people and norm *interpretation*, or the *application* of norms, pertains to the appropriate level of the judiciary – argues Michelman – for the simple reason that the 'People's higher-law ministrations are *always interpretive*, never orig- inary' (1995a: 247). Even the framing of the constitution, let alone the act of amending it, is in fact to be seen as a (self-)interpretive act directed at the core of the political identity of the people. Thus another criterion must be sought as the basis on which to rest the distinction. At this juncture I believe that the aesthetic analogy, as well as a parallel with the fulfilment of an individual identity, become relevant. The lower-level 'higher-law ministrations' entrusted to the Supreme Court or their equivalent can be understood as including the treatment of questions concerning the best way of *understanding* the project embedded in the constitution. The upper-level 'higher-law ministrations' that ought to remain the prerogative of the people *qua* collectivity endowed with a political identity, instead, can be understood as including those questions that call for a *reassessment* of the project and as such are (potentially) trans- formative. If reconstructed along these lines, the criterion underlying the distinction remains fully consistent with the attribution of an interpretive character to both kinds of questions. In fact, in the case of lower-level 'higher-law ministrations' what stands in need of interpretation is the consti- tution as a reflection of the political identity of the people *qua* collectivity endowed with a *political* identity, and in the case of upper-level 'higher law ministrations' what stands in need of interpretation is the interpretive align- ment of the political identity reflected in the constitution with the broader cultural and historical identity of the people. Under liberal and republican- liberal premises, however, the people *qua* collectivity endowed with a cultural identity cannot be the subject of any political decision, except for the one which, via the enactment of a constitution, calls the people *qua* collectivity endowed with a political identity into being. This is why, at subsequent times, it is incumbent on the already constituted people *qua* collectivity endowed with a political identity to act as a fully authorized trustee and interpreter of the people *qua* collectivity endowed with a cultural identity – a prerogative which includes the possible reassessment of the political project embedded in the constitution – just as the Supreme Court or an equivalent institution can legitimately act as a trustee of the People *qua* collectivity endowed with a political identity and as an interpreter of the constitutional project as it stands at any point in the history of the political community.

It is worth noting that the above illustrated distinction between an upper and a lower level of higher lawmaking does not imply a relapse into the positivist democratic view according to which the people is the sole and final arbiter of the normative legitimacy of constitutional amendments. This unwelcome consequence can be avoided if one understands Michelman's distinction as allowing also for criticism of the self-interpretation eventually adopted by the people. To be sure, no *legal* evaluation by judges *qua* judges could possibly be allowed. But legal philosophers, political philosophers, historians of law, social critics and judges *qua* private persons can all conceivably develop arguments in a public space on why a certain self-understanding of the People is dubious or flawed. The 'People's Court' is thus the final one only in a *legal* sense. Above it stands a *still higher-order* kind of judgment – judgment *on the congruity of the People's self-understanding with the People itself*, a judgment that, just as is the case with individual identities and the symbolic identities metaphorically possessed by works of art, can be rendered by participants and observers alike. Such a 'History's Court' or 'Judgment's Court' as a separate legal-philosophical, if not politically effectual, level is what must be presupposed if Michelman's idea of a 'People's Court' standing above the Supreme Court is not to result in the introduction of an element of legal positivism in the form of the unquestionability of the will of the People.

An example from the legal history of the United States that illustrates the interplay of these levels of higher lawmaking is provided by the vicissitudes of the Eighteenth Amendment on prohibitionism. To introduce the prohibition of the 'manufacture, sale, transportation and importation' of 'intoxicating liquors' was perceived as something that exceeded the mere interpretation of the Constitution and thus went beyond the proper jurisdiction of the Supreme Court. Such a prohibition was made higher law through the formal amendment of the Constitution, via the procedure outlined in Article Five.[14] This was what occurred in 1919. Yet the amendment was to be shortlived. In 1933, merely 14 years after its enactment, the amendment was repealed through the same process by the People. Unless one finds it appealing to account for this process as an instance of the People's changing their mind *for no reason* other than pure arbitrary preference – a preference which happened to be oriented in one direction in 1919 and in the opposite direction in 1933 – the sensible account seems to have to include in one way or other the notion that the interpretive judgment rendered by the People in 1919 in the context of their participating in higher lawmaking was after all mistaken and that the mistake was corrected at a subsequent time. This account need not be retrospective. The judgment view of higher lawmaking can allow for the possibility that a judgment of this sort on the adequacy of the People's judgment can be formulated by a legal philosopher or any other concerned person at any time, also prior to the recognition of the mistake on the part of the People, which is after all a merely contingent fact – a valid judgment on the unsoundness of the Eighteenth Amendment could have been made in 1925 no less cogently than in 1933. Only the *legal* cogency of that judgment would have to wait for a pronouncement of the People.

PART II

COMPLETING THE TURN: THE PROSPECT FOR THE JUDGMENT MODEL

6

Traces of Modern Universalism in Contemporary Liberalism

However far reaching they might seem, the modifications brought by Rawls and Habermas to their earlier frameworks, as well as the more decidedly judgment-based conceptions of normative validity propounded by Dworkin, Ackerman and Michelman – thus I would continue our historical narrative – should not mislead us into thinking that a sudden and thorough paradigm revolution is under way in political philosophy. These transformations and new conceptions are to be taken, instead, as an indicator of a growing uneasiness with the early modern model of generalizing universalism and of a growing, but still somehow reluctant, willingness to come to terms with and partially integrate a view of normative universalism based on the model of reflective judgment. While in the previous chapters I have tried to highlight some aspects of the work of Rawls, Habermas, Dworkin, Ackerman and Michelman that point to a newly developing understanding of normative validity as linked with the exemplary universalism of judgment, in the present chapter the focus will be on those aspects of their work which testify to a reluctance in fully adhering to the new paradigm – a reluctance which takes the form either of relapses into figures of thought linked with the older model of generalizing universalism or of the persistence of significant residues of it.

The Cumulativity of the Political

If the political conception of justice presented in *Political Liberalism* (Rawls 1993) is examined in light of the three features of determinant judgment specified in the Introduction, it appears that for all his decided rejection of perfectionism and intuitionism, for all his rejection of a foundationalist and deductivist view of the principles of justice, Rawls's view of justice remains entangled in lingering remnants of the model of determinant judgment. This is the fundamental source of the questions raised by it and of the difficulties which still await a solution. Of the three distinctive features of the determinant judgment model of validity, only the quality of necessity associated with the universal – the role of the universal being played in our case by the two principles of justice – is unambiguously rejected by Rawls.

Justice in a complex society, as Rawls reminds us time and again, cannot be a matter of simply applying to the facts of the matter principles that have been previously *proven* or *demonstrated* valid. The idea of a strong *deductive* specification of the conditions of subsumption – i.e. the idea that in matters of justice propositions can be proven valid in the same way as a theorem in geometry – is also rejected by Rawls, but significant traces of it can be found at various junctures. In order to detect such traces, however, we have to recall one of the implications of that idea – namely, the implication that the *deductive* or *analytic* quality of the relation between the nature of a universal on the one hand, and the conditions under which a particular can be subsumed under it on the other, constitute the cornerstones on which a *method* can be built. Only disciplines – be they empirical or analytical – which allow for such a relation can generate a 'method' of inquiry, where by 'method' is meant a procedure which in a specifiable sequence of predetermined steps can lead a practitioner to results that are valid, reliable and reproducible over time by other practitioners. It has been argued by Richard Rorty (1988) that this ideal, still somehow pervading *A Theory of Justice*, in Rawls's subsequent work is abandoned in favour of an anti-foundational contextualism. In *Political Liberalism*, however, we can still find a few traces of the ideal of the demonstrability of truth and validity alongside, and in tension with, a contextualist defence of justice as fairness as the conception of justice 'most reasonable for us' (Rawls 1993: 28).

One of these traces can be found in Rawls's defence of the legitimacy of the abolitionist's struggle against slavery – a passage mentioned above in discussing Rawls's implicit view of political change. The struggle for abolition is the case of a conflict in which it is impossible to identify a 'political' ground 'thick' enough to support an institutionally stable solution – indeed, a civil war was needed to end the conflict. Rawls does not elude this basic fact. He neither pretends that the abolition of slavery could be compatible with both the contending points of view, nor pretends that the notions of human dignity, human rights and liberty invoked by the abolitionists found support in some privileged access to the reality of human nature, the human subject, moral rationality or any such notion. He defends the abolitionists' drawing on their own (religious) comprehensive conceptions of the person on the assumption that their political movement constituted one of the *necessary historical conditions* for the eventual establishment of political justice (1993: 251). Rawls here presupposes the possibility of ascertaining – in a manner which remains to be clarified consistently with the anti-intuitionist premises

underlying the whole project – the necessary quality of the necessary historical conditions for the establishment of a just society.

A second trace of the model of validity based on determinant judgment
can be found in the discussion of the so-called 'publicity condition' (1993:
66–71). Here the idea of the methodical and *a priori* nature of the specification of the conditions under which the particular can be subsumed under the
universal takes the form of the assumption that the citizens of a well-ordered
society share *substantive* beliefs about human nature and the functioning of
society, as well as *formal* beliefs about the 'forms of reasoning' and the 'methods of inquiry'. The tension between the requirements of the publicity
condition and the burdens of judgment has already been mentioned above.
For the purposes of the present discussion it is relevant to note that the function of the publicity condition is to ensure that, by virtue of sharing the
evaluative standards that serve as benchmarks for assessing principles, citizens are enabled to reach the same conclusions from the same premises. This
function is structurally equivalent to the shared quality of those categories
assumed by Kant, on the naturalistic basis of a precultural setup of the
human subject, to allow determinant judgment to generate universally valid
results.

Differently from the two aspects connected with the necessity associated
with the universal and with the deductive nature of the relation of subsumption, the third aspect of the model of determinant judgment – namely, the
notion of a *conceptual separability* of the universal from its particular
instances as well as the related idea of a *priority* of the universal over the particular – seems to be retained *explicitly* and *completely* by Rawls. In order to
understand this aspect it is necessary to recall the contrast between the model
of universalism based on determinant judgment and the one based on reflective judgment.

In reflective judgment, as we may recall, 'only the particular is given and
the universal has to be found for it' (Kant 1986: 18). Such process of 'ascending from the particular in nature to the universal' must be guided by a
'principle', as Kant calls it, but this principle cannot be borrowed from experience or from 'any other quarter', lest we fall back into the model of
determinant judgment: judgment, as Kant puts it, 'must be a principle to
itself' (1986: 36). One of the consequences of this model is that the 'universal'
draws its normative force entirely from its immanence in the particular. To be
sure, its nature can be elucidated independently of reference to a particular
for purposes of expository expedience, but in such case the universal thus presented has no normative force. It cannot lead to an unambiguous recognition
or rejection of the validity of a particular.

Full consistency with the model of normativity based on reflective judgment would then suggest treating the principles of justice – understood in
Rawls's case as self-standing moral theoretical constructions that (a) sum up
the logic underlying our considered judgments concerning the fairness of
institutional arrangements and (b) are compatible with these considered judgments in *reflective equilibrium* – as if they related to the concrete institutional

reality of a given society in the same way as a poetic manifesto relates to the aesthetic quality of a concrete work of art. Consequently, even as the hypothetical winner of the contest among theories of justice for the title of 'best reconstruction of the pattern underlying *our* considered judgments in moral matters', justice as fairness would no more constitute a set of principles on the basis of which we could legitimately deny or establish the legitimacy of the basic structure of a given historical society than the requirements of a realist, surrealist, hyper-realist, minimalist, pop art or Dadaist manifesto provide a basis for assessing the aesthetic quality of a painting. Failure to meet the principles embedded in justice as fairness could no more disqualify institutional arrangements as unjust than failure to meet the standards of a Dadaist poetics could automatically disqualify the aesthetic quality of a painting.

Of the new normative status that his political conception of justice would acquire if the older model of generalizing universalism were to be thoroughly and consistently rejected, Rawls certainly seems to be aware. His awareness of the shift toward a model of normative validity based on reflective judgment emerges most clearly when he points out that if, in the long run, an overlapping consensus over his political conception of justice were *not* to emerge within the political culture of our societies, that would not be a sufficient ground for considering the institutional structure of that society 'unjust' or 'unfair', but would more modestly have to be considered an indicator of the fact that the 'hope' that justice as fairness would be recognized as the political conception of justice most adequate for a democratic society was not well grounded. Such awareness, however, should not be mistaken for what it clearly is not. It is not part of a complete and explicit change in perspective on the part of Rawls. Rather, it is simply part of a growing awareness of the difficulties of the old model accompanied by a somewhat hesitating adoption of a few aspects of a universalism based on the model of reflective judgment. The result is a *mixed model* of normative validity still laden with implicit assumptions that draw on the notion of the independence of the universal from, and of its normative priority over, the particular.

An example of such hesitancy is provided by Rawls's distinction between the *normative* valence of a political conception of justice corroborated by an overlapping consensus, which generates 'stability for the right reasons', and the *prudential* expediency of establishing a *modus vivendi* between warring factions.

A *modus vivendi* is an agreement between parties involved in a conflict, in which 'the terms and the conditions are drawn up in such a way that it is public knowledge that it is not advantageous' (Rawls 1993: 147) for any of the parties to violate them. The agreement is honoured because it is in each party's interests to honour it, including among those interests also the interest in appearing an agreement-honouring party. Yet, it is also part of the notion of a *modus vivendi* that the parties 'are ready to pursue their goals at the expense of the other, and should conditions change they may do so' (1993: 147).

In the case of the *overlapping consensus* on the basic structure for a society shaped by justice as fairness, instead, the object of the agreement 'is itself a moral conception' and the motives for entering the agreement are *moral* grounds, not pragmatic ones. The parties enter the agreement, and subsequently abide by it, because they believe that this is *morally right*, not because they think it is *expedient* for them to do so. The third aspect under which a *modus vivendi* and an overlapping consensus differ is their respectively low or relatively high potential for ensuring stability. The higher potential typical of the overlapping consensus is linked with the *moral* nature of the parties' motivation for entering the agreement. Because they enter the agreement on the basis of their considering it *morally* and not just prudentially worth while, the parties' subsequent allegiance to the pact is independent of the contingencies of interests and of the 'balance of respective forces'.

Yet, what does it mean exactly for a ground or a motive to be *moral*, as opposed to pragmatical or prudential? In this context the term 'moral' can only mean: most consistent with the actor's conviction that to act in a certain way in turn is consistent with the principles of justice that would be selected in the original position and can reasonably be expected to form the object of a reasonable overlapping consensus. The reason why this motivation generates more stability than the motivation underlying a compromise, however, is unclear. Configurations of interests can be fairly stable over long periods, and certainly there is no intrinsic necessity why they should be more likely to change than our moral convictions, which also undergo momentous transformations. In light of this fact, the claim that an overlapping consensus has a sort of stronger normative status than a *modus vivendi* – in that it resists changes of the context without itself changing – makes sense only if we assume, drawing implicitly on the determinant judgment model of normativity, that an overlapping consensus somehow brings to realization a 'universal' or simply a set of principles of justice whose normative cogency can be established separately from, and prior to, the context at hand.

Rawls must be credited, however, with distancing himself, in a passage of his 'Reply to Habermas', from any such way of understanding the overlapping consensus. For example, when spelling out the idea of 'stability for the right reasons' he makes the preservation of the overlapping consensus over time depend on such contingencies as the fact that the reasonable comprehensive conceptions continue over time to outnumber the unreasonable conceptions that reject the political conception of justice (1995: 147).

Finally, a fourth and quite significant residue of the model of universalism based on determinant judgment is constituted by the quality of 'cumulativity' which inheres in the 'political' as conceived by Rawls. According to Rawls, the possibility for issues, reasons and values to move from one to the other side of the border which separates the political from the other realms is always unidirectional. Some of those issues, reasons and values which are controversial may over time meet with solutions or reformulations susceptible of rendering them uncontroversial and thus of relocating them onto the other side of the boundary, into the realm of possible objects of public reason. It remains unclear, however, how – within Rawls's model of public reason –

issues, reasons and values which at some point in time are 'political' may over time cross the border in the opposite direction and turn into, or return to be, controversial and thus 'non-political' ones. Within Rawls's conception of public reason we can thus still find a residue of the *cumulativity* of modern reason: what is controversial and non-political can become public and political, but what has once become political and public is supposed to remain such for ever.

To sum up, despite the presence of lingering remnants of an older model of universalism which bring a note of incomplete consistency to his argument, Rawls's political conception of justice is certainly one of the liberal approaches which come closest to a full appreciation of the *contingency of justice*, of its inherent relation to reflective judgment and of its uneliminable situatedness. The normative cogency of justice rests ultimately, for Rawls, on a reasonable account of the reasonable which in turn is based on the hope that it will be accepted by reasonable people. This has been considered by many commentators, including Kukathas and Habermas, as an unfortunate development, a loss in the overall clarity and compellingness of justice as fairness. There is reason to believe that the opposite is true.[1] The underlying strategy of extending the 'method of avoidance' to the entire realm of political philosophy represents an innovative approach to the problem of reconciling transcontextual validity with the situated quality of our moral judgments. We have seen some of the problems that it leaves open and some of the remnants of the older model of universalism which are still present in it. These problems and these residues, however, do not undermine the status of Rawls's view of justice as the metaphysically least demanding conception of justice, within the gamut of the contemporary liberal theories here considered, that is up for consideration as the best reconstruction of the principles underlying our considered judgments in matters of justice.

The Ambiguity of Habermas's Notion of Generalizability

As in Rawls's case, also in Habermas's work the transition from a stronger to a fully postfoundational model of reason and validity is not complete, as the presence of several residues of the older paradigm and of one central ambiguity underlying his conception of moral validity as generalizability indicate. For example, despite his discursive reformulation of the concept of justice, Habermas is still willing to commit himself to the possibility of *a priori* assigning certain kinds of practical dilemmas to one or another type of practical *discourse*. Thus he lists issues of social policy, matters of tax law, and questions concerning the health system and the educational institutions among the *moral* issues. Among the *ethical* issues he lists ecological questions concerning the protection of the environment and of endangered species, questions of traffic control and city planning, questions of immigration policy, the protection of cultural and ethnic minorities, and, more generally, questions of political culture.[2] The basis on which such partition rests appears unclear. If one reads the passage as meaning that issues which are either ethically or morally relevant are so in an *exclusive* way, then Habermas's point is plainly indefensible. For there obviously are moral implications in immigration policy, in city planning and even in questions of traffic control, as well as ethical implications in questions of social and educational policy, not to mention the case of legislation concerning abortion. On the other hand, if moral and ethical discourses turn out to be only *primarily relevant* in either set of issues, still the question remains: what basis other than discourse can justify the sorting of complex problems into the two categories? Habermas seems here to neglect to apply to his own framework the point that he appropriately raised against Rawls. Just as is the case with the boundary between private and public central in Rawls's understanding of public reason, also the proper boundary between kinds of practical discourses and the distribution of specific topics under the headings of the moral or the ethical are often controversial. There is no reason, except Habermas's own propensity toward salvaging as much as possible of the determinant judgment model, why such controversies could not, consistently with the postmetaphysical premises put by Habermas at the centre of his view, be left for the participants to solve in light of their considered judgments.

Other remnants of the stronger model of universalism and of reason show up in Habermas's understanding of normative validity in the context of his view of deliberative democracy. The new version of Habermas's moral theory presented in *Between Facts and Norms* contains a number of very interesting points, over and beyond the systematic differentiation of the three practical standpoints and related types of practical discourse. For example, coming to terms with the reality of the cultural diversity of contemporary society, Habermas acknowledges that 'in complex societies it is often the case that even under ideal conditions' the successful carrying out of moral or ethical discourses on certain issues might prove impossible. It may happen, and it often does happen, 'that all the proposed regulations touch on the diverse interests in respectively different ways without any generalizable interest or clear priority of some one value being able to vindicate itself' (Habermas 1996a: 165). This statement indicates a major theoretical shift in the direction of a sober realism and of a total embrace of liberalism. Habermas here implicitly abandons a long and strenuously defended stronghold of moral universalism, namely the idea that moral discourses, *if* conducted under ideal conditions, normally do generate a rational consensus on the legitimacy of a norm and allow for the identification of truly generalizable interests. Now Habermas seems to fully accept the Rawlsian 'fact of pluralism'. Under conditions of cultural diversity, that is, conflicts of value or of interest may arise which are simply not susceptible of a rational solution *even* if the strong idealizations of discourse were satisfied. They are not amenable to a rational *moral* solution not just because of limitations inherent in discourses conducted in the 'real world', but because there exists no actual common interest or not enough of a common ground between the contending parties. It is at this juncture that Habermas introduces his notion of an *acceptable* or *fair* 'compromise', a rough equivalent of Rawls's *modus vivendi*. Just as Rawls's *modus vivendi* stands in opposition to a morally motivated *overlapping consensus*, so the acceptance of a norm on the basis of a 'fair compromise' stands, for Habermas, in opposition to the acceptance of a norm out of a rational consensus reached in discourse. While Rawls singles out the prudential quality of a *modus vivendi* and the ensuing instability of the resulting arrangements as distinctive features, in his account of a *fair compromise* Habermas characterizes compromise in more positive terms. He allows for *fair* compromise, which takes place when three conditions are satisfied. First, the existence of a compromise is more advantageous to *all* than a situation in which no arrangement exists at all. Second, the compromise is so arranged that free-riders are excluded. Third, the compromise is so arranged that exploitation of the weakest party is prevented, where exploitation is defined as contributing more to the cooperative effort than one gains from it.

On Habermas's new approach, there is no limit to the number and quality of the decision-making processes that in a democratic society can be left up to fair bargaining – with one proviso and one restriction though. The proviso is that 'from a normative perspective fair compromise-formation does not stand on its own', but needs to be buttressed by moral discourse concerning the framework within which bargaining occurs.[3] This dependency on a morally secured framework is explained by Habermas on two grounds. First, since bargaining is a strategic game in which power is used in order to influence the opponent, the fairness of each bargaining process can only be established via a morally grounded procedure which (a) provides all the interested parties with 'equal chances to take part in the bargaining process', (b) grants them equal chances to exert influence on one another during the actual bargaining, and (c) thereby creates generally equal chances for the assertion of all the affected interests.[4] Second, bargaining is acceptable in lieu of a moral or ethical process of will formation only when no generalizable interests, but only particular interests, are at stake in the problem at hand, and, as Habermas is ready to admit – without fully realizing that this move introduces a moment of circularity into his argument – the general or particular quality of interests 'can be tested only in moral discourses' (1996a: 167).

The restriction, instead, concerns political will formation and also ethical-political discourses. According to Habermas, they cannot be replaced entirely by bargaining processes aimed at reaching compromises. The reason is that 'their results must be at least compatible with moral principles' (1996a: 167). In fact, within the democratic political process, Habermas understands legislative and parliamentary debates as the sum total of the three forms of discourse such as bargaining, ethical and moral discourse. Aside from pragmatically determining what is concretely feasible, observes Habermas,

> political opinion- and will-formation must first of all clarify three questions: the question underlying compromise-formation, that is how we *can reconcile* competing preferences; the ethical-political question of who we are and who we seriously *want to be*; and the moral-practical question of how we *ought to act* in accordance with principles of justice. (1996a: 180)

To these three aspects of the formation of a political will correspond three properties of the collective political will: in bargaining we observe the emergence of an *aggregated* will, in ethical discourses of an *authentic* will and in moral discourses of an *autonomous* will (1996a: 180).

Two questions are raised by Habermas's account of fair compromises, which point to two residues of the model of generalizing universalism based on determinant judgment. First, if moral discourse has to ascertain the inexistence of a generalizable interest before fair bargaining can *legitimately* take place, does this not presuppose, contrary to what is explicitly stated in other passages, that on the whole moral discourse is *unaffected* by cultural situatedness? For otherwise, in all those cases in which the object of contention is exactly the existence of a universalizable interest – affirmed by one party, denied by the other – Habermas's account would lead to a stalemate. In fact, no moral deliberation could take place because the existence of a generalizable interest is uncertain, and no fair bargaining could legitimately take place because the existence of a generalizable interest is not *ruled out* either.

Second, at one point Habermas states that what distinguishes a fair compromise from rational agreement on moral issues is the fact that 'whereas a rationally motivated consensus rests on reasons that convince all the parties *in the same way*, a compromise can be accepted by the different parties each for its own *different* reasons' (1996a: 166). Under conditions of cultural pluralism, however, and assuming that the meaning acquired by a motivation or an argument is also a function of the cultural background presupposed by it, it is hard to understand how the reasons for agreeing can be *exactly the same*. In the context of a multicultural state, for instance, we could envisage a rational agreement of people belonging to quite different cultures on protecting the dignity and the privacy of the individual. In this case, is it not an excessively stringent requirement that the reasons for valuing dignity or privacy be *exactly the same*? Furthermore, doesn't this standard commit Habermas to the universal translatability of all vocabularies into each other or into a metavocabulary? And in any case, given that the choice of the vocabulary to be used for the purpose of comparing the parties' reasons for agreeing cannot be *irrelevant*, at least under the premises of the linguistic turn, in which vocabulary are we to ascertain whether the reasons for accepting a norm on the part of actors who subscribe to rival worldviews or conceptions of the good are the same?[5]

Aside from these local resurgences of the older model of generalizing universalism, Habermas's discursive conception of normative validity remains affected by an ambiguity located at its core – an ambiguity affecting the notion of generalization underlying the test of dialogical generalization. The ambiguity in question is part and parcel both of the principle 'D' and of its moral specification, but for simplicity's sake I will develop my point mainly with reference to the specification of 'D' for the *moral* realm, which runs: 'A norm is just only if all can will that it be obeyed by each in comparable situations' (1996a: 161). My point, however, holds just as well in the more general case of principle 'D', according to which: 'Just those action norms are valid to which all possibly affected persons could agree as participants in rational discourses' (1996a: 107). The ambiguity concerns the terms 'will' and 'agree'.

What does it really mean that everyone can *will* or *agree* that a norm be generally observed by everybody in comparable situations? Does it mean that everyone can *tolerate* that everybody else observes the norm in comparable contexts? Does it mean that everyone can *accept*, consistently with all their preferences, that the norm be observed by everybody else? Does it mean that the general observance of the norm is compatible with everyone's maintaining their self-respect? Does it mean that everyone can *authentically* will that the norm be universally observed? The list of questions could be extended further. The absence of whatever indication on Habermas's part leaves the meaning of the terms 'will' and 'agree' open to almost *any* interpretation. Two of these readings, however, stand out as more plausible than any other, though there is no clear indication that Habermas has chosen one over the other, and there is also reason to believe that were he to choose between these two meanings of 'D' and of its moral specification 'Dm', the whole edifice of the communicative paradigm would suffer severe damage – so much does it depend, for its stability, on exploiting this ambiguity.

While one of these two interpretations supports the sharp distinctions thus far drawn by Habermas between *grounding* and *applying* norms, the *right* and the *good, morality* and *ethics*, but is almost indefensible, the other reading conversely appears a much more plausible reconstruction of our intuitions concerning the generalizing moment in moral validity, but ends up undermining the dichotomous understanding of the moral-practical realm that Habermas wishes to defend. Let us briefly consider these two interpretations.

According to the first interpretation, the terms 'will' (occurring in 'Dm') and 'agree' (occurring in 'D') can be interpreted as meaning 'to wish or to consent to, on the basis of the totality of one's volitions, preferences and *interests*'. This reading brings the test close to an inquiry into whether a candidate norm can meet what Rousseau would call 'the will of all', as opposed to the general will. The universalization test so conceived takes on the features of a *consistency* test fully internal to the determinant judgment model of validity. When we assess the fairness or moral validity of a norm, according to this interpretation, we try to determine – in a dialogical context that satisfies certain ideal conditions – whether everyone can reasonably be said to will, *on the basis of his present volitions, preferences and interests*, the state of affairs that presumably, to the best of our empirical knowledge, will result from the general observance of the given norm in comparable situations. We could introduce further restrictions, for example to the effect that the preferences and volitions that we take into account be not precipitous or formed on the basis of first impressions, but preferences and volitions submitted to critical scrutiny and formulated in a state of 'reflective equilibrium'. The problematic quality of this interpretation of 'D' would not be thereby significantly changed.

The good news is that, if understood along these lines, the principle of universalization fully supports the sharp distinction that Habermas wants to draw between ethics and morality. In fact, the universalism of *moral* validity, impartiality, fairness or justice remains solidly anchored to the consistency of the consequences of the norm and the preferences, taken in equal consideration, of all the concerned ones. The kind of universalism implicit in this first interpretation of the generalization test is indeed radically discontinuous with the 'softer' normativity implicit in our 'clinical intuitions' concerning the state of an identity and what is *good* for it. In principle – no matter how distant 'principle' in this case is from 'reality' – one can always imagine a state of the world, considered from the perspective of the preferences and volitions entertained by its inhabitants, such that the universal validity of a given norm would be irrefutable.

The bad news is that there is a price to be paid for purchasing this strong, 'context-transcending' view of moral validity. The price consists in the fact that the adoption of this interpretation of 'D' and 'Dm' would implicitly undermine the *intersubjective* and *communicative* dimension of what would then remain a '*discourse* ethics' only by virtue of its name. If we read 'D' and 'Dm' in this way we could run the generalization test in terms of formal logic, as the search for inconsistencies that arise *between two lists of propositions*: (a) the list of the propositions which specify, to the best of our present knowledge, the foreseeable consequences and side-effects of the observance of a given norm, and (b) the list of the propositions which specify, to the best of our present knowledge, the volitions and preferences that everyone brings into the deliberative process. This interpretation not only would require that we bring the cultural plurality of the preferences of the members of humanity down to the unity of one language of universal commensuration without any significant loss of meaning. It would also render discourse *superfluous* for moral purposes. Discourse could still keep a relevance as a heuristic tool for better compiling the two lists and possibly for revising them in light of critical considerations, but not for actually comparing the two lists. It would be useful for operating *within* each list, but useless for operating *between* lists. In fact, it is hard to see what the *discursive*, *communicative* or *dialogical* quality of the comparison between the list of the consequences and the list of the preferences would or could add to the factual presence or absence of semantic inconsistencies between them. Rational consensus on the examined norm would not *constitute* its validity, but would merely *follow* from the fact that the effects of the norm do not actually contradict any volition or preference of the participants.[6]

The other possible interpretation of 'D' (and 'Dm') avoids these difficulties. According to this alternative reading, to say that a norm is fair, impartial or just means that it has passed a generalization test conceived as the mental experiment of aggregating the foreseeable consequences and side-effects of the general observance of the norm into a synthetic and holistic image of 'the way the world would look if the norm were generally observed' and then asking each and every moral actor whether the way in which things would go,

the state of the world, would be such that all of us – *qua* citizens of a hypothetical world republic – would still recognize in it the image of who we want
to be, of the life that we want to lead together. To affirm that a norm is valid
means, from the standpoint of a principle of generalization reinterpreted
along these lines, that everyone can equally want to live in a world shaped,
among other things, by the norm in question – that we all would still recognize this world as 'our own' and not as an 'alien' one.

The good news now is that under this interpretation 'D' and 'Dm' become
genuinely dialogical or intersubjective. In so far as they embed also a project-
constitutive and 'evaluative' moment concerning who we want to be, the
outcome of the test really depends on the outcome of discourse. There is no
way in which one could claim to know the outcome of such discourse – a discourse which, of course, could be envisaged as being conducted
hypothetically or counterfactually – in the same way as one could claim to
know, antecedently to any real discourse, whether the two lists which record
the foreseeable effects of a norm and the parties' preferences are consistent
with one another. While – on the first reading of 'D' and 'Dm' – knowing the
contents of the two lists would be strictly equivalent to knowing whether they
are mutually consistent, in the holistic reading of the generalization test
knowing what the world would look like and knowing the preferences of
people would not put us in the position of knowing whether, starting from
'these' preferences, everyone would want to live 'there', in 'that' world.

The bad news, however, is that the greater plausibility of this version of the
principles 'D' and 'Dm', as well as their truly intersubjective quality, are not
without costs. By adopting this reading we could no longer consistently subscribe to the Habermasian distinctions between the logic of moral discourse
and that of ethical discourse, between the universalism of the former and the
context boundedness of the latter – certainly not in the formulations that
these distinctions have received thus far.

While in *Between Facts and Norms* Habermas had already characterized
moral questions as questions concerning *what is equally good for all*, but such
formulation appeared in the special context of his discussion of the justness
of a policy,[7] in a more recent essay Habermas has adopted a more general formulation, which seems to finally dissipate the ambiguity. 'Ethical questions,'
writes Habermas, 'cannot be judged from the "moral" standpoint of whether
something is "equally good for everybody"' (1993a: 137).

This reformulation, however, does not eliminate all the difficulties. First, it
is hard to see in what sense a moral judgment about what is 'equally good for
everybody' can be independent from an ethical conception of the good, and
more specifically from an ethical understanding 'of the kind of society we
want to live in', unless 'equally good' is interpreted once again reductively as
'equally compatible with everybody's preferences'. In his response to a similar objection raised by McCarthy,[8] Habermas calls this point 'trivial' as a
sociological statement and ambiguous as a philosophical one. Philosophically
it allows for two interpretations: a stronger and less acceptable one, according to which a conception of the right conceptually *depends on* (and

presumably is *inseparable from*) a conception of the good, and a weaker one according to which our articulation of a notion of justice must inevitably find *its point of departure* in a conception of the good, but then in the course of the critical confrontation between the partial approaches to justice the fluctuating general concept of justice can still be unfolded in a way which is, *in principle*, context-independent. I find this response problematic. In fact, to argue, as Habermas does, that while the perspective boundedness of our running of the generalization test is only an inescapable *starting point*, the parties' initially dissonant perspectives may change in the course of discourse as a result of discourse – for example, because the parties become aware of the intrinsic worthiness of other perspectives as well as of the weakness of their own – and that in this reflexive relativization of perspectives lies our best bet for a universalistic notion of justice, means to concede my own and McCarthy's main point: namely, that our chances of ever coming to an agreement on justice do depend on the modifications undergone by our conceptions of the good, and therefore that justice or the right is really *not independent of the good*, at least not in the way Habermas wants it to be.

It seems to me that there could be another way of solving the tension that arises between the non-reductive interpretation of the generalization test on the one hand and our desire to keep a distinction between ethical and moral discourse on the other hand. We could say that while in ethical judgment the 'we' whose good is being evaluated is a *particular* we, in moral judgment it is a sort of *universal* 'we', a 'we' in which every living human being (and possibly the future generations) is included. To be sure, we could still distinguish between morality and ethics but this distinction would hardly be a distinction in kind. It would be just a matter of degree, of the scope of the 'we' whose good we evaluate. The moral, as opposed to ethical, validity, impartiality or fairness of a norm, according to this interpretation, would then be measured by its compatibility with our intuitions concerning the *good* for humankind.

Under this interpretation of the generalization test, moral judgment would indeed be somehow more universalistic than ethical judgment, but in a sense that would make the internal consistency of Habermas's position very precarious. The apparent capacity of moral judgment to 'burst the provinciality of contexts asunder' would take on the character of an illusion, a *trompe-l'oeil*, a mirage in which the desires of the desert wayfarer are reflected. Moral judgment would indeed be more universalistic than ethical judgment, but only because it takes into account the good of an identity which by definition is the largest imaginable one and includes all others, not because its internal logic, its presuppositions and the way in which it is reached are any different and any less *situated* or context-dependent than those typical of ethical judgment. While truly doing justice to the intersubjective character of the test of dialogical generalization, this way of understanding the universality of moral judgments would then clash with Habermas's initial programme of a *cognitivistic* and *formal* discourse ethics. In fact, moral judgment understood as judgment as to what is equally good for everybody cannot be cognitivistic, in that if we follow the second reading of the generalization test the candidate norms need neither be valid or non-valid (goodness for everybody appears rather to be a matter of degree), nor be demonstrably good or not good (the goodness for everybody of a norm depends on an evaluative standpoint which, differently from consistency with existent preferences, cannot be made the object of demonstration). Similarly, moral judgment so understood cannot be formal because there is simply no way of rendering such a judgment without assuming a substantive, evaluative stance concerning the desirability of the state of the world to which the observance of a norm would lead.[9]

Despite this persisting ambiguity and the several remnants of an older model of universalism and validity, however, Habermas's discursive account of justice remains, along with Rawls's political conception of justice as fairness, one of the most significant attempts, in our century, to provide a non-relativist framework for conceiving of normative validity. Habermas must be also credited for having succeeded in differentiating his original intuition in such a way as to create a dynamic framework capable of encompassing and integrating all the aspects of the practical sphere – from distributive justice to politics, from law to the notion of the good life. The suspicion remains, however, that the keystone on which the solidity of the entire construction rests – the dialogical reformulation of the Kantian test of generalization – might itself be less firm than Habermas would have us think.

The Tension within Dworkin's View of Normative Validity

The case of Dworkin's view of normative validity reflects a somewhat different balance of motifs. Differently from Rawls and Habermas, Dworkin's theoretical trajectory cannot be described in terms of a transition from an earlier understanding of normative validity enmeshed in the logic of modern generalizing universalism to a subsequent reformulation along lines more inspired by the model of reflective judgment universalism. Dworkin's legal theory has consistently been interpretive, and thus intrinsically related to the reflective judgment model, from the outset. As has been argued in Chapter 3, Dworkin's constant referring to the notion of 'principles' by no means represents an endorsement of a view of normative validity as subsumption of the particular under the right principles. Even in the most explicitly and polemically anti-relativist piece written by him – 'What Justice Isn't' in *A Matter of Principle* (1985: 214–20) – Dworkin never defends the idea that a viable notion of justice could be formulated in merely procedural terms. To the extent that we strive for generality and reflexivity, we do so in order to decide 'which of our traditional distinctions and discriminations are genuine and which spurious, which contribute to the flourishing of the ideals we want, after reflection, to embrace, and which serve only to protect us from the personal costs of that demanding process' (1985: 220).

Also in Dworkin's approach, however, it is possible to find a few traces of the older model of generalizing universalism, which most of the time take the form of incongruities, internal tensions and, in one instance, of the longing for some kind of intuitionist moral realism.[10] The influence of the determinant judgment conception of validity can be observed also in the form of a reluctance, on Dworkin's part, to follow all the implications of his aesthetic model of justice.

One of the advantages of Dworkin's *integrity* or authenticity approach to questions of normative validity and of justice over other approaches – such as Habermas's discursive approach or Rawls's 'method of avoiding' – is that it enables us to choose between different solutions to moral conflict which appear *equally successful* in bracketing the controversial issues or in satisfying the criterion of being 'equally good for everyone'. However, the integrity or authenticity approach reveals its superiority also in the converse case, namely when the tenuousness of the common ground shared by the rival positions makes it hard to find *any* way of bracketing successfully the controversial issues or any solution that is consensually recognized to be in the equal interest of everyone. In a case such as the abolition of slavery, for example, the Rawlsian notion of the political as uncontroversial seems impotent to capture our intuitions concerning the rightness of a political decision – on which more will be said in the next chapter – which was neither uncontroversial among the parties nor justifiable by reference to some Archimedean point outside history. Equally impotent seems the discourse approach: for the test of dialogical generalization can only be applied if we agree on who is a suitable participant and thus has a right to be included – which is precisely what is controversial between the supporters of slavery and the abolitionists. Dworkin's view of normative validity in terms of integrity proves more helpful, but only if a certain internal tension, which in turn reflects a significant trace of generalizing universalism, is dissolved.

The text where such tension, internal to the integrity approach, can be found is *Foundations of Liberal Equality*. In the account of justice developed there Dworkin introduces some modifications in the aesthetic model of justice previously articulated in *Law's Empire*. On the one hand, he advocates a strategy of *continuity* in opposition to the Rawlsian and Habermasian attempt to sharply distinguish the logic of arguments about justice from the logic of arguments about the good. This strategy aims at making 'liberal political morality seem continuous rather than discontinuous with appealing philosophical views about the good life' (1990: 6). On the other hand, the aesthetic approach to the *good*, epitomized by the 'challenge' view of the good life, is now combined by Dworkin with a kind of intuitionist moral realism when matters of *justice* are concerned.

In the opening sections of *Foundations of Liberal Equality* Dworkin defends convincingly what he calls 'the model of challenge' over the 'model of impact' as a framework for making sense of the goodness of a good life. While according to the model of impact the value of a good life consists in the greatness, importance, or exceptional quality of the objective results that it leaves behind when it is completed, according to the model of challenge a good life 'has the kind of value a brilliant dive has and retains when

the ripples have died away' (1990: 8). The first model has the elitist implication that a life which for any reason fails to make any 'big difference' to the
course of the world has not been worthy at all, even if its failing cannot be
imputed to a lack of moral qualities on the part of the actor.[11] The model of
challenge, instead, considers 'living a human life' as a practice with its own
inherent standards of excellence. One can do a great job at living in the conditions one happens to find oneself in even though what one achieves has no
impact on the external world. This way of thinking about the value of a
good life is called *aesthetic* by Dworkin because it incorporates an irreducibly reflective standard – from this perspective 'good', as an adjective
applicable to 'life', ultimately means 'congruent with itself', 'authentic' – but
also because, like the more complex aesthetic practices, it presupposes the
challenge of defining the object of the practice (in this case the living of a
human life) each time anew.[12] In a good life we admire not just the skilful-
ness in carrying out a plan but also and especially the actor's ability to form
an imaginative, creative life-project out of the available symbolic material.[13]

Judgments about justice at first sight do not seem to follow a different
logic. When it comes to the contest between competing conceptions of justice, Dworkin points out, the consensual paradigm offers no solution.
Neither in the Rawlsian nor in the Habermasian version does the notion of
consensus offer any advice to anyone who has to choose between rival conceptions of justice.[14] In the first-person attitude of a participant who has to
contribute to the formation of a not yet existent consensus, obviously the
consensus models offer no help – their nightmare is the tiebreaker's situation.
On the other hand, if we adopted 'consistency with the tradition and history
of a community' as the guideline for orienting our assessment of competing
conceptions of justice, then, given the fact that 'the history of any community includes controversy as well as tradition' we can find ourselves in a
situation in which

> two very different political conceptions, which would justify very different contro-
> versial political decisions now, might each fit the record and rhetoric of a
> community's political history roughly equally well. (1990: 32)

For example, justice as fairness could very well provide an account of our settled beliefs about religious toleration and the rejection of slavery, while
utilitarianism could provide a superior reconstruction of equally widespread
and deepseated beliefs concerning the acceptability of economic inequalities
for the sake of the general welfare. A contest of arguments and counter-
arguments must then be run to decide which conception of justice provides
the *better* reconstruction of our intuitions, *all things considered.* Dworkin
points out, still in the vein of *Law's Empire*, that

> we can mean only one thing by 'better' in this context: one conception is better
> than its rival if the justification it offers is superior as a matter of political moral-
> ity: it makes the rhetoric and history it interprets a more attractive story politically.
> (1990: 33)

Dworkin stops short, however, of fully drawing out the consequences of his position and in the end relapses back into a kind of intuitionist foundationalism. Shying away from accounting for the normative force of justice in terms of the attractiveness of a narrative – the truly consistent conclusion to be derived from the premises of his interpretive approach – Dworkin proceeds to note that the political attractiveness of a certain version of the history of a community will itself be controversial and that, in order to decide 'which of two general theories of justice . . . provides a more just interpretation of [a] community's history', one 'would need a further theory of justice, more abstract still, to decide that question, and so forth into higher and higher levels' (1990: 34). In order to break out of the circle, Dworkin concludes, we must fall back on 'some conception of justice whose categorical force we can defend in some *other* way, as not dependent on or derived from its congruence with the community's traditions' (1990: 34). Justice cannot be a matter of convention, at least from a first-person perspective: 'we must rely on what (we believe) is *true* about matters of justice' (1990: 34). The fact that some principle or set of principles is what we traditionally believe justice to be or, in a corrected version, what we believe helps us 'make the most' of our tradition, *cannot* for Dworkin count for an independent argument in favour of a specific view of justice.

How this passage fits with the bulk of what Dworkin has been saying about justice in his previous work remains unclear. Three problems come immediately to mind. First, if such a thing exists as an independent 'truth' in matters of justice, namely a truth of the matter independent of our own communal perspective (and tradition), then why would we need an interpretive perspective of the kind outlined in *A Matter of Principle* and *Law's Empire* at all? In fact, a kind of Platonist intuitionism would seem then our best choice for reconstructing our understanding of justice. For *interpretation* – as opposed to revelation, intuition and deduction from self-evident principles – seems to be a meaningful perspective only where no objective truths are assumed to exist.

Second, the argument that the process of assessing 'which of two general theories of justice . . . provides a more just interpretation of [a] community's history' would generate an infinite regress of theories of justice of higher and higher order seems unwarranted. In fact, it appears that the contestants would differ on their interpretations of the community's legal and political history but would nonetheless share a common uncontested criterion – namely 'fit'. If they didn't, there wouldn't be any controversy at all, just as there is no controversy but mere diversity between totally unrelated life-worlds, paradigms, language games or cultures. Thus, it is unclear what grounds Dworkin's assumption to the effect that linking the notion of justice with fit or consistency with the overall background culture would entrap us into an infinite regress.

Third, in his claim that justice possesses a dimension of moral truth independent of narratives Dworkin seems to conflate two different positions which need to be carefully distinguished. He conflates a premodern kind of conventionalism or traditionalism – best epitomized by the proposition (a)

'This principle or set of principles is what we traditionally believe justice to be' – with a postmetaphysical recourse to the conditions of the realization of an identity understood as the only 'foundations' left after the fall of all Archimedean points. This latter position is best epitomized by proposition (b) 'This principle or set of principles is what we believe helps us *make the most of our tradition.*' In rightly rejecting (a), but failing to distinguish it from (b), Dworkin misses the possibility of reconciling his aesthetic model of ethics, as developed in *Foundations of Liberal Equality*, with a reflective judgment view of justice consistent with the integrity approach developed in his previous works.

The tension between Dworkin's moral realist understanding of justice and his integrity approach to normative validity, however, can be dissolved through a different strategy. Applying Dworkin's theory of interpretation to his own work and trying to make the most of it, a different account of the meaning of the expression 'true about matters of justice' can be developed. In this new account the meaning of 'true about matters of justice' is still different from that of the phrase 'congruent with the community's traditions', but remains consistent with the integrity approach. This alternative account includes two steps.

The first step consists of acknowledging that also the communal life of communities – as defined by Dworkin in 'Liberal Community' (1989a) – can succeed or fail, and that, just like individual success or failure, also communal failure or success must be understood in terms of the model of challenge. The enduring fascination exerted by the Athenian democracy or the Roman republic rests ultimately on the notion of succeeding uniquely well at a task (in this case: communal living) which someone (in this case: an entire political community) has done an exceptionally good job of defining anew. And, certainly, Dworkin's account of the 'liberal community' allows us to include a certain view of justice as part and parcel of the communal life which belongs to the whole of a society.

The second step consists of drawing an important distinction. When, at particular junctures of the history of a community so conceived, conflicts arise – such as the conflict over slavery in the United States of the mid nineteenth century – which reveal that underneath a seemingly shared political culture rival conceptions of justice exist, and it is impossible to identify a common ground 'thick' enough to support a practically and institutionally viable solution, then Dworkin's contention that we can only solve the controversy by appealing to what we believe to be 'true about matters of justice' can be vindicated – *consistently* with his interpretive approach – by introducing a distinction between identities of different scope. It would be tempting to say that justice requires us to adopt the solution which makes that communal life more valuable in terms of the challenge model. That move, however, would dedifferentiate our practical vocabulary: the right and the good would become not just continuous, but actually *indistinguishable*. Instead, to anticipate here a point which I will develop more fully in Chapter 7, the distinction between the standpoint of the right and that of the good can be rearticulated with reference to the *scope* of the identities submitted to critical evaluation. We can say that the abolition of slavery was *good* for the United States because it made the history of the United States 'a more attractive story politically' than it would have been otherwise. On the other hand, we could say that abolition was also *right*, *just* or *fair* because it made the *history of humankind* better – i.e. once again 'a more attractive story, politically' – than it would have been otherwise. Now, the validity of the two judgments expressed by propositions (a) 'The history of the United States would have been less attractive had slavery continued to exist' and (b) 'The history of humankind would have been less attractive had slavery continued to exist' can no more be the object of *demonstration* than any aesthetic judgment. But the difficulty of demonstrating to sceptical opponents what justice requires is beside the point. Undemonstrability does not undermine the legitimacy of claiming that a certain view of justice is the one which fits most with whom we (as members of this community, citizens of this country or members of humanity) are and want to be. As Robert Nozick aptly put it: 'The lack of a procedure guaranteed to answer a question does not show the question has no correct answer' (1981: 482).

The important point is that such a reformulation of Dworkin's view of justice would bring it in line with his contention that ultimately our conception of what justice requires must be defended on grounds other than congruency with the tradition of the community. In fact, our sense of what justice requires is defended in terms of its congruency not with the community's traditions, but with a certain idea of the flourishing of humanity as a whole. Furthermore, such reformulated view presupposes no privileged access to any kind of truth independent of our interpretations and narratives.

A similar radicalization of the theses and implications left not worked out by Dworkin is required if we want to solve another internal difficulty of his interpretive approach. Let us go back to one point which remained only cursorily addressed in Chapter 3: the distinction between rules and principles. The exemplary, as opposed to generalizing, model of normative validity underlying Dworkin's approach leads him to account for constitutional adjudication in terms of *balancing principles*, rather than *applying rules*. Yet Dworkin is very parsimonious in offering indications concerning how it is possible for us to tell principles from rules and deciding controversies on the status of normative provisions. As we have seen in Chapter 3, Dworkin maintains that the status of a normative and, more specifically, constitutional provision is 'a question of interpretation or, if you prefer, translation', to be settled with reference to what the framers of a constitution 'meant to say'. Once again, a different, more elegant and consistent solution to the problem can be drawn from Dworkin's integrity approach to normative validity. Applying the central insight of that approach in a reflexive way, it becomes possible to claim that a normative expression counts as a rule or as a principle depending on which alternative, in the judge's considered judgment, would make the most of the legal culture as a whole. Our arguments and controversies then revolve around questions such as: what legal consequences would derive from considering the minimum age of 18 years for obtaining a driver's licence a principle? For example, we would have to balance the principle against competing principles, such as the right to mobility. Perhaps we would also have to determine which complex of competencies is implicitly presupposed to have been acquired by an 18-year-old, so that their proven possession on the part of, for instance, a 16-year-old would entitle her to legitimately obtain a driver's licence. The practical applicability of the provision would then almost vanish and the reflection of thus interpreting the norm on the overall legal culture would be to render it almost ludicrous. On the other hand, if we interpreted the provision of freedom of speech as a rule we would generate equally absurd consequences. Unless we were prepared to reject all exceptions to the rule, the very breadth and ubiquitousness of the phenomenon that the norm aims at regulating – as opposed to the conceptually more easily definable act of 'driving an automobile' – would entrap us in the task of setting up a casuistry of all the possible concrete cases which potentially require a suspension of the rule, a casuistry that would approximate in complexity the task of mapping all the possible instances of social interaction.

The kind of radical interpretive reflexivity underlying this solution to the problem of telling rules from principles can be found at other junctures of Dworkin's theory. In *Law's Empire*, for instance, he rejects the idea that the type of judgment presupposed by his approach might concern, as some of Dworkin's critics have claimed, the degree of freedom that a judge can avail herself of in departing from the American Constitution as a historical document. A judge, rightly claims Dworkin, 'has nothing he *can* depart from or cleave to until he has constructed a novel-in-progress from the text, and the various decisions we have canvassed are all decisions he must make just to do this' (1986: 238). The same radically reflexive perspective can be applied to the problem of distinguishing principles and rules. A judge cannot, strictly speaking, be said to misperceive the status of a norm as a rule or a principle, because that status does not pre-exist her judgment like an essence pre-exists its manifestations. Rather, such status is determined by a metajudgment that the judge is in principle required to render – though, in practice, most of the time takes for granted or derives from the legal tradition – on whether assigning the status of a rule or of a principle to the provision at issue would fit best with his interpretive vision of law as a whole 'at its best'. This solution to the problem of distinguishing rules and principles would bring Dworkin's integrity approach to the question of normative validity truly in line with its own underlying hermeneutic inspiration.

Beyond Constitutional Majoritarianism

As we move on to consider once again the work of Bruce Ackerman, we can see a peculiar way of combining the reflective and the determinant judgment models of normative validity. On the one hand, the transition from the kind of questions addressed in *Social Justice in the Liberal State* (1980) to the framework developed in the two volumes thus far published of *We the People* signals, as we have seen, the rising of the model of judgment to a position of pre-eminence – a change that appeared somehow necessitated by the substantive shift of Ackerman's inquiry. On the other hand, despite its taking the form of a *situated judgment* about whether the conservation or a specific transformation of the Constitution is most appropriate for a given historical identity, despite the impossibility of invoking external criteria for determining when it is appropriate to initiate a process of deliberation concerning possible constitutional changes, and despite the impossibility of determining, on the basis of objective criteria, when the People have spoken their mind, the dualist view of democracy falls short of explicitly articulating a reflective judgment view of normative validity. It seems to remain in a sort of paradigmatic limbo, a kind of approach to normative validity that naturally rests on judgment but lacks an understanding of the workings of reflective judgment – a paradoxical judgment approach without judgment. How is this possible?

In a way, Ackerman's approach brings to its extreme consequences a view of normative validity as contingent which we have already found in *Political Liberalism* (Rawls 1993). Within Rawls's political conception of justice a certain tension still subsisted – which Habermas has critically highlighted from his own point of view[15] – between the contingency of the formation of the overlapping consensus on which the operating of political justice depends and the standards of reasonableness which any form of public use of reason has to fulfil. It is instructive to compare Rawls and Ackerman on the legitimacy of higher lawmaking. In his discussion of the legitimate avenues to constitutional change Rawls dissents from the idea that there are no structural internal limits to what the People can legitimately and validly will. The limits are to be found, in his opinion, in the intrinsic meaning of the practice of higher lawmaking: the formal following of the procedures of Article Five of the Constitution of the United States is not sufficient, according to Rawls, to ground the normative legitimacy of an amendment. The practice of amendment thus far, argues Rawls, has been aimed at adjusting 'basic constitutional values to changing political and social circumstances', or at incorporating 'into the constitution a broader and more inclusive understanding of those values' (1993: 238–9), or at removing certain weaknesses of institutional design that have become manifest in constitutional practice. In all the cases that have thus far occurred it is possible to say that 'the amendments brought the Constitution more in line with its original promise' (1993: 238–9). This 'long historical practice,' according to Rawls, has acquired enough *normative force* over two centuries to 'place restrictions on what can now count as an amendment, whatever was true at the beginning' (1993: 239). The normative force of past practice, for example, would authorize the Supreme Court to strike down an amendment that abolished freedom of conscience and established Christianity as a state religion on the ground that such an amendment, even if approved through the procedure specified in Article Five, would simply run against the meaning of the Constitution as established through historical record and amount to its *subversion* rather than to an act of bringing it more in line with itself or of adapting it to a changed historical context. Ironically, if we pressed Rawls's text with the further question 'How are we to determine whether a given amendment amounts to a completion or a subversion of the "original promise" of the Constitution?', the answer that we could gather – consistently with the whole of Rawls's approach – would point in the direction of a reflective judgment approach. The answer, namely, would make reference not to a set of external criteria, but to some notion of congruity similar to Dworkin's 'integrity'.

In Ackerman's approach as articulated in *Foundations* (1991), instead, apparently the Constitution has to match solely the will of the People as manifested in acts of considered judgment occurring in the forms discussed in Chapter 4. As the will of the People changes, the Constitution can legitimately change in whatever direction, provided that the new amendment reflects that will. In this total openness of normative validity to contingency, what gets undermined is precisely the dimension of judgment. For the very distinction between the *empirical* substance of the People's will and the *normative* 'ought' to which such will should be responsive is eliminated. The conception of constitutional politics spelled out by Ackerman, in fact, only preserves the distinction between the 'considerate' and the 'immediate' or 'unreflective' quality of the People's judgment in constitutional matters, but at the price of eliminating any sense in which the validity of that considered judgment obeys anything beyond the empirical, subjective will of the ones who judge. The right constitutional decision is in the end what is willed by the appropriate majority of the People, alerted, informed and duly mobilized about the matter. All moment of universalism, even in the singular, exemplary and undemonstrable sense of reflective judgment universalism, seems to become lost in this *constitutional*, as opposed to *ordinary*, *majoritarianism*.[16] In fact, if the Constitution is understood as reflecting an unchallengeable will, it becomes hard to account for the sense in which we might feel that we can learn from the constitutional history of other peoples or from our own past history of constitutional debates. Also, it becomes impossible conceptually to form the notion of the People's *being mistaken* in making a certain choice, except in the reductive sense of their rendering a premature, less than considerate, judgment.

There is an explanation for this eventual loss of all normative content in a view of normative validity which at various junctures of its development includes significant elements of a reflective judgment approach. The explanation can be found in the thread that links Ackerman's anti-utilitarian argument in *Social Justice in the Liberal State* with the constitutional majoritarianism of *Foundations*. Underlying both is a reductive notion of the fulfilment, realization or authenticity of an identity. In *Social Justice in the Liberal State*, Ackerman criticized a utilitarian view centred on 'equal fulfilment' for generating distributive schemes that discriminate people whose notion of fulfilment is not amenable to the same quantitative kind of assessment applicable to those who build their identity around, for instance, mountain climbing. He could not have considered his critique conclusive, however, had he himself had a notion of fulfilment broader than the one he imputes to utilitarianism – had he had a conception of fulfilment not just as the measurable extent to which given wishes are met, but rather as the extent to which observable conduct can be apprehended as part and parcel of one and the same intended pattern, much in the same way as a series of facial features is holistically apprehended as the uniqueness of a 'face', or as a series of sentences is holistically apprehended as one specific 'text'. Under this more differentiated view of fulfilment, self-realization or authenticity, the bearer of an identity is the author of her identity project, but by no means the final arbiter in assessing the extent to which her conduct fits her identity. The predicament of the actor resembles, once again, the case of the artist: no one can suggest what work of art she should conceive, but once she sets a project under way, it becomes possible for critics and fellow artists to comment on the quality of its execution. If we adopt this broader and more sensible conception of fulfilment, Ackerman's anti-utilitarian objection against distributing resources in such a way as to ensure equal chances for fulfilment ceases to apply.

This reductive view of fulfilment or authenticity is operative also underneath the argument for dualism in *Foundations*. Problematic is not so much Ackerman's rejection of structural entrenchment as understood by Rawls.[17] For it may well be that Rawls, by understanding the legitimacy of higher lawmaking only as a function of bringing the Constitution more in line with its initial promise, errs too much on the conservative side: after all, the New Deal produced a *new* understanding of 'due process' and rights rather than a better alignment of the Constitution with its initial project. Problematic is the idea that the rightful rejection of foundationalism implies that there are no substantive limits whatever to the People's will, provided that such will is formed in the canonical sequence of signalling, proposing, mobilizing consensus and codification. Problematic is Ackerman's notion that there is no legitimate standpoint from which the congruence of the People's will with the People's project can be assessed because the People's project is analytically defined away as whatever the People (in their considered judgment) want at a certain point in time. Problematic is the move according to which the rejection of an external standpoint, in the name of which the philosopher could indicate to the People the constitutional revisions that they should pursue, translates in an analytical coincidence of what the People want with what the People should want. The single most important residue of the modern view of universalism in Ackerman's view of normative validity lies in the recurrence, within his framework, of a dichotomical universe in which we have either the compellingness of external standards and criteria or the total subjectivism of an unchallengeable will. This crude dichotomy in the end stands in the way of unfolding the broad potentials of the dualist approach – and reduces it to the dimension of a constitutional majoritarianism.

A different picture seems to emerge as the project of *We the People* reaches its second stage with the publication of *Transformations* (1998). Underlying Ackerman's account of the 'unconventional' aspects of important constitutional moments such as the Founding, the Reconstruction and the New Deal is a view of normative validity in the realm of higher lawmaking that certainly goes beyond the limits of a constitutional majoritarianism. In fact, Ackerman carefully emphasizes the distance that separates the American constitutional actors' attempt to bring about a significant realignment of the political identity of the People through the unconventional use of existing institutions from the French and the Russian revolutionaries' understanding of their praxis as a *total rupture* with the institutional past of their countries.

In the transformations reconstructed by Ackerman, the actors' attempt to change existing constitutional provisions is in the service of creatively transforming, and not of remaking anew, the political identity of the American people. In this sense, the validity of the new normative achievements is not simply a function of their mirroring a consensus that can arguably be attributed to the People, but appears to be also somehow dependent on their coherence with pre-existent patterns and with an overall project. Within Ackerman's new perspective, the notion of the flourishing of the political identity of the American People as a politically, as opposed to ethnically or culturally, integrated nation throughout its changing constitutional cultures functions as a unifying normative framework that sets limits to the unconventionality of the unconventional means deployed by the actors in order to bring about the consensus necessary for higher lawmaking. At the same time, the notion of the flourishing of the political identity of the American People provides that evaluative backdrop for assessing the normative validity of the transformations sanctioned by the alerted, informed, mobilized and considered will of the People which seemed altogether missing from the framework of *Foundations*. It seems premature, at this stage, to guess whether this correction of the majoritarian overtones of *Foundations* will proceed to completion in the context of the announced third volume of *We the People* or whether *Transformations* in the end will just be the locus of transient dissonances in a melody characterized by the theme of constitutional majoritarianism.

Michelman's Problem of Infinite Regress: a Residue of Externalism?

Also in Michelman's 'judgment view of higher lawmaking' it is possible to find one residue of the older paradigm of generalizing universalism. Let me first recall the gist of Michelman's approach to what he understands as the problem of infinite regress. The founding of a deliberative democratic polity – the *legal big bang* that the framing of a constitution represents – is hard to subsume under the category of a jurisgenerative, democratic process, according to Michelman, because the democratic quality of such a process can be so characterized only on the basis of a constitution yet to be enacted. In a belated political-philosophical reincarnation of Gödel's theorem, we discover that the founding of a deliberative democracy cannot be part of the democratic process. To this realization Michelman responds with a complex strategy of neutralization, which in the end does not lead him out of the dead end but reveals the presence of an – inessential, in my opinion – element of modern generalizing universalism within his genuinely judgment-based approach.

Michelman first distinguishes *justice* as an absolute kind of concept and *validity*, understood as a kind of relative or historicized rightness – rightness for us. Then he transforms the ideal of justice, as a standard by which to measure the adequacy of a constitution, into that of 'validity for us' and argues that validity so conceived is of value to us because it ensures *stability*. Conduciveness to stability, in turn, is a prized quality of constitutional essentials, because stability allows the individuals to reconcile the exercise of their capacity for justice with their effort to pursue their vision of the good. At this point Michelman raises the question of whether such a conception of the person can really be neutral and comes to the sombre conclusion that:

> either we are critically disposed toward any and all philosophical specifications of the relevant ('political') notion of the person, hence epistemically committed to democratic procedures all the way up and caught in the immobilizing regress, or we stop the regress with a philosophical-foundational conception of the political person. (1996b: 33)

This bleak conclusion follows from, and gives out, a residue of *externalism* in Michelman's conception of normative validity. The whole matter appears in a somewhat different light if we think of the democratic process and the democratic standard of validity thoroughly along *internalist* and *immanent* lines, in terms of a model of validity consistently based on judgment. The aesthetic analogy of justice and art, which will be explored in more depth below, can again be helpful. In the case of a work of art there is no separate ground for the validity of the aesthetic intention on which the well-formed work of art rests. Self-validation through the exceptional ability to produce an aesthetic experience covers both the work of art and the inspiration on which it rests. There is no need to provide a separate justification for engaging in the activity of painting and no need to justify the initial brush stroke. When we paint, the justification of the initial brush stroke comes from the whole of the work to which it belongs.

I don't want to follow this tack, however, because it draws on premises not entirely internal to Michelman's framework. An equally cogent case against the thesis that the notion of deliberative democracy entails an infinite regress can be developed along fully immanent lines, by drawing on other parts of Michelman's work. In 'Can Constitutional Democrats Be Legal Positivists?' Michelman notes that because they attribute higher-law authorship to the People themselves conceived as self-governing, constitutional democrats 'cannot ever conceive higher lawmaking either as total revolution or as writing on a clean slate', but rather are bound to conceive of it as 'a product of a framed political interaction, an interaction framed by some already present, politically grounded, idea of reason or right' (1996a: 302).

In 'Always under Law?' (1995a), Michelman speaks of the 'political identity of the People', a term borrowed from Ackerman, as something that pre-exists the constitution and allows us to regard even the framing of a constitution as an act that takes its place within a *broader* normative frame of reference to which it has to be responsive. At the end of that paper, Michelman calls into question the distinction between norm origination and norm interpretation. One consequence of the 'always under law' thesis is that 'the People's higher-law ministrations are always *interpretive*' (1995a: 247, my emphasis). In order to understand what the object of this interpretive activity is, we have to go back to 'Can Constitutional Democrats Be Legal Positivists?' (1996a). Such higher-law ministrations, which the People take to themselves in the form of suggested constitutional amendments and do not entrust even to the Supreme Court, are interpretations 'of the community's ultimate law or proto-law of which the from-time-to-time enacted and amended Constitution is to be understood as a series of representations and interpretations' (1996a: 303).

From these lines we get a different picture from the one suggested in 'How Can the People Ever Make the Laws?' (1996b). On this picture, instead of having a legal 'big bang' – the framing of the constitution – we have a *continuum*, a gradient of transformation undergone by a human group which is initially thrown together by accidental reasons, some of which are natural, others historical, and then in the process of intragroup and intergroup interaction comes to acquire a *communal identity*, understood as a self-conscious representation of its characteristics and circumstances. Out of differentiation there soon grows a representation of the communal way of regulating the relation between members – perhaps primarily, as Herbert Spencer has suggested, of regulating the relation between those in power and the governed. The framing of a constitution then appears to be an act of *interpretation* as well as one of *norm generation* – in that it brings to expression, in an objectified form, a normative content which was only implicit in the identity of the people beforehand. In this picture, adumbrated by Michelman in 'Always under Law?', is contained an alternative solution to the problem of infinite regress, a solution that follows a route quite different from invoking a comprehensive view of the person.

This route is the 'judgment and authenticity' route. According to it, we never get out of the circle of the 'for us', nor do we need to. Even the justification for the value of stability – namely, the fact that it allows us to exercise in a conflict-free way our sense of justice and our capacity for choosing a view of the good – is a justification *for us*, given *who we are*. In this case, the notion of conflict-free individuation, of 'being at one with oneself', is so ingrained in the identity of any Western modern political community – though Dionysian views of subjectivity are also present – that it is hard to imagine a political conception of justice or a constitution that wouldn't be responsive to it. Then the validity of the attribution of value to validity – for that is ultimately the question addressed by Michelman – need not be understood as being based on a standard external to us and thus as entailing a relapse into the older model of generalizing universalism. On the reflective judgment view of universalism, our cherishing validity understood as 'justice relative to a context' rests on the optimal, exemplary congruency that such a conception has with us. We are not 'we' without that notion. If someone objected that this is a relativist view of validity, we could contend that, on the contrary, precisely this optimal and exemplary congruence between who we are and the constitutional essentials that we converge on – between who we are as a collectivity endowed with a *cultural* identity and who we are as a collectivity endowed with a *political* identity – is what makes our constitutional essentials so inspiring also to other people. Evidence for this is the fact that whoever we are, in whichever context we discuss a constitution, we usually take the American experience, among other experiences, as exemplary – not as something that we *must* follow, but as something in which we *might* find something of great value to us. In this exemplariness, not different from the inspiring exemplariness of the work of art, lies the best chance for a certain view – deliberative democracy – to project its influence beyond the provincial context in which it first arose. If we adopt this line of thought, then we simply don't have the problem of infinite regress and we are able to keep a universalistic understanding of validity, albeit an *exemplary* universalist one.

7

The Judgment View of Justice

As the reconstruction outlined in the preceding chapters indicates, there is no revolution under way in political philosophy. The paradigm of judgment is just gradually and slowly emerging in a process marked by hesitations and constant relapses into the old kind of universalism as well as by counter-tendencies and resistances to change. In the following two chapters I will try to contribute to the further consolidation of this new way of thinking about justice by way of drafting a judgment-based conception of justice that builds on the different suggestions gleaned from our examination of the works of Rawls, Habermas, Dworkin, Ackerman and Michelman and is designed for fitting coherently with the implications of the linguistic turn – primarily for fitting with the way of understanding universalism left open by it.

Rethinking the Problem of Justice: Two Formulations

The problem that constitutes the object of the judgment view of justice can be stated as a variation on a Rawlsian theme: how can we conceive of a notion of justice that can ensure the stability or integration over time of a society of free and equal citizens who subscribe to profoundly divergent visions of the good?

This Rawlsian formulation of the problem of justice represents a good starting point. In fact, while all of its underlying assumptions are shared by the judgment view, the judgment view contains an extra assumption not to be found in Rawls's formulation. Among the shared premises are: first, the 'fact of pluralism' and the acceptance thereof on the part of the citizens; second, a condition of moderate scarcity which sets limits on the possibility of satisfying all preferences and interests and of realizing all values, and yet is not so severe as to render futile all attempts to peacefully settle various conflicting claims.

Furthermore, like the Rawlsian conception known as 'justice as fairness', also the judgment view of justice is to be responsive to a set of requisites. First, our conception of justice must be general in nature, namely it must not contain explicit or implicit reference to individuals or groups. Second, it must be 'universally applicable', i.e. perfectly compatible with everyone's following it. Third, it must be 'public' in the Kantian sense, i.e. its functioning must not rest on secret clauses. Fourth, it must be able to assign a rank in terms of degrees of justness to the various alternatives being tested in its light. And fifth, it must be such that the citizens who subscribe to the various rival conceptions of the good can recognize in it the 'final court of appeal' when practical controversies demand adjudication in terms of justice.

Differently from Rawls's and the other conceptions of justice and normative validity discussed above, however, a fully fledged judgment view of justice will have to meet an *additional* requisite. It must be fully *immanent*: namely, in exerting the function of mirroring our intuitions concerning the fair solution of practical controversies, it must not appeal to any notion, principle or standpoint external to the context where the controversy has arisen. The problem that constitutes the object of a judgment view of justice and of normative validity in general can then be reformulated in the following terms: what notion of justice can ensure the integration of a society of free and equal citizens who subscribe to different conceptions of the good by means of helping these citizens to solve their controversies of interest and value without appealing to any standpoint, criterion or principle external to the parties involved in the contention?

In Part I, I have discussed various attempts to provide a conception of justice or normative validity which in different ways are all guided by the intention to avoid what has been called 'foundationalism', but nonetheless for different reasons do not offer a convincing answer to this question. Even Michelman's republican-liberal conception of justice, while thoroughly based on the reflective judgment interpretation of a normative framework – be it the constitution or the political identity of the people – in the end neglects to clarify how justice or normative validity so understood can cogently confer priority to one among several conflicting claims in a practical controversy, without invoking principles external to the context at hand. This clarification of the *impartiality* aspect of justice will constitute the object of the reflective judgment view of justice outlined in the present and in the following chapter.

Such clarification includes several steps. First, I will elucidate the received view of the 'context of justice' and will discuss an alternative understanding of it. Then I will consider the *source of cogency* or normativity for a view of justice that dispenses with general principles and yet retains the ordering function typical of deontological views of justice. Subsequently I will draw a distinction between 'political' and 'moral', 'elementary' and 'fully fledged' conceptions of justice and, finally, I will elucidate the analogy of justice and aesthetic judgment. In the next chapter, then, I will take the discussion of the ordering function exerted by a judgment view of justice as my starting point and will offer a reconstruction of the ideal of equal respect that enables justice so conceived to help us sort out better and worse solutions to practical alternatives. Subsequently I will explore two of the broader philosophical implications of the judgment view of justice: its relation to the good and to a radically self-reflexive mode of grounding centred around the notion of authenticity.

The Context of Justice: the Received Liberal Conception

Central to the judgment view is the idea that the meaning of justice cannot be understood apart from the meaning of the self-realization of a collective identity. Justice, in other words, is not as *radically different* from the pursuit of the good on the part of a collective identity as the deontological conceptions of Kantian descent would invite us to think. The difference between these conceptions of justice and the one based on reflective judgment that I try to defend in this book is best illustrated with reference to the paradigmatic picture of the *context* in which a problem of justice arises. For the conceptions of justice based on generalizing universalism, modern questions of justice arise, as we have seen, in a context where a number of contending parties lay conflicting claims to some resource, material or ideal, and have no common substantive teleological vision of the good by reference to which the contest could be solved. In such a context, and given the assumption of an equal respect due to each party's conception, the standpoint of justice is best envisaged as the application of some *impartial* principle to the dispute at hand – a principle that no one could reasonably reject (Scanlon) or a principle from which a solution can be derived which is equally good for everybody (Habermas). The problem, from the perspective of a judgment view of justice, is not raised by associating justice with impartiality or neutrality: indeed, the judgment view purports to provide the most defensible understanding of what the impartiality or neutrality of justice means, if we take the 'fact of pluralism' seriously. The problem lies rather in the *externality* of the source from which the impartial standpoint is supposed to gain its cogency: the presuppositions of discourse for Habermas, the principles of rational choice in *A Theory of Justice*, the very notion of 'equal respect' as Dworkin construes it, the three conversational constraints in *Social Justice and the Liberal State*, and so on. Alternatively, the liberal theories seem to weaken their normative core up to the point of almost losing their normative cogency. In *Political Liberalism*, the point of view of 'what justice requires' arises only *after* the formation, contingent and not normatively commanded, of an overlapping consensus on a political conception of justice among the conceptions of the good contingently present in a given context. In *We the People* there is still uncertainty as to the normative backdrop against which the will of the People can be assessed.

Yet how can an *impartial* standpoint be gained from within the perspective of the contending parties, as the judgment view suggests, and consistently with the assumption of the fact of pluralism – for example without adopting the standpoint of a future convergence or presupposing the possibility of a neutral language that ensures commensuration without loss? The classical doctrines of judgment – Aristotle's conception of *phronesis* and Kant's notion of *reflective judgment* – were aimed at developing a notion of validity severed from the postulation of general principles. They are of no *immediate* help, however, because they are intertwined with and depend on assumptions that cannot be easily reconciled with the linguistic turn.

Kant, for example, himself struggled with the problem of identifying the source of the universalistic normativity inherent in the judgment of taste. In paragraph 33 of *The Critique of Judgment*, Kant notes that the judgment of taste 'is invariably laid down as a singular judgment upon the Object' (1986: 140), includes no reference to principles and concepts and yet *raises a universalistic claim to the effect that everyone ought to feel pleasure in taking notice of a certain object*. How can this be possible? The answer is offered in paragraph 39. There he suggests that the pleasure which the judgment of taste claims to be linked with the mental representation of an object

> must of necessity depend for everyone upon the same conditions, seeing that they are the subjective conditions of the possibility of a cognition in general, and the proportion of these cognitive faculties which is requisite for taste is requisite also for ordinary sound understanding, the presence of which we are entitled to presuppose in everyone. (1986: 150)

Two aspects of this answer come into an obvious tension with our postmetaphysical sensibility and thus render it unviable for us. On the one hand, Kant's thesis implies a cognitive naturalism which reduces the shared basis of human cognition, on which rests the possibility of intersubjective agreement, to a *natural* endowment of man. On the other hand, Kant asks us to subscribe to the whole of his analysis of the categories of cognition in the *Critique of Pure Reason* in order to understand how pleasure arises from the congruence of perceived objects with our cognitive apparatus in the absence of interest.

With respect to our task, more helpful than a philological revisitation of the classical doctrines of principle-free normativity is a critical examination of another assumption implicit in the views of justice reconstructed in Part I.[1] While none of the authors considered is committed to an *atomistic* notion of the individual of the kind criticized by the communitarian critics of liberalism, their views of justice or normative validity continue to share one important element in common with the atomistic conception of subjectivity. Even in Rawls's political conception of the person, which is formulated in such a way as to be *neutral* with respect to any substantive conception of subjectivity, and even in Habermas's conception of the individual as *intersubjectively constituted*, the relation between the parties to whom justice is to be rendered – be they individuals or groups of individuals, be they the originary units of all intersubjective processes of communication and interaction or themselves the product of intersubjective processes – is understood to be as *tenuous*, for the purpose of the assessment of competing practical claims, as the relation between the atomistically conceived individuals of modern political philosophy from Hobbes to Mill. However intense that relation might be in a number of other respects – from a psychological, sociological, political or economic standpoint – it is assumed to be *irrelevant* for the purpose of defining the nature of justice. In fact, the distinction between the right and the good as drawn from the perspective of generalizing universalism – we will see below the new meaning that it acquires when drawn from the perspective of exemplary universalism – rests on the assumption that any conflict between parties, individual or collective, that pursue different and rival conceptions of the good can only be solved if we abstract from all notions of the good, which cannot but be particular, in that they must be indexed to specific identities, and accede to a more general point of view, called the 'moral point of view', the 'view from nowhere'[2] or the point of view of 'impartiality' or 'fairness', which is not the reflection of *any* identity, individual or collective, as such.

The judgment view of justice starts from a different view of the context of justice and reaches an altogether different understanding of impartiality. The idea underlying the judgment view of justice is that whenever a number of parties, individual or collective, clash over their incompatible visions of the good and the competing demands for resources following therefrom, we must presuppose, in order to make sense of the idea of a conflict, not only that they must be involved in a common interaction – a presupposition which poses no difficulty also to the other conceptions of justice – but also that such interaction possesses a *normative valence*. Its normative, and not just factual, significance lies in its constituting a foothold for the normative, impartial but *immanent*, standpoint that we are looking for.[3] Let us take a closer look at the common substance and some versions of this alternative view of the context of justice before trying to unpack its implications.

An Alternative View of the Context of Justice

Let me first enunciate the basic idea underlying the alternative understanding of the context of justice. In the process of interacting with one another, the parties for whom a question of justice arises cannot but give rise to a common overarching identity, however thin or minimal, whose *good* understood as fulfilment is somehow *equivalent* to what deontological theorists call 'justice'. For the good of a superordinate collective identity to be *equivalent* with what justice requires when a number of rival identities embedded in it come to clash over practical issues means that a certain property – which for lack of a better term I will continue to call *impartiality* – inheres in both notions. It is by virtue of this property that the area of overlapping between contending conceptions of the good can serve the same functions that the traditional concept of justice is usually supposed to serve: (a) setting limits on the non-overlapping goals that can legitimately be pursued, (b) outlining ways of adjudicating conflict of interest and of value in the service of continuing peaceful cooperation, and (c) providing some sort of a criterion acceptable to all for the evaluation of the legitimacy of norms.

There are two separate claims in this basic idea underlying the judgment view of justice that need to be considered. The first is the claim that there cannot be 'pure conflict' without the obtaining, at the same time, of a horizon of shared orientations which functions as a condition of the possibility of conflict. This idea has been developed as an argument against relativism from a variety of standpoints, including the theory of conceptual schemes (Davidson), anthropology (Geertz), hermeneutics (Gadamer), the notion of 'incommensurable exclusivity' (Williams), and analytical pragmatism (Putnam).[4] In all these different versions, the same point has been made: namely, that the idea of *total incommensurability* is ultimately incoherent. For people who articulate their understanding of the matter at hand from within vocabularies that are totally unrelated could not, strictly speaking, make sense of their being in any kind of relation with one another. As Peter J. Steinberger has nicely put this point, common to the authors mentioned above: 'Interpretation always involves at least some distance to be bridged, and also some solid points of contact on the basis of which bridges may be built' (1993: 268). We can apply this insight to the case of justice. No two conceptions of the good can be so incommensurable as to contain no points of intersection whatsoever and yet allow those who embrace them to understand their mutual relation as one of being involved in a conflict over matters of justice.

The second claim concerns the normative relevance of the overlap between identities. That such overlap can be treated as an identity, however minimal, in its own right and extends a *normative cogency* over the claims of the contending parties is not obvious. Among the authors who provide important anticipations of this idea are Durkheim, Taylor, Walzer and Rorty. In *The Division of Labor in Society* (1964), Durkheim repeatedly and insistently stresses the close connection that links the division of labour as a social phenomenon with the moral life of a society. The integrative effects of a highly developed division of labour turn into divisive and anomic outcomes if the allocation of tasks and rewards is too removed from what the sense of justice inherent in the members of society regards as a just distribution. In the 'Conclusion' Durkheim offers some interesting considerations on the justness of that local sense of justice. Looking favourably at the 'formation of continually larger societies', for example at the incipient formation of a 'European society', and considering that the notion of the impossibility of a single human society 'has not been proven', Durkheim appears to envisage a hierarchy of normative, increasingly general but always situated standpoints from which the particularism of the individual and group interests can be regulated. In his words,

> Just as private conflicts can be regulated only by the action of the society in which the individuals live, so intersocial conflicts can be regulated only by a society which comprises in its scope all others. (1964: 405)

The *source of normativity* in this case is given by the fact that by virtue of participating in the same division of labour we are already in some sort of common moral space, however thin, which can both 'moderate' the individuals' or collective parties' particularism and exert an ordering function with respect to their claims. In Durkheim's notion of a 'society which comprises in its scope all others' we find a powerful foreshadowing of the idea that ultimately the *normative but situated* anchoring for the standpoint of justice is to be found in the concrete, historically contingent, but nonetheless not further transcendable requirements for the fulfilment of humanity in its entirety.

From a different angle and within a different vocabulary a similar idea is presupposed by Charles Taylor when, in his essay 'Atomism', from the premise that 'outside society, or in some variants outside certain kinds of society, our distinctively human capacities could not develop' (1985: 191) he draws the conclusion that we have a certain obligation toward the maintenance of the kind of society that allows the development of such capacities. In his words,

> If we cannot ascribe natural rights without affirming the worth of certain human capacities, and if this affirmation has other normative consequences (i.e. that we should foster and nurture these capacities in ourselves and others), then any proof that these capacities can only develop in society or in a society of a certain kind is a proof that we ought to belong to or sustain society or this kind of society. (1985: 197)

Taylor's point is part of a broader argument against the liberal thesis of the primacy of rights-as-trumps – an argument that need not concern us here – but significant for our purposes is his understanding of the 'duty to sustain' the social bond that enables us to be who we are. For example, it is part of this 'duty to society', which we could reinterpret as a duty to the larger whole which contains the contending parties, that we could not 'unreservedly assert our right in the face of, or at the expense of, such a society': rather, 'in the event of a conflict we should have to acknowledge that we were legitimately pulled both ways' (1985: 198). Should we fail to attend this duty and instead assert our particular interest, we would thereby contribute, in a contradictory way, to undermine the conditions of the possibility for our fundamental capacities to flourish and we would condemn ourselves to a 'truncated mode of existence'. Taylor's argument is designed to counter the objection that we owe an attitude of care not to society in its entirety but only to the institutional segment of society that most directly bears a significance for the growth of our capacities, namely the family. He points out that our families in turn can exert such formative function only in so far as they are not isolated patriarchal units but are enmeshed in the larger society and indeed in the whole of Western civilization. In so far as one thinks of protecting the capacity for considered and autonomous judgment in matters of great existential impact and not just in selecting trivial alternatives on a restaurant menu, it is doubtful that such capacity may develop within a purely familial horizon. It seems much more plausible to state that the development of such capacities presupposes the formative influence of an entire civilization, including its arts, its culture, its philosophies, its sciences, its political practices, its institutions and its religious beliefs and rituals.[5] There is no reason, however, why this line of reasoning could not be extended one step further, so as to generate the conclusion that even Western civilization could not be what it is and exert its formative function without the contrasting plane of other civilizations. In that case the individual would be under a duty to attend the flourishing of the human community as such and to use this regulative notion for assessing the merits of conflicting regional interests.

In a more self-conscious way the idea of replacing abstract justice with situated justice understood as the requirements of the fulfilment of a superordinate identity has also been put forward by Walzer and Rorty. In *Thick and Thin: Moral Argument at Home and Abroad* (1994) Walzer starts with a familiar picture. A demonstration in a foreign city, which happens to be Prague, is being shown on TV. We can read the signs that the demonstrators are carrying. Some of these signs say 'truth', others 'justice'. The question is: what is meant by these words? Walzer's point is that we can have accounts of that meaning that are variously 'thick' or 'thin'. The thin meaning is what can get across to distant actors. What the word 'justice' written on a placard means is 'an end to arbitrary arrests, equal and impartial law enforcement, the abolition of the privileges and prerogatives of the party elite' (1994: 2). This is only a minimal or thin account of the meaning of 'justice'. At both ends of the communication model, the sender and the receiver, the meaning thickens. For both the Prague marchers and the American TV watcher justice carries a thicker web of associations. These associations often do not get across to the other side. They remain intertwined with a local historical-cultural-religious-political context. This is true on both sides. The Czech marchers embed what they mean by justice in the context of their experience of the past regime, and the distant onlookers in interpreting what they read on the signs are bracketing away, for the time being, the equally local understanding of justice which they bring to bear in their discussions about, for example, zoning regulations or the by-laws of the Parents–Teachers Association.

The question is: how do the more universal but thinner and the local and thicker understandings of justice relate to one another? Walzer's point is constructed by exclusion. First, they certainly do not relate as a principle and its applications. It is not the case that the thick intuitions about justice are derived from some 'freestanding' principle or some set of independently established 'conversational constraints' or 'presuppositions of communication', because there is no way to go deductively from abstract principles to the rich substantive representations of concrete moralities. Nor can it be shown that our species started out from a unique moral code which subsequently underwent the same fate that Babel supposedly has inflicted on our linguistic ability to understand each other. Rather, the opposite seems to be true: 'morality is thick from the beginning, culturally integrated, fully resonant, and it reveals itself thinly only on special occasions, when moral language is turned to specific purposes' (1994: 4). 'The moral minimum,' argues Walzer, cannot be understood as 'a freestanding morality', such as the political conception of justice proposed by Rawls. Rather, it 'simply designates some reiterated features of particular thick or maximal moralities' (1994: 10). The thin morality of 'justice' genealogically grows out of, and normatively draws its cogency from, the contingent overlapping of many thicker and local moralities.

At the same time, we should not understand thick as *real* and thin as *artificial*. For we usually have very strong feelings about 'thin' moral concepts such as dignity, freedom, human rights and the like. These are the moral notions that move us the most when we see them betrayed or attacked anywhere in the world. So, argues Walzer, 'thinness and intensity go together, whereas with thickness comes qualification, compromise, complexity and disagreement' (1994: 6). Also we should be wary, according to Walzer, of associating *thin* moral principles with reason and *thick* accounts of the good with intuitions and prudence.

The relation between the thin and the thick should rather be understood in terms of 'reiteration'. Walzer here provides a further elaboration of the distinction drawn in 1990 between 'covering law' and 'reiterative' universalism.[6] The fact that moral actors who are distantly located nonetheless converge on minimal standards of justice must be understood as a matter of 'repetition': minimal or thin moral discourse

> consists in principles and rules that are reiterated in different times and places, and that are seen to be similar even though they are expressed in different idioms and reflect different histories and different versions of the world. (1994: 17)

In 'Justice as a Larger Loyalty' (1997) Rorty starts from a set of examples of conflicts between justice and loyalty. For example,

> all of us would expect help if, pursued by the police, we asked our family to hide us. Most of us would extend such help even when we know our child or our parent to be guilty of a sordid crime. But if an innocent person is wrongly convicted as a result of our perjury, most of us will be torn by a conflict between loyalty and justice. (1997: 9)

Another example:

> sharing food with impoverished people down the street is natural and right in normal times, but perhaps not in a famine, when doing so may amount to disloyalty to one's own family. (1997: 9)

And a third: according to some analysts a complete globalization of the labour market could spell an end to democracy in the West. On the one hand, justice would require 'exporting capital and jobs until everything is leveled out – until an honest day's work, in a ditch or at a computer, earns no higher a wage in São Paulo or Paris than in a small town in Botswana'. On the other, points out Rorty, 'the inhabitants of the industrialized democracies will turn fascist and militarist long before they let their present standard of living dwindle away'. In light of the preceding three examples the problem of justice is stated by Rorty in the following general terms:

> Would it be a good idea to treat 'justice' as the name for loyalty to a certain very large group, the name for our largest current loyalty, rather than the name of something distinct from loyalty? Could we replace the notion of 'justice' with that of loyalty to that group – for example, one's fellow-citizens, or the human species, or all living things? Would anything be lost by this replacement? (1997: 11)

In answering the question in the negative Rorty draws on Walzer (1994) and enlists Rawls as well among the advocates of a specific distinction between the *thick*, i.e. the comprehensive, and the *thin*, i.e. the political, conception of justice – a distinction which allows him to say that conflicts between justice and loyalty are ultimately conflicts between 'two self-descriptions, two ways of giving meaning to one's life' (1997: 12) – a description of the self as belonging to a smaller circle or to a wider one. To be sure, the thin moral discourse enjoins us not to make arbitrary distinctions between moral subjects, but this intuition, argues Rorty, is articulated

> only on special occasions. On such occasions, the thin concept can often be turned against one of the thick conceptions from which it emerged, in the form of critical questions about whether it may not be merely arbitrary to think that certain people matter more than others. (1997: 13)

However, continues Rorty, neither Walzer nor Rawls think that 'unpacking the thin concept of justice will by itself resolve such critical questions' (1997: 13), which is the same as saying that the conflict between larger and more restricted loyalties cannot be solved by invoking any principle external to the context of conflict itself.

But if the criterion for assigning priority and thereby solving the conflict has to be found within the context in which the conflict originates, what can it be? Not surprisingly, even in Rorty we find some equivalent of a normative notion of authenticity invoked at this point. For example, in urging all the other societies in the world to respect certain human rights, should Western societies appeal to something *not merely Western*, for example notions of morality, humanity or rationality that *ought to be shared by everyone*? Or shouldn't they rather base such demands, addressed to non-Western societies, on the authenticity claim that in so doing they are being true to themselves? Rorty concludes that

> if by rationality we mean simply the sort of activity which Walzer thinks of as a thinning out process – the sort that, with luck, achieves the recognition and utilization of an overlapping consensus – then the idea that justice has a different source than loyalty no longer seems plausible. For, on this account of rationality, being rational and acquiring a larger loyalty are two descriptions of the same activity. This is because *any* unforced agreement between individuals or groups about what to do creates a form of community, and will, with luck, be the initial stage in expanding the circles of those whom each party to the agreement had previously taken to be 'people like ourselves'. (1997: 18)

The problem with all the approaches mentioned above is that, despite their incorporating, in one way or other, a notion of justice as related to the requirement to attend the good of the superordinate identity which includes the partial identities involved in a contention over interests or values, they fail to adequately specify what the *source* of the cogency of justice so conceived might be, along which lines the *ordering function* of a view of justice ought to be then understood, and what kind of relation should then be assumed to connect the right and the good.

The Problem of the Source of Cogency

Let me start with highlighting a number of implications of our reformulation of the context of justice along judgment lines. First, from the standpoint of the judgment view justice appears to be as context-bound, as 'local' as the good for an identity, and to depend on reflective judgment just as much as the determination of the good for an identity does.[7] Drawing on Simmel's seminal idea of an 'individual law',[8] the central intuition underlying the judgment view of justice can be expressed as the proposition:

> *What justice requires is equivalent with what the superordinate identity formed at the intersection of the contending identities requires in order to attain its own fulfilment.*

The acceptance of this proposition somehow orients our attempt to identify the source of normativity from which the judgment view of justice draws its cogency. Its cogency comes entirely from an immanent source in that such cogency is located – as in the classical and contemporary Aristotelian ethics of the good – in the *eudaemonistic self-reflection* of the actor.

Second, when considered from the vantage point captured by the proposition enunciated above, the impartial standpoint of justice has a powerful motivating force of its own in that it directly hooks up with the good – a good which today we understand in formal terms as 'self-fulfilment'.[9] Yet two aspects of Aristotelian and neo-Aristotelian approaches that make their contemporary use somewhat problematic are (a) their dependency on substantive visions of the good life and (b) their difficulty in specifying a credible notion of a 'duty to others', over and beyond the eudaemonistic duty to live one's life well.[10]

The judgment view of justice is designed to avoid these two shortcomings. It does not take for granted any substantive view of the good for human beings as such, but takes the actors' own understanding of the good as its starting point and then tries to keep the parochialism of such view under check by means of requiring the adoption of an *enlarged point of view*: namely, the point of view of a superordinate collectivity which ideally, in the case of the *moral* point of view, can be coextensive with humanity in its entirety.

Furthermore, by means of requiring the adoption of such an enlarged point of view, the judgment approach to justice introduces the idea of duties to other people without ever deriving such duties from any source that does not possess an internal anchoring for the actor, in the form of his or her participating, however minimally, in the intersection. By virtue of that participation, in fact, aspects of the superordinate identity contribute to the constitution of the identity of the actor – for example, via the actor's self-constitution through seeing herself through the eyes of the generalized other – and cannot be ignored in the actor's reflections on her good without paying the price of subtracting something from that understanding. From this interconnection of the individual and the collective identity – through the intersubjective constitution of subjectivity – the judgment notion of justice draws its own normativity.

The answer developed above to the question 'What grounds the adoption of the enlarged standpoint?' requires a word of clarification. If a view of justice has to exert an ordering function and help us sort out claims that are justified from those which are less so, then its normative standpoint must be justifiable to everyone. But what claim to universality can be raised by the enlarged standpoint? What if someone rejects it? Why are we bound to adopt it?

Many attempts to work out a postmetaphysical and non-foundationalist view of morality incur difficulties in trying to answer these questions. For too strong is the temptation, at this juncture, to invoke some kind of true description of an uninterpreted aspect of reality – be it structures of practical rationality, the presuppositions of communication embedded in language use, the requirements of relations of reciprocal recognition, a kind of natural aversion to being submitted to cruelty or even a kind of drive toward self-realization inherent in all human individuals. On the other hand, that we must take these questions seriously is not obvious. Some authors claim the opposite and dismiss the question as unanswerable and thus irrelevant. On this view, no one can explain why one should be moral to someone who is not already within the circle of morality – or, in other words, morality cannot be justified 'from ground up' (Williams 1985: 28–9). I think that there is certainly some truth in Williams's position, in the sense that no one could conclusively prove that, simply by being immoral, the member of a fictive 'race of devils' is bound to be inconsistent. Following this line of thought, the attempt to ground the moral point of view or the enlarged standpoint from the outside, namely starting from premises that are not themselves moral, is as senseless as trying to provide a *non-aesthetic* answer to the questions 'Why be interested in art?' or 'What is the use of art?' Although art can of course be of use in a variety of respects, 'being of use' cannot be claimed to be its *raison d'être* without at the same time forfeiting the aesthetic quality of art. Similarly, no justification can be provided of why we cannot but embrace an enlarged standpoint without reducing the moral nature of that standpoint to something non-moral – for example, to the enlightened self-interested attempt to secure all the conditions of satisfaction for an imprinted drive toward self-realization.

These considerations would suggest keeping the moral point of view and the perspective of justice within the safe boundaries of one language game among others – the discourse of morality as the jargon of those who are already receptive to the call of the moral point of view. The question 'Why play the language game of morality and justice?' would then have to be dismissed as irremediably misleading – as a question that inevitably would lead us straight into foundationalism, into a quest for something non-moral to which morality can and ought to be reduced.

The judgment view of justice embeds a more sanguine understanding of the possibility of accounting for the source of its own normative premises.

The above considerations are not so much incorrect as they are *incomplete*. There is another side to the matter of justifying the enlarged standpoint that the defenders of the strictly autonomistic conception of morality tend to overlook. Both the moral phenomenon, which includes our intuitions concerning what justice requires, and the realm of the aesthetic are part of *human praxis*. And human praxis, as a dynamic foreground figure on the background canvas of human life, is always enmeshed with the concern that life, the individual lives of human beings, go well or at least be saved from the horror of being wasted. Evidence for this claim comes from the fact that we could not possibly make sense of an autonomistic affirmation of the value of justice or art *to the detriment* of life. Even those who extol the point of view of justice or the aesthetic attitude as the paramount horizon of value at the same time maintain that the meaningful, worthy, fully human life is *coextensive* with the exercise of the moral or the aesthetic faculties. They could not possibly claim that art or moral conduct are the epitome of value and yet detrimental to a human life well lived or, in other words, to *eudaemonia*. The modern differentiation of the value spheres, which instils in us 'modernlings' an aversion to assessing any of the value spheres against standards other than their own, is itself a cultural phenomenon that we, the same 'we', differently appraise in terms of its potential to enhance human life as such. As a matter of historical fact, some modern thinkers have been enthusiastic about the exhilarating opening up of a new dynamism following from such differentiation, others have felt uneasy and uncomfortable with it, others have sought refuge in compensatory monotheisms of various sorts, others have advocated a stoic endurance of the rifts induced by the new polytheism, and still others have sought ways of rearticulating some kind of interconnection between the various value spheres without dedifferentiating them. This variety of reactions shows that under modern premises even partitions of this magnitude – cognition, morality and the aesthetic – are perceived not as ultimate realities, worlds of their own, but still as spheres of meaning responsive to the somehow higher standpoint of *eudaemonia* or the human life worth living. In his essays on the sociology of religion and especially in 'Religious Rejections of the World and their Directions',[11] Max Weber pointed out how the modern condition has led to a cultural predicament best summed up by the notion of a renewed, yet deanthropomorphized, polytheism. The space of modern culture has taken on once again the semblance of an arena for the warring gods. What Weber failed to emphasize, owing among other things to his interest in sharply contrasting tradition and modernity, is the fact that before making her 'undemonstrable', irreducibly personal choice, each of us 'modernlings' can ask her prospective god: 'In what ways will you enhance my life?' Differently from the foundational God of the Christian tradition and in a renewed consonance with the polytheism of the Greek world, we can always ask each realm of value that demands our unconditional and undivided allegiance: 'What will my life be like if I serve you?'

Going back to our initial question concerning the source of cogency for a notion of justice conceived along judgment lines, the considerations outlined above are designed to chart a third course between the equally undesirable alternatives of cognitivizing, naturalizing or somehow reducing the normativity of justice to something other than itself on the one hand, and sealing that normativity in the self-contained normativity of a language game which we are under no obligation to play on the other. In the same spirit as we can interrogate the Weberian gods of modernity, we can legitimately raise again the questions 'Why worry about justice? Why care about the claims of others?', if by that we mean not 'Which principles of rationality or structures of human subjectivity enjoin us to entertain those concerns?' but rather something like 'Would a human life lived without concern for justice be as well lived as one which included such a concern?' A negative answer is suggested by the consideration that if we assume that identities, both individual and collective, are constituted via significant relations of recognition with other identities and, even when they are in conflict with one another, nonetheless do intersect to some extent, then for the bearer of any identity to take into account, in the formation of the future-oriented project that orients the identity, that moment of intersection and the needs connected with the maintenance of the relations of recognition means by definition to have access to a more complete fulfilment than would be the case should those aspects be deliberately neglected. In this purely formal sense it is possible to say that the source from which the judgment view of justice draws the normative cogency that allows it to perform the ordering function usually associated with any conception of justice is once again the actor's eudaemonistic self-reflection conceived now along postmetaphysical lines.

The Ordering Function

Having so accounted for the problem of the source of the cogency that this enlarged standpoint can claim on whoever considers a problem of justice, it remains to be clarified how that standpoint – the standpoint of the fulfilment of the superordinate identity that includes the intersection between the contending identities – can actually exert, without resorting to the authority of principles, the ordering function that the judgment view of justice is supposed to be able to exert.

The aesthetic analogy to which I have often had recourse proves useful once again. While a more complete consideration of this analogy will be postponed to later in this chapter, one particular facet of it which can shed light on our problem can be discussed here: that aspect is the practice of solving aesthetic controversies as they arise in the process of artistic production. Just as in the production of a work of art – let us take the example of some artistic practice which requires the cooperation of a number of differently talented individual artists, such as the production of a movie, the staging of a play, the construction of a cathedral, the staging of a ballet – controversies over alternative procedures or alternative ways of completing the work of art are settled with reference to a *project* assumed to be common, so in the case of controversies over what political justice requires the political project enshrined in the constitution can play a similar role. Noteworthy is the fact that neither the commonality of a shared artistic project nor the commonality of a *political* project have anything to do, in this context, with that commonality of *ends*, constitutive of the 'community of saints', which Rawls sets in opposition to the fact of pluralism. The commonality of an artistic as well as of a 'political' project represents a sharing in a limited and 'reflective' construction which acquires its sense only against the background of a pluralistic culture traversed by reasonable disagreements. It resembles the commonality of the artistic project pursued by an orchestra, as in Dworkin's example of a liberal community, or of the political project captured by Habermas's expression 'constitutional patriotism'. The ordering function of the artistic project with respect to the alternative procedures and strategies for completion is exerted via a reflective judgment concerning how any given solution will affect the overall well-formedness of the work of art or, in other words, its potential for arousing an *aesthetic experience*, where the expression 'aesthetic experience' is meant to be neutral between four distinct accounts of aesthetic validity: (1) the account that equates the work of art's aesthetic validity with its potential for 'setting the imagination in motion' (Kant in paragraph 49 of the *Critique of Judgment*); (2) the account that equates the work of art's aesthetic validity with its potential for 'disclosing a world' (Heidegger); (3) the account that equates it with the work of art's potential for bringing an experience to its fulfilment (Dewey); and (4) the account that equates the work of art's aesthetic validity with its potential for eliciting the feeling of the 'furtherance of life' in its perceiver (Kant in paragraph 23 of the *Critique of Judgment*).

In a similar way, the ordering function of justice conceived along judgment lines *vis-à-vis* conflicting claims is exerted via a reflective judgment concerning how a given solution to the practical problem at hand will affect the overall chance of the political project institutionalized in the political community to lead the identity of that political community to a fully fledged fulfilment.

One obvious objection to this view would point to a basic difference between an artistic and a political project. In any artistic communal enterprise, be it the repertoire of a philharmonic orchestra or a movie, each member voluntarily subscribes to the initial project in a sense that does not immediately apply to the case of the citizen of a polity. As citizens we grow up and develop our political autonomy within the space of a preformed political project, embedded in the constitution of our country. At some point, coming of age, we find ourselves in the midst of an ongoing political practice. In what sense is our position similar to that of an artist who assesses alternative solutions to the problems raised by the stylistic encoding of the initial project in some medium? It is similar in that we can assume that an implicit consensus to that project is expressed by the citizen who resides in his country, exercises her right to vote, collects the benefits of her participation in the division of labour and exerts the prerogatives of citizenship.

Particularly interesting is a second aspect under which we can draw an analogy between the settling of artistic controversies and of those controversies that concern justice when justice is conceived along judgment lines. In both cases the solution to a controversy is assumed to be in some sense 'better' or 'more valid' than the alternatives – as opposed to being just a solution that the totality or majority of the parties involved happens to *prefer* – and yet its superior validity cannot be understood as the property of better fitting a preordained impartial principle. Given that the source of the normativity of the better solution lies in its perceived potential for better bringing to fulfilment the project-like moment of the superordinate identity which contains the contending parties, if we want to make sense of how the ordering function can be exerted by a notion of justice whose normative force is so conceived it is necessary to understand the nature of the kind of judgment at work here. In fact, if we can't resort to the notion of applying a yardstick to the available alternative solutions to a practical or aesthetic controversy, how are we to make sense of an alternative being better than another?

After a long detour through the context of justice and the source of normativity for the cogency of justice, we are once again back to Kant's question. Consistently with the linguistic turn we can only assume that our notion of justice enables us to discriminate better and worse solutions to practical controversies because our judgment on the impact of the various alternatives on the chances of fulfilment of the relevant political identity draws on certain shared intuitions concerning the authenticity of an identity or, in another terminology, is an *oriented reflective judgment*. The ordering function rests then on the orienting function exerted by certain guidelines on our judgment. In *Reflective Authenticity: Rethinking the Project of Modernity* I have tried to spell out the nature of oriented reflective judgment[12] as a kind of judgment which is not principle-bound but, on the other hand, is not completely unbound either – a kind of judgment in which certain guidelines *orient*, without dictating, the processes whereby we come to valid conclusions. In that context, the argument was developed with reference to aesthetic judgment and judgment concerning the fulfilment of identities. The orienting factors were described in terms of a number of dimensions – coherence, vitality, depth and maturity – which can be shown to be constitutive of our intuitive idea of the authentic fulfilment of an identity. These dimensions function not as criteria, but rather as ways of articulating different facets – which sometimes may be in tension with one another – of a basic sense of the 'furtherance of life'. They help us articulate our sense that one alternative, aesthetic or practical, better 'furthers life', to use Kant's expression. In a similar way, reflective judgments concerning justice do not amount to an infinitely open search for a 'universal under which to include the particular', but are rather *oriented* reflective judgments concerning the best way to bring to fulfilment the identity growing at the intersection of two or more contending parties. Orienting factors in this case not only are the general dimensions of the fulfilment of any identity, reconstructed in Chapter 5 of *Reflective Authenticity*, but include also a much more specific guideline: the *ideal of equal respect*. It is the operation of this ideal which ensures that the case of assessing what justice requires appears equally distant from the paradigmatic cases of solving an equation and interpreting a work of art and appears closer to the case of appraising instances of martial valour, politically responsible action, friendly care, interpretive skill, success in child-rearing, therapeutic help, effective legal assistance, educational effectiveness and the like – all instances of conduct which cannot be assessed on the basis of rules, yet whose assessment seems to rest on intuitively shared meanings. A judgment view of *justice* can exert its ordering function because our judgments concerning the merits of the alternatives are guided not only, as every other reflective judgment, by the dimensions of the fulfilment of identities in general, but also by the ideal of equal respect for all human beings.

This consideration shifts now the focus of our discussion on the new notion introduced: what is the ideal of equal respect? Before addressing this question in Chapter 8, however, I will introduce a pair of distinctions aimed at making more specific the undifferentiated notion of 'justice' used thus far and will explore in more detail some further facets of the aesthetic analogy.

Moral and Political, Elementary and Fully Fledged Conceptions of Justice

Thus far 'justice' has been treated as synonymous with *normative validity* or *rightness* in general. The judgment view, however, offers the possibility of differentiating levels of normative validity according to the *scope* of the superordinate identity implicated. More specifically, we can distinguish justice in a *political* sense and justice in a *moral* sense. In a political sense justice designates what is required by the fulfilment of the identity of the political community which includes the citizens, the social groups or the factions that are involved in a practical controversy over interests or values. Such a formulation may seem open to the accusation of paving the way to a totalitarian outcome – justice as the primacy of the good for a collectivity over the good for the individuals who belong to it. This false impression can be quickly dispelled by pointing out that totalitarianism is a political category – it refers to the oppressiveness of certain political arrangements – and to that extent immediately sets the discussion at the level of the political legitimacy of institutions. When the question of the meaning of justice is posed from that angle, the judgment view takes the dualist constitutionalist approach, with its emphasis on the 'inauspicious conditions', as its starting point and consequently understands the phrase 'what is required by the fulfilment of the identity of the political community' as denoting a range of symbolic objects located at the level of what Rawls has called 'constitutional essentials'. Among these symbolic objects are different orders of 'rights'. Far from embedding totalitarian overtones, the judgment view of justice enjoins whoever inquires into what political justice requires to address also the issue of rights – an issue which the judgment perspective has no trouble addressing from a reformulated Habermasian perspective, namely in terms of the question: what rights should free and equal citizens grant one another if they want to regulate their common life in such a way as to render it most conducive to the Pareto optimal flourishing and fulfilment of the political community to which they together belong?[13]

Not all the questions of justice with which we can be confronted are so broad and general. Below this level of generality, however, for instance when we deal with such cases as solving a controversy between neighbours or friends or local communities, perhaps we should rather use terms like *impartiality* or *fairness*, though we can certainly speak, in a looser sense, of a 'sense of justice'.

What is fair or impartial in a *political* sense, however, may not be just in a stronger *moral* sense. For example, the institutional practices of 'precautionary imprisonment' before trial and of capital punishment as found respectively in Italy and in the United States may meet the criteria of 'local justice' in a *political* sense, yet may fail to meet the more stringent requirements of justice in a *moral* sense. The *moral* point of view can be understood as the attending of the good or fulfilment for the broadest possible identity that we can envisage: the identity of humankind in its entirety. The 'view from nowhere', the impartial stance which so many authors have seen as a privileged standpoint for solving controversies about values or interests, if understood as the view of the matter from the standpoint of humanity, turns out to be then a view from *somewhere*, though not from *anywhere*. The standpoint of humanity is not a formula, an abstract principle of reciprocity or consistency, but a kind of 'concrete universal' bound up with substantive presuppositions that change over time. It was substantively different in the era before nuclear weapons, in the era when the total aggregate output of the production processes still posed a limited threat to the integrity of the natural environment, or when science was in no position to interfere with genetic processes, or in the time when population growth posed no threat to the survival of the species. Thus justice conceived along judgment lines is as contextual and particular as the good, because humankind is not immutable in the characteristics that are relevant for justice, but at the same time it also has the power – as the theorists who lean toward the model of generalizing universalism like to emphasize – to 'transcend' the particularity of all local contexts. This is possible not because our notion of justice can be disentangled from all context dependency – strictly speaking, the very idea of a normative notion 'transcending' all contextual determinations makes no sense from a standpoint internal to the linguistic turn – but because the context wherefrom it arises and within which it is operative is the largest imaginable context, which includes all other human contexts. In this sense the so-called 'view from nowhere' can be said to be always a view from somewhere, while being no less neutral (in the *situated* sense of the term) and 'transcontextual' because of that.

The distinction between the moral and the political conception of justice and their interconnection can be further highlighted in the following terms. There is no human political community whose members are not part of humanity as well and, for this reason, a political conception of normative validity – for example, as embedded in the constitutional essentials underlying the higher law of some specific polity – that does not include some reflection, however minimal or implicit, of an understanding of the good for humanity is a conception that fails to be true to that part of the people's collective identity which overlaps, however minimally or implicity, with the identity of humanity in its entirety. In this sense, a political conception of justice that is consistent with our moral conception of justice is always truer to us than one that is not. The only exception to this generalization would be provided by the radical opposition of justice and identity or authenticity to be found in the 'race of devils' counterfactually hypothesized by Kant – provided that such a race decided to live in a political community.[14]

On the other hand, the two conceptions of justice are differentiated in the sense that lack of reflection of the moral standpoint, the point of view of the good for humanity, in the political conception embraced by a given polity is not cause for automatically disqualifying the latter as a possibly valid conception – for the relation cannot be one of subsumption in the sense of the determinant judgment model of validity. A conception of justice embraced by a political community that fails to make it consistent with *some* kind of vision of the good for humanity – namely, their own – will only be less adequate to that community than a conception of justice that vindicates also the overlap aspect of the collective identity of the community, except once again in the case of a 'race of devils'.

From this perspective we can also understand the sense in which it is possible to say that a judgment view of justice continues to possess a *universalistic* dimension of cogency. It is a cogency quite different from the one that the notion of justice was supposed to exert from within the determinant judgment model of validity. It is not cogency by subsumption or a cogency that can be made the object of demonstration. It is the kind of *exemplary* cogency that the well-formed work of art possesses. It certainly projects an element of normativity – we have a sense of the *inner necessity* or non-contingency of certain artistic solutions that belong together in a fusion of meaning and form – but that necessity cannot be demonstrated and does not command automatic replication to other contexts.

From the same perspective we can make sense of what can be called the *elementary* conception of justice: dividing a cake in equal shares by having a person cut it and another choosing the portions. It is the elementary form because it is justice in the context of a distributive controversy such that the parties have a minimal interest in attending the overlapping sector of their identities. *Minimal* or *elementary justice* is adherence to the ideal of equal respect understood as a device for ensuring that the solution provides everyone with the same chances for attaining her own individual good. Notice that the parties in this case continue to share a minimal interest in the preservation of the overall thinner area of intersection. It is a *minimal* interest because they are not concerned with the *flourishing* of that identity, yet it is an *interest* in so far as the parties, by virtue of their decision to follow a consensually agreed procedure rather than unleashing a conflict over the contended resource, manifest their desire *not to disrupt* the thin framework of 'peaceful interaction based on indifference' which pre-exists their coming to a distributive contest. The mistake of most deontological theories of justice of liberal inspiration is to unduly generalize this special case, and to present 'minimal justice' or 'the elementary form of justice' as synonymous with justice as such.

The Aesthetic Analogy Taken Seriously

Time and again in the course of this book I have been making reference to aesthetic notions in order to elucidate various aspects of the relation of justice to judgment. This represents no novelty. The aesthetic analogy between the work of art and justice is explicitly used by Dworkin in order to elucidate the inner dynamic of constitutional adjudication, and a similar reference is used by Michelman in order to illustrate the difficulties of the model of jurisgenerative politics. In this chapter, I have drawn on the aesthetic analogy in order to show how the ordering function that we usually associate with a political conception of justice can be conceived as resting on the same kind of 'impartiality without principles' that guides our judgments and choices in matters of aesthetic production. It is now time to explore somewhat more closely, but still quite tentatively, the potential inherent in this analogy for helping us to make sense of our intuitions concerning justice. A fully developed discussion of the issue would require a volume of its own.

The explanatory potential of the aesthetic analogy reaches much further than providing illustrations for the dimension of judgment involved in constitutional adjudication and jurisgenerative politics. It sheds light on the nature of judgments about what political justice requires. Let us take the example of impressionism. It has never been the case, in aesthetics, that our judgments about the exceptional well-formedness of Degas's *Leçon de dance*, Manet's *Le déjeuner sur l'herbe* or Renoir's *La grenouillère* are thought to be valid by virtue of their tracing a connection between the single paintings and something called 'impressionism', which has been previously and independently established as being a valid pictorial manifesto. On the contrary, because we find in Degas's, Manet's and Renoir's paintings a quality of exemplary self-congruence which produces a powerful aesthetic experience and because we realize that there are certain aspects that these paintings share in common, we become interested in a reconstruction of certain underlying constitutive patterns of their production – a reconstruction of what we now take to be a set of pictorial patterns to which we give the conventional name of 'impressionism' – and we regard the impressionist style of painting as a valuable aesthetic tradition. The interesting point, from the vantage point of understanding justice in terms of the 'aesthetic analogy', is that we never assess the worthiness of the ideas of impressionism – for example, the idea of combining a rejection of historical, mythological and heroic subjects, a predilection for outdoor, everyday scenes, a great attention to the representation of the nuances of light and their effects on the perception of colours, a certain holistic accentuation of the power of colour to convey feeling and a correspondent lack of emphasis on pictorial details – aside from the single works of art that embed them. Indeed the 'aesthetic validity' of those ideas consists in their potential for inspiring pictorial works that do generate an aesthetic experience and in nothing else.

Let us now consider the case of 'democratic constitutionalism'. In this case as well we have on the one hand certain historically exemplary experiences such as the parliamentary practice of Britain, the republican *république* in France and the constitutional history of the United States and, on the other hand, a number of reconstructions of the principles underlying the political practice of democratic constitutionalism in these countries – a series of reconstructions, still competing with each other, to which we give the names of liberalism, republicanism, deliberative democracy and the like. Differently from aesthetics, it has long been believed that the normative validity of the institutions and practices of these countries was a reflection of their embedding principles contained in doctrines called 'liberalism' or 'republicanism' and independently established as valid. From this standpoint, the interesting quality of these experiences has traditionally been understood as coming from their constituting an actualization 'in practice' – with various degrees of approximation – of the right guiding principles of political justice. From this perspective, based on the model of generalizing universalism, the contest among institutional orders for recognition as normatively valid shifts onto the level of the general doctrines that provided justification. It becomes a contest among 'isms'. For a long time, for example, the defenders of orthodox Marxism dismissed the oppressive character of Eastern European polities as not really indicative of what Marxian principles of state organization entail. The term 'really existing socialist states' was coined in order to sever the link between the legitimating theory and its practical forms of institutionalization.

Now, the *diagnostic* thesis underlying this book is that this model of justification has gradually been set aside. The most prominent theorists within the liberal and republican traditions are less and less sure – as attested by the reconstruction, conducted in Part I, of their recent work – about the meaning of an expression such as the 'independently established validity' of a liberal or republican conception of justice. The *affirmative* thesis being advanced in Part II is that the understanding of justice most consistent with the recognition of the 'fact of pluralism' is an understanding that, as in the case of 'aesthetic validity', proceeds from the exemplary self-congruence of the concrete institutional order or practice. As with the impressionist paintings in their relation to the poetics of impressionism, the only thing which can be considered, so to speak, 'independently valid' is the optimally self-congruent nexus of an institutional order or, in Rawls's words, a 'basic structure' and 'who we are'. 'Liberalism', 'republicanism' and other such terms are understood as names that we attribute to reconstructions of the principles underlying the institutional orders that we evaluate. These reconstructions can be valid in two ways. They can be accurate or less accurate relative to the principles embedded in the institutional orders examined: our reconstructed principles of liberalism can match or fail to capture the functioning of polities that we intuitively recognize as liberal. In another sense, however, to take the aesthetic analogy seriously means that we conceive of the validity of such reconstructions as derivative with respect to the exemplary self-congruence possessed by the historical institutional constellations which they try to capture.

Another illustration of the aesthetic analogy comes from the psychological side of the aesthetic. A consideration developed by Simmel on the subject of love can be of help. We do not love a person because of the qualities possessed by her. If it were so, we would be bound to fall in love anew whenever we find an equivalent or larger concentration of the same psychological elements in another individual. Rather, we love someone for the uniqueness of her way of being: love, no differently than the sacred, admits of no arithmetics, no counting, no adding up of features, but is radically holistic. At the same time, the interesting feature, to which Simmel draws our attention, is that such 'uniqueness' is *created* by love. It is not the case that first the 'love object' exists, then comes within our perceptive range, and finally causes love to arise.[15] Rather, love arises and at the same time creates its own object. The other person, in other words, 'is not an invariable element that enters the status of being loved just as it enters all other configurations, or to which love is, as this might be expressed, appended. On the contrary, as "my love", the other person is a primordial and integral entity that did not exist before' (Simmel 1984: 160). In a formula, the love object 'does not exist prior to love itself but only by means of it'. This particularity of erotic love is true of a whole host of phenomena that we group sometimes under the rubric of 'love', sometimes under that of 'loyalty'. Also the loyalty to one's community, the love for one's idiom and the love for one's culture are directed at their own objects not so much in so far as these objects possess certain traits, but *unconditionally* – and, like erotic love, also these other forms of love are not shifted onto different objects simply because these new objects possess the 'loved' traits to a larger extent. Certain aspects of one's country, one's language, one's culture are loved because they are part and parcel of the country, language or culture with which one's biography is intertwined – not 'in general' or 'prescinding from' the object which embeds them. Between these traits and the object of our love a relation of mutual exemplarity obtains. Our love object exemplifies these traits in an exceptional way, but at the same time the single traits symbolize the love object – as for example the light or sounds or odours of certain urban scenes may come to symbolize the entire feel of a certain metropolitan life. This potential for symbolization – for being in an exemplary relation with something else – is instead missing in the possible substitutes for the original traits, for example in the not very different lights, sounds and odours that can be found in another city. In the latter case, in fact, the spark of love fails to fire off. The object – a new city to which we might have moved – may possess the features we love most, but these remain traits that we abstractly 'prefer' over others, and never become metaphors of a concrete love object, at least not for quite some time.

This quality of *agent-relatedness* inherent in the distinctive traits of the love object – their possessing value not independently but because they are traits of an object to which I am related in a certain significant way – somehow sheds light also on a way of understanding justice that can truly reconcile the universalist thrust associated with the idea of justice and the genuine acceptance of pluralism that originates in our being heirs to the linguistic turn. In modern political philosophy the idea of justice has traditionally been seen as something which imposes itself on us by virtue of an external cogency, a cogency that somehow *forces* us to recognize it. We are learning to see justice with different eyes, as something that commands respect by virtue not only of the fact that it proceeds from us – after all, many things proceed from us which don't command respect – but because of the special way in which it proceeds from us. As the lover's gaze creates his love where we, who are not within the circle of love, just see a person like any other; as the gaze of the nostalgic exile creates the spell possessed by certain lights, sounds, and odours where we, who come from a different city, see an urban scene like many others, so we participants in a political culture and in a political community create *justice* where others, differently situated, see mere opinions like any other.

It would be wrong to conclude that this is a relativistic way of understanding justice. The experience of exceptional congruency that links the lover and her object, in fact, possesses a relevance – the relevance of the psychologically exemplary, the other side of the exemplarity of the work of art – that extends beyond the original context and the original circle of persons within which such experience arose. Generally we do not remain impassive when it occurs to us to be the spectators of a love, of a moment of authentic reminiscence of the past or of a community that lives according to justice. We are somehow moved and experience a feeling of admiration. The object of our admiration is similar in all three cases. In the case of love, we admire and are moved not by the exceptionality of the love object – an exceptionality that exists only in the eyes of the lover – but by the extraordinary quality of the relation of the lover to the loved object, a relation marked by an exemplary congruence that can be perceived even by us who are beyond its context. Thus when we read about Benjamin's childhood memories of Berlin we are somehow moved by the exemplary congruence between the reminiscer and the objects of reminiscence. Today, when the old paradigm of generalizing universalism is losing ground, we are learning to follow the commands of justice not on account of the context-transcendent validity which ancient and modern conceptions attributed to it, but on account of the exemplarily congruent relation that we establish with one of its forms, and others establish with other among its forms.

As I have said time and again, however, judgments about justice are not as open as judgments about the congruence of an identity or the exemplary authenticity of a work of art. Just imagine how ludicrous it would be – within the realm of aesthetic judgment – to draw a line between the aesthetic manifesto put forward by impressionism and 'really existing' impressionist paintings, in the same way as a distinction used to be drawn between the ideal institutionalization of Marx's view of the socialist society and the 'really existing socialist countries'. Impressionism simply does not have a life of its own apart from the works of art in which its pictorial principles are embedded. On the other hand, we don't find it ludicrous to refer to 'really existing socialist countries', or even to 'really existing democracies' as opposed to democracy as envisaged by liberal and democratic theorists. The reason for this difference is that while in artistic production no extra-aesthetic concern can be imported into the creative or the evaluative process without thereby endangering the aesthetic well-formedness of the result, in the case of institutions and institutional orders, including clusters of 'constitutional essentials', we do legitimately try to 'realize in practice' ideals that we hold in theory – in a way that in the case of works of art does not apply. This fact should not be taken as counter-evidence against the aesthetic analogy as such. In fact, the suggestive force of the aesthetic analogy rests on the manifest difficulties of conceiving judgments about justice in terms of application of context-free principles to the facts of the matter. The fact that we can assess institutional realities at least *in the light* of principles that we hold to be justifiable should simply be taken as evidence that our judgments concerning justice and normative validity are *oriented* reflective judgments in the sense specified above: they are judgments on possible solutions to practical controversies which are rendered from the perspective of the fulfilment of the superordinate identity that includes the parties to the controversy – where the assessment of prospective avenues of fulfilment is conducted in light of the ideal of an equal respect owed to all the parties involved. To the specification of what this ideal entails we must now turn.

8

Impartiality without Principles and the Ideal of Equal Respect

The sort of impartiality without principles that grounds the normative force of our judgments concerning what justice requires is made possible – as we have seen in the preceding chapter – by the overlapping of our diverse conceptions of the fulfilment of identities over some dimensions that orient our judgment. What makes judgments about justice distinct from judgments about the well-formedness of works of art, the fulfilment of individual or collective identities, or the interpretation of texts, however, is the fact that our judgment is *oriented* – when we concern ourselves with matters of justice – by an *additional* element, to which I have referred above as the 'ideal of equal respect'. In the modern world it is the orienting force of this ideal that gives judgments about justice their specific colouring and grounds the ubiquitous expectation, destined to be so many times disappointed, that such judgments be closer, on a scale of predictability, to the case of assessing martial valour than to the more pronounced openness of aesthetic judgments.

Justice and Equal Respect

The ideal of an equal respect due to all human beings is a quite ancient and glorious one. In its purest form it can be found at the core of the Christian message of the Gospel, at the basis of the Protestant notion that even in matters of religious doctrine no believer should feel bound by any prescriptions other than those that he himself could freely read into God's scriptures, in the Christian idea that we are all creatures of the same God and, of course, underneath Kant's moral philosophy. Those versions of the ideal, however, are not, to put it in Rawlsian terms, 'political'. Rather, because they are enmeshed with substantive and highly controversial views of the nature of human beings understood as creatures of God or moral actors, they seem unable to function as reconstructions of the intuitions that guide the judgments about justice rendered by members of cultures other than Christian and other than Western. The ideal of equal respect that can serve the purpose of orienting our judgments concerning justice has a different genealogy: it constitutes the basic premise underlying the most representative contemporary conceptions of liberalism.

Underlying the models of justice or normative validity defended by Rawls, Habermas, Dworkin, Ackerman and Michelman we can see at work the notion that each citizen, when *political* justice is at issue, or every human being, when *moral* justice is at issue, is due the same respect as any other.[1] In a sense, the notion of equal respect represents a neutral terrain on which diverse theories of justice and normative validity overlap, in analogy with the Rawlsian image of a neutral area of overlap at the crossroads of different comprehensive, reasonable conceptions of the good. In its most general meaning, equal respect means that no one should be treated in a way that directly or indirectly suggests that his or her human dignity is of less import than that of anyone else. Beyond this point, however, the various versions of this ideal differ on a number of scores: for example, they embed different and sometimes competing understandings of what it is that constitutes human dignity, of the source of human dignity, or of the proper way to express such basic respect. Thus for some the ideal of equal respect is attained when basic resources are distributed in an egalitarian way, for others it translates in a fundamental right to obtain justification, for others it entails a symmetry of chances to put forward justifications and to criticize the arguments of others.

Equal Respect as an Implicit Assumption

In Chapter 1, I have reconstructed the intellectual trajectory that has led John Rawls from the philosophically more traditional normative standpoint of *A Theory of Justice* (1971) to the truly innovative standpoint of *Political Liberalism* (1993). I have emphasized the switch of perspective that underlies the different understanding of the validity of justice as fairness. In the former book the validity of Rawls's own view of justice is conceived as the potential, inherent in justice as fairness, to defeat the most important rivals in a philosophical contest for the title of 'best reconstruction of our intuitions concerning justice'. In the latter, the claim to validity raised by justice as fairness rests on its potential, unparalleled by any of its rivals, for constituting the core of an overlapping consensus among the otherwise diverging moral doctrines. The reasons that motivate such transition on Rawls's part are not just of biographical import, but on the contrary possess a crucial philosophical relevance. They reveal to us the nature of Rawls's deeper philosophical commitment – a commitment that never comes into focus and never leaves the status of a tacit premise. One of these reasons is certainly the realization of the extreme difficulty of bringing not just religious doctrines and conceptions of life, but also comprehensive *moral* perspectives, to an agreement concerning the principles of justice and political association.

As Larmore points out, the step from this realization to the adoption of the standpoint of 'political liberalism' is not a necessary one and reveals a deeper albeit unthematized commitment:

> After all, we may intelligibly ask why liberalism's response to this controversy [about the atomistic assumptions typical of 'metaphysical' liberalism] should be a reformulation of its principles. Why should liberalism become 'political', in the sense that Rawls and I intend? Why should liberal thinkers not dig in their heels and, observing rightly that no political conception can accommodate every point

of view, maintain that liberalism stands or falls with a general commitment to individualism? (1997: 10–11)

The answer is that deeper underneath the freestanding formulation of justice
as fairness lies a basic commitment to a certain version of the ideal of equal
respect – the 'moral heart of liberal thought' – which Larmore correctly
assumes to be presupposed by 'the idea that basic political principles should
be rationally acceptable to those whom they are to bind' (1997: 11). In fact, as
Larmore points out, the reason why the acceptance of political principles on
the basis of force would be regarded as fundamentally unjust by us cannot be
that the use of force is in and of itself wrong or unjust. For otherwise political association – which, as Weber taught us, always embeds within itself the
element of force and the possibility of its use – would not be possible. The
reason is rather that to seek compliance on a forced basis, without engaging
the person's ability to think on her own and for herself, or engaging that
person's ability only to the limited extent of appraising the threat of a
prospective use of force against her, means to treat that person *in a demean-
ingly different way from the way in which we consider ourselves*. It means to
engage that person's distinctive capacity to choose principles of conduct and
action in a different, much more *limited* way. Thus, concludes Larmore, in so
far as political justice is concerned, 'to respect another person as an end is to
require that coercive or political principles be as justifiable to that person as
they presumably are to us' (1997: 14).

The reconstruction of Rawls's most basic moral principle, however, is
given by Larmore a moral realist twist which creates some difficulties.
According to his view,

> it would be wrong to suppose that the moral principle of respect for persons plays
> the political role it does because reasonable people share a commitment to it. On
> the contrary, the idea of respect is what directs us to seek the principles of our
> political life in the area of reasonable agreement. Respect for persons lies at the
> heart of political liberalism, not because looking for common ground we find it
> there, but because it is what impels us to look for common ground. (1997: 25)

Consequently, what Larmore calls the *principle* of equal respect must be
'understood as having more than just political authority', indeed an authority 'that we have not fashioned ourselves' and that is 'binding on us
independently of our will as citizens' (1997: 16). It seems to me that two
claims which should be kept separate are here conflated: namely, the recognition that underneath the principles of justice as fairness lies a deeper
commitment to an ideal of equal respect on the one hand, and the idea that
such commitment originates in the discovery of the cogency of a principle
independent of our moral will on the other. The first thesis offers us insight
into a fundamental orienting element that gives our judgments concerning
justice those characteristics which make them appear closer to oriented reflective judgments about martial valour or friendly care than to purely aesthetic
judgments on the work of art, though in fact the basic structures of judgment
at work are the same. The second claim, instead, is more problematic. It

brings a view of justice so conceived into an unsolvable tension with our post linguistic turn pluralistic ontology and with the Rawlsian basic premise, following from a thorough acceptance of the 'fact of pluralism', that the justification of a conception of justice does not rest on its 'being true to an order antecedent to and given to us' – in this case, to a principle of equal respect that we *discover* to be binding on us – but rather on 'its congruence with our deeper understanding of ourselves and our aspirations, and our realization that, given our history and the traditions embedded in our public life, it is the most reasonable doctrine for us' (Rawls 1980: 519). Furthermore, if we accept also Larmore's second claim it would remain unclear in which sense a liberalism conceived as embedding a view of justice responsive to objective principles could still claim to be a *political* liberalism. Finally, Larmore's interpretation of Rawls sits uneasily with Rawls's understanding that what grounds the status of justice as fairness as the doctrine *most reasonable for us* is its compatibility with all the reasonable conceptions of the good – a compatibility which it is *up to the citizens* and not to the philosopher to establish. It is up to the citizens to determine whether justice as fairness or any other political conception of justice is compatible with all the reasonable conceptions of the good because every such assessment requires the weighing of political and non-political values and, if a philosophical conception of justice were to include such a ranking of political and non-political values, that conception would immediately forfeit its 'political' character and turn into just another comprehensive doctrine. From the standpoint of Larmore's interpretation, instead, the status of justice as fairness as the doctrine most reasonable for us would depend on its superior responsiveness, relative to its competitors, to the principle of equal respect – and, once again, the assessment of this quality of 'superior responsiveness' would become the philosopher's, and not the citizens', task.

In the case of Habermas, a similar argument can be developed. At two crucial junctures of his thought the ideal of equal respect appears to be a necessary presupposition. First, according to Habermas's principle 'D', as we have seen, valid are those norms 'to which all possibly affected persons could agree as participants in rational discourses' (1996a: 107). 'Rational discourses' are those discourses, in turn, which satisfy a number of idealized conditions. Among these idealized conditions, formerly listed as 'unavoidable presuppositions of discourse' and still earlier grouped under the rubric – later abandoned by Habermas because of its misleadingly concretistic assonances – of the 'ideal speech situation', we find the requirement that all the potential participants must have (a) equal opportunities to use communicative speech acts (i.e. to open and to continue the discussion through theses and counter-theses, questions and answers) and (b) equal opportunities to put forward interpretations, assertions, recommendations, explanations and justifications and to problematize, ground or rebut the validity claims thereby raised. These requirements in turn make sense only against the background of a deeper-lying assumption, namely that the participants in discourse ought to respect one another in the same way. The outcome of discourse counts as valid only in so far as such a mutual attitude of equal respect has obtained.

Second, Habermas's view of deliberative democracy and especially his conception of the co-originality of public and private autonomy, of rights and popular sovereignty, appears to presuppose the notion of equal respect. Habermas makes a point of rejecting the liberal priority of rights – a priority which, according to Habermas, is anchored in the crucial theoretical choice of starting from assuming that state power is already constituted. Instead, he starts his construction of a view of the modern polity from the 'horizontal' standpoint of the citizens who first create, through an act of collective will formation, the state power that they at the same time wish to curb. The crucial question is then 'What rights should citizens who recognize each other as equals confer on each other if they want to regulate their living together in the form of a rule of law?' It appears at first sight that we are faced with an eminently democratic rather than liberal view: rights are created via self-determination for the sake of self-determination, for the contribution that they can give to a well-ordered and non-degenerating process of democratic will formation. On closer inspection, however, it appears that the opposite is the case. The democratic process of deliberation is to be channelled by rights reciprocally and voluntarily granted by citizens who have granted each other a more fundamental right to have rights. However, as Larmore points out, the Habermasian view of deliberative democracy makes sense only if we understand that process as oriented by an even more fundamental right than that of having rights – namely the right, possessed by every citizen, 'to be bound only by political principles whose justification he can rationally accept' (Larmore 1997: 36). Habermas appears then a liberal *malgré lui*, since 'an individual right sets limits to democratic self-rule, determining as it does the sort of expression of the popular will that shall count as "democratic"' (1997: 36). The horizontal relation among citizens 'who recognize each other as equals' – the relation on which the whole construction rests – obviously presupposes the primacy of an implicit principle of equal respect. For the citizens' commitment to regard each other as equals cannot be *acquired* within political association: it is not one of the fruits of democracy but, on the contrary, is a commitment that constitutes and defines the kind of (democratic) political association that the citizens intend to form.[2] Also in *Between Facts and Norms*, then, we find a normative ideal of equal respect which is not understood as the product of communal, democratic will or, in other words, as the creation of the citizens' public autonomy but 'has an independent authority which individuals must acknowledge if they are to form a *democratic* will' (1997: 37–8, my emphasis).

Of all the authors considered in this book, Ronald Dworkin is certainly the one whose work demands less hermeneutical exercise in order to uncover an underlying commitment to the ideal of equal respect. In fact, the normative notion of equal respect is explicitly posited by Dworkin as the regulative ideal for democratic life and for orienting our selection of a principle of distributive justice. 'Equality of resources' is argued by Dworkin to be a more adequate view of distributive justice than the competing notion of 'equality of welfare' precisely on account of its embedding a higher potential for realizing the ideal of an equal respect due to all the citizens.[3] The two devices illustrated in the article on equality of resources – the equal initial distribution of clamshells and the auction – are designed in order to prevent individual differences, when combined with the accidents of luck, from resulting in the feeling of a different worthiness of each person, such as it is presupposed in all grievances about discrimination. Furthermore, the 'no-envy test' – according to which, if the auction has worked out properly, no one will end up envying the bundle of resources allotted to anyone else – would not be able to operate unless every citizen submitted to it was not assumed to be assessing the distribution under premises that include an ideal of equal respect.

Dworkin's account of democracy embeds an even more explicit reference to the notion of equal respect. Often accused of espousing a hyper-liberal perspective characterized by the absolute priority of rights over democratic self-rule, Dworkin has recently begun to develop an equality-oriented view of *democracy*, called the 'constitutional conception of democracy'. Distinctive of this view is the fact that the democratic rule of law is justified not so much in terms of the basic notions of public autonomy, self-determination or self-government, as in terms of a deeper ideal of equal concern and respect. Democracy appears to be the form of government most likely to fulfil the ideal that the state should speak with one voice to all the citizens. The defining aim of democracy is summed up by Dworkin as the bringing about of a predicament in which 'collective decisions be made by political institutions whose structure, composition, and practices treat all members of the community, as individuals, with *equal concern and respect*' (1996: 17). The immediate target of Dworkin is here what he calls the majoritarian conception of democracy – democracy as a form of government primarily designed in order to make collective decisions 'that a majority or plurality of citizens would favor if fully informed and rational' (1996: 17) – but obviously his formulation enters a tension also with other conceptions, such as Habermas's or Michelman's view of deliberative democracy. While the latter explicitly make the idea of self-government play a definitional role with respect to democracy, Dworkin's 'constitutional conception' adopts as an explicit starting point the notion that only implicitly runs underneath Habermas's complementarity thesis – namely, the notion that ultimately the ideal of equal respect is not the outcome of the exercise of democratic self-rule but, on the contrary, democracy is the best political arrangement for any collectivity of citizens who wish to base their political association on terms of equal respect for each other. The instrumental and derived status of democracy with respect to the ideal of equal respect is further highlighted by the advantage that, according to Dworkin, makes his account of democracy more attractive than the majoritarian one: namely, while all the cases in which majority rule has to give way to some other scheme for collective decision making are a source of difficulty for majoritarian approaches – a loss of democracy appears to be inevitably associated with these cases – the constitutional view has no trouble accommodating those cases, and suffers no internal tension, because it conceptualizes them as cases in which the overarching ideal to which democracy is responsive is better served by forms of decision making other than majority rule.

In the case of Bruce Ackerman, we find a fundamental commitment to the ideal of equal respect underlying both his model of the constrained conversation and his dualist conception of constitutional politics. The 'principle of rationality', which enjoins any 'power holder' to respond to any question concerning the legitimacy of his power 'not by suppressing the questioner but by giving a reason that explains why he is more entitled to the resource than the questioner is' (Ackerman 1980: 4), obviously presupposes the notion of an equal and mutual respect as the foundation of the vertical relation between the rulers and the ruled citizens. A similar consideration holds for the horizontal relation between citizens. The 'principle of neutrality' prevents any participant in the conversation from justifying his claims to resources in ways that imply either that 'his conception of the good is better than that asserted by any of his fellow citizens' or that 'he is intrinsically superior to one or more of his fellows' (1980: 11). It takes no arduous philosophical analysis to realize that a principle so conceived rests on the prior and more fundamental assumption that the citizens of a just polity possess a right to equal consideration – a right which does not result from, but is rather presupposed by, a constrained conversation about the distribution of resources.

Less obvious is the implicit presence of the ideal of equal respect in the framework developed by Ackerman in the *We the People* volumes. At first sight, in fact, the normative validity of the framing or transformation of a constitution seems to depend only on its capacity to reflect the will of the people, as formed after a protracted period of mobilization, debate and considered deliberation. On closer inspection, however, it becomes evident that the ideal of equal respect is presupposed within the framework of *We the People* in two important senses. The first sense is connected with the formal aspects of the process of constitutional transformation. As time and again Ackerman points out, the difference that sets the kind of bold constitutional transformations pursued by Madison, Lincoln and Roosevelt apart from the total rupture with the previous institutional order pursued by Robespierre or Lenin is the persistence, in the first case, of a strong and unabated commitment to the view that even institutional change of the highest order ought to be brought about in a consensual manner and to be justified with reasons that can prove convincing to all those concerned. Even during the darkest moments of constitutional transformation – for example, when the presidential ambitions of local politicians were kindled in order to keep the ratification process in motion, or when the threat of a continued exclusion from representation in Congress was used as a form of pressure on the legislative assemblies of the Southern states in order to induce them to approve the Thirteenth Amendment – the use of outright coercion was never contemplated. Despite the use of forms of unorthodox pressure, at least a formal fidelity to the ideal of a dialogue between equals bound by a relation of mutual respect was preserved.

The second sense in which the idea of equal respect underlies the framework of *We the People* has to do with the substance of the process of constitutional change investigated by Ackerman. The substantive theme that underlies and unifies the three salient moments of the Founding, the Reconstruction and the New Deal as episodes of one and the same narrative is the gradual construction of the national identity of the American people. The abolition of the veto power attributed to each single state under the Articles of Confederation; the priority, sanctioned by the Reconstruction, of the national quality of citizenship over local and more restrictive definitions of it; and the New Deal conception of a right, on the part of the government, to intervene in the economy for the good of the entire national community, all point to the overcoming of a narrower conception of the American polity as a federation of state-based local polities acting in their capacity as sovereign bodies – i.e. to the overcoming of a *modus vivendi* in the direction of an integrated national body politic in which each citizen counts for one. If we extend our consideration to the contemporary scene, the reorientation of constitutional politics from the formal path traced by Article Five to the practice of constitutional change via transformative judicial appointments also points in the same direction – the Presidency being at the same time the institutional source of the judicial appointments and the only office elected by one undivided national electoral body. Finally, Ackerman's own proposal for a transformation of the practice of constitutional amendment is clearly designed to eliminate the residual elements of the old 'anti-federalist' conception of the democratic process and to place the crucial constitutional choices concerning the ratification of proposals in the hands of an electoral body no longer segmented along local lines. This proposal is presented by him as a reflection of the ideal of conferring on the vote of a single citizen of populous California the same quota of influence on the shaping of a collective political will as the vote of a citizen of less populous Idaho. From this vantage point, the linkage between Ackerman's interpretation of American constitutional history, his proposal for the future and the idea of an equal respect, in this case concretized in the notion of an equal influence of each citizen on democratic will formation, appears under full light.

Finally, in the work of Frank Michelman we find that the ideal of an equal respect for and among all citizens is at the centre of his conception of deliberative democracy as one kind of democracy that fully reconciles the two guiding notions of 'government by consent' and 'government by the governed'. More specifically, the ideal of equal respect must be necessarily presupposed in order to make sense of what Michelman calls the *deontological* notion of political rightness embedded in his view of deliberative democracy. The deontological moment of deliberative democracy consists, in Michelman's view, in the fact that deliberative democracy subordinates any pursuit of a social or collective or aggregate *good* to a prior distributive constraint of *right*, namely of 'doing justice to each taken severally of as many as there are to be considered of some set of supposedly free and equal individuals or other social entities' (1996b: 7). Here too, as in Dworkin's account, the goodness of democracy is implicitly connected with its representing the political arrangement that carries the greater potential for 'doing justice' to the claims raised by each 'taken severally' of a set of 'free and equal' citizens.

The list of authors underneath whose basic categories we could find a deeper commitment to the notion of equal respect could be easily extended far beyond the five authors most closely taken into consideration in this book. Certainly, conceptions of justice and normative validity such as those put forward by Thomas Scanlon, Alan Gewirth, Brian Barry, Stephen Holmes, William Galston and Thomas Nagel would qualify as examples of conceptions of justice or normative validity as 'impartiality' that rest on the assumption of equal respect.[4] It would not be surprising if we discovered that it is much more difficult to find contemporary liberal conceptions of justice and normative validity that are *not* premised on the ideal of equal respect. Our inquiry then necessarily shifts onto another plane. What are we to make of this realization? Does the ideal of equal respect possess a significance that goes beyond that of being a moral ideal on which there fortuitously happens to be such a broad convergence?

The Meaning of the Ideal of Equal Respect

The ideal of equal respect has thus far been shown to assume a variety of meanings and to resist being reduced to just one of them. In some cases the fulfilment of this ideal has been interpreted as meaning that each and every citizen has an equal right to demand a justification of any normative arrangement. In other cases the ideal of equal respect seems to imply an equal distribution of the initial resources with which each generation of citizens negotiates its journey through the life-cycle. From another perspective equal respect means an equal share of influence over the processes of will formation that are under way in the political life of a collectivity. This diversity of meanings, however, does not speak against the use of the concept. On the contrary, it indicates an important potential inherent in it.

Potentially the notion of equal respect can play, with respect to the plurality of reasonable conceptions of justice and normative validity existing today, the same function of constituting an overlapping area that a political conception of justice has been shown to be capable of playing with respect to the diversity of reasonable comprehensive conceptions of the good. The notion of equal respect represents, in other words, an area of overlapping consensus in terms of which we can, as from a shared vantage point, assess the various claims raised within the more partial perspectives. The ordering function that 'political' theories of justice are supposed to exert with respect to claims raised from within ethically comprehensive standpoints can be exerted by the ideal of 'equal respect' in relation to the plurality of understandings of the notion of justice that the various approaches put forward. The ideal of equal respect cannot function as a criterion or a yardstick, and for that reason the use of the term 'principle' has here been avoided, but it certainly can be understood as the main guideline which *orients* the kind of reflective judgment with which we assess the merits of the competing reconstructions of the notion of justice available to us. It is the significance, for we moderns at the end of the twentieth century and the beginning of the twenty-first, of the idea that everyone should be treated with an equal concern for his or her human dignity that allows us to make sense of the variety of approaches to questions of justice and normative validity as variations around the same theme and, at the same time, gives us the feeling that judgments about what justice requires – for all their imperviousness to subsumption under principles – do nonetheless resemble more closely the relatively less controversial assessment of martial valour than the more indeterminate assessment of aesthetic congruence or well-formedness.

This interpretation of the significance of equal respect poses two tasks: on the one hand, it requires an elucidation of the meaning of equal respect that is itself *neutral* or *uncontroversial* with respect to the partial meanings illustrated above; and, on the other hand, it requires an elucidation of the ground for conferring such a deep normative value to 'equal respect'. If equal respect is not an ideal that within a just political order we democratically *decide* to adopt, but an ideal whose authority on us we *recognize* via a reflection on the presuppositions of a just political order, we need to address the question: whence does the ideal of equal respect draw its normative cogency?

While the second task will be taken up later in this chapter, a tentative outline of a reformulated notion of 'equal respect' will be offered here. One way of going about this reformulation is to interrogate ourselves about the reasons that seem to us more compelling for a justification of our commitment to equal respect. As we look for an answer to the question 'Why is equal respect due to all human beings?', our strategy for finding an answer seems almost inevitably to revolve around the search for some exclusively human characteristic, the possession of which might be a sufficient reason for claiming that an equal measure of respect is due to any possessor of it. 'Freedom', 'self-determination', 'autonomy', 'human dignity' are among the first candidates that come to mind. It is of crucial importance, however, to realize that when we speak of the possession of characteristics we are not in the process of describing something that happens to be objectively true about the constitution of the human agent: the moment we think that this is what we are doing, the judgment view of justice built around the notion of equal respect would lose its 'political' status and become one of the many comprehensive moral conceptions that ground a notion of justice on some controversial philosophical anthropology. The lesson to be drawn from Rawls is, on the contrary, that our chances of outlining a viable conception of justice rest on our avoiding any such controversial claims. I suggest that we start from a notion, which I hope will be uncontroversial, of the human being as possessor of a human life-course. That finite human life-course is endowed with a certain meaning which, under the conditions of modernity, is understood as being generated by the possessor of the life-course. We react with horror to the prospect of a human life devoid of any meaning whatsoever, lived in the total absence of any frame of reference – be it even the Dionysian idea of life dedicated to the pursuit of 'limit experiences' or to nomadic drifting[5] – against which the possessor of that life evaluates its course. The sense in which Heidegger has claimed that death gives meaning to life rests precisely on the horror of a life in which, because of the lack of a temporal frame, any action may be made to assume any meaning and thus in the end has *no* meaning. Now, the human ability to create that meaning – an ability somewhat more extended than the ability to form a conception of the good, which Rawls considers one of the two essential moral powers of the human being – and to make that meaning *unique*, something like what I have called the ability for *reflective authenticity*, is what we direct our respect to. It is an ability, a potential[6] for living one's life creatively amidst the human context of norms, values, social expectations and technical constraints on action – a potential that as such commands our respect even when it fails to be realized owing to external circumstances. The idea that an *equal* respect is due to every human being in matters of moral justice, and to every citizen in matters of political justice, is rooted ultimately in the intuition of the invaluable salience of the one irreplaceable life each of us has to the human being who lives it. Each of us is situated before the world in the predicament of having one and only one earthly life to live as an embodied human being – a formulation which is neutral with respect to religious worldviews that include a belief in a disembodied life after life, though admittedly not neutral with respect to religious views that admit of reincarnation.

In the end, equal respect is due to every human being on account of this very feature of human life: that each of us stands before his or her own life as the one context given to him or her for making use of that potential for creating meaning that he or she comes into the world with. This account of the reasons why equal respect is owed to each and every human being can function as a neutral reformulation of the intuition which the various conceptions of justice and normative validity try to articulate, each from a specific vantage point. It neither coincides with nor contradicts any of the particular understandings of the ideal of equal concern that were shown to undergird the conceptions of justice or normative validity put forward by the authors discussed above. Considered from the standpoint of a theory of democracy and of political freedom, the ideal of equal respect so conceived implies that individuals can be bound only by rules of which they are themselves the authors – hence equal respect translates into a right to demand and obtain justification, into a right to be a partner in dialogue with all the other fellow citizens. Considered from the standpoint of distributive justice, equal respect so conceived implies that each member of a political community ought to receive an equivalent share of initial resources. Considered from the standpoint of moral justice, equal respect implies that everyone ought never to be treated 'solely as a means' and his or her dignity ought never to be denied or humiliated. Today's multiculturalist sensibility extends the consequences of this intuition to a collective dimension. Assuming that each individual is constituted by a web of relations of recognition mediated by a culture, equal respect for the individual means that equal respect is also due to that web of relations and that culture that allow that individual to 'be born psychologically' and be herself.

At the same time, this reformulated version of the ideal of equal respect ought to be completed with a specification of what respect is not. Equal respect cannot mean 'equal worth'. Individuals do differ with respect to what they do with their potential for pervading their life with meaning: some people succeed in creating a unique matrix of meaning out of the mix of their life-project and the circumstances of their existence, others fail owing partly to the imperviousness of their circumstances and partly to their own weaknesses. The worthiness of a life is a function of all these factors and is not something that an individual can lay a claim to in the same way as she can claim a right to equal respect just on account of being a human individual. Similarly, equal respect cannot mean equal entitlement to an equal amount of welfare or an equal share of self-realization. For, once again, actual welfare and self-realization are a function of motivational, cognitive, environmental, historical and ultimately contingent elements on which no one can sensibly impose the expectation of a uniformity without thereby threatening the very conceivability of the individuality of each individual life.

It remains to be seen what credentials the ideal of equal respect so conceived can put forward in order to justify its status as the ultimate normative commitment that orients our judgments in matters of justice. What is the status of the reformulation offered above? Even granting that such reformulation could indeed be taken as a common denominator underlying the different and more specific understandings of equal respect, why should the mere fact of convergence or the substance on which the overlap among theories of justice and normative validity occurs command our allegiance? Why does the sameness of the predicament or condition under which in certain respects each human being faces her life – which after all is just one element of sameness in an ocean of differences relating to all sorts of aspects of human existence – enjoin equality of respect? As anticipated above, these questions will be addressed later, because the type of argument used for vindicating the normative ground of the ideal of equal respect has a broader significance: indeed, it provides a pattern for vindicating the plausibility of the judgment view of justice as a whole.

The Right and the Good Revisited

The modern reflection on justice is inaugurated by the rise of a sharp distinction – not to be found in the tradition of classical philosophy – between the standpoint of the right or justice and the standpoint of the good. While an explicit formulation of that distinction was offered for the first time only in the 1930 essay by Ross *The Right and the Good*, in Sidgwick's *The Methods of Ethics* (1907) we find a statement of the problem that has decisively contributed to shape the perception, so common in the majority of contemporary philosophers, that there is indeed, as Rawls puts it, a 'priority problem'. Those who have insisted on the sharpness of the distinction have also been those who have argued mostly for the priority of the right. In this section I want to rethink both the distinction between the right and the good and the priority issue from the standpoint of the judgment view. Does the judgment view of justice entail a questioning of the distinction? Does it entail a shifting of the priority back to the good?

While in many contemporary authors it is possible to find reflections on this distinction, one of the clearest statements of the issues involved is offered by Larmore. I will follow his argument, which may be taken as representative of a liberal approach to justice, for it offers a convenient backdrop for contrasting the received liberal understanding and the judgment view of this issue. Larmore's argument proceeds in three steps. First, we find a reconstructive claim based on Sidgwick, to the effect that while ancient philosophy by and large emphasized the priority of the good over that of the right, modern philosophy by and large has embraced the opposite thesis, namely the priority of the right over the good. This generalization is not entirely accurate. While it is certainly true that no classical philosopher has ever built his ethical thought around the notion of the right, the exceptions to the modern centrality of the right are more numerous than the figures mentioned by Larmore – Hume, Schopenhauer, Anscombe and Foot. The thinkers whose ethical thought revolves around the notion of authenticity are essentially 'virtue thinkers' – the classical virtues become concentrated and summed up in one central virtue of self-congruence. Despite the many differences that cannot be accounted for in this context, this is the case with Rousseau, Schiller and Kierkegaard. Then the whole existentialist tradition – and especially Sartre and Jaspers – is difficult to capture under the heading of the priority of the right. Equally difficult appears the attempt to grasp the ethical implications of Hegel's, Nietzsche's and Wittgenstein's thought in terms of the priority of the right. The whole pragmatist tradition appears recalcitrant to being classified within the Kantian morality of principle: Dewey's ethics, both in its 1908 and in its 1932 formulations, appears to be an explicit attempt to link morality and the actor's self-fulfilment. Finally, the argument through which Larmore calls into question the traditional understanding of utilitarianism as an ethics centred on the good is not entirely convincing: the assumption of an equal consideration owed to the consequences of an action for the good of each individual considered severally does not suffice to eliminate the standpoint of the good from the central place it occupies in the utilitarian perspective. The right-theoretical precept that individuals ought to be given equal consideration just affects the *mode* or the *how* of judgment, but in no sense contributes to the substantive determination of what is ethically worthy.

In a second step, Larmore offers a reconstruction of Kant's defence of the priority of right. Such defence, to be found in the *Critique of Practical Reason* (1997), is occasioned by Kant's need to clarify the status of the claim, previously advanced in the *Foundations of the Metaphysics of Morals* (1959), to the effect that the only thing unconditionally good is a will which orients itself to the moral principle. As Larmore points out, one of the early reviewers of the *Foundations* had objected that the thesis of the priority of the right, in so far as it presupposes that the principle of morality to which the good will is oriented is itself a good one, fails to overcome the classical priority of the good. In the context of the *Critique of Practical Reason*, Larmore identifies two separate arguments for reaffirming the priority of the right over such an objection. First, Kant observes that if the notion of the good is made the ground of the right – namely, by claiming that the cogency of the moral principle derives from its ability to promote the good – then, in so far as every notion of the good must somehow be connected with the agent's desires, also the moral will become connected with the agent's desire and pleasure. This conclusion Kant takes to be untenable. According to even the most charitable interpretation, in fact, the reason why the linkage of morality and the satisfaction of desire is to be rejected rests not so much with the intrinsic selfishness of desire – in fact, it is possible to imagine conceptions of happiness that are based on altruistic desires – as with the extreme variability of the objects of desire and the conceptions of happiness across individuals. Literally, 'every person has a different conception of his own happiness, shaped by his own constitution and particular experiences' (Larmore 1990: 22). Such an extreme variability makes the notion of happiness, and consequently the notion of desire, unsuitable as a basis for a moral principle that supposedly must apply to all. Larmore directs our attention to the distinctively modern quality of Kant's point: what motivates his rejection of the classical Platonic and Aristotelian view that all human beings orient themselves to a search for fulfilment guided by a notion of fulfilment unitary enough to serve as a criterion for discerning the virtues, after all, is his 'pluralistic awareness of the great variety of forms of human self-fulfillment and the absence of any ranking among them acknowledged by all' (1990: 22–3).

Second, Kant observes that because our knowledge of what satisfies our desires can only be empirical and never *a priori*, building the edifice of morality on desire and happiness, via conferring primacy on the good over the right, would be tantamount to forfeiting the 'categorical' or 'unconditional' quality that we intuitively associate with the commands of the moral law. Only the priority of the right over the good can vindicate this intuition. Since the categorical, as opposed to hypothetical, character of the moral principle is not beyond dispute, but is what needs to be established, Kant's second argument in practice seems to amount to begging the question. As Larmore reconstructs Kant's position, however, Kant was able to avoid this outcome by entrenching, so to speak, the categorical character of the moral law in the domain of the indisputably self-evident 'facts of reason' – truths that we are immediately aware of in our conscience, without being able to justify them by means of anything else.[7] I call this an entrenchment because while on the one hand it entails a renunciation of the ambition – still part and parcel of the eudaemonistic approach prevailing in ancient philosophy – to justify the moral point of view to those who don't already share it, on the other hand by fiat it puts the unconditional character of the moral law beyond dispute. Moral theory, from this perspective, can only explicate intuitions that it lies not within its powers to create. As Larmore puts it, from this point on Kant's claim will become that 'only the priority of the right over the good can make sense of what we know in our conscience to be the nature of moral duties' (1990: 24).

Finally, in a third step Larmore gives the argument for the priority of the right a very interesting intersubjective twist. Moral ideas and doctrines do function, like all other vocabularies, against a larger backdrop of assumptions. Sometimes entire clusters of these background assumptions suddenly undergo transformations and thereby introduce new tensions into previously consistent doctrines. In the case of Kant's argument, one of the background ideas that has undergone significant modifications is our conception of the individual. While atomistic conceptions of the individual – necessary in order to make sense of the notion of moral intuitions shared by every human being as such – have become increasingly problematical to us, the notion of an intersubjective constitution of the individual via culture-bound processes of mutual recognition has come to better match our intuitions. Consistently with this modification of the background, Larmore points out that the role of 'socialization' must be included. As he puts it: 'Categorical duties need then no longer appeal to a metaphysically obscure interest in morality, one which is supposedly ours whatever our experience may have been; rather, they pre-suppose only that there is an interest in categorical duties into which everyone can be socialized' (1990: 24–5). In other words, in accordance with Kant's argument, we can assume that the standpoint of the right is independent of, and prior to, the standpoint of the good; differently from Kant, however, the actor is supposed to partake of the moral standpoint not *a priori*, namely by virtue of her presocial constitution as moral subject, but *a posteriori*, namely by virtue of her experience as a member of society. The *a posteriori* quality of our access to the moral standpoint – continues Larmore – does not taint the unconditional quality of our commitment to morality. Even though we learn in a socialization process to *recognize* our interest in categorical duties, this recognition is totally independent of the empirical interests we may have: what we recognize is our interest in what we *ought* to do. For this reason, to link conceptually the unconditional quality of moral duty with the discovery of this socialization-induced interest in morality is not tantamount to subordinating the notion of the right to an overarching notion of the good.

A new difficulty, however, awaits the postmetaphysical or 'political' vindication of the priority of the right. As Larmore warns us, the unconditional precepts of a conscience redefined as the product of socialization could be challenged by refusing allegiance to the life-form or, more specifically, the worldview reflected in the socialization process within which we come to recognize the unconditional quality of our moral interests. To his credit, Larmore at this point refrains from resorting to two common but equally problematic argumentative strategies. The first alternative – the 'view from nowhere' alternative, understood in a looser sense than that attributed to it by Thomas Nagel – tries to overcome this difficulty by positing the viability of a standpoint of impartiality from which, detached by all local and contextual commitments that we may have, we gain the ability to assess, on the basis of our commitment to reason alone, all the other 'partial' commitments 'from the same distance from which we evaluate the commitments of anyone else' (1990: 27). From this privileged standpoint, thus, morally rational conduct can be said to have an unconditional claim on all rational agents independently of their empirical interests. Against this strategy, Larmore objects that a 'commitment to rationality' is 'too slender a basis for justifying the validity of any moral obligation, if it may not rely upon the validity of others' (1990: 27). It is ultimately unreasonable to claim – argues Larmore – that moral reason demands that our decisions 'rely upon reason alone' and exclude reference to all other sorts of beliefs that we may have concerning the subject matter (1990: 28). It is unreasonable because on this view very little could be justified, in morality or in any other domain.[8]

The other common strategy consists in a positive reappraisal of the classical idea of morality as a normative standpoint which ultimately is in the service of the agent's self-fulfilment – the rehabilitation of Aristotle's perspective. This strategy runs into the difficulty, already examined by Kant, of the plurality of notions of the good available to the modern actor.

Larmore tries to develop a third argumentative strategy:

> if the idea of a core morality applicable to all does indeed figure among our most settled convictions, and if it cannot be understood in terms of the priority of the good, then these convictions also commit us to a belief in the priority of the right. Why can these convictions not stand on their own? If we place at the center of our moral thought the fact that these are convictions from which we will not budge, then there will be something we can adduce as the source of these categorical obligations. Not God, nor practical reason, but rather the way of life expressed in these convictions. There will no longer be any positive reason to doubt the authority of conscience, when it speaks of duties that are unconditionally ours, once it is taken to be no more than the voice of the way of life to which we hold. (1990: 30)

I have followed closely Larmore's argument because it offers a very good entry point for a discussion of the right and the good from the standpoint of judgment. On the one hand, the judgment view of justice cannot be understood as a mere restatement of the priority of the good. Despite the connection, illustrated in Chapter 7, between justice and the authenticity of an identity, there is no way of deriving what justice requires from a *formal* view of the good – the only kind of view acceptable to us until the bells announce that God has resuscitated – in the same way as classical moral philosophy suggested that we draw a view of justice from a *substantive* understanding of the good for human beings. The guidelines of the fulfilment of an identity reconstructed in *Reflective Authenticity* (Ferrara 1998a), even when combined with the ideal of equal respect, are too thin for that purpose. And luckily so. But it is important to understand the reason why the good, when considered from the standpoint of the judgment view of justice, cannot be restored as the privileged standpoint *vis-à-vis* the right. This reason cannot be the one mentioned by Kant and reconstructed by Larmore. The reason why the good cannot be prior is connected neither with its being plural nor with its depending on experience. In fact, in aesthetics a pluralistic understanding of value has always prevailed – even centuries before the linguistic turn – and has never constituted an obstacle to dialogue between adherents of different schools or to the possibility of assessing the aesthetic validity of concrete works of art. It is not the dimension of plurality as such that prevents the good from being a suitable 'elementary' concept for morality, but only its plurality *if combined* with a principle-based and generalizing, as opposed to a judgment-based and exemplary, perspective.

Equally implausible appears the argument to the effect that the *a posteriori* quality of the good would render it disturbingly contingent. Kant's philosophy has been one of the most authoritative among the sources that have taught us to radically question the classical equation of empirical experience and contingency. Haven't we learned from the *Critique of Pure Reason* that necessity can inhabit the world of the *a posteriori* just as much as that of the *a priori*? I suspect that there simply isn't an *objective* or external reason of the kind sought by Kant that can force us to think, under penalty of being 'unreasonable', that the good cannot be prior to the right. We rather have to turn inward and ask ourselves whether we, given who we are, can truly *want* to articulate a moral and political philosophy centred around a substantive vision of the good. We might then discover that the strongest reason why the good cannot be prior with respect to the right is not an *external* one – namely, a reason bound up with necessary relations between concepts – but is a reason connected with our own *will*, our will as being formed in the context of our modern experience of religious and, more recently, ethnic wars.

On the other hand, as we have seen above, our understanding of the cogency of justice cannot be entirely detached from the notion of a life well lived, or eudaemonia, either. Justice cannot be 'categorical' or unconditional for us in the sense intended by Kant – namely, *independently of who we are*. It makes no sense for us to think of justice as something so detached and independent from the idea of a life well lived that an actor's effort first to determine, and then to follow, what justice requires leaves the quality of his life, under the aspect of fulfilment and meaning, unaffected.

The judgment view of justice, thus, cannot be easily placed under the rubric of either those conceptions that presuppose a priority of the right or those that presuppose a priority of the good. It rather belongs in the category of those conceptions of morality and justice which try to overcome not the distinction between the right and the good as such, but the rigid hierarchization of these two equally constitutive and essential notions.[9]

Far from questioning the distinction between the two standpoints of the right and good, the judgment view of justice purports to offer a better rendition of it – namely, an interpretation which fits our intuitions better than the competing deontological and neo-Aristotelian accounts. The core of the reformulation of the distinction from the perspective of judgment is constituted by the idea that the right and the good are not as radically discontinuous as the defenders of the priority of the right – from Kant to Habermas – have invited us to think.

In fact, from the argument developed in the previous chapters, it follows that no different kinds of practical rationality underlie our understanding of what the right and what the good require: in both cases that understanding is based on oriented reflective judgments.

Furthermore, the argument indicates that we cannot legitimately associate the standpoint of the right with abstractness and context independence (in fact, the requirements of the fulfilment of the superordinate identity are no less concrete and context-bound than the requirement of the fulfilment of the conflicting identities) and the standpoint of the good with particularism and context-boundedness (in fact, the fulfilment of any identity is all the more complete in so far as it takes into account all the aspects of the identity, and thus also the involvements with superordinate identities of which it partakes and the practical implications of these involvements). Even moral justice conceived as 'the good for humankind' is context-bound. For, as we have noted above, the standpoint of the good for humankind substantively changes over time.

Finally, justice appears, in light of the reconstruction offered in the previous chapters, as *contingent* as the good. While in any contest of normative orientations it is always possible to identify a comparatively better orientation, where 'better' means 'more conducive to the realization of the concerned superordinate identity', the capacity to allow for an actual settling of the conflict among followers of rival conceptions of the good depends on the existence of a sufficiently extended area of overlap and of the fact that the area of normative overlap is robust enough to sustain institutional implementation of the solution to the initial conflict. Rawls points out that the modern notion of justice is heir to the end of the religious wars. Justice as fairness, impartiality or neutrality begins when comprehensive religious visions are bracketed away for the sake of peaceful cooperation. Today, after three centuries, however, a certain cycle may be coming to a close. On abortion, the death penalty, and similar issues no neutral ground may exist which is thick enough for supporting an institutionally viable solution acceptable to all the reasonable contending parties. Then we will just have the *fact of conflict*, and what justice requires may once again resemble what the old gods required – namely, that we take up arms and fight on behalf of our visions of the good. With one major difference, however: this time the solution will come from a *democratic conflict*, the weapons will be ballots cast in democratic polls, and the battle theatre will be a public sphere in which we try to clarify to ourselves the sort of values by which we want to lead our life together.

The considerations developed above on these three points of contact between the good and the right should not blind us, however, to the more fundamental yet obvious fact that what the good for me, my family, my profession, my city, my country requires cannot be conflated – despite occasional and fortuitous instances of total coincidence – with what I ought to do when my understanding of my good clashes with other individuals', families', professions', cities' or countries' understanding of their own good. The point of my argument is not to deny the necessity of distinguishing the right and the good, but rather that such a distinction need not necessarily be associated, as has been commonly been assumed, with the priority of either notion. It is quite possible to combine the distinction of the right and the good with a *complementarity thesis*. In the remainder of this section I will try to illustrate the meaning of such a thesis.

As an individual moral actor, by definition I am interested in *eudaemonia*, living well or fulfilment – where these terms are to be understood in fully formal terms, such that even my choice to forgo 'fulfilment' in its everyday meaning still counts, in philosophical terms, as a choice made for the purpose of attaining fulfilment, albeit a fulfilment conceived along self-abnegating lines.[10] This initial consideration seems to make the good prior. However, in so far as – owing to my intersubjective view of subjectivity – I see my identity as not entirely independent of processes of recognition that originate in other, equally autonomous and fulfilment-seeking, individuals, I come to an understanding that the many aspects of my identity contain internal references and linkages to these identities as well and that I cannot achieve a complete fulfilment except by trying to bring to realization also those parts of my identity where the sediments of these relations of recognition are reflected. There are many ways of attaining my own good or fulfilment, but those which also further the realization of the parts of my identity in which the external involvements are contained will always be *more complete*. Hence the deontological moment of doing justice to the claims of other identities comes into the picture. The more complete, as opposed to partial, the fulfilment to which I aspire, the more I have to take the claims of others into account.

This consideration would seem to reverse the priority and to make once again the right prior. The claims of others, however, could be argued to impinge *normatively*, and not just affectively, on me – i.e. to generate an *ought* for me – only in so far as they are not simply another individual's claims, clashing with mine, but are also susceptible of being somehow included or reflected in the claims of a superordinate identity in which both I and the other, by virtue of our interaction, are involved. These claims, like all claims directed at the fulfilment of an identity, are oriented not to an abstract *right* but to a concrete *good*, albeit a good that goes beyond, includes and in some aspects may clash with my own, more limited good. And yet again, ultimately the good for a superordinate identity is not to be conceived as the summation of individual preferences directed at some object of collective desire – be it liberty, equality or some other equally lofty value – but rather must be conceived as itself the product of an oriented reflective judgment concerning what would 'make the most' of, and be optimally congruent with, the most crucially constitutive aspects of that identity. In this sense even the notion of the 'good for humanity in its entirety', which underlies our intuitions about moral justice, is not altogether independent of the unconditional character that we associate with the right. In fact, unless we are prepared to equate the good for a collective identity with what a majority of those who partake of that identity *believe*, at a given point in time, the good to be and we are prepared to accept all the relativistic implications of this move, it seems plausible to claim that the good for any identity – including that of humanity – is somehow connected to a judgment, rendered from a first-person as well as from a third-person perspective, concerning the optimal unfolding of its potential. In the impartiality *sui generis* of that oriented reflective judgment concerning the good, as the aesthetic analogy shows, there survives a crucial moment of the unconditional 'ought' built in the notion of right, and this moment of unconditionality manifests itself in the subjective perception, typical of those who render such judgments, that, at the very moment they exercise a supreme freedom, they are but obeying a *necessity* which stems from no external sources and yet, no less than all other sorts of necessity, leads them to say 'I can do no other'. This moment of unconditionality, impartiality or lawlikeness, independent of external principles and in the service of the fulfilment of an identity, is what Simmel has tried to capture with the expression 'individual moral law'.[11]

To sum up, although the judgment view of justice presupposes and reformulates along new lines the distinction between the standpoint of the right and that of the good, it operates with a combination of these two viewpoints – a combination that takes the form of an alternation and a complementarity under which it is difficult to discern a pattern of definite predominance. After the linguistic turn the right can no longer, for us, be grounded by a principle which rests on some piece of 'objective reality' – be it even the 'noumenal' reality of the moral subject. For this reason the right is bound up with our interpretation of who we are and by way of including this inevitable moment of interpretation it ends up containing a moment of the good. To interpret, in fact, is always to try to make the most of the interpreted thing, to see it in light of its optimal fulfilment. On the other hand, in so far as we wish the good to remain distinct from arbitrary preference we must think of it in *reflective* terms, as linked with a moment of judgment and, through that characteristic, our notion of the good ends up importing a certain connection with the dimension of 'ought' or with the right.

Radically Reflexive Self-Grounding

We have reached the last leg of a long journey. One more loose end needs to be tied up. Let me first recapitulate. By looking at the course taken by the work of important figures of contemporary political philosophy – John Rawls, Jürgen Habermas, Ronald Dworkin, Bruce Ackerman and Frank Michelman – an awareness emerges of the increasing uneasiness with which we consider the idea that 'what justice requires' is to be understood as the application of a general principle to a local context. The diversity of the philosophical agenda and thematic focus of these figures' work makes it difficult to evince one coherent alternative view of justice. I hope I have made a convincing case for the plausibility of just one quite modest claim: namely, that underneath such diversity it is possible to grasp one single moment of convergence – the increased salience, sometimes only implicitly acknowledged, of the relation of justice to the process and faculty of judgment. In the recent work of Frank Michelman, in particular, such relation gains a central role in his judgment approach to normative validity in higher lawmaking. In Chapter 6, I have tried to highlight the tensions that a judgment-based, as opposed to a principle-based, model of justice and of normative validity introduces in the framework of these authors. In this and the previous chapter I have tried to indicate possible ways of solving these tensions in the direction of a coherent *judgment view of justice*. I have started from a reconstruction of the 'context of justice' as understood by liberal political philosophy and have offered a reformulation of it designed to make it more consistent with those intuitions concerning the fact of pluralism which, by hypothesis, form our shared horizon. In the process of outlining such an alternative conception of justice a number of problems had to be addressed: first, the problem of identifying a source of cogency alternative to general and context-independent principles; second, the problem of accounting for the way in which a notion of justice reformulated along these lines can exert the 'ordering function' that theories of justice are designed and expected to exert. It is now time to address a problem which was merely mentioned in Chapter 7.

The alternative source of cogency for a notion of justice based on judgment was located in the kind of 'impartiality without principles' – parallel to the 'aesthetic impartiality' possessed by the better solution to an artistic controversy – which inheres in the better solution to a practical controversy, where 'better' means 'embedding the highest potential for bringing to fulfilment the project-like moment of the superordinate identity which includes the contending parties'. The possibility for an agreement among members of competing ethical cultures on the fact that a certain solution possesses such a potential to a greater extent was argued to rest, in the absence of common yardsticks, criteria or substantive shared orientations, on the nature of the *oriented reflective judgment* with which judgments about matters of justice can be associated. The guidelines which orient the otherwise total openness of our reflective judgment in matters of justice were argued to include not only the general dimensions of the fulfilment of identities – namely, the dimensions of *coherence, vitality, depth* and *maturity* specified in *Reflective Authenticity* – but also the *ideal of equal respect*. The problem left open can thus be summed up in the following question: what justifies the judgment conception of justice and, more specifically, what grounds the cogency of the ideal of equal respect as an orienting guideline for our assessment of competing solutions to practical controversies?

Let me start by pointing out that it would be a performative contradiction for a *judgment* view of justice to seek justification in terms of *principles*, in terms of a *substantive* conception of the moral subject, in terms of idealized conditions of dialogical conflict-solving embedded in the communicative use of language, or indeed in any terms other than judgment itself. In *Reflective Authenticity* I have tried to outline an analogously self-reflexive justification for a conception of validity centred on authenticity. I traced out two models of radically self-reflexive validation in Hegel's dialectic of the finite and infinity and in Heidegger's analytics of *Dasein* but tried to avoid their entrapments in the pre-postmetaphysical notion of *conceptual necessity* – a notion which seems to contain a residue of that idea of necessity *sub specie aeternitatis* of which we, the heirs to Quine's critique of the absolute distinction between analytic and synthetic, cannot but be quite wary.[12] Alternatively, I advanced the claim that the authenticity conception of validity cannot ultimately be vindicated, if we care to be consistent with the premises of the linguistic turn, but by a philosophical account of why it is authentic for us – authentic in the sense of 'exemplarily congruent with who we want to be' – to adopt this view of validity. This account must take the shape of a concrete narrative concerning the turning points in our history that have brought us to a predicament in which, if we want to be true to ourselves, we can only think of validity as bound up with authenticity. Over and beyond this narrative, our account of validity was argued to have to include also an elucidation of those *future-oriented* and *project-like* elements of our identity which receive their sense from, and contain constitutive references to, those turning points, even if only in order to subvert their direction. In the end, from the reconstructive and the prospective components of this philosophical account – of which in *Reflective Authenticity* I tried to give only a methodologically angled description, not a fully fledged version – ideally we should be able to derive, as an implication, the proposition 'For these reasons the authenticity view of validity is the only conception of validity that beings like us can adopt'; or, putting Luther's famous saying to a new use, 'Here we stand. We can do no other.'

This approach can be applied also to the problem of justifying the judgment view of justice and normative validity, as well as to the problem of explicating the source of cogency for the ideal of equal respect. We had encountered problems of justification susceptible of being addressed on the basis of the same radically reflexive strategy also when considering the reasons why we would *not* want to articulate a view of morality based on the priority of the good, when considering a way of avoiding Michelman's problem of infinite regress, and when reconstructing Ackerman's defence of a reform of Article Five procedures for constitutional amendment. Let me begin to illustrate how the argument could go by recalling Ackerman's case, which actually provides an example, fully immanent to the liberal tradition of political philosophy, of the kind of normative bootstrapping that is at issue here.

As was pointed out at the end of Chapter 4, in the concluding section of *Transformations* Ackerman reveals the actual status of his reconstruction of three essential transformative moments in the constitutional history of the

United States. His reconstruction is designed to serve as a supporting historical argument to be used by the Supreme Court in upholding a special statute
called the Popular Sovereignty Initiative – a statute proposed by a (second-
term) President and aimed at making it possible to change the Constitution
also by a new procedure as well as by the more traditional Article Five procedure. According to this new procedure a second-term President could put
forward a formal proposal for constitutional amendment. If the proposal is
approved by a two-thirds majority in Congress, it is then placed on the ballot
in two national referenda to be held in conjunction with two consecutive
presidential elections. If approved both times by the national electorate –
thus by an electorate no longer segmented along state lines – by a three-fifths
majority, the presidential proposal becomes then higher law. Interesting from
our angle here is the kind of argument that Ackerman envisages the Supreme
Court to develop – an argument tacitly anticipated in its main lines by
Ackerman, for it to make sense to present the historical reconstruction at the
centre of *Transformations* as possible supporting evidence. Such an argument
is an argument about the best way of fulfilling a concrete identity – the
constitutional identity of the people of the United States. About this identity
it is said that two features of it – (a) its *national*, as opposed to federal,
dimension and (b) its making room, ever since the Civil War, for an active role
of the Presidency in constitutional change – are not adequately allowed to
unfold under the premises of Article Five, at least since the time of the Civil
War, and that instead the Popular Sovereignty Initiative would allow such
aspects of the constitutional identity of the People of the United States to
come to an adequate expression. A deeper-seated assumption of the argument that Ackerman envisages the Supreme Court to develop concerns the
positive valence of the growth in salience of the nation-centredness of the
identity of the American People, as a process obviously connected with the
fuller realization of the ideal of equal respect owed to each citizen.

I call this an instance of normative bootstrapping because, notwithstanding the implicit reference to a fuller realization of the ideal of equal respect,
ultimately the highest-order justification mobilized by Ackerman in support
of the normative validity of his proposal is an argument about the best way
of bringing the constitutional process in line with the requirements of the fulfilment of the political identity of the people. The optimal self-congruence or
authenticity of such an identity provides the ultimate evaluative horizon
against which to check the validity both of the *diagnosis* – namely, the existence
and growing frustration of a need for a nation-based, unitary process of collective will formation – and of the proposed *remedy*, namely the new procedure
for revising the Constitution. It is an instance of normative *bootstrapping*
because the normatively coloured notion of congruence or optimal realization of an identity on the one hand serves the function of justifying the
argument in favour of the Popular Sovereignty Initiative and its related ideas,
but on the other hand *qua* ultimate justificatory horizon is also supposed to
self-validate itself as the framework within which the matter addressed by the
initiative ought to be considered. As in aesthetic judgment, there is no need

assumed by Ackerman for a separate argument establishing the legitimacy of that way of considering things.

In Frank Michelman's work we find an analogous juncture at which a radically self-reflexive form of justification could be developed – that is, the problem of infinite regress in the chain of democratic legitimation. How can there ever be a *democratic* founding of a deliberative democracy or a *constitutionally* legitimate framing of a constitution? Drawing on Michelman's 'Always under Law?' as well as on his 'Can Constitutional Democrats Be Legal Positivists?', higher lawmaking, including the framing of a constitution, can be understood as something that never amounts to 'writing on a clean slate' but, on the contrary, always builds on 'some already present, politically grounded, idea of reason or right' (Michelman 1996a: 302) and enters an *interpretive relation* with some other normative framework. In this sense even the framing of a constitution is not the 'legal big bang' that it appears at first sight to be, but an act of interpretation, transformation and objectification of an intuitive understanding of right which the people perceive as bound up with their communal identity. There is no need, if we follow this line of reasoning, to presuppose external criteria for assessing the rightness of a constitution or to anchor its legitimacy in its potential for ensuring a *stability* that will enable the members of the polity to reconcile the exercise of their capacity for justice and their effort to pursue their vision of the good. Rather, applying a radically self-reflexive mode of justification to Michelman's premises, we could reinterpret his view of the 'goodness of validity as conducive to stability' as a goodness that exists only *for us*, given *who we are*. Being able to avoid tragic conflicts between our capacity to pursue a conception of the good and our having a sense of justice is something of value not independently of our history and the 'spiritual situation of our time', but *because of* who we are and of the salience that the value of 'being at one with oneself' has acquired and, despite the occasional resurgence of Dionysian-oriented 'critiques of the subject', maintains in Western culture. Once again, on this reading – which is perfectly compatible with the spirit of Michelman's judgment view of higher lawmaking – the validity of our attribution of value to validity is recursively justified in terms of the congruence of 'validity' so conceived with our identity. The ultimate justification of the judgment view of higher lawmaking is that we would not be 'we' or we would be less 'we' if we adopted a different view. Once again, in the end we encounter a kind of collective 'We can do no other' that rests on a thick account – that by no means can be offered here – of the authenticity of our identity.

In a negative vein, a similarly self-reflexive argumentative structure underlies the conclusion, generated in the context of my effort to disconnect the modern distinction of the right and the good from any unnecessary and indefensible priority thesis, that the judgment view of justice does not imply a restoration of the standpoint of the good as the privileged one. Among the reasons in support of this reconstruction of our moral intuitions, Kant's objections against the priority of the good were considered and found wanting.

If judgments on matters of justice are conceived as oriented reflective and not as determinant judgments, then neither the plurality of conceptions of the good nor the rootedness of the good in experience constitute insurmountable obstacles. Rather than with reasons that are *external* to our identity and compel us to deny the priority of the good under penalty of being unreasonable, the justification of such denial is best supported with reasons that are entirely *internal* to our identity. As the descendants of those who survived the religious wars that raged through Europe a few centuries ago and of those who witnessed the horrors of the Inquisition; as the sons and grandchildren of those who survived the wars unleashed in this century by totalitarian nationalism and the horrors produced by the institutionalization of the idea of 'reason in history'; and as contemporary witnesses to the resurgence of ethnic intolerance, to the horrors of 'ethnic cleansing' in former socialist countries and of tribal strife on the African continent, we find it hard to reconcile the priority of the good with who we have come to be through this long and tormented historical process. In other words, we can't regard it as good for us – in the sense of being not compatible, let alone conducive, to an optimal fulfilment of our identity – to embrace a vision of justice and normative validity based on the priority of the good. Also in this case, I have only offered here a description of how the argument for distancing our judgment view of justice from the thesis of the priority of the good *could* be developed in a radically self-reflexive way. The actual outlining of the argument would require an interpretive case based on nothing less than a reading of the history of the West between the Reformation and the end of the 'short century' – an interpretation angled from the vantage point of the relation between moral culture and political ideas.

The clearest example, however, of a radically self-reflexive grounding comes from the argument through which we can account for the cogency of that ideal of equal respect which plays a special orienting function when we form our judgments about what justice requires – that is, the argument which fulfils the second task posed by the elucidation of the significance of the ideal of equal respect as specified above in the first section of this chapter.

If 'equal respect' is not the name of an ideal that we *choose* or *prefer* to embrace over other equally possible political and moral ideals, but designates an ideal that we *discover* to be binding on us in matters political and moral, how can we conceive of the source of its bindingness? The argument which can both justify the cogency of this ideal and at the same time avoid reference to general principles is an argument that leads to a reflective judgment, partly historical and partly ethical, about who we are and the constitutive relation that the notion of equal respect bears with certain traits of our identity. For the same reasons as *Reflective Authenticity* could not include an exhaustive argument concerning the authenticity for us of conceiving of validity in terms of authenticity, but is rather to be counted as a long methodological premise to such an argument, so in the context of the present book I have limited my objective to presenting an interpretive and diagnostic argument concerning the direction toward which recent political philosophy seems to be headed and a reflection on how to complete the transition toward a conception of justice more in line with our postmetaphysical intuitions. It goes beyond the scope of this objective to provide a fully fledged justification, corroborated by all the necessary elements of historical detail concerning who we are, for the judgment view of justice. Nevertheless, with the intent of at least showing the form that such an argument should ideally take, I will briefly mention, in closing, three reasons that militate in favour of the judgment about the inevitability for us, if we want to be as true to ourselves as we can, of adopting a judgment view of justice centred around the notion of 'equal respect'.

First, the ideal of equal respect, as an 'orienting factor' for reflective judgments in matters of justice, has the advantage, over other possible competitors, of an unsurpassed inclusivity. It provides a terrain of overlap not just among the five conceptions of justice or normative validity discussed in this book but, under one rubric or other, among all of the modern conceptions of justice – whether deontological or consequentialist. Although I cannot develop the point in this context, I believe that even in the case of Nietzsche the notion of equal respect could be shown to play a role. To be sure, it is a notion of equal respect with a very restricted domain, implanted in an elitist conception which sets the ethics of the few *exceptional men* in opposition to the morality of the *herd men*. Despite this problematic aspect of his ethical conception, however, it is at least dubious that the moral relations of the exceptional men with one another should recede – in Nietzsche's view – to a kind of Hobbesian war of all against all where might makes right. In a passage where Nietzsche addresses the issue, we are led to imagine (a) that the exceptional men do interact with one another and (b) that the moral relations among them 'overcome' the petty and invidious metrics of justice typical of herd men and herd men's relations with the exceptional[13] not in the sense of regressing to a sheer contest of power, but in the sense of including a finer appreciation of the transvalued values. The exceptional men do recognize each other as *equally self-creating* creatures and in that recognition is embedded the same kind of respect that the conceptions of justice despised by Nietzsche meant to extend to every human being.

Second, the notion of 'equal respect' appears to be located at the centre of a Quinean holistic network of interrelated meanings with which we negotiate our relation to moral phenomena. It possesses a potential, unparalleled by any other notion in that symbolic network, for affecting the formation of a great number of neighbouring concepts, which could not be conceived in the way they are if we didn't presuppose the ideal of 'equal respect'. Let us just think, for example, of how impoverished our concept of the *person*, as a source of autonomous action, thought and value, would be if we didn't associate it with the idea of a basic and equal respect owed to every person as an irreplaceable source of action, thought and value. Let us think, furthermore, of the idea of human dignity as a focus of recognition and respect among individuals. How could the idea of *human dignity* retain its intuitive meaning if detached from the idea of equality in the attribution of it? In fact, within

Nietzsche's framework, the unequal dignity of the exceptional and the herd men is inevitably combined with an understanding of the mass of common human beings as less fully human than the exceptional. A third example is provided by the idea of democracy. A notion of *democracy* which did not include that of an equal respect owed to every citizen would not allow us to make sense of the rule of law and of the majority principle. Fourthly, the idea of the *legitimacy* of institutions, of the political order and of authority would be difficult to conceive in the terms in which legitimacy is usually understood if we didn't presuppose the notion of equal respect. This list could be expanded much further, but let me just briefly mention the most obvious case: *justice*. The idea of rendering justice to someone without the idea of an equal respect between the parties to the controversy is an incoherent idea. Even those authors who, like Hegel and Nietzsche, envisaged the possibility of denying that equal respect is owed to common human beings and world-historical figures, herd men and exceptional ones, were correspondingly forced to operate implicitly with *two* distinct notions of justice – a 'base' and 'petty' one for one kind of human beings, and a more sublime kind of justice for the superior kind. In the view of justice that I have tried to outline above, the connection between justice and equal respect manifests itself in the difficulty of conceiving justice as an oriented reflective judgment concerning the optimal fulfilment of an identity encompassing the contending parties unless the total openness – and thus also potential oppressiveness – of such a judgment is kept under check by the understanding that equal respect is owed to each of the parties involved.

Third, the significance of the ideal of equal respect for us is bound up not just with a conceptual and philosophical dimension but also with a *histori-cal* one. Equal respect is a historical product of the end of the religious wars that ravaged through Europe in the sixteenth and seventeenth cen-turies. It is a common heritage to all those born in the West that after the religious unity of Europe under Roman Catholicism was broken, owing to the rise of the several branches of the Reformation, the forces of the Counter-Reformation, instigated by the Council of Trento and by the influ-ence of several Popes, for nearly a century pursued the fatal project of restoring that religious unity by force, through the political hegemony of the Austrian Habsburgs and the military might of the Catholic Crown of Spain. The result was a continental bloodbath fuelled by the clash of dynastic, commercial and geopolitical interests grafted on either side of the religious divide – an unprecedented carnage that started in France in 1562 and 1567 (on the night of St Bartholomew) and brought destruction and desolation to most territories of Europe, from Flanders to Bohemia, from Denmark to Sweden, from Germany to northern Italy and northern Spain, until the Peace of Westphalia put an end to the Thirty Years War in 1648 and the Treaty of the Pyrenees to the war between France and Spain in 1659. These events provide the backdrop against which the modern exclusion of reli-gious issues from the arena of a secularized politics was achieved. Understood as a principle of equal respect applied to matters of religious conscience, the principle of tolerance – first institutionalized in the Edict of Nantes of 1598, but soon swept away by the upcoming conflict – became part and parcel of the political culture and the common conscience of the peoples of Europe. Thus the claim that we wouldn't be 'we' if we embraced a conception of justice that didn't include the ideal of equal respect entails much more than the idea of remaining faithful to the conceptual core of a philosophical tradition. It includes a dimension of faithfulness to certain fundamental formative experiences of the Western modern consciousness.

Similarly, the notion of equal respect has played a central role in many important social movements of the modern West, starting with the workers' movement and continuing with anarchism and radical syndicalism, and including the abolitionists, the suffrage movement, the civil rights movement, the feminist movement, the animal rights movement, the gay movement, up to today's multiculturalist sensibility. While it is certainly true that many other movements have arisen which do not orient themselves to the ideal of equal respect or actually loathe it – the fascist and Nazi movements before the consolidation of the respective regimes, the Ku-Klux-Klan, the OAS in France in the wake of the Algerian crisis, the racist and anti-immigration movements in contemporary France and Germany, and many others – these movements by and large, with the notable exception of the racist anti-immigration movements, either no longer play any significant role in today's politics, and their past successes are perceived as sources of embarrassment for the citizens of their countries, or operate in an illegal way. The impact of these two kinds of social movements on our political culture could not be more different. While the former movements, even when they died out, have seen significant aspects of their central claims incorporated and institutionalized in the contemporary democratic polity, though often in an imperfect way – and, as some undoubtedly would maintain, in a somewhat enervated way – the latter movements not only cannot be said to have contributed to the shaping of our political life to any comparable extent, but their views and claims actually stand out as negative examples to which the democratic polity defines itself in outright opposition.

The considerations outlined above illustrate how closely the ideal of equal respect is bound up with who we Western moderns of the beginning of the twenty-first century are. Yet it would be misleading to think of the unsurpassed potential, inherent in the ideal of equal respect, for bridging the gap between the most diverse traditions of moral and ethical thought, of the constitutive role that the ideal of equal respect plays in our understanding of many normative concepts, of its relation with certain historical experiences that have shaped our cultural and political identity, and of its central role in many of the social movements that have stimulated the social learning of our societies, as a set of sufficient reasons for claiming the necessity for us to place equal respect at the centre of our conception of justice and normative validity. For there cannot be any such necessity proceeding from the outside – from a description of things that are true of us independently of what we want to be true of us. In fact, we cannot think of our relation to ourselves along merely cognitive, descriptive lines.[14] We also have a *practical* relation to ourselves, embedded in the project-like moment of our identity, the 'who we want to be' that completes the appraisal of 'who we are'. The 'who we are' moment of our identity can never *dictate* to us what we ought to become, because it lies within our power to change – or, at least, to direct our efforts to change – what we have been up to a certain point. But one of the basic ways of making ourselves one way or another consists of beginning to *see* ourselves in a certain way, namely to adopt a certain *description* of ourselves, a description that allows us to reconcile 'who we are' and 'who we want to be' in a coherent picture. This is the sense in which the considerations about equal respect offered above must be understood. They are meant as a possible description of aspects of who we are that dovetail with our judgment that the best reconstruction of our intuitions on justice is a view of justice as bound up with a reflective judgment oriented by the ideal of equal respect – an oriented reflective judgment on the fulfilment of the superordinate identity which includes the contending parties. These considerations are also meant to highlight the indispensability for us of this notion of justice by way of allowing us to see with what aspects of ourselves, of our history, and of our institutions we would lose touch if we adopted a reconstruction of our intuitions about justice that did *not* hinge on equal respect. The appeal that such dovetailing of our view of justice with a certain description of who we are is expected to exert, both on us and on those who are not us, is ultimately to be understood not as linked with an *external* necessity that impinges on us – against whose intrusive compellingness we would rebel – but as the kind of *internal* necessity experienced by those who come to the judgment that a certain answer to their question (whether an aesthetic, an ethical, a moral, a political question) carries a superior potential, relative to other answers, for eliciting that feeling which Kant has called the *furtherance of life*. In that sense, and only in that sense, the judgment view of justice is supposed to induce in us the feeling that we truly 'can do no other'.

Notes

Introduction

1 See Durkheim (1967: 23–5).

2 See Rorty (1989: 5).

3 Converging but from a different perspective see also Dancy (1993: 55–8).

4 See Rawls (1987a). A similar conception is propounded in the chapter 'The Idea of Public Reason' in Rawls (1993: 212–54).

5 Kant (1986: 18).

6 See Kant (1986: 35–6).

7 See Simmel (1987).

8 I am indebted to Charles Larmore for having drawn my attention to the risk of overemphasizing the rigidity of determinant judgment and the openness of reflective judgment. A similar point was raised by Axel Honneth. Though they may not agree with my own response to their objection, their remarks were very helpful to me.

9 More on this will be said in Chapter 3.

10 See Wittgenstein (1953: sections 201–41).

11 Hannah Arendt has tried, unsuccessfully in my opinion, to reconstruct the exemplary form of universalism underlying reflective judgment in her *Lectures on Kant's Political Philosophy* (1982). See also Beiner (1982; 1983; 1997). However, by construing the relevance of examples to 'exemplary' validity in a way that parallels the relevance of schemata to cognition, Arendt fails to highlight the distinctive 'orienting' nature of general notions in reflective judgment. For a more detailed argument, see Ferrara (1998b).

12 On the convergence of the deontological and consequentialist moral-theoretical paradigms from the standpoint of generalizing universalism, see Williams (1985) and Larmore (1987: ix).

13 Here I follow the considerations put forward in Scanlon (1982: 111–12) and in Nagel (1991: 33–40). On the merits of Scanlon's solution see Barry (1995: 67–72).

14 On this distinction see Dworkin (1989a: 484–7). For a critical appraisal, see Williams (1989).

Chapter 1

1 The notion of the basic structure, thus understood, is discussed also in *Political Liberalism*. See Rawls (1993: 258).

2 For a critique of Rawls's notion of the self, see Sandel (1982: 54–9, 62–5, 179–83). For Rawls's response, see Rawls (1985a: 238–9). On the constitutive relation of justice to the present distributive arrangements, as opposed to the legitimacy of the transactions that have led to the present distribution, see Nozick (1974: 183–231). On the difficulties of justifying the adoption of a maximin strategy in the original position, see Barber (1989: 297–301) and Williams (1981: 94–100; 1985: 77–80). On the moral-psychological presuppositions of the second principle of justice, see Nozick (1974: 239–46). On the cogency of the 'thought experiment' argument applied to real dilemmas, see Dworkin (1989b: 16–53). On the relation of Rawls's position to Kant, see Höffe (1984; 1987). See also Daniels (1989) and Reath, Herman and Korsgaard (1997).

3 This view is further elaborated in Rawls (1993: 72–3), where the deliberation in the original position is reconceived as a case of pure procedural justice.

4 For an interesting account of this stage in Rawls's thought, see also Pogge (1989).

5 Cf. Kukathas and Pettit (1990: 60–3).

6 See also Rawls (1974; 1975; 1979).

7 See Rorty (1988: 262–8). For a counter-interpretation, see Brink (1989).

8 See Rawls (1985a: 224).

9 See Rawls (1985a: 224; 1988: 252–3).

10 See Rawls (1993: 24–5, n. 27).

11 See Rawls (1993: 36).

12 For an issue to be removed from the political agenda means that it is no longer regarded as an appropriate subject for political decision by majority or other plurality voting. In other words, the relevant provisions of liberty of conscience or personal liberty are assumed to be 'set once and for all' (Rawls 1993: 151).

13 On the formation of the *overlapping consensus* see Rawls (1993: 164–8).

14 For a discussion of this moment with reference to the articles antecedent to *Political Liberalism*, see Kukathas and Pettit (1990: 124–5). On the Humean elements in Rawls's early conception of justice as fairness, see Barry (1978).

15 Rawls's new understanding of the grounds on which the validity of justice as fairness rest shows here more than a family resemblance with the notions of *reasonable* or *unanimous* 'non-rejectability' suggested respectively by Scanlon (1982) and Nagel (1991).

16 For an interesting alternative to Rawls's view of the politicalness as uncontroversiality, see Gaus's notion of the 'robustness' of a theory of justice (1996: 9–10).

17 The idea of goodness as rationality, the idea of permissible comprehensive conceptions of the good, the idea of political virtues, and the idea of the good of a well-ordered society. See Rawls (1993: 176ff).

18 See Rawls (1993: 28).

19 The standpoint constituted by the original position serves the function of bridging the gap between the principles of justice that we recognize as binding (the 'principle of equal liberties' and the 'principle of difference') and the ideals which underlie our own conception of a well-ordered society. The standpoint of the citizens of a well-ordered society includes the normative conception of the moral actor as endowed with a capacity for a sense of justice and a capacity to entertain a conception of the good, and contains as well the normative idea of society as a fair system of cooperation that spans over several generations.

20 See Rawls (1993: 28).

21 Among the different interpretations of wide reflective equilibrium, see Daniels (1979; 1980), Sosa (1991), DePaul (1986), D'Agostino (1988) and Raz (1982).

22 See Rawls (1993: 99–101).

23 On the nature of the burdens of judgment see below in this chapter.

24 See Rawls (1993: 39–40).

25 For a different view see Nozick (1974).

26 Rawls points out that Habermas does himself acknowledge the substantive dimension of his own discursive view of justice in *Faktizität und Geltung* (1996a: 536). The difference with Rawls is only in the more reduced extent to which substantive assumptions are allowed within the conception of justice.

27 See Rawls (1993: 250–1).

28 See also Raz (1990).

29 See Rawls (1993: 65–6; 1995: 147).

30 The burdens of judgment are discussed in Rawls (1993: 56–7).

31 See Habermas (1996a), Ackerman (1980) and Larmore (1987).

Chapter 2

1 For accurate and detailed reconstructions of this central intuition, see Baynes (1989: 77–121) and Rehg (1994). See also Forst (1994: 289–306).

2 See Habermas (1990: 197).

3 See Habermas (1990: 108).

4 See Habermas (1990: 108).

5 I am grateful to Rainer Forst for having alerted me, in private correspondence, to the need for such a justification, with the substance of which he may not necessarily agree.

6 This lecture was later included in *Justification and Application*, with the title 'On the Pragmatic, the Ethical and the Moral Employments of Practical Reason' (Habermas 1993b: 1–17).

7 See Habermas (1993b: 5).

8 Between the ethical sphere and the moral point of view proper lies the intermediate area of 'concrete universalism' – the universalism of the Golden Rule. The Golden Rule already represents a *moral* principle, in that it enjoins the actor to take the good for others into the same consideration as the good for herself, but still contains an egocentric residue in that the acceptability of the generalized maxim is still assessed with reference to what is acceptable to 'me' and not to what is acceptable to 'everyone else'. See Habermas (1993b: 8).

9 See Habermas (1996a: 161).

10 For succinct and accurate reconstructions, see also Rasmussen (1994), Baynes (1995) and Rehg (1996). Very useful are also White (1995), Rasmussen (1996b).

11 See Habermas (1994a: 139).

12 See Rousseau (1967: 30–5, 55). For a commentary, see Ferrara (1993a: 55–60).

13 According to Larmore, Habermas fails to produce a convincing argument concerning *why* we should want that the lawgivers be coextensive with the lawtakers. Underneath the discourse principle, objects Larmore, lies an implicit principle, unacknowledged by Habermas – the principle of equal respect. Habermas's derivation of rights from the communicative conditions of the exercise of political autonomy works only because, in a circular way, he understands the exercise of political autonomy as presupposing (a) a recognition of this principle and (b) an acceptance of the limitations that it imposes on the autonomous communal will of the legal consociates. See Larmore (1993: 326–7).

14 See Habermas (1994a: 49).

15 'At the same time immigration, i.e. the expansion of the legal community through the inclusion of aliens who would like to acquire the rights of membership, requires a regulation in the equal interest of members and petitioners' (Habermas 1996a: 125). On the same issue, see also Habermas (1993a).

16 These two aspects of the function of the constitutional state are explored by Habermas in the last two sections of Chapter 4 of *Between Facts and Norms*.

17 For a more balanced conception of the connection between the three powers in a deliberative democracy, see Ackerman (1991: 104–62).

18 The proposal would allow the President to nominate an extra justice whenever a current justice reached age 70 and chose not to retire, up to a new total number of justices of 16.

19 This is the gist of Habermas's criticism against Joshua Cohen's conception of deliberative democracy, as outlined in Cohen (1989; 1993). For an interesting commentary, see Bohman (1994: 915–16; also 1996). Of related interest are also Mansbridge (1980), Fishkin (1991) and some of the essays collected in Mouffe (1992).

20 See also Habermas (1989).

21 While the basic tenets of *mainstream* liberalism are somehow reflected in Habermas's reconstruction – though the central figures of *liberal* liberalism, discussed in this book, are ignored perhaps because their closeness to his own position would somehow undermine the 'third-course' argument that Habermas is trying to develop – the republican tradition is virtually caricaturized. The Arendtian, Pocockian and neo-Aristotelian strand of republicanism (best illustrated by Pocock 1975) is arbitrarily taken as representative of the whole of republicanism. Instead the existence of a Ciceronian, Machiavellian, Tocquevillian strand that by no means

shares the premises called in question by Habermas is systematically ignored. For interesting reconstructions of this alternative strand of republicanism, see Skinner (1978a; 1978b; 1983; 1984; 1986; 1992), Skinner and Viroli (1990), Pettit (1997), Spitz (1994; 1995a; 1995b) and Viroli (1992). For a critique of the Habermasian interpretation of republicanism, see Viroli (1995). For one of the few examples of a kind of 'communitarian republicanism' that somewhat fits Habermas's description, see Sandel (1996).

22   This makes Habermas's proposal distinctively different from the democratic-participatory emphasis to be found in Barber (1984; 1987). See Habermas (1996a: 300–1 and 1994b). For Habermas's response to Joshua Cohen's (1989) version of deliberative politics, see Habermas (1996a: 304–6).

23   On the distinction between 'strong' and 'weak' publics, see Fraser (1992).

24   See Habermas (1996a: 373–4).

25   Bohman (1994: 924–5). For a different interpretation, see McCarthy (1994: 49). McCarthy points out that 'independent public forums . . . are for Habermas the basis of popular sovereignty': they provide the locus for the exercise of public reason, and the results of that exercise are 'translated via legally institutionalized decision-making procedures . . . into the legitimate administrative power of the state' (1994: 49). For a very interesting collection of essays on the public sphere see Calhoun (1992).

26   Bohman suggests that one of the points of contention between a liberal and a radical view of democracy is the locus of public reason: while for liberal democrats like Rawls public reason is exercised in the state institutions, for radical democrats public reason is exercised 'in the public sphere of free and equal citizens', as was the case, for example, with the civil rights movement Bohman (1994: 926).

27   See Habermas (1996a: 310). The same point is made by Nancy Fraser (1992).

28   See Ackerman (1983; 1989; 1990) and Holmes (1988). See also Moon (1991), Barry (1995) and Waldron (1993).

29   On this point, see also Benhabib (1989a: 149–54).

30   In a similar vein, see also Ackerman (1994a: 369–71).

31   Habermas (1990: 88). On the relation between the discursive notion of validity and Habermas's philosophy of language, see Rasmussen (1996a; also 1990: 56–74).

32   Occasional resurgences of this aspect can still be observed in *Between Facts and Norms*. One of the most interesting proposals for 'weakening' the determinant judgment premises of this version of the discourse ethics has been put forward by Seyla Benhabib (1989b: 381–3; 1992: 26–38). See also Ingram (1987). Very interesting also is the suggestion to cast the universalization test in a negative form, as a test for screening out norms that cannot be universally accepted (i.e. at least one of the concerned persons would presumably object): see Wellmer (1991: 201–2). In a similar direction points O'Neill's version of constructivism (1989: 211–13). The idea of a fallibilistic principle of universalization is also at the centre of Scanlon (1982) and Nagel (1991).

33   On this point, see McCarthy (1996) and Bernstein (1996).

Chapter 3

1   On this point, see Covell (1993). See also *Social Theory and Practice* (1980).

2   See Murphy (1990), Guest (1992) and Burke (1992).

3   See Dworkin (1977: 7).

4   See Dworkin (1977: 24–5).

5   See Dworkin (1977: 27).

6   See Dworkin (1977: 26).

7   See Nozick (1981: 294ff).

8   See Dworkin (1977: 40).

9   See Dworkin (1977: 43–4).

10   See Dworkin (1977: 44).

11   See Dworkin (1986: 318).

12   See Dworkin (1986: 322).

13 On the relation of *integrity* to the notion, equally central in Dworkin's approach, of *rights*, see Gaffney (1996). For a critical appraisal of the integrity approach, see Ackerman (1994b: 520–1).

14 See Dworkin (1986: 228–32).

15 See Dworkin (1986: 234).

16 See Dworkin (1993: 67).

17 See Dworkin (1993: 18–19, 30–60).

18 See Dworkin (1990: 55–8).

19 A further distinction is needed, argues Dworkin, 'between what we value incrementally – what we want more of, no matter how much we already have – and what we value only once it already exists' (1993: 73). Our longing for knowledge is an example of the first type of importance, and human life and art are examples of the second. We do not wish that there be as many works of art as possible, but once one exists, we feel we owe it special protection on account of its being intrinsically valuable. Aside from the case of something becoming sacred out of association with something else already sacred, something acquires sanctity by virtue of the way in which it came into being. Works of art and cultures are intrinsically valuable 'because they embody processes of human creation we consider important and admirable' (1993: 75). Much in the same way we think of animal and vegetal species as intrinsically valuable on account of the creativity implicit in the process of natural evolution that has produced them.

20 See Dworkin (1993: 88).

21 See Dworkin (1989a: 484–5; 1990: 42–7).

22 Rousseau was the first to point out the moral import of the dynamics of identity formation and identity change, in his novel *Julie, or the New Héloise*. See Ferrara (1993a: 93–109).

23 On the distinction between the communal life of a community and its political life, see Dworkin (1989a: 492–9). For an interesting appraisal, see Honeyball and Walter (1998).

Chapter 4

1 See Parsons (1990: 323–4).

2 See Chapter 1 in Walzer (1983).

3 See Rawls's argument against the dependency of even pure procedural justice on an uncontested notion of the good (1995: 170–3).

4 See Ackerman (1980: 50–1).

5 See Chapter 5 of Ferrara (1998a).

6 On the relation of fulfilment to hedonism and authenticity, see Chapters 1, 4 and 5 of Ferrara (1998a). See also Seel (1995).

7 For a reconstruction of this view of the good, see Jay (1995).

8 For interesting considerations on Ackerman's constitutionalism in relation to Dworkin's, see Bellamy (1996).

9 See Ackerman (1991: 6; also 1992). For critical appraisals of Ackerman's dualist model of politics, see Galston and Galston (1994) and Herzog (1994). For a response, see Ackerman (1994b).

10 For a view of this sort see Michelman (1995a; 1996a; 1996b).

11 See Ackerman (1991: 14–15). The point is further elaborated in Ackerman (1994b: 531–3), where the author introduces a distinction between his own point of view, not unfavourable in principle to the entrenching of certain fundamental rights, and the point of view actually reflected in the Constitution, which contains no such entrenching of any core of inalienable rights.

12 Michelman distances himself from Ackerman's version of the distinction between higher lawmaking and ordinary, in that in his opinion Ackerman tends to convey an overly conformist view of normal politics and to overlook how under the ashes of its routines often the seeds of constitutional transformation are already implanted. See Michelman (1988: 1522–3).

13 Equivalents of these three types can be found in the series of emblematic portraits of con-

temporary individuals occupying various positions on the spectrum from involvement to privatism drawn in Bellah et al. (1985); see also Bellah et al. (1992) and Bellah (1991).

14 See Ackerman (1991: 267–8).

15 For example, some states allowed for conventions to make constitutional proposals, but not for ratifying conventions. See Ackerman (1998: 37).

16 See Ackerman (1998: 126).

17 In fact, Mississippi and other states did say 'No' to the Thirteenth Amendment.

18 The former provided relief for the emancipated blacks and the latter granted them the 'full and equal benefit of all laws and proceedings for the security of person and property, as is enjoyed by white citizens' (quoted in Ackerman 1998: 170).

19 See Ackerman (1998: 182).

20 Ackerman (1998: 311).

21 I can only refer the reader to Chapters 5 and 8 of Ferrara (1998a), where the question is addressed in general philosophical terms.

22 On this point see Ackerman (1998: 403–6).

23 See Ackerman (1991: 54–5).

24 This trend is also confirmed by Ackerman (1997).

Chapter 5

1 See Michelman (1995c: 16). Throughout this chapter I will quote, with Frank Michelman's kind permission, from unpublished drafts of his that are still undergoing extensive revision.

2 See Michelman (1995c: 55–6; also 1997b).

3 See also Michelman (1986; 1988).

4 See Michelman (1986: 47).

5 For a critical appraisal of Michelman's reconstruction of republicanism, see Fallon (1989: 1725–30).

6 See Michelman (1995a: 246–7).

7 For Michelman's understanding of the concept of community, see Michelman (1994b: 69–72). On the perfect compatibility of a certain republican (namely, more Machiavellian than Aristotelian) view of democracy with a certain liberal (namely deliberative, as opposed to 'pluralist' *à la* Dahl or Schumpeter) conception of democracy, see also Sunstein (1989: 1567–8; 1990; 1996) and Sullivan (1988).

8 See Rawls (1971) and Habermas (1990). For interesting defences of this view, see Forst (1992) and Baynes (1988).

9 See Dworkin (1990), Raz (1986) and Kateb's (1992) account of 'democratic individuality'.

10 See Michelman (1996c: 310–12).

11 See Dworkin (1996: 16–17).

12 On the notion of exemplary universalistic validity implicit in Simmel's notion of the 'individual law', see Ferrara (1997: 85–7).

13 See Michelman (1995a: 244–7). See also Michelman (1995c: 88–90), where the distinction is implicitly drawn via a discussion of the respective roles of the Supreme Court and the so-called 'People's Court'.

14 On the political movement that led to the Eighteenth Amendment, see Hamm (1995) and Ashbury (1968).

Chapter 6

1 For a partially convergent reconstruction, see also Josefson and Bach (1997).

2 See Habermas (1996a: 165). Significantly, in the German original edition (*Faktizität und Geltung: Beiträge zur Diskurstheorie des Rechts und des demokratischen Rechtsstaats*, Frankfurt, Suhrkamp, 1992, p. 204), Habermas listed also abortion and issues of criminal procedural law

(e.g. the prohibition against certain methods of presenting evidence) as instances of moral problems. These examples have disappeared in the English edition, which has been supervised by Habermas himself. On the same problem, see Bernstein (1996: 1143).

3 See Habermas (1996a: 166–7).

4 See Habermas (1996a: 166–7).

5 Even in Habermas (1993a), an essay largely concerned with multiculturalism, the issue remains unaddressed. See also the interesting considerations on cultural incommensurability in Ingram (1995; 1996). See also the contributions collected in Passerin and Benhabib (1996).

6 What is really surprising about this interpretation is that, even in the face of its obvious difficulties, rejection of it is not unanimous in the literature. While McCarthy explicitly rejects it when he states that '[Habermas] is not talking of the aggregation of individual interests but of the transcendence of merely particular interests in a search for the common good' (1991: 184), Wellmer appears inclined to accept it in holding that a valid norm is 'equally in the interest of all those affected'(1991: 148ff), and Habermas (1993b: 143–5) seems to corroborate this reading when he extensively and approvingly quotes Klaus Günther's (1988: 45–59) reconstruction of 'U' – a reconstruction entirely couched from the standpoint of 'interests'.

7 See Habermas (1996a: 161).

8 See McCarthy (1996: 1120–5) and Habermas (1996b: 1499–1501).

9 Rawls makes the same point against Habermas's idea of a purely procedural understanding of justice: see Rawls (1995: 170–5). Also McCarthy points out that in so far as different substantive worldviews and ethical perspectives 'figure in judgments regarding the common good, they will translate into differences on substantive questions of justice, that is, on whether specific laws or policies are equally in the interest of, or equally good for, all' (1994: 57).

10 Some of the internal tensions and ambiguities as well as the difficulties connected with intuitionist moral realism are highlighted in the essays collected in Cohen (1984) and Hunt (1992).

11 I have discussed this point more extensively in Ferrara (1993a: 145–7).

12 This, however, seems hardly sufficient to qualify the model of challenge as an aesthetic view of the good life. The same point is made by MacIntyre (1981: 180–1) in his discussion of the concept of a practice in relation to the notion of a skill, and his account of the model of challenge, understood as 'the model of the quest', has no aesthetic connotation.

13 See MacIntyre (1981: 63–4).

14 See Dworkin (1990: 32–3).

15 See Habermas (1996c).

16 For criticism along similar lines, see Bellamy and Castiglione (1997).

17 Indeed, Ackerman's claim is not that such entrenchment is undesirable or unjust, but simply that it finds no anchoring in any plausible interpretation of the present American Constitution. On the need for a new and entrenched Bill of Rights, see Ackerman (1991: 319–20).

Chapter 7

1 I have tried to offer a more detailed appraisal of the problematic and the still relevant aspects of Aristotle's notion of phronesis and of Kant's notion of reflective judgment in Chapters 2 and 3 of Ferrara (1998a).

2 The expression is Thomas Nagel's: see Nagel (1986) and, for the more recent version of his perspective, Nagel (1997).

3 I first developed this idea in Ferrara (1993b).

4 See Williams (1981: 135), Davidson (1984: 184), Geertz (1973; 1983), Gadamer (1975: 404–6) and Putnam (1983: 191–7, 234–8).

5 See Taylor (1985: 204).

6 See Walzer (1990).

7 The notion of situated impartiality underlying the judgment view of justice and reflected in the central proposition of the judgment view, thus, does not fall under the objections raised against the ideal of impartiality by Iris M. Young (1990: Chapter 4) and against liberal theories

⬛⬛⬛

of justice by Susan M. Okin (1986; 1989). See also the critique of liberal notions articulated in Shanley and Pateman (1991), Pateman (1985; 1988) and Phillips (1993); and the critique of the Habermasian 'subject of discourse' in Meehan (1995). On the other hand, the judgment view of justice is designed to offer that perspective for passing judgment on the merit of the various 'differences' which Nancy Fraser (1997) has invoked against the 'pluralist' or 'uncritical' conception of difference. See also Benhabib et al. (1995), Nicholson (1997) and Lara (1998).

8   See Simmel (1987). For a commentary of its significance for a view of validity centred on authenticity and judgment, see Chapter 4 of Ferrara (1998a).

9   On this point see Chapter 5 in Ferrara (1998a).

10   On this point, see Honneth (1997a). For an English, but not exactly equivalent, version of the same paper, see Honneth (1997b).

11   See Weber (1975).

12   See Ferrara (1998a: 90–7 MS).

13   Pareto distinguished between the good *for* a collectivity and the good *of* a collectivity. While the latter notion admits of the totalitarian possibility of an increased fulfilment of the collectivity at the expense of some individuals, the former understands the good *for* a collectivity as that state which is optimal in the sense that any further change will result in a worsening of the fulfilment of some individual in the collectivity.

14   See Kant (1957: 30).

15   See Simmel (1984: 160).

Chapter 8

1   Charles Larmore has developed this point with reference to the work of Rawls and Habermas in his paper 'The Moral Basis of Political Liberalism' (1997). His argument has influenced my own thinking on the subject in a deep way and I wish here to thank him for having suggested to me this idea, which however I am putting here to uses with which he most likely would not agree.

2   See Larmore (1997: 37).

3   See Dworkin (1981a; 1981b). See also Varian (1985) and Gosepath (1995).

4   See Scanlon (1982; 1999), Barry (1989; 1995), Nagel (1991), Gewirth (1978), Galston (1980; 1991) and Holmes (1995).

5   See Foucault (1991) and Deleuze and Guattari (1972).

6   This aspect is emphasized in Taylor (1992: 41).

7   See Larmore (1990: 23).

8   See Larmore (1990: 28).

9   Among the other attempts to explode the dichotomy between right-premised and good-premised conceptions of the moral point of view, see Honneth (1997a).

10   See Nozick (1981: 352–62) on the notion of self-choosing.

11   See Simmel (1987: 217).

12   See Ferrara (1998a).

13   The kind of relations in which justice appears to be a 'development of the drive to revenge' (Nietzsche 1968: 148, aphorism 255).

14   I am indebted here to Larmore's (1995) reconstruction of the two sides of the relation of the self to itself.

References

Ackerman, Bruce (1980) *Social Justice in the Liberal State*. New Haven, CT: Yale University Press.

Ackerman, Bruce (1983) 'What Is Neutral about Neutrality?', *Ethics*, 93 (2).

Ackerman, Bruce (1989) 'Why Dialogue?', *The Journal of Philosophy*, 86 (1).

Ackerman, Bruce (1990) 'Neutralities', in R.B. Douglass, G.M. Mara and H. Richardson (eds), *Liberalism and the Good*. New York: Routledge.

Ackerman, Bruce (1991) *We the People*, Vol. 1, *Foundations*. Cambridge, MA: Harvard University Press.

Ackerman, Bruce (1992) *The Future of the Liberal Revolution*. New Haven, CT: Yale University Press.

Ackerman, Bruce (1994a) 'Political Liberalism', *Journal of Philosophy*, 91: 364–86.

Ackerman, Bruce (1994b) 'Rooted Cosmopolitanism', *Ethics*, 104: 516–35.

Ackerman, Bruce (1997) 'The Rise of World Constitutionalism', *Virginia Law Review*, 83.

Ackerman, Bruce (1998) *We the People*, Vol. 2, *Transformations*. Manuscript.

Arendt, Hannah (1982) *Lectures on Kant's Political Philosophy*, edited and with an interpretive essay by R. Beiner. Chicago: University of Chicago Press.

Ashbury, H. (1968) *Great Illusion: An Informal History of Prohibition*. Greenwood, NY: Greenwood.

Barber, Benjamin R. (1984) *Strong Democracy: Participatory Politics for a New Age*. Berkeley, CA: University of California Press.

Barber, Benjamin R. (1987) *The Conquest of Politics*. Princeton, NJ: Princeton University Press.

Barber, Benjamin R. (1989) 'Justifying Justice: Problems of Psychology, Politics and Measurement in Rawls', in N. Daniels (ed.), *Reading Rawls*. Stanford, CA: Stanford University Press.

Barry, Brian (1978) 'Circumstances of Justice and Future Generations', in R. Sikora and B. Barry (eds), *Obligations to Future Generations*. Philadelphia: Temple University Press. pp. 204–47.

Barry, Brian (1989) *Theories of Justice*. Berkeley, CA: University of California Press.

Barry, Brian (1995) *Justice as Impartiality*. Oxford: Clarendon.

Baynes, Kenneth (1988) 'The Liberal/Communitarian Controversy and Communicative Ethics', *Philosophy and Social Criticism*. 14 (3–4). pp. 61–81.

Baynes, Kenneth (1989) *The Normative Grounds of Social Criticism*. Albany, NY: State University of New York Press.

Baynes, Kenneth (1995) 'Democracy and the *Rechtstaat*: Habermas's *Faktizitätcund Geltung*', in S.K. White (ed.), *The Cambridge Companion to Habermas*. Cambridge: Cambridge University Press. pp. 201–32.

Beiner, Ronald (1982) 'Hannah Arendt on Judging', in H. Arendt, *Lectures on Kant's Political Philosophy*. Chicago: University of Chicago Press. pp. 89–156.

Beiner, Ronald (1983) *Political Judgment*. Chicago: University of Chicago Press.

Beiner, Ronald (1997) 'Rereading Hannah Arendt's Kant Lectures', *Philosophy and Social Criticism*, 23 (1): 21–32.

Bellah, N. Robert (1991) 'Citizenship, Diversity and the Search for the Common Good', in R.E. Calvert (ed.), *The Constitution of People: Reflections on Citizens and Civil Society*. Kansas: University of Kansas Press.

Bellah, N. Robert et al. (1985) *Habits of the Heart: Individualism and Commitment in American Life*. Berkeley, CA: University of California Press.

Bellah, N. Robert et al. (1992) *The Good Society*. New York: Random House.

Bellamy, Richard (1996) 'The Political Form of the Constitution: The Separation of Powers, Rights and Representative Democracy', in R. Bellamy and D. Castiglione (eds), *Constitutionalism in Transformation: European and Theoretical Perspectives*. Oxford: Blackwell. pp. 24–44.

Bellamy, Richard and Castiglione, Dario (1997) 'Constitutionalism and Democracy: Political Theory and the American Constitution', *British Journal of Political Science*, 27: 595–618.

Benhabib, Seyla (1989a) 'Liberal Dialogue versus a Critical Theory of Discursive Legitimation', in N.L. Rosenblum (ed.) *Liberalism and the Moral Life*. Cambridge, MA: Harvard University Press.

Benhabib, Seyla (1989b) 'Autonomy, Modernity and Community: Communitarianism and Critical Social Theory in Dialogue', in A. Honneth, T. McCarthy, C. Offe and A. Wellmer (eds), *Zwischenbetrachtung in Prozebder Autkläring: Jürgen Habermas zum 60. Geburstag*, Frankfurt: Suhrkamp.

Benhabib, Seyla (1992) *Situating the Self: Gender, Community and Postmodernism in Contemporary Ethics*. Cambridge: Polity.

Benhabib, Seyla, Butler, Judith, Cornell, Drucilla and Fraser, Nancy (1995) *Feminists' Contentions: A Philosophical Exchange*, with an introduction by Linda Nicholson. London: Routledge.

Bernstein, Richard (1996) 'The Retrieval of the Democratic Ethos', *Cardozo Law Review*, 17: 1127–46.

Bohman, James (1994) 'Complexity, Pluralism, and the Constitutional State: On Habermas's *Faktizität und Geltung*', *Law & Society Review*, 28 (4): 897–930.

Bohman, James (1996) *Public Deliberation: Pluralism, Complexity, and Democracy*. Cambridge, MA: MIT Press.

Brink, David O. (1989) *Moral Realism and the Foundations of Ethics*. Cambridge: Cambridge University Press.

Burke, John A. (1992) *Political Foundation of Law and the Need for Theory with Practical Value: The Theories of Ronald Dworkin and Roberto Unger*. Lanham, MD: Austin & Winfield.

Calhoun, Craig (ed.) (1992) *Habermas and the Public Sphere*. Cambridge, MA: MIT Press.

Calvert, Robert E. (ed.) (1992) *The Constitution of People: Reflections on Citizens and Civil Society*. Kansas: University of Kansas Press.

Cohen, Jean L. and Arato, A. (1992) *Civil Society and Political Theory*. Cambridge, MA: MIT Press.

Cohen, Joshua (1989) 'Deliberation and Democratic Legitimacy', in A. Hamlin and P. Pettit (eds), *The Good Polity*. Oxford: Oxford University Press.

Cohen, Joshua (1993) 'Moral Pluralism and Political Consensus', in D. Copp, J. Hampton and J.E. Roemer (eds), *The Idea of Democracy*. Cambridge: Cambridge University Press.

Cohen, Marshall (ed.) (1984) *Ronald Dworkin and Contemporary Jurisprudence*. Totowa, NJ: Rowman and Littlefield.

Covell, Charles (1993) *The Defence of Natural Law: A Study of the Ideas of Law and Justice in the Writings of Lon L. Fuller, Michael Oakeshott, Frederik A. Hayek, Ronald Dworkin and John Finnis*. New York: St Martin's.

D'Agostino, Fred B. (1988) 'Relativism and Reflective Equilibrium', *Monist*, 71: 420–36.

Dancy, Jonathan (1993) *Moral Reasons*. Oxford: Blackwell.

Daniels, Norman (1979) 'Wide Reflective Equilibrium and Theory Acceptance in Ethics', *Journal of Philosophy*, 76: 256–82.

Daniels, Norman (1980) 'Reflective Equilibrium and Archimedean Points', *Canadian Journal of Philosophy*, no. 10: 83–103.

Daniels, Norman (ed.) (1989) *Reading Rawls*. Stanford, CA: Stanford University Press.

Davidson, Donald (1984) 'On the Very Idea of a Conceptual Schema' (1974), in D. Davidson, *Inquiries into Truth and Interpretation*. Oxford: Clarendon. pp. 183–98.

Deleuze, Gilles and Guattari, Félix (1972) *L'Anti-Oedipe*. Paris: Minuit.

DePaul, Michael R. (1986) 'Reflective Equilibrium and Foundationalism', *American Philosophical Quarterly,* 23: 59–69.

Durkheim, Emile (1964) *The Division of Labor in Society.* New York: Free Press.

Durkheim, Emile (1967) *The Elementary Forms of the Religious Life.* New York: Free Press.

Dworkin, Ronald (1977) *Taking Rights Seriously.* London: Duckworth.

Dworkin, Ronald (1981a) 'What is Equality? Part 1: Equality of Welfare', *Philosophy and Public Affairs,* 10 (3): 185–246.

Dworkin, Ronald (1981b) 'What is Equality? Part 2: Equality of Resources', *Philosophy and Public Affairs,* 10 (3): 283–345.

Dworkin, Ronald (1985) *A Matter of Principle.* Cambridge, MA: Harvard University Press.

Dworkin, Ronald (1986) *Law's Empire.* Cambridge, MA: Harvard University Press.

Dworkin, Ronald (1989a) 'Liberal Community', *California Law Review,* 77 (3): 479–504.

Dworkin, Ronald (1989b) 'The Original Position', in N. Daniels (ed.), *Reading Rawls.* Stanford, CA: Stanford University Press.

Dworkin, Ronald (1990) *Foundations of Liberal Equality* (1988), in *The Tanner Lectures on Human Values.* Salt Lake City, UT: University of Utah Press. pp. 3–119.

Dworkin, Ronald (1993) *Life's Dominion: An Argument about Abortion, Euthanasia, and Individual Freedom.* New York: Knopf.

Dworkin, Ronald (1996) *Freedom's Law: The Moral Reading of the American Constitution.* Cambridge, MA: Harvard University Press.

Fallon, Richard H. (1989) 'What is Republicanism, and Is It Worth Reviving?', *Harvard Law Review,* 102 (2): 1695–735.

Federalist Papers, The (by Alexander Hamilton, James Madison and John Jay) edited and with an introduction by Clinton Rossiter. New York: Penguin.

Ferrara, Alessandro (1993a) *Modernity and Authenticity: A Study in the Social and Ethical Thought of Jean-Jacques Rousseau.* Albany, NY: State University of New York Press.

Ferrara, Alessandro (1993b) 'Justice and the Good from a Eudaemonistic Standpoint', *Philosophy and Social Criticism,* 18 (3/4): 333–54.

Ferrara, Alessandro (1997) 'Authenticity as a Normative Category', *Philosophy and Social Criticism,* 23 (3): 77–92.

Ferrara, Alessandro (1998a) *Reflective Authenticity: Rethinking the Project of Modernity.* London: Routledge.

Ferrara, Alessandro (1998b) 'Judgment, Identity and Authenticity: A Reconstruction of Hannah Arendt's Interpretation of Kant', *Philosophy and Social Criticism,* 24 (2–3): 1–24.

Fishkin, James (1991) *Democracy and Deliberation.* New Haven, CT: Yale University Press.

Forst, Reiner (1992) 'How (Not) to Speak about Identity: The Concept of the Person in *A Theory of Justice*', *Philosophy and Social Criticism,* 18 (3–4): 293–312.

Forst, Reiner (1994) *Kontexte der Gerechtigkeit: Politische Philosophie jenseits von Liberalismus und Kommunitarismus.* Frankfurt: Suhrkamp.

Foucault, M. (1991) 'How an "Experience-Book" is Born', in *Remarks on Marx: Conversations with Duccio Trombadori.* New York.

Frankenberg, Günther (ed.) (1994) *Auf der Suche nach der gerechten Gesellschaft.* Frankfurt: Fischer.

Fraser, Nancy (1992) 'Rethinking the Public Sphere', in C. Calhoun (ed.) *Habermas and the Public Sphere.* Cambridge, MA: MIT Press.

Fraser, Nancy (1997) *Justice Interruptus: Critical Reflections on the 'Postsocialist' Condition.* London: Routledge.

Fullinwider, Robert and Mills, Claudia (eds) (1986) *The Moral Foundations of Civil Rights.* Totowa, NJ: Rowman and Littlefield.

Gadamer, Hans-Georg (1975) *Truth and Method.* New York: Continuum.

Gaffney, Paul (1996) *Ronald Dworkin on Law as Integrity: Rights as Principles of Adjudication.* Lewiston, NY: Mellen.

Galston, Miriam and Galston, William A. (1994) 'Reason, Consent and the US Constitution: Bruce Ackerman's *We the People*', *Ethics,* 104: 467–79.

Galston, William A. (1980) *Justice and the Human Good.* Chicago: University of Chicago Press.

Galston, William A. (1991) *Liberal Purposes: Goods, Virtues and Diversity in the Liberal State.* Cambridge: Cambridge University Press.

Gaus, Gerald F. (1996) *Justificatory Liberalism: An Essay on Epistemology and Political Theory.* Oxford: Oxford University Press.

Geertz, Clifford (1973) *The Interpretation of Cultures.* New York: Basic.

Geertz, Clifford (1983) *Local Knowledge.* New York: Basic.

Gewirth, Alan (1978) *Reason and Morality.* Chicago: University of Chicago Press.

Gosepath, Stefan (1995) 'The Place of Equality in Habermas' and Dworkin's Theories of Justice', *European Journal of Philosophy*, 3 (1): 21–35.

Guest, Stephen (1992) *Ronald Dworkin.* Stanford, CA: Stanford University Press.

Günther, Klaus (1988) *Der Sinn für Angemessenheit: Anwendungsdiskurse in Moral und Recht.* Frankfurt: Suhrkamp.

Habermas, Jürgen (1972) 'Wahrheitstheorien', in J. Habermas, *Vorstudien und Ergänzungen zur Theorie des kommunikativen Handelns* (1984). Frankfurt: Suhrkamp. pp. 127–83.

Habermas, Jürgen (1975) *Legitimation Crisis.* Boston: Beacon.

Habermas, Jürgen (1979) *Communication and the Evolution of Society.* Boston: Beacon.

Habermas, Jürgen (1982) 'A Reply to my Critics', in J.B. Thompson and D. Held (eds), *Habermas: Critical Debates* (1982). London: Macmillan.

Habermas, Jürgen (1984) *The Theory of Communicative Action,* Vol. I, *Reason and the Rationalization of Society.* Boston: Beacon.

Habermas, Jürgen (1985) 'Treffen Hegels Einwände gegen Kant auch auf die Diskursethik zu?', in J. Habermas, *Justification and Application: Remarks on Discourse Ethics* (1993). Cambridge, MA: MIT Press.

Habermas, Jürgen (1987) *The Philosophical Discourse of Modernity.* Cambridge, MA: MIT Press.

Habermas, Jürgen (1989) 'Volkssouveränität als Verfahren: Ein Normativer Begriff von Öffentlichkeit', in Forum für Philosophie Bad Homburg (ed.), *Die Ideen von 1789.* Frankfurt: Suhrkamp. pp. 7–36.

Habermas, Jürgen (1990) *Moral Consciousness and Communicative Action.* Cambridge, MA: MIT Press.

Habermas, Jürgen (1993a) 'Struggles for Recognition in Constitutional States', *European Journal of Philosophy*, 1 (2): 128–55.

Habermas, Jürgen (1993b) *Justification and Application.* Cambridge, MA: MIT Press.

Habermas, Jürgen (1994a) 'Postscript to *Faktizität und Geltung*', *Philosophy and Social Criticism*, 20 (4): 135–50.

Habermas, Jürgen (1994b) 'Three Normative Models of Democracy', *Constellations*, 1 (1): 1–10.

Habermas, Jürgen (1995a) 'Reconciliation through the Public Use of Reason: Remarks on John Rawls's Political Liberalism', *Journal of Philosophy*, XCII (3): 109–31.

Habermas, Jürgen (1995b) 'Ein Gespräch über Fragen der politischen Theorie', in J. Habermas, *Die Normalität einer Berliner Republik.* Frankfurt: Suhrkamp. pp. 135–64.

Habermas, Jürgen (1996a) *Between Facts and Norms: Contributions to a Discourse Theory of Law and Democracy,* translated by William Rehg. Cambridge: Polity. Original *Faktizität und Geltung: Beiträge zur Diskurstheorie des Rechts und des demokratischen Rechtsstaats.* Frankfurt: Suhrkamp, 1992.

Habermas, Jürgen (1996b) 'Reply to Symposium Participants, Cardozo School of Law', *Cardozo Law Review*, 17: 1083–125.

Habermas, Jürgen (1996c) 'Die Moral der Weltbilder – "Vernunft" und "Wahrheit" in Rawls Politischem Liberalismus?', in Manuscript.

Hamm, Richard F. (1995) *Shaping the Eighteenth Amendment: Temperance, Reform, Legal Culture and the Polity (1880–1920).* Durham, NC: University of North Carolina Press.

Herzog, Don (1994) 'Democratic Credentials', *Ethics*, 104: 467–79.

Höffe, Otfried (1984) 'Is Rawls's Theory of Justice Really Kantian?', *Ratio*, 26 (2).

Höffe, Otfried (1987) *Politische Gerechtigkeit: Grundlegung einer kritischen Philosophie von Recht und Staat.* Frankfurt: Suhrkamp.

Holmes, Stephen (1988) 'Gag Rules or the Politics of Omission', in J. Elster and R. Slagstad (eds), *Constitutionalism and Democracy.* New York: Cambridge University Press.

Holmes, Stephen (1995) *Passions and Constraint: On the Theory of Liberal Democracy*. Chicago: University of Chicago Press.

Honeyball, Simon and Walter, James (1998) *Integrity, Community, and Interpretation: A Critical Analysis of Ronald Dworkin's Theory of Law*. Ashgate.

Honneth, Axel (1997a) 'La morale del riconoscimento', in *Micromega*, no. 3.

Honneth, Axel (1997b) 'Recognition and Moral Obligation', *Social Research*, 64 (1): 16–35.

Honneth, Axel, McCarthy, Thomas, Offe, Claus and Wellmer, Albrecht (eds) (1989) *Zwischenbetrachtung im Prozeb der Aufklärung: Jürgen Habermas zum 60. Geburtstag*. Frankfurt: Suhrkamp.

Hunt, Alain (ed.) (1992) *Reading Dworkin Critically*. New York: Berg.

Ingram, David (1987) *Habermas and the Dialectic of Reason*. New Haven, CT: Yale University Press.

Ingram, David (1995) *Reason, History and Politics*. Albany, NY: State University of New York Press.

Ingram, David (1996) 'The Subject of Reason in Postmodern Discourse: Aesthetic Judgment and Political Rationality', in Maurizio Passerin d'Entrèves and Seyla Benhabib (eds), *Habermas and the Unfinished Project of Modernity*. Cambridge: Polity. pp. 269–301.

Jay, Martin (1995) 'The Limits of Limit-Experience: Bataille and Foucault', *Constellations*, 2 (2): 155–74.

Josefson, Jim and Bach, Jonathan (1997) 'A Critique of Rawls's Hermeneutics of Translation', *Philosophy and Social Criticism*, 23 (1): 99–124.

Kant, Immanuel (1957) *Perpetual Peace*, edited and with an introduction by Lewis W. Beck. Indianapolis: Bobbs-Merrill.

Kant, Immanuel (1959) *Foundations of the Metaphysics of Morals*. Indianapolis: Merrill.

Kant, Immanuel (1986) *Critique of Judgment*, translated and with analytical indexes by James Creed Meredith. Oxford: Clarendon.

Kant, Immanuel (1997) *Critique of Practical Reason*. Cambridge: Cambridge University Press.

Kateb, George (1992) *The Inner Ocean: Individualism and Democratic Culture*. Ithaca, NY: Cornell University Press.

Kukathas, Chandran and Pettit, Philip (1990) *Rawls: A Theory of Justice and its Critics*. Cambridge: Polity.

Lara, Maria Pia (1998) *Moral Textures*. Cambridge: Polity.

Larmore, Charles (1987) *Patterns of Moral Complexity*. Cambridge: Cambridge University Press.

Larmore, Charles (1990) 'The Right and the Good', *Philosophia*, 20 (1–2): 15–32.

Larmore, Charles (1993) 'Die Wurzeln radikaler Demokratie', *Deutsche Zeitschrift für Philosophie*, 41 (2): 321–7.

Larmore, Charles (1995) 'Une théorie du moi, de son instabilité et de la liberté d'esprit', in H. Grivois and J.P. Dupuy (eds), *Mécanismes mentaux, mécanismes sociaux*. Paris: Editions La Découvert. pp. 127–45.

Larmore, Charles (1996) *The Morals of Modernity*. Cambridge: Cambridge University Press.

Larmore, Charles (1997) 'The Moral Basis of Political Liberalism'. Manuscript.

MacIntyre, Alasdair C. (1981) *After Virtue*. Notre Dame, IL: Notre Dame University Press.

Mansbridge, Jane J. (1980) *Beyond Adversary Democracy*. New York: Basic.

McCarthy, Thomas (1991) *Ideals and Illusions: On Reconstruction and Deconstruction in Contemporary Critical Theory*. Cambridge, MA: MIT Press.

McCarthy, Thomas (1994) 'Kantian Constructivism and Reconstructivism: Rawls and Habermas in Dialogue', *Ethics*, 105: 44–63.

McCarthy, Thomas (1996) 'Legitimacy and Diversity: Dialectical Reflections on Analytical Distinctions', *Cardozo Law Review*, 17: 1083–125.

Meehan, Johanna (ed.) (1995) *Feminists Read Habermas: Gendering the Subject of Discourse*. London: Routledge.

Michelman, Frank I. (1986) 'Traces of Self-Government', *Harvard Law Review*, 100 (4): 4–77.

Michelman, Frank I. (1988) 'Law's Republic', *The Yale Law Journal*, 97: 1493–537.

Michelman, Frank I. (1994a) 'The Subject of Liberalism', *Stanford Law Review*, 46: 1807–33.

Michelman, Frank I. (1994b) 'Kollektiv, Gemeinschaft und das liberale Denken in

Verfassungen', in G. Frankenberg (ed.), *Auf der Suche nach der gerechten Gesellschaft.* Frankfurt: Fischer. pp. 55–73.

Michelman, Frank I. (1995a) 'Always under Law?', *Constitutional Commentary*, 12 (2): 227–47.

Michelman, Frank I. (1995b) 'Thirteen Easy Pieces', *Michigan Law Review*, 93: 1297–332.

Michelman, Frank I. (1995c) *Higher Law: On the Legal Theory of Constitutional Democracy.* Manuscript.

Michelman, Frank I. (1996a) 'Can Constitutional Democrats Be Legal Positivists?', *Constellations*, 2 (3): 293–308.

Michelman, Frank I. (1996b) 'How Can the People Ever Make the Laws?' Paper read at the Conference on Contested Terrains: Social Conflict and Critique, Prague, 20–25 May.

Michelman, Frank I. (1996c) 'Review of Jürgen Habermas's *Between Facts and Norms*', *Journal of Philosophy*, 93: 307–13.

Michelman, Frank I. (1997a) 'How Can the People Ever Make the Laws? A Critique of Deliberative Democracy', reduced version of Michelman (1996b) in J. Bohman and W. Rehg (eds), *Deliberative Democracy*. Boston: MIT Press.

Michelman, Frank I. (1997b) 'Constitutional Authorship'. Unpublished manuscript.

Moon, Donald (1991) 'Constrained Discourse and Public Life', *Political Theory*, 19.

Mouffe, Chantal (ed.) (1992) *Dimensions of Radical Democracy: Pluralism, Citizenship, Community.* London: Verso.

Murphy, Cornelius F. (1990) *Descent into Subjectivity: Studies of Rawls, Dworkin, and Unger in the Context of Modern Thought.* Aperture.

Nagel, Thomas (1986) *The View from Nowhere.* Oxford: Oxford University Press.

Nagel, Thomas (1991) *Equality and Partiality.* Oxford: Oxford University Press.

Nagel, Thomas (1997) *The Last Word.* Oxford: Oxford University Press.

Nicholson, Linda (ed.) (1997) *The Second Wave: A Reader in Feminist Theory.* London: Routledge.

Nietzsche, Friedrich (1968) *The Will to Power*, translated by W. Kaufmann and R.J. Hollingdale. New York: Random House.

Nozick, Robert (1974) *Anarchy, State and Utopia.* New York: Basic.

Nozick, Robert (1981) *Philosophical Explanations.* Oxford: Clarendon Press.

Okin, Susan Moller (1986) 'Are our Theories of Justice Gender-Neutral?', in R. Fulliwider and C. Mills (eds), *The Moral Foundations of Civil Rights.* Totowa, NJ: Rowman and Littlefield.

Okin, Susan Moller (1989) *Justice, Gender and the Family.* London: Harper.

O'Neill, Onora (1989) *Constructions of Reason.* New York: Cambridge University Press.

Pareyson, Luigi (1988) *Estetica: Teoria della formatività.* Milan: Bompiani.

Parsons, T. (1990) 'Prolegomena to a Theory of Social Institutions' (1934), *American Sociological Review*, 55: 319–33.

Passerin d'Entrèves, Maurizio and Benhabib, Seyla (eds) (1996) *Habermas and the Unfinished Project of Modernity.* Cambridge: Polity.

Pateman, Carole (1985) *The Problem of Political Obligation: A Critique of Liberal Theory.* Berkeley, CA: University of California Press.

Pateman, Carole (1988) *The Sexual Contract.* Stanford, CA: Stanford University Press.

Pettit, Philip (1997) *Republicanism: A Theory of Freedom and Government.* Oxford: Clarendon.

Phillips, Anne (1993) *Democracy and Difference.* Cambridge: Polity.

Pocock, John G.A. (1975) *The Machiavellian Moment: Florentine Political Theory and the Atlantic Republican Tradition.* Princeton, NJ: Princeton University Press.

Pogge, T.W. (1989) *Realizing Rawls.* Ithaca, NY: Cornell University Press.

Putnam, Hilary (1983) *Realism and Reason*, Vol. 3 of *Philosophical Papers*. Cambridge: Cambridge University Press.

Rasmussen, David (1990) *Reading Habermas.* Oxford: Blackwell.

Rasmussen, David (1994) 'How is Valid Law Possible?', *Philosophy and Social Criticism*, 20: 21–44.

Rasmussen, David (1996a) 'Jurisprudence and Validity', *Cardozo Law Review*, 17.

Rasmussen, David (ed.) (1996b) *Handbook of Critical Theory.* Oxford: Blackwell.

Rawls, John (1951) 'Outline of a Decision Procedure for Ethics', *Philosophical Review*, no. 60: 177–97.

Rawls, John (1971) *A Theory of Justice.* Cambridge, MA: Harvard University Press.

Rawls, John (1974) 'The Independence of Moral Theory', in *Proceedings and Addresses of the American Philosophical Association.*

Rawls, John (1975) 'Fairness to Goodness', *Philosophical Review*, no. 84: 536–54.

Rawls, John (1978) 'The Basic Structure as Subject', in A. Goldman and J. Kim (eds), *Values and Morals.* Boston: Reidel. pp. 47–71.

Rawls, John (1979) 'A Well-Ordered Society', in P. Laslett and J. Fishkin (eds), *Philosophy, Politics and Society.* pp. 6–20.

Rawls, John (1980) 'Kantian Constructivism in Moral Theory', *The Journal of Philosophy*, no. 88: 512–72.

Rawls, John (1982) 'The Basic Liberties and their Priorities', in S. McMurrin (ed.), *The Tanner Lectures on Human Values*, Vol. 3. Salt Lake City, UT: University of Utah Press.

Rawls, John (1985a) 'Justice as Fairness: Political Not Metaphysical', *Philosophy and Public Affairs*, 14 (3): 223–51.

Rawls, John (1985b) 'A Kantian Conception of Equality', in J. Raijchman and C. West (eds), *Post-Analytic Philosophy.* New York: Columbia University Press.

Rawls, John (1987a) 'The Idea of an Overlapping Consensus', *Oxford Journal of Legal Studies*, 7 (1): 1–25.

Rawls, John (1987b) 'Foundationalism in Political Theory', *Philosophy and Public Affairs*, 16: 115–37.

Rawls, John (1988) 'The Priority of the Right and Ideas of the Good', *Philosophy and Public Affairs*, 17 (4): 251–76.

Rawls, John (1993) *Political Liberalism.* New York: Columbia University Press.

Rawls, John (1995) 'Reply to Habermas', *Journal of Philosophy*, XCII (3): 132–80.

Raz, Joseph (1982) 'The Claims of Reflective Equilibrium', *Inquiry*, 2: 307–30.

Raz, Joseph (1986) *The Morality of Freedom.* Oxford: Clarendon.

Raz, Joseph (1990) 'Facing Diversity: The Case of Epistemic Abstinence', *Philosophy and Public Affairs*, 19: 3–46.

Reath, Andrew, Herman, Barbara and Korsgaard Christine M. (eds) (1997) *Reclaiming the History of Ethics: Essays for John Rawls.* Cambridge: Cambridge University Press.

Rehg, William (1994) *Insight and Solidarity: The Discourse Ethics of Jürgen Habermas.* Berkeley: University of California Press.

Rehg, William (1996) 'Habermas's Discourse Theory of Law and Democracy: An Overview of the Argument', in D. Rasmussen (ed.), *Handbook of Critical Theory.* Oxford: Blackwell. pp. 166–89.

Roosevelt, Franklin D. (1937) 'Presidential Speech of March 9, 1937', Senate Report no. 711, 75th Congress, 1st Session, pp. 41–4. Quoted in F.M. Murphy, J.E. Fleming and W. F. Harris II (eds), *American Constitutional Interpretation.* Mineola, NY: Foundation.

Rorty, Richard (1988) 'The Priority of Democracy over Philosophy', in R. Vaughan (ed.), *The Virginia Statute of Religious Freedom: Two Hundred Years After.* Madison, WI: University of Wisconsin Press. pp. 262–8.

Rorty, Richard (1989) *Contingency, Irony, and Solidarity.* Cambridge: Cambridge University Press.

Rorty, Richard (1997) 'Justice as a Larger Loyalty', in R. Bontekoe and M. Stepaniants (eds), *Justice and Democracy: Cross-Cultural Perspectives.* Honolulu: University of Hawaii Press. pp. 9–22.

Rorty, Richard, Schneewind, J.B. and Skinner, Quentin (eds) (1984) *Philosophy in History: Essays on the Historiography of Philosophy.* New York: Cambridge University Press.

Ross, W.D. (1930) *The Right and the Good.* Oxford: Clarendon.

Rousseau, Jean Jacques (1967) *The Social Contract*, in J.J. Rousseau, *The Social Contract and the Discourse on the Origin of Inequality*, edited by L.G. Crocker. New York: Simon and Schuster.

Sandel, Michael (1982) *Liberalism and the Limits of Justice.* Cambridge: Cambridge University Press.

Sandel, Michael (1996) *Democracy's Discontent: America in Search of a Public Philosophy.* Cambridge, MA: Harvard University Press.

Scanlon, Thomas M. (1982) 'Contractualism and Utilitarianism', in A. Sen and B. Williams (eds), *Utilitarianism and Beyond.* Cambridge: Cambridge University Press. pp. 103–28.

Scanlon, Thomas M. (1999) *What We Owe to Each Other*. Cambridge, MA: Harvard University Press.

Seel, Martin (1995) *Versuch über die Form des Glücks: Studien zur Ethik*. Frankfurt: Suhrkamp.

Shanley, Mary L. and Pateman, Carole (eds) (1991) *Feminist Interpretations and Political Theory*. Pittsburg, PA: Pennsylvania State University Press.

Sidgwick, Henry (1907) *The Methods of Ethics*. London: Macmillan.

Simmel, Georg (1984) *On Women, Sexuality and Love*, translated and introduced by G. Oakes. New Haven, CT: Yale University Press.

Simmel, Georg (1987) 'Das individuelle Gesetz' (1913), in G. Simmel, *Das Individuelle Gesetz: Philosophische Exkurse*. Frankfurt: Suhrkamp.

Skinner, Quentin (1978a) *The Foundations of Modern Political Thought*, Vol. 1, *The Renaissance*. Cambridge: Cambridge University Press.

Skinner, Quentin (1978b) *The Foundations of Modern Political Thought*, Vol. 2, *The Age of Reformation*. Cambridge: Cambridge University Press.

Skinner, Quentin (1983) 'Machiavelli on the Maintenance of Liberty', *Politics*, 18: 3–15.

Skinner, Quentin (1984) 'The Idea of Negative Liberty: Philosophical and Historical Perspectives', in R. Rorty, J.B. Schneewind and Q. Skinner (eds), *Philosophy in History: Essays on the Historiography of Philosophy*. New York: Cambridge University Press.

Skinner, Quentin (1986) 'The Paradoxes of Political Liberty', in *The Tanner Lectures on Human Values*, Vol. VII. Salt Lake City, UT: University of Utah Press. pp. 225–50.

Skinner, Quentin (1992) 'On Justice, the Common Good and the Priority of Liberty', in C. Mouffe (ed.), *Dimensions of Radical Democracy: Pluralism, Citizenship, Community*. London: Verso.

Skinner, Quentin and Viroli, Maurizio (eds) (1990) *Machiavelli and Republicanism*. Cambridge: Cambridge University Press.

Sosa, Ernest (1991) 'Equilibrium in Coherence?', in E. Sosa, *Knowledge in Perspective*. Cambridge: Cambridge University Press. pp. 257–69.

Spitz, Jean-Fabien (1994) 'The Concept of Liberty in "A Theory of Justice" and its Republican Version', *Ratio Juris*, 7: 331–47.

Spitz, Jean-Fabien (1995a) *La Liberté Politique*. Paris: Presses Universitaires de France.

Spitz, Jean-Fabien (1995b) 'Le Républicanisme, une troisieme voie entre libéralisme et communautarianisme', *Le Banquet*, 7 (2): 215–38.

Steinberger, Peter J. (1993) *The Concept of Political Judgment*. Chicago: University of Chicago Press.

Sullivan, Kathleen M. (1988) 'Rainbow Republicanism', *Yale Law Journal*, 97.

Sunstein, Cass R. (1989) 'Beyond the Republican Revival', *Harvard Law Review*, 102 (2): 1539–90.

Sunstein, Cass R. (1990) *After the Rights Revolution: Reconceiving the Regulatory State*. Cambridge, MA: Cambridge University Press.

Sunstein, Cass R. (1996) *Legal Reasoning and Political Conflict*. Oxford: Oxford University Press.

Taylor, Charles (1985) 'Atomism', in *Philosophy and the Human Sciences*, Vol. 2 of *Philosophical Papers*. Cambridge: Cambridge University Press.

Taylor, Charles (1992) 'The Politics of Recognition', in C. Taylor, *Multiculturalism and the Politics of Recognition*. Princeton, NJ: Princeton University Press.

Varian, H.R. (1985) 'Dworkin on Equality of Resources', *Economics and Philosophy*, 1: 110–25.

Viroli, Maurizio (1992) *From Politics to Reason of State: The Acquisition and Transformation of the Language of Politics 1250–1600*. Cambridge: Cambridge University Press.

Viroli, Maurizio (1995) *For Love of Country*. Oxford: Oxford University Press.

Waldron, Jeremy (1993) *Liberal Rights: Collected Papers 1981–1991*. Cambridge: Cambridge University Press.

Walzer, Michael (1983) *Spheres of Justice. A Defense of Pluralism and Equality*. New York: Basic.

Walzer, Michael (1990) 'Two Kinds of Universalism', in *Nation and Universe, The Tanner Lectures on Human Values*. Salt Lake City, UT: University of Utah Press.

Walzer, Michael (1994) *Thick and Thin: Moral Argument at Home and Abroad*. Notre Dame, IL: University of Notre Dame Press.

Weber, Max (1975) 'Religious Rejections of the World and their Directions', in H. Gerth and C. Wright Mills (eds), *From Max Weber: Essays in Sociology*. New York: Oxford University Press.

Wellmer, Albrecht (1991) 'Ethics and Dialogue: Elements of Moral Judgment in Kant and Discourse Ethics', in A. Wellmer, *The Persistence of Modernity: Essays on Aesthetics, Ethics, and Postmodernism*. Cambridge, MA: MIT Press.

White, Stephen K. (ed.) (1995) *The Cambridge Companion to Habermas*. Cambridge: Cambridge University Press.

Williams, Bernard (1981) *Moral Luck*. Cambridge: Cambridge University Press.

Williams, Bernard (1985) *Ethics and the Limits of Philosophy*. London: Fontana.

Williams, Bernard (1989) 'Dworkin on Community and Critical Interests', *California Law Review*, 77 (3): 515–20.

Wittgenstein, Ludwig (1953) *Philosophical Investigations*. London: Macmillan.

Young, Iris M. (1990) *Justice and the Politics of Difference*. Princeton: Princeton University Press.

Index